NATIVE AMERICAN
in the LAND of the
SHOGUN

*Ranald MacDonald
and the Opening of Japan*

FREDERIK L. SCHODT

Stone Bridge Press • *Berkeley, California*

Published by
Stone Bridge Press, P.O. Box 8208, Berkeley, CA 94707
TEL. 510-524-8732 • sbp@stonebridge.com • www.stonebridge.com

Publication of this book was generously assisted by a grant from the Suntory Foundation.

The publisher would like to thank the Hudson's Bay Company for permission to reproduce its trademark on page 85.

Cover and jacket design by Linda Ronan. Chinook Tribe logo by Tony A. Johnson, used with permission of the Chinook Indian Tribe. Background text from MacDonald's Nagasaki deposition, used with permission of the Matsuki Collection, Kyūshū University. Image of MacDonald from the Ranald MacDonald monument in Nagasaki, sculpted by Kazukuni Yamazaki.

Credits and copyright notices accompany their images throughout.

Printed in the United States of America.
10 9 8 7 6 5 4 3 2 1   2008 2007 2006 2005 2004 2003

LIBRARY OF CONGRESS CATALOGING-IN-PUBLICATION DATA
Schodt, Frederik L., 1950–
    Native American in the land of the shogun: Ranald MacDonald and the opening of
Japan / Frederik L. Schodt.
        p. cm.
    ISBN 1-880656-77-9 (pb); 1-880656-78-7 (cb).
        1. MacDonald, Ranald, 1824–1894. 2. Pioneers—Columbia River Valley—Biogra-
phy. 3. Adventure and adventurers—Pacific Area—Biography. 4. Japan—Description and
travel. 5. Americans—Japan—History—19th century. I. Title.

F853.S38 2003
915.204'25'092—dc21

                                                                                2003003856

To
Masakatsu Tomita
(1949–96)

Contents

List of Illustrations

Maps

Introduction

This is a book about a man who did an extraordinary thing, and then fell through the cracks of history. Ranald MacDonald was of Chinook Indian and Scottish origin, born at the mouth of the Columbia River. In 1848, at the age of twenty-four, he risked his life to go to faraway, feudal Japan, which had rigid policies prohibiting contact with foreigners. How he conceived of and executed his adventure, and what it means to us today, is the subject of this book.

I first learned of MacDonald around 1990. I was doing research for a book later dedicated to him, titled *America and the Four Japans: Friend, Foe, Model, Mirror,* about the convoluted nature of U.S.-Japan relations. After coming across a brief mention of him, I went to my local public library and discovered a dusty, original-edition copy of what is regarded as his "autobiography"—*Ranald MacDonald,* edited by William S. Lewis and Naojirō Murakami and published by the Eastern Washington State Historical Society in 1923.

Having spent most of my adult life working with Japan, I was amazed that I had never before heard of such an interesting person—the first North American to go to Japan alone, of his own volition. But I wasn't the only one. Most people I then knew had never heard of him either, even if they were experts in Japanese history. I felt as though I had stumbled across a secret, lost history.

Every book I have written has been a personal odyssey of sorts, but this one has been the longest of all, requiring twelve years from conception to completion. It became something of an obsession, requiring multiple trips around the United States, Canada, and Japan to visit the places that MacDonald lived or visited. It meant long hours in archives and libraries, reading books and newspapers and musty old letters and records, and staring bleary-eyed at roll upon roll of scratchy microfilm. And it involved talking and corresponding with innumerable people.

In the process, I discovered that there were quite a few others like me, people who had also "discovered" MacDonald and felt his story resonated with them on some deep personal level. Some had even formed tiny "Friends of MacDonald" societies in both the United States and Japan to preserve his memory and encourage awareness of him. Moreover, I found that—while there were many mysteries surrounding MacDonald's life—for an individual born in 1824 and unaffiliated with any organization, he is remarkably well documented, in English, Japanese, and Dutch primary source materials. There is also a considerable body of work about MacDonald written after his death, in the form of articles and books in both English and Japanese. And yet MacDonald remains an extremely marginal figure in "orthodox" histories.

Which raises the question, why write another book on someone who has failed to generate sustained interest? The simple and selfish answer is that I think MacDonald should be much better known. The more complex answer is that new information on his life is now available, and it is possible to view his life and his adventure in a broader context.

The story of Ranald MacDonald, as readers will discover, is an extremely tangled one, in need of a renewed effort to sort myth and speculation from fact. But in doing so, it may be possible to achieve something larger. Most recorded histories are an attempt to make sense of an infinitely complex past. They are assembled from available information, and may change radically as our understanding and needs change. By re-examining MacDonald's story, we can also enjoy a new view of early connections between North America and Japan, and a new view of the nineteenth-century world.

❖   ❖   ❖

Before plunging into this book, a few words are in order about what it is about, and what it is not about, as well as a few housekeeping details.

Since this book is mainly about MacDonald's Japan adventure, some readers may be disappointed to find that I have glossed over his years in Australia (about which little is yet known) and his later activities in British Columbia (about which quite a bit is known). Instead, I have tried to provide more detail on the environments that helped propel him on his course in life, and the context in which his adventure occurred.

The temptation to speculate about gaps in our knowledge of MacDonald's life is enormous. More than a few writers have tripped by relying too heavily on his posthumously published "autobiography," the 1923 *Ranald MacDonald*. Often regarded as the "bible" on him because it contains what is presented as his own writing (as well as invaluable supplementary information), it contains significant errors and can be quite misleading.

This book also makes frequent references to MacDonald's "autobiography," but only with great care. To understand the context of the statements in it and to evaluate their accuracy, wherever possible I have done a type of historical triangulation, using other contemporary and primary sources, and making comparisons with earlier drafts of his manuscript (copies of which survive in the Oregon Historical Society in Portland, the Eastern Washington Historical Society in Spokane, and the British Columbia Archives in Victoria, B.C.). I refer to MacDonald's story of his adventure to Japan as the *Narrative*, which encompasses all drafts or versions that survive of his story, with endnotes identifying the source. When specifically referring to the version included in the 1923 book edited by Lewis and Murakami, I refer to it as the posthumously "published *Narrative*," or the "published autobiography."

On a more mundane level, quoted material has been reproduced verbatim. Readers will note occasional variations in the spellings and punctuation of names and places in quotations and in the text, the consequence of writers at that time in history writing without unified or standardized spellings. This occasionally extends even to the names of the most central parties in the story. MacDonald and his half-siblings, for example, generally spelled their surname with a "Mac" instead of their father's "Mc." And as most readers will by now also have deduced, Ranald MacDonald's name is spelled differently from that of a similar-sounding mascot of a certain famous fast-food chain; in fact, the two have absolutely nothing in common.

In English-language academic publications, Japanese names are often written in Japanese order, surname first and given-name last. For a general audience, however, this approach can become extremely confusing, especially in a story where there appear not only Japanese and North Americans, but also Japanese-Americans and Japanese permanent residents of the United States visiting Japan. To avoid confusion, I have used the usual English-language name order of first-name first and last-name last.

On the subject of nomenclature, I should also note that the term "Native American" is used in a broad sense, to include all natives of North America, not just the United States.

Finally, this book could not have been written without the help of a great number of people in the United States, Japan, Canada, and Holland. They include members of libraries, archives, historical societies, the Chinook Indian Tribe, and ordinary individuals. I am grateful to all who have encouraged me, especially to my long-time publisher and friend, Peter Goodman, and the readers who consented to read and critique all or parts of my manuscript. They include Bruce Berney, Jennifer S. H. Brown, Jean Murray Cole, Fiammetta Hsu, Tony A. Johnson, Yumiko Kawamoto, Stephen Kohl, Leonard Rifas, and Eddie and Margaret Schodt. For interviews, general assistance, and spiritual support over the years, the following people also deserve mention and eternal good karma: Yūji Aisaka, Amy Barach, Lisa Barksdale, Jeffrey Booth, David H. Cory and family, Paul Cyr, Joan Druett, Denise Fuchs, Kyōji Furukawa, Shawna Gandy, Joan Goddard, Michi Gotō, Hisayuki Ishimatsu, Judy Hayama, Mamoru Inagami, Yoshitaka Inoue, Akiko and Masatoshi Kakikoshi, Misao Mizuno, Jim Mockford, Tomisato Nagata, Ken Nakano, May Namba, Eiji Nishiya, Shinkichi Nohtomi, Masami Obama, Barbara Peeples, Laura C. Pereira, Ron Romano, Kōichi Saito, Takeyoshi Sakai, Natsuo Sekikawa, Dick Slagle, Kenji Sonoda, Yasuo Takeuchi, Francisca Tausk, Keiko Tokioka, Machiko Tomita, Masakatsu Tomita, Massie Tomita, Torao Tomita, Atsumi Tsukimori, Victor Van den Berg, Mary S. Warring, and Akira Yoshimura. The Suntory Foundation, it should be noted, not only provided publication assistance, but was also extremely patient with my delays. A tip of the hat in gratitude also to Bonnie Dehler and Linda Ronan and to Stone Bridge Press employees Dulcey Antonucci, Barry Harris, and Ayako Willen.

Frederik L. Schodt
San Francisco, May 2003

Artwork on previous page based on Lewis and Murakami's 1923 *Ranald MacDonald* daguerreotype, originally in the possession of A. T. MacDonald, Great Falls, Montana. Background text from MacDonald's Nagasaki deposition, used with permission of the Matsuki Collection, Kyūshū University.

CHAPTER 1

Fort Colvile and the Custer Interview

When we drew up in front of the larger house, an old man came out, bowing and smiling, while half-breed children, chickens, and dogs scattered on either side. The men said, "Here comes old Ron, old McDonald himself," but I had not heard his history, and consequently could not account for his courteous manner and marked individuality.[1]

Thus Elizabeth B. Custer described her first reaction to Ranald Mac-Donald, after coming across him quite by accident while on assignment for *Harper's Weekly*. It was one of the more incongruous meetings in the Old West. Custer was reporting on the new rail line just laid between Spokane Falls, Washington, and Revelstoke, Canada. Her article, titled "An Out-of-the-Way 'Outing,'" appeared in the July 18, 1891, issue of the magazine and included one of the last first-hand descriptions of MacDonald.

Elizabeth Custer was the widow of General George Armstrong Custer, the flamboyant Civil War hero and Indian fighter who, in 1876, had inadvertently led 210 of his men into slaughter at the Battle of Little Big Horn. A celebrity in life, George Custer had been elevated to near sainthood in death, and no one had helped ensure this more than Elizabeth. Left a meager pen-sion, a famous name, and a talent for writing, she wrote mostly glowing books about her husband and clever, breezy articles, often about the American West.

By 1891 the American West was no longer wild and, for the most part, had been tamed. Railroads crisscrossed the continent, towns had sprung up in the former wilderness, and once proud tribes of Native Americans—whose armed resistance to the United States government had largely ended after Little Big Horn—were now subjugated peoples confined to living on reservations, desperately adjusting to the white communities pressing in on all sides. In this environment, with her ex-soldier's-wife background, Elizabeth Custer was the perfect reporter. She satisfied readers on the East Coast who hungered for information on both the exotic, rapidly changing West and its romantic past. Ranald MacDonald's life bridged both worlds, and for Mrs. General Custer (as she was addressed in public) he was the perfect subject.

The trip between Spokane Falls and Revelstoke took Mrs. Custer and her readers through the Colville Valley region of northeast Washington. A beautiful and brand-new part of the United States, Washington had only achieved statehood a year and a half earlier, in November 1889, after a long period of territorial status. The young United States could only assert a tenuous cultural claim to the area, despite waves of invading gold miners and settlers from the East. Native Americans had been nurtured there for millennia, sustained by the bounty of the Columbia River. For over a century and a half, the valley also had functioned as a critical hub for the Hudson's Bay Company (HBC), a vast and powerful London-based, fur-trading empire that had long asserted nominal control over the entire North American Northwest through its network of trading posts. A common border with British-controlled Canada lay only twenty-five miles north at the 49th parallel and had been drawn, after much squabbling, with the signing of the Oregon Treaty in 1846.

Mrs. Custer's visit to the area in 1891 was freighted with nuance. As an educated white female from the East, she represented "polite," "civilized" United States society. As General George A. Custer's widow, she also symbolized the nation's belief in its "manifest destiny"—the duty to expand westward—as well as the scorched-earth policies of the government when indigenous peoples got in the way. Her first observation of Colville Valley presaged some of the problems she would have in her interview with Mac-

Donald. "The harvest was stacked in the fields," she wrote, "and all this golden grain was being garnered by the Indians, to whom it belongs. I cannot express what a peculiar sight it was to me to witness the first savages I had ever seen at work in a wheat field."[2]

Mrs. Custer's initial impressions of Native Americans had been mainly formed through tales of armed conflict or scenes of dissolution around Army posts. But in the Colville Valley, she found with astonishment, many of the Indians had been taught agriculture. They had been trained not just by the Jesuits at the local mission of St. Ignatius, she realized, but by the men of the longer-established Hudson's Bay Company, for Company officers "were decided promoters of progress, and many of the half-breed sons of these educated men are now tilling the soil."[3] In fact, the whole area challenged prevailing preconceptions of American ideology of the era, that a wild and savage West had been tamed by brave Euro-American pioneers from the eastern United States. In reality, the road to more modern ways had long ago been paved by the Hudson's Bay Company. But by 1891, American-style progress in Colville Valley, as in much of the West, was nonetheless represented by Protestant missionaries, gold seekers, farmers and ranchers, soldiers, and modern technology. Along with the railroad, brand-new towns were springing up everywhere. Mrs. Custer wrote about one of them:

> All the streets of Marcus were carefully laid out through the forest. One looked down these vistas without so much as seeing a board as the beginning of a house. The trees looked affronted at the highways cut through their midst, but they will soon be much more so when the cabins and canvas houses begin to line the road. We named these streets Faith and Hope as we passed them, and the third we called Charity, for there the saloons had planted their shacks and tents, and surely they need the greatest of these.[4]

After lunch at the only hotel in town, Mrs. Custer and her entourage left by wagon to visit the older sights in the valley, including the old Hudson's Bay Company fort, described as a "square surrounded by the low log huts, but individualized by the block house that still stands as firm as if it were a stone tower."[5] Here, the forty-nine-year-old widow first met MacDonald, a sixty-seven-year-old bachelor.

After wandering the world and working for years in the Northwest as a

Photo No. 562 [13-28]. Courtesy Museum of N.W. History Collection, K. Ross Toole Archives, University of Montana, Missoula.

Ranald MacDonald, July 5, 1891.

prospector, guide, and entrepreneur, MacDonald had finally settled down in 1885 on 153 acres in the Colville Valley. First living in a rough-board shack that burned down in 1891, and then erecting a log house on the Colville Indian Reservation land nearby, he spent much of his time at his cousin's place; Donald MacDonald owned the old Hudson's Bay Company fort land and Ranald helped with the ranching there. It appears to have been a happy time for him, for as he wrote to a friend, "I yearn for nothing more than to live according to the whims of my nature. If I need meat for my dogs, in the foothills there is plenty of game. If it is flour that I lack, there is a store at the nearest settlement. My books furnish diversion, and in my solitude I am free to write and meditate."[6] If anything, MacDonald's biggest headaches in the last few years of his life were caused by a chronic inability to get his story about his adventures in Japan published, and by his meeting with Elizabeth Custer.

At sixty-seven MacDonald still cut quite a figure. According to one account, he had thick and curly gray hair, wore a trimmed beard, and, while not particularly tall, had broad shoulders and proportions that made him an imposing presence. His eyes were small and deep set with gray irises outlined in hazel-brown, and his Pacific Northwest Indian ancestry was revealed mainly by his high cheekbones and broad, flat nose.[7] To Mrs. Custer, he seemed already ancient, but very polite. "No one," she wrote, "could have invited us to descend from our anything but dignified perch on the high seats [of the wagon], with more grace than did this coarsely dressed antiquarian."[8]

MacDonald had had good reason to settle in such an out-of-the-way

Fort Colvile, with blockhouse and surrounding buildings, ca. late 1890s.

place as Colville Valley. He had lived there briefly as a boy, and he had strong family ties to the land. Between 1833–44, his father, Archibald McDonald, had been the Hudson's Bay Company's chief trader and then chief factor at Fort Colvile,[9] ruling over a vast portion of the wilderness like a potentate. Two of MacDonald's half-brothers also lay buried there. After 1846 the region had fallen under the control of the United States, and the Company's influence had slowly waned. MacDonald's distant cousin Angus McDonald had served as Fort Colvile's last chief factor, even as trade became more and more difficult. The Company depended on Indians for pelts, but the population of the fur-bearing animals was in decline. As American settlers moved farther into the Northwest, bloody wars broke out between them and the Indians; the U.S. government eventually required the Indians to forgo hunting in the area and move onto reservations. Finally, in 1871, the Hudson's Bay Company sold all of its forts south of the 49th parallel. Angus MacDonald took over the operation of Fort Colvile as his own property, later turning it over to his own son, Donald.[10]

History is replete with early visitors' glowing descriptions of the land. Mrs. Custer herself described it as "lovely" and an "Arcadia." Built in 1825 where the Kettle River merges with the mighty Columbia, close by the ever-roaring Kettle Falls—the most popular salmon fishing spot for local Native American tribes—the fort was blessed with timber and good soil for farming. In fact, until 1846 it dominated trade in the area, purchasing furs from

Indians to be shipped back to England and supplying other forts throughout the Northwest with food. Before the advent of the railroad, the river had been the primary means to reach far-flung trading posts in the Northwest. Nearly all of the Company's boats had been made at the fort out of local yellow pine.

Angus MacDonald, who died two years before Mrs. Custer's visit, left recollections of the area before and after the arrival of American settlers, writing: "When the Columbia is up in June the sound of the Colvile Falls on a silent summer night is very grand. . . . Salmon as heavy as one hundred pounds have been caught in these falls." As fisheries became newly established on the lower Columbia by whites to can and export salmon, Angus observed critically how they were "fast at work in destroying the noble supply. . . . Wherefore, if not otherwise provided for[,] the extinction of the Columbian River salmon is only a question of time." At one point, he noted, the valley had been a virtual Indian Mecca, with the hallmark of peaceful relations with whites during the fur trade era. "Annual gatherings of the Columbian Indians were wont to meet here. Foot-racing, horse-racing, wrestling and archery used to be the fun. Adultery was punished by death, and the moral commands instilled into their children by these wild and hospitable red men were equal to anything that either Moses or Christ ever said." But in recent years, Angus added, "[T]he insidious and overbearing evils of the white man, have been making heavy raids on their descendants, always the result with weaker nations before the strong." Still, while some of the ugliest fighting between Americans and Indians had taken place around Fort Colvile, the fort itself had never been attacked. "There was a report, probably true, that one tribe of the Colvile tribes intended to kill all the English-speaking people of the Fort, but they never put their intention into practice."[11]

The presence of the Hudson's Bay Company was a major reason that peace reigned in the area. Incorporated in 1670, the Company had slowly spread south and west throughout the North American wilderness from its namesake bay in the far north. In the process, the Company had learned that peace was good for business. Its policies generally encouraged good relations among diverse Indian tribes, discouraged white settlers, and, for part of its history, actively encouraged intermarriage between traders and Indians. In this sense, the Company's approach was dramatically different from that of the United States. In the latter's westward land rush, the underlying culture supporting settlers' claims made miscegenation a social taboo, often a crime, and warfare with Indians was almost constant. As Peter C. Newman, Canadian author of a popular history on the HBC, writes, "[A]t least the HBC's greed for ever more furs, which required constant harnessing of the Indian labor force, prevented the kind of indiscriminate slaughter of the native peoples that fouled the American frontier."[12]

Like many American arrivals, Mrs. Custer was quick to notice the results of intermarriage around the old Hudson's Bay Company fort. Typically in the Pacific North-

Elizabeth Custer, ca. 1900.

Photo No. 468. Courtesy Little Bighorn Battlefield National Monument, National Park Service.

west, the Company's forts were manned by Scottish or English officers, and employees of Orkney Islander, French Canadian, Hawaiian Islander, and Iroquois descent. Most of the men, including the officers, eventually wound up marrying women of local native tribes, and the ensuing children reflected all sorts of exotic mixtures. Fort Colvile was no exception, and a true hybrid culture had grown up in the area long before American settlers arrived. Ranald MacDonald and his relatives epitomized this. Angus MacDonald had married a Catholic Nez Perce woman, and their half-Indian son Donald was married to a part-Indian woman.[13] The world-traveled Ranald Mac-Donald himself was half-Scottish and half-Chinook. Under the Chinook name of Cum Cum li-ti no, he would later register himself as a member of the Lake Tribe, one of the confederated tribes of the Colville Indian Reservation.[14] In late-nineteenth-century America, the mixed hybrid culture of the Colville Valley area was under assault from members of a new, more racially polarized society—one in which half-breeds and "squaw men" (the American term for whites who took native companions) were increasingly viewed less than favorably. But to those of mixed ancestry, the region remained an oasis.

A Courtly Meeting

MacDonald guided Mrs. Custer around Fort Colvile, explaining with great flourish what it had been like in the old days. There was an initial attraction between the two, even though they came from completely different worlds. Mrs. Custer was quickly charmed, describing MacDonald as "stately," and "elegant," noting his polished manner, expressiveness, and the "twinkle" in his eyes. Early in her article, she referred to him as "a descendant of Scottish kings." Completely "overcome," she declared him to be a "prince of paupers" and a man completely outside the realm of her experience. She caught the slips he occasionally made "into everyday talk, and the introduction, in the very midst of his most lofty flights of rhetoric, of slang phrases, which seemed all the more absurd associated as they were with the stately language of by-gone days."

After inquiring about MacDonald's background, Mrs. Custer learned for the first time of his prominent father, Archibald, a powerful Hudson's Bay Company chief factor who "had married a squaw, as was the custom of the country." Ranald MacDonald, she concluded, "had all his early life been associated with the English and Scotch, which accounted for the grandiose style of the old-school gentleman, and the evidence of vivacity and foreign polish were traceable to the many French Canadians who were in the employ of the company in its prosperous years."[15]

If Mrs. Custer was puzzled by MacDonald, he, too, was somewhat puzzled by her, for he was at first unaware of her identity. In writing that betrays a remarkable egocentricity, she described their first encounter in *Harper's*, noting that, after a pause in the conversation,

> the old courtier, *sans* several articles of toilet that civilization might require, came back as hurriedly as his many years would permit . . . [saying] "I must make my compliments if it is really she," and such obeisance and lordly bending of his ancient back made me aware that he had not heard who I was at our introduction, and had come back to pay reverence to my husband's name. I can scarcely think of anything more incongruous than this aristocratic old man, with his

high-flown expressions . . . and the tumbled-down, dilapidated, untidy old buildings around him.[16]

Despite the suddenness of the unexpected visit, MacDonald graciously invited Mrs. Custer into his home. When asked to tell his life story, he more than willingly obliged, spending considerable time telling her of his birth in Astoria; of his famous Chinook chief grandfather, Comcomly; of trips crossing the Rockies as a child; and of his education in what is today's Winnipeg, Canada. The highlight of his life, however, had been his adventure to Japan in 1848, and he delighted in recounting it in great detail, even referring to himself as possibly being "the instigator of Commodore Perry's expedition to Japan." Had Mrs. Custer actually listened to what MacDonald was saying, her article might have turned out quite differently. But as she later confessed, "I found that it made little difference what he said, his manner of telling what he had to say was something that I was not likely to encounter every day." She further wrote,

> It suddenly came over me how some people I know at the East would enjoy this witty, dramatic, and versatile man, and how I should like to take the droll old fellow and set him in the midst of people who get so tired of each other and long for novelty. So I said, suddenly,
>
> "Oh, Mr. McDonald, how I should like to take you home with me!"
>
> In return, I received such an impressive bow, and his hand went instinctively over his heart as he said:
>
> "Oh, Madam, take possession of me. I am yours."[17]

MacDonald tried his best to play along with Mrs. Custer, but it was a doomed effort. Although progressive for a woman of her era, Elizabeth functioned in a world where people were measured against the yardstick of northern European civilization. If different in culture or color, they always came up short. In the end, Mrs. Custer was unable to view MacDonald's world without condescension. After being introduced to a "bright-eyed half-breed woman" and "dark-skinned children," she mistakenly believed them to be his own family. As she wrote, she glanced "at the squaw, wondering if any of the savage instinct remained in her, and how she would look upon this rather open trespassing upon her preserves; but she smiled on me. . . . I found out afterwards that she was not Mrs. McDonald, but the wife of the older man's [similarly named] nephew; so the tomahawks ceased to float in the air before my eyes."[18]

Betrayal

MacDonald later read Mrs. Custer's article when it appeared as a reprint in the August 6, 1891, issue of the *Kettle Falls Pioneer*, the leading newspaper in his area. Reflecting the local pride taken in the visit, the paper ran the enthusiastic headlines "The New Eden, First Glimpse of a Glorious Land; Like a Paradise, Seen By a Revered Hero's Widow, Mrs. General Custer; Her Charming Sketch of the Upper Columbia Region and a Quaint Pioneer."[19]

To say that the article did not sit well with MacDonald would be an understatement, however, for resentment festered in his bosom and boiled over into his own writings until the day he died. Around this time, he was engaged in almost daily correspondence with his old friend Malcolm McLeod, a lawyer in Ottawa, Canada. McLeod had edited and partially ghost-written MacDonald's story of adventure in Japan, and the two were desperately seeking to get the manuscript published. In an August 10 letter, in clear, precise handwriting, MacDonald complained about Custer's depiction of his cousin's wife and her descriptions of him. On August 29 he attempted to explain why he had acted so gallantly, "offering himself" to Mrs. Custer when she left. "It struck me," he wrote, "that she had come to the wooly west to pull wool over me and exhibit me as a show, as Barnum would his Wooly Horse. The offer of myself was the only way out of the dilemma."[20]

Mrs. Custer's attitude toward race particularly offended him. Concerning her disparagement of his cousin's wife, he declared, "[H]ow could we overlook the wantonly deliberate and dastardly insult to Mrs. MacDonald, her only crime being her skin, a shade or two darker than her own, believing perhaps that no notice would be taken she could do it with impunity so she just let loose the bridle of her imagination." Mrs. Custer's remark about him, that "perhaps the subdued, obedient, and servile squaw is his only idea of women," he found especially insulting. By late-nineteenth-century American society, the epithet "squaw man" usually referred to white males not high enough on the social ladder to gain white wives, men who tended to abuse their Indian partners. MacDonald reminded his friend how he (MacDonald) had associated with far more than servile "squaws" in his life, how years earlier, in fact, he had received recommendations for employment in British Columbia from British royalty itself—from the Duchess of Gordon and the Duchess of Manchester. In condemning Custer's ignorance of his life, community, and the Hudson's Bay Company, he wrote sarcastically that it was, "too good, putting it in Black and White of a subject she knew nothing of."[21] In another letter penned two days earlier, he had already summed up his opinion about her, describing the reporter as "Mrs. Mustard Custer violating all the established rules of decency and common politeness—too much of the garrison—I was going to say HACK, but you might construe that to mean too severe to apply to a woman of her pretensions."[22]

Rebuttal

On August 31, MacDonald submitted a letter to the editor of the *Kettle Falls Pioneer*. He started out diplomatically, praising the universally admired Mrs. Custer, but he quickly got to the point, carefully rebutting many of her statements. He asserted that he had never been a "pauper" nor had any of his family. To the contrary, as the first "white inhabitants" his relations possessed and rightfully owned the area and "by the sweat of our brows and enterprises, filled or at least largely covered every valley and plain with the fruits of our industry in herds and flocks and bands of horses for hundreds of miles in every direction." Of Custer's description of him wearing only two articles of apparel, he countered with some humor that "[s]he forgot the moccasins and clean under-clothing." He also noted, however, that he had been at work when she had rudely appeared without warning and he affirmed that "clothes I had in abundance and of the finest quality wherewith to stand before kings." Then he defended his cousin's wife, writing that the "application of the word 'squaw' to the lady of the house was utterly inappropriate. Mrs. MacDonald, the wife of my cousin Donald, was well born as well educated and with as fine a literary taste . . . and with as fine an appreciation of habit of the proprieties and duties of civilized life as any of the circle to which Mrs. Custer belongs." Mrs. MacDonald, he noted, was the daughter of a respected Hudson's Bay Company official and her mother was only part Indian. "There was no white woman in the country at the time, so she was of semi-Indian blood—but then, if not still, the red blood was the true blue in sovereign lordship of the country. My own mother was a daughter of King

Kum Kumly, immortalized in the pages of Washington Irving's 'Astoria.' "[23]

In response, on September 3 the *Kettle Falls Pioneer* ran another article, "Was uncalled for—a cutting rebuke to Mrs. General Custer's Criticism of The Oldest of Pioneers. An Interesting Letter from Our Honoured and Respected Patriarch, Ranald MacDonald." Standing up for him, the editor wrote,

> Why this lady should have so turned against and so sneeringly commented on the dress and even doubted the veracity of Mr. MacDonald is a mystery, unless, since her brave and fearless husband was so foully butchered by the Indians, she has an abhorrence for anyone with Indian blood coursing through their veins. We think the lady must have certainly known better. Then again she may have thought it funny and that class of literature would suit the readers of Harper's Weekly; but in our minds the dubbing of Mr. MacDonald as the "Prince of Paupers" was uncalled for.[24]

The Facts of the Matter

In her carelessness, Mrs. Custer could never have imagined how deeply insulting her use of the phrase "Prince of Paupers" would be. In reality MacDonald had little reason to take offense at being called "poor," for in letters to others at the time, he often and openly acknowledged his near-destitute state. But "pauper" carried a strong connotation of someone living on charity, which was especially galling to one so self-reliant. The phrase, "Prince of Paupers," moreover, maligned his relatives and made him honor-bound to defend them. As landowners they were, after all, hardly paupers. Furthermore, only two years earlier his friend McLeod had told MacDonald how his father, Archibald, had once attempted to pursue on his son's behalf a claim against the United States government under an 1846 land settlement with Britain over the Northwest country. Nothing had ever come of it, McLeod said, because the then-young Ranald had been at sea and his father could not locate him. But according to McLeod (a lawyer), MacDonald was heir, through his mother, to the famous Oregonian Chinook Chief Comcomly and as such was a true "prince," the rightful owner of vast tracts of land and presumably entitled to compensation.[25]

Although the legal claim may have been shaky, as Comcomly had a great many progeny, at this point in his life MacDonald was serious about it. While never really believing he would be given vast swaths of already settled land in Oregon and Washington, he stood by his claim as a matter of principle. It figured importantly in his still-unpublished autobiography and had already generated a certain amount of notoriety for him in the American West. MacDonald was well aware of the relative advantages that could be gained from notoriety, writing McLeod that "[t]he KumKumly business is going the rounds of the press and may advertise the book more than we think."[26]

Six months before the meeting with Mrs. Custer, both the *Astorian* and the Portland-based *Morning Oregonian* had run an article entitled "The Oldest Native Astorian: A Brief Sketch of the Life of the Grandson of King Kumkumly, the Old Indian Chief." In an entertaining and somewhat exaggerated fashion, the writer described MacDonald's life, his adventure to Japan, and how his Chinook grandfather had been "in command of all the tribes from the mouth of the Columbia River to the Flathead country, and was the only chief recognized by the Hudson's Bay Company, on account of his great influence with all the tribes." MacDonald, it said, was "the only lineal descendant of King Kumkumly, and is still looked upon by all the Indian tribes, particularly down this way, as their only chief, although he cannot speak any of the Indian dialects with fluency."[27]

To American settlers who believed they had just conquered the Northwest, the notion that someone else might own part of it was potentially inflammatory, and preposterous. Later, in 1893, MacDonald would meet with ridicule from editors of newspapers like the *Oregonian* and the *Spokane Review*. The latter (with a mocking allusion to the Hawaiian monarchy that had just been deposed by Americans in the Pacific) would write,

When the widow of the lamented Custer was here a few years ago she was presented to the old king, and was much impressed with his bearing.

We advise Mr. MacDonald, or, rather, Comcomly II, to lay his case before the President and demand his just rights as recognized in the Hawaiian precedent.

Down with the stars and stripes and up with the royal standard! Long live the king, and God save the house of Com-comly![28]

The summer after Elizabeth Custer's visit, author-historian Eva Emery Dye corresponded with MacDonald to inquire about the famous Hudson's Bay Company Chief Factor, John McLoughlin, whom he had known as a child. She planned to write a book about McLoughlin and to refer to him as the "King of the Columbia," but when she told MacDonald this she received the following reply:

[I] consider myself the only living descendant of the once powerful King Kum Kumly, so as his only surviving representative you will excuse me if I dutifully and loyally enter my protest (for all the good it will do) in this usurping the rights and prerogatives of another. Don't laugh. I mean what I say. Although I may not have enough to jingle on a tombstone, but such is the case nonetheless.

In case she ever decided to write anything about him, MacDonald also closed his letter with the postscript, "Don't be so hard on me as Mrs. General Custer."[29]

What the Records Show

MacDonald's bad feelings about Mrs. Custer never did go away. The William S. Lewis and Naojirō Murakami edition of MacDonald's manuscript, published posthumously by the Eastern Washington State Historical Society in 1923, has the following passage:

For my part: proud, and with no reason to be ashamed of my native "blue" blood of Indian in America, I feel no contumely towards any of different hue of humanity. At the same time, I must plead guilty to the soft impeachment of being naturally quick to resent an insult on this score; or on any score. However, I have never had occasion to do so.[30]

Yet an earlier draft in the Eastern Washington State Historical Society's archives reveals that the following lines had actually been deleted from the Lewis and Murakami edition:

. . . save once, and that was from an American woman—a lady, so called—who, abusing my hospitality to her, when unexpectedly obtruding on it, chose, with a flippant disregard of truth and literary propriety, to paint me up as a pauper prince, for ridicule, in the columns of Harper's Weekly some two years ago.[31]

❖ ❖ ❖

Nearly lost in the controversy over the racial and pecuniary slurs made in Mrs. Custer's article was her equally great offense as a journalist. MacDonald's adventure to Japan in 1848 at age twenty-four was the highlight of his life and the central theme of his unpublished autobiography. He had described it to her in considerable detail, even referring to himself as possibly being "the instigator of Commodore Perry's expedition to Japan." That statement should have had a powerful impact on Mrs. Custer and dominated her article. For over two hundred years, Japan had adhered to a draconian policy of national isolation, banning trade and communication with all European nations except Holland, at pain of death forbidding visits by most foreigners and travel abroad by its own citizens. But in 1853, acting on orders of President Millard Fillmore, Commodore Matthew Perry had led a United States Navy squadron into Edo (today's Tōkyō) Bay and, without firing a gun, forced Japan to end its isolation. The opening of this feudal nation, about which Americans had become intensely curious, was one of the major events in mid-nineteenth-century U.S. history. And for a while, the media had been deluged with accounts of the trip.

Mrs. Custer was familiar with this history and already knew far more about Japan than most Americans. In 1885 she had written a piece about a Japanese village on special display in Madison Square Garden, describing its quaint buildings and crafts, and the "coffee-colored" workers, whom she found to be "the cleanest little creatures." (Later in life, Mrs. Custer would become one of the early female tourists to Japan.)[32] Yet, despite such knowledge and interest, her reporting in the 1891 *Harper's* article completely mangled the most important part of MacDonald's life story. While recording most of the details he told her with reasonable accuracy, she omitted a key point. Instead of having him infiltrate Japan, and during his ten-month sojourn contribute to the subsequent opening of the hermit nation, she placed him in China. In his later letters to Malcolm McLeod and in his rebuttal letter to the *Kettle Falls Pioneer*, MacDonald complained about Elizabeth Custer's error, reasserting how he had gone to Japan, not China. But the ensuing controversy over her racial and economic insults would over-shadow the point he made about her abysmal reporting skills.

A Journey into the Past

MacDonald sometimes referred to himself as a "Columbian," in the broad sense of someone who had spent much of his life in the watershed of the giant Columbia River, an area incorporating most of the Pacific Northwest, and even the Colville Valley. He lived in an era of great convulsions and, like the river, his life was filled with dramatic twists and turns. He was born in Astoria in 1824 by the river's mouth and, after traveling the world, lived many years in British Columbia. In 1894, he died in northeastern Washington, also near the river's shore.

One hundred years after his death, in August 1994, I finally had a chance to explore MacDonald's country, by land and air, and to visit the Colville Valley area where Mrs. Custer had interviewed him. I have long been fasci-nated by MacDonald's bold adventure to Japan, partly for a very personal reason. One of his stated goals in going there in 1848 was to become an interpreter and, for most of my adult life, I have supported myself as a pro-fessional Japanese-English interpreter. It seemed appropriate that my visit to MacDonald country would begin with an unusual interpreting job.

Hired by a Japanese engineering firm, I first flew into Portland, Oregon, a hundred miles inland from the mouth of the Columbia. Then, on a tiny propeller aircraft that required me to crouch in the aisle before reaching my seat, I headed east, tracing the long river upstream over lush forests, the spec-tacular Columbia River Gorge, then farmlands, and finally the near desert. Along the way, the 11,245-foot Mt. Hood towered in the distance like an American version of Japan's famous volcano, Mt. Fuji. I arrived at Pasco Air-port in the Tri Cities region of Washington that evening.

The next day, I was taken out to the U.S. Department of Energy's nearby Hanford site, which straddles the Columbia River for over fifty miles. Han-ford is where the United States produced the plutonium for the "Little Boy" atomic bomb that wasted much of the city of Nagasaki and killed or wound-ed over 75,000 people—the same city where MacDonald had been impris-oned a century earlier. After decades of Cold War–related production, the 560-square-mile area is now one of the most heavily contaminated spots on earth. Access is strictly limited, and radiation badges are required at all times to monitor exposure. Nearby, long-term residents live with the same fear of thyroid illness and cancers as the residents of Nagasaki. Projected cleanup costs range as high as $300 billion.[33] In 1994, in an oddity of history, Japanese engineering firms were playing a significant role in the mega-cleanup of the site.

The interpreting work for the project proved to be grueling. There were unfamiliar terms such as "vitrification," "site remediation," and "carbon tetrachloride," and there was the additional stress of security clearances and escorts and the danger of walking off a narrow pathway between engineering offices into contaminated ground. It was a relief when the job was over, and I flew back along the Columbia to Portland, Oregon.

I joined a bus tour there, sponsored by the Oregon Historical Society and the Astoria-based Friends of MacDonald society, or FOM, as it is often called. A year or so prior to this, I had been surprised to learn that such a group even existed. First formed in 1988, FOM was particularly active around 1994, and the goal of the tour that year was to commemorate the one-hundredth anniversary of MacDonald's death by visiting his gravesite in northeastern Washington, stopping at Colville Valley and other sites of interest. Sitting with twenty-two other fans of Ranald MacDonald in a modern, air-conditioned bus, I again left Portland, rolling over much of the same territory I had just flown above the day before, along Highway 30 on the Oregon side of the Columbia. Not too far from the Tri Cities area we left the river to cut overland through the arid interior of Washington to Spokane. There, we visited the Eastern Washington Historical Society (where a copy of the manuscript of MacDonald's autobiography is kept), stayed a night, and continued north.

My companions included founding members of FOM, such as then-chairman, Mas Tomita, a Japanese resident of Portland and an indefatigable promoter of MacDonald's story; Bruce Berney, then director of Astoria's Public Library; and Dr. Stephen Kohl, an associate professor from the East Asian Languages and Literature Department at the University of Oregon. Others on the trip included Canadian Jean Murray Cole, the great-great-granddaughter and biographer of MacDonald's father, Archibald; Jonathan Kahananui, a Hawaiian veteran of World War Two who identified with MacDonald's adventures and the Hawaiians in his story; and Homer Yasui, a retired surgeon and descendant of the famous Yasui Clan of Japanese Americans, who early on had settled the Hood River area along the Columbia. As

I was to learn over and over, Ranald MacDonald's story appeals to a wide variety of people, each of whom "discovers" him in his or her own way and derives a unique personal message from the man's experience.

Were Ranald MacDonald a better-known figure, perhaps this personal sense of "discovery" would not be so strong. And in that regard, the environment in which Mrs. Custer's interview with MacDonald was conducted provides important clues not only as to why her interview was problematic, but also why the story of his adventure to Japan fell through the cracks of history.

Northeastern Washington in the late Nineteenth Century

To most Americans visiting eastern Washington State around 1891, Fort Colvile already seemed to be a ghost of the distant past, as control of the area had long ago shifted from the Hudson's Bay Company to the new, settler-based culture of the United States. Yet it was still a time of considerable transition. Even though relations were good around the Colville Indian Reservation, local newspapers reflected white settlers' continuing nervousness about Indians. The last major conflict in the West had occurred only six months earlier at Wounded Knee in South Dakota; after Chief Sitting Bull (the nemesis of Mrs. Custer's late husband) was assassinated, U.S. troops had turned their Gatling guns on rebellious, largely unarmed Indians involved in the Ghost Dance Movement. In contrast, at the same time in Spokane—about seventy-five miles south of where MacDonald lived—newspapers were running advertisements for electric trolleys. One ad taken out by the Rochester Hotel in the *Kettle Falls Pioneer*, which was published only a few miles from MacDonald's home, boasted of amenities such as hot and cold water, electric bells, and telephones.

Nascent globalization had also begun to affect this once remote and isolated area. There were increasing mentions of Japan in the local newspapers, which MacDonald read avidly. No Japanese yet lived in the Colville Valley area and Japan seemed a world away to most people, so the articles largely focused on the exotic aspects of Japanese culture. Yet some citizens already talked about Japanese immigrants arriving in West Coast cities.

As odd as it may seem today, in 1891 the Chinese had begun to replace Indians as the threat uppermost in the minds of settlers in northeastern

Washington. Many Chinese workers ("coolies") had been imported to help build railroads or had come to mine gold. But an anti-Chinese movement was already in full swing (just as an anti-Japanese movement would be later). Three years before Mrs. Custer's visit, the paper most local to Ranald Mac-Donald, the Colville-based *Steven's County Miner*, ran a diatribe, proclaiming that "Colville is one of the burgs of Washington territory whose people detest the idea of a Chinese population, still the festive pigtail is slowly and surely worming himself into the good graces of our citizens and will finally be numbered among our business fraternity if something is not done to repulse the detestable creatures. Anything but a Chinaman!" On September 27, 1890, the *Spokane Falls Review* ran an inflammatory article titled, "The Chinese Evil," about a local meeting held by a congressional subcommittee investigating the Chinese "problem." Reports were made about rumors of Chinese arriving in British Columbia, then being "smuggled into the Colville Indian Reservation by their fellow country-men who live there and have squaw wives and half-caste families."[34]

These articles were emblematic of a shift in racial attitudes occurring in the area. During the reign of the Hudson's Bay Company (when only European men and Indians were present), class and upbringing came to be even more important than race, religion, or ethnicity. In contrast, many U.S. settlers brought with them a new fixation on skin color and a far more narrow definition of what it meant to be an "American." In the last article quoted above, one local witness defined "whites" as being only "German, Irish, and Americans," and advocated excluding all "Italians, Chinese, Hungarians and Poles" in immigration.

What Ranald MacDonald thought of this local paranoia is unknown, but it held deep implications for him personally. He was of both European and Indian descent. In his early years, he had considered himself "white" in relation to the native societies around him. Later in life, he began publicly identifying himself as an American "Indian." In the early 1890s, MacDonald was respected in the Colville Valley area as one of its oldest pioneers. Increasingly though, he was surrounded by newcomers with extreme bias against Indians and mixed bloods. In fact, when an excerpt of his autobiography was finally published in the local *Kettle Falls Pioneer* in 1893, it was prefaced with an article by a writer using the nom de plume of "Traveler." The writer introduced MacDonald as an example of a respectable "half-breed" and used him to rebut an earlier article by a Christian reverend named Munday, who had viciously attacked the long-established half-breed and non-Protestant populations.[35]

As Traveler's article symbolized, Americans had begun to create a new history of the Pacific Northwest below the 49th parallel. In this version, settlers from the eastern United States played the starring role, vanquishing the Indians and developing the land. The previous achievements of Native Americans, mixed bloods, French Canadians, Hawaiians, and even the Scottish and English men who worked for the Hudson's Bay Company were downplayed, ignored, and eventually almost forgotten. If, in Mrs. Custer's interview with MacDonald, she was unable to capture the essence of what he was trying to tell her, it is not surprising. She was an active creator of the new history, and as such the significance of MacDonald's extraordinary visit to Japan was at odds with her agenda and beyond her ability to put into context.

* * *

On August 12, 1994, I finally arrived in the Colville Valley area at the intersection of Highways 385 and 20. Along with my fellow admirers of MacDonald on the centennial tour, I had hoped, perhaps, to see vestiges of the old fort where Mrs. Custer conducted her interview. But this was not to be. Even MacDonald would have been amazed; not only is the once-sturdy old Fort Colvile gone, but so is everything else, including the town of Marcus, where he used to mail his letters in the 1890s. The entire area has been submerged by the construction of the Grand Coulee Dam, which backs up the Columbia for over one hundred miles, creating the largest lake in the area and ruining the former salmon fisheries more completely than Angus MacDonald could ever have imagined. Like Ranald MacDonald, and like the story of his extraordinary life and adventure to Japan, the site of the old fort is only rarely revealed, when the waters of what is now known as Franklin D. Roosevelt Lake occasionally recede.

Artwork based on OrHi62601. Courtesy Oregon Historical Society.

CHAPTER 2

The Mouth of the Columbia River

The 1,210-mile-long Columbia River begins humbly on the western slope of the Canadian Rockies. It meanders through the interior of the Northwest, growing increasingly straight and muscular in its travel westward, eventually cutting the border between today's Washington and Oregon states. When nearly five miles across, it suddenly narrows to empty into the vast Pacific, pointed straight at Asia and northern Japan. Right by the mouth of the river, in a graveyard near the town of today's Ilwaco, Washington, lies the skull of Ranald MacDonald's ancestor, Comcomly, famous chief of the once-powerful Chinook Tribe.

Comcomly died around 1831 and four years later, Meredith Gairdner, a young British physician in the employ of the Hudson's Bay Company, decided to rob his grave, decapitate the head, and send it back to England for study. Whites often robbed Indian graves in the nineteenth century, not just for souvenirs but out of a general interest in theories of racial origins, and this was especially true of Chinook graves. The Chinook Indians flattened the heads of their infants and thus retained uniquely shaped skulls. Chinook graves were also relatively easy to rob (as long as one wasn't caught) for the important dead were usually laid to rest initially on supports above ground in canoes, laden with treasured effects.

Perhaps to prevent robbers, Comcomly's family had buried their chief in the ground, and Gairdner—who suffered from a severe case of tuberculosis—so overexerted himself digging up the corpse that he began coughing up blood. Nonetheless, on November 21, 1835, he excitedly wrote the recipient of his present in England:

> [T]he accompanying head in a small box is that of Com-com-ly, the old chief of the Chinook nation at the mouth of the Columbia, who died four or five years ago. You may have heard of this character for he is mentioned in most of the narratives relating to the Columbia. By his ability? cunning? or what you please to call it, he raised himself & family to a power and influence which no Indian has since possessed in the districts of the Columbia below the first rapids 150 miles from the sea. When the phrenologists look at this frontal development what will they say to this? . . . I will endeavor to [later] procure you the whole skeleton.[1]

Gairdner never did send the skeleton, and a year later he died of his disease. As for Comcomly's skull, it was displayed in a museum in England for over a hundred years. The lower jawbone was lost in a World War II bombing raid, but the rest of the skull was sent to the Smithsonian Institute for study in 1946. In 1972 it was finally returned to Chinook tribal members for reburial.

As Gairdner indicated in his letter, Comcomly was one of the better-documented Indian chiefs in North America. To early European visitors, his tribe's customs and appearances seemed exotic and thus worthy of recording. And during his long life of sixty-six years, Comcomly personally welcomed British and American visitors to the Columbia River, becoming their ally and protector. It was a strategy that yielded short-term rewards for his people but could not prevent their eventual destruction.

Quest for a Northwest Passage

In the sixteenth century, Europeans had begun dreaming of finding a "Northwest Passage"—a practical shortcut by water from the Atlantic to the Pacific Ocean—that would bring the wealth of Asia closer. The dream took a very long time to die and in the late eighteenth century it was bolstered by rumors of a giant river flowing in the still poorly understood American Northwest. In addition to explorations by land, British, Spanish, American, and Russian ships all began searching for the

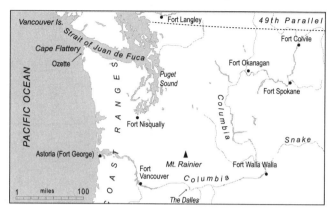

The Pacific Northwest of MacDonald's youth.

mouth of this river on the coast. In fact, it was a £20,000 reward for discovery of the Northwest Passage that helped bring British explorer Captain James Cook into the area in 1778, on his third and last "voyage of discovery." Cook explored much of the coastline of today's Canada and Alaska but never found the passage. Nor was he able to survey the eastern coast of Japan on his return as he had hoped, for he was killed in a confrontation with angry natives in Hawaii.

In 1792 George Vancouver—a young midshipman on Cook's expedition—returned to explore the North Pacific, hoping to find the Northwest Passage. In the spring, on his way up the Pacific Coast to Nootka Sound (on the island in today's British Columbia that bears his name), Vancouver unwittingly sailed right by the Columbia River. The narrow opening contained treacherous sand bars and had deceived or intimidated many ship captains (and later caused innumerable wrecks). Not until October, after an American sea captain gave him a rough sketch, did Vancouver return to the area and finally discover what he had been looking for. Eventually, his main ship, the *Discovery*, proved to be too large to safely cross the bar. With a gale on the way, Vancouver ordered his second-in-command, William R. Broughton, to cross in a smaller vessel, the *Chatman*.

Broughton and his men immediately found themselves afloat on a grand river. As they sailed past a Chinook village of wooden houses (with faces painted on their fronts, and openings through their mouths), the seamen quickly noted how populated the area was. Friendly Indians began to follow them, hawking delicious salmon and fresh vegetables. On October 28, the explorers met twenty-three canoes carrying warriors dressed for combat. But these natives also proved friendly and willing to trade, except that they "would neither part with their copper swords nor a kind of battle-axe made of iron." One elderly Indian chief, presumably a Chinook, was particularly friendly and traveled with the explorers a considerable distance.[2]

The Columbia was not the Northwest Passage, but it was one of the biggest rivers in North America. Having traveled over eighty miles upstream, convinced that he was the first subject of a "civilized nation or state" on the river, Broughton did what the British then typically did. On October 29, he took formal "possession of the river in His Britannic Majesty's name." Oblivious to the cruelty of the situation, he recorded that "the friendly old chief . . . assisted at the ceremony and drank His Majesty's health on the occasion."[3]

As it turned out, the real claim to being "first" on the Columbia went not to Broughton but to the American sea captain, Robert Gray, who had provided Broughton with a rough map to the river's entrance in the first place. Unbeknown to the latter, Gray had already crossed the bar months earlier (and had he not done so the area today might not be U.S. territory). As for Broughton, he would become better known for accomplishing some of Cook's unfinished business in the North Pacific, exploring and surveying the coasts of Japan's northern frontier in 1796. In 1804, when Broughton published a widely read book of his observations, he included one of the first English descriptions of the small island of Rishiri, upon which Ranald MacDonald would land almost a half century later.

Unlike the professional explorers, Gray was an aggressive American trader engaged in the booming new trade of sea-otter skins—a trade sparked by none other than Captain Cook, who had accidentally created a direct link between the Pacific Northwest and Asia. Along the coast of Alaska and today's British Columbia, Cook and his men had bought quantities of excellent furs from the natives for a pittance. On their way home in 1779, after the death of their captain, the ship's crew had stopped at Canton and discovered how much these furs were worth to the Chinese. As Cook's successor, Captain King, would write, "The rage with which our seamen were possessed to return to Cook Inlet [in Alaska] and buy another cargo of skins to make their fortunes, at one time was not far short of mutiny. And, I must own, I could not help indulging myself with the thought of the project."[4]

Riches of the Pacific Northwest

The exceptionally soft and fine sea-otter furs from the Pacific Northwest were highly sought after in Europe as well as China. As a result, European powers soon began jockeying for control of the still poorly understood area. The Russians already had outposts in southern Alaska and were about to expand into California; the Spanish, probing up from their California colonies, had already formed an outpost at Nootka. But after reports of Cook's voyage were published in 1784, ships from Britain and the young United States soon created a new sea-based trade. Captains simply sailed up land to barter simple trinkets and manufactures for pelts with the Indians.

China was the main Asian market for furs, but early traders always kept Japan in mind, too. Since the beginning of the 1600s, Japan had been ruled by the Tokugawa Shogunate, or military dictatorship, which had enacted a series of Seclusion edicts prohibiting contact with most foreigners on pain of death. Only a token trade was allowed with the Chinese and Dutch in the southern port of Nagasaki. Europeans and Americans knew next to nothing about Japan, but ignorance amplified their imaginations and the island country was presumed to be rich. One man on a British voyage to Nootka Sound in 1786 later remarked that another British ship had sailed along the coasts of Korea, Japan, and today's Hokkaidō, meeting with "[v]essels of different kinds, some of which [had been] sent on board without any restraint." He recommended that Britain should become much more involved in the local fur trade, because by "means of it we may open a Trade to Japan." The Chinese, he predicted, would resell what they did not need to the Japanese, "for enormous Sums."[5]

Ultimately, it was not the British but the Americans who began to pursue furs in the Northwest most actively. In 1787 the newly independent "United States" was a tiny collection of former colonies hugging the North American East Coast. Nonetheless, after hearing reports of Cook's expedition, Boston-based merchants sent out two ships—the Columbia Rediviva and the sloop Lady Washington, commanded by John Kendrick and Robert Gray, respectively—to trade with the Indians along the Northwest coast. Scores of East Coast–based ships later followed, sailing around South America's treacherous Cape Horn to get to the Pacific Northwest. The traders would spend up to two years collecting furs on the coast, winter in the Hawaiian Islands, then sell the furs in Canton and bring home Chinese tea and manufactures.

After considerable success at trading (at one point bartering two hundred sea-otter skins for an equivalent number of cheap chisels "in a very fue moments"), Kendrick and Gray switched ships, and the *Lady Washington* sailed to China to sell its furs. Eventually, in 1791, the vessel, with Kendrick in command, became the first U.S. ship to visit Japan, stopping briefly in the south after getting caught in bad weather but wisely leaving before the crew could be arrested, imprisoned, or worse.[6]

Gray, on the other hand, continued sailing the *Columbia* back to Boston via China (his ship becoming the first U.S. vessel to circumnavigate the globe). Then in 1790 he embarked on yet another trading venture. It was on this second expedition, around May 11, 1792 (more than half a year before Broughton), that Gray sailed over the bar into the river that today bears his ship's name.

First Impressions of the Lower Columbia

Gray and his crew quickly realized that they were not on a bay but a huge freshwater river. The log of the fifth mate, John Boit, reported that they berthed the ship "abrest the Village *Chinoak*, command'd by a cheif name *Polack*. Vast many Canoes full of Indians from different parts of the river where constantly along side. . . . The Indians . . . appear'd very civill (not even offering to steal). During our short stay we collected 150 otter, 300 beaver, and twice the Number of other land furs."[7] In fact, the river teemed with fish, nearby woods were filled with deer and elk, and alongside the water's banks grew delicious edible roots. With considerable prescience, Boit speculated that a trading post (or "factory") on the Columbia River could easily grow its own food and, with one or two other posts, dominate trade on the entire Northwest Coast.

Of the Indians' appearance, Boit gave a glowing review: "The Men at Columbia's River are strait limb'd, fine looking fellows, and the women are very pretty. They are all in a state of Nature, except the females, who wear a leaf Apron (perhaps '*twas* a fig leaf)."[8] His description was quite a contrast to that of later visitors, who often negatively compared the Chinooks to Hawaiians or to the tall, regal-looking Plains Indians they had encountered on overland trips. One fur trader who arrived twenty years later described the Chinooks as being:

the most uncouth-looking objects. . . . Their eyes were black, piercing, and treacherous; their ears slit up, and ornamented with strings of beads; the cartilage of their nostrils perforated . . . while their heads presented an inclined plane from the crown to the upper part of the nose, totally unlike our European rotundity of cranium; and their bodies besmeared with whale oil gave them an appearance horribly disgusting. They the women,—O ye gods! With the same auricular, olfactory, and craniological peculiarities, they exhibited loose hanging breasts, short dirty teeth, skin saturated with blubber, bandy legs, and a waddling gait, while their only dress consisted of a kind of petticoat . . . [that] . . . formed a miserable shield in defence of decency.[9]

We have no written record of what the Chinooks thought of the first European Americans they encountered. Yet given the sanitation habits of sailors and frontiersmen, and their general hairiness and unkemptness, it was certainly not as favorable as the whites would like to have thought. The Chinooks were excellent swimmers and bathed regularly, whereas the whites almost never did.

Comcomly is not mentioned in the logs of either the *Columbia* or *Chatham*, but as a young man back then he would have witnessed the explorers' arrival. Shortly thereafter, his name does appear in other records, often in the context of the intense international rivalry in the region and the growing interest in further linking the Northwest fur trade with Asia and the perceived wealth of Japan.

❖ ❖ ❖

In 1785, also acting on Cook's discoveries, London investors had formed the King George's Sound Company to pursue fur trade on the Northwest Coast themselves, hoping to create a trading post at Nootka and trade throughout the North Pacific, including Japan. Compared to the Americans, these financiers were at a disadvantage, as the British Empire had at that stage already divvied up the world into trading blocs for which it parceled out monopolies. Nonetheless, the East India Company (which handled Asia) agreed to specially license a ship "to proceed from the North West Coast of America to the Japanese islands and China."[10] Charles Bishop was made captain of an American-built vessel, the *Ruby*, and on September 24, 1794, he was given the following instructions:

> I have appointed you to the command of my ship the Ruby, on an intended voyage to the North West Coast of America, Japan and China . . . you will proceed examining the Coast to Deception Bay, which lies in 46°20' North Latitude. I advise your going over the Bar into this bay on the flood tide, as the River Choonock and two other considerable Rivers empties them selves into this bay. There are very fine Sea Otter, River Otter, Fox, Martin, Racoon, Lynx cat, Beavers, Wolves and Bear skins to be procured there.[11]

After obtaining as many furs as possible, Bishop was then to sail on to Japan and China, with the first stop contingent on a "favourable account of the trade at the Japanese Islands."

The British financiers must have known of Japan's harsh prohibitions against foreign visitors, but they were dreaming the old dream of wealth. Two centuries earlier, prior to Japan's Seclusion edicts, the East India Company had maintained a small trading post at Hirado in Japan; the British had long schemed to somehow get back in. Bishop's instructions were specific, requiring him to go back and forth from the Northwest and Asia twice. To keep faith with the trading license, when arriving at Canton in China he was to provide the East India Company's supercargo representative there an accurate ship manifest not only of all the furs and merchandise on board the *Ruby* but any "gold and silver" that might have been procured in Japan. Bishop was sternly warned not to do any harm to the natives in Japan or China.[12]

On May 22, 1795, the *Ruby* sailed over the bar into the Columbia and promptly began trading. The first Indians met were peaceful. The next day though, Bishop complained that no one was interested in his best wares—including tea kettles, sheet copper, and fine cloth—because two other trading sea captains had recently wintered at the site. Nonetheless, trade soon picked up, and near the mouth of the Columbia Bishop sometimes had two hundred Indians visiting at a time, "plentifully arm'd with Bows & arrows, spears and some Muskets." He had to post extra guards to ensure piece of mind, but all went well.[13]

After a foray up north for more furs, Bishop returned again on December 10, and on this date his log first mentions Comcomly. The ship was visited by then head chief, Taucum, with Comcomly and another chief named Shelathwell. Bishop tried hard to win their confidence and had great success. When one of his crewmen was found to have stolen an arrow from the Indians, he had the man tied up and flogged. "A trifling present now and then," he also wrote, "gratifies their Desires, and which is generally returned by a Present of Fish or Cranberries, nor do they withhold their Daughters, some of whom are well Featured young Women."[14]

Comcomly, in particular, developed a remarkable friendship with Bishop. The captain wrote of Comcomly that the "little one Eyed man has en-

Comcomly, Chief of the Chinooks. From a drawing in Duncan McDougal's Astoria journal, 1810–13.

deared him Self to every one on board. He often sleeps in my Cabin and gives me many Proofs of his disinterested kindness. I have had a Jackett and Trousers fitted for him, and this day he first Putt them on to his great delight." In another log entry, Bishop added, "The chief has ever deserved our warmest Friendship and Praise. His Pacific manners, Truth and honesty are seldom met with in Savage life."[15]

As Bishop and other captains discovered, Comcomly could offer protection. On the frontier Pacific Northwest Coast, security was extremely important, as trading from ships was fraught with risk for both Indians and sailors. The *Columbia*, for example, had stopped in Gray's Harbor, near today's Aberdeen, just before finding the Columbia River. According to John Boit, when too many Indians came too close one midnight,

> We fi'd sevrall cannon over them, but still [they] persisted to advance with the war Hoop. At length a large Canoe with at least 20 Men in

her got within $^1\!/_2$ pistol shot of the quarter, and with a Nine pounder, loaded with langerege and about 10 Musketts, loaded with Buck shot, we dash'd her all to peices, and no doubt kill'd every soul in her. . . . I do not think that they had aney Conception of the power of Artillery. But they was too near us for to admit of any hesitation how to proceed.[16]

If a trading ship killed or mistreated natives on its visit, a vicious cycle of revenge could start, wherein the next, unrelated ship might be attacked. In the most famous incident of this nature, occurring in June 1811, the *Tonquin* sailed north from the Columbia to trade for pelts along the Northwest Coast, only to become embroiled in a dispute with Indians. According to the sole survivor, after most of the crew had been massacred one or more men retreated to the powder room, "lit a fire there and ended their lives in a heroic manner by exploding the ship with some hundred savages who were on board."[17]

Comcomly and his people offered protection from attacks, but they also provided other services, too. As those arriving by sea soon learned, the Chinooks had an intimate knowledge of the Columbia River and its tricky entrance; so much so that Comcomly later officially piloted most of the ships entering the river, saving many lives in the process. And if there were advantages for the whites in allying with the Chinooks, the reverse was also true. The Chinooks had long been traders rather than warriors, intermediaries between inland tribes and the traditional bounty of the lower Columbia. New technology helped them amass power and influence far in excess of their actual number. In his log entry of December 7, 1795, Bishop described how Comcomly and Shelathwell once took off up the Columbia River in a large canoe paddled by ten men, each armed with a musket, Comcomly dressed in a jacket and trousers. The Chinooks, Bishop learned, regularly sailed two to three hundred miles up river to trade with Indian villages that had had no exposure to civilization. They offered trade in trifling pieces of copper or iron for skins and other goods:

The strangers naturally demand more. The chief then gives the Signal and they all discharge their Pieces laden with Powder, into the Air. These people never having heard or seen such a Strange Phenomema throw of[f] their Skins and Leather War Dresses and fly into the woods, while the others Pick them up, and leave on the Spott the articles first offered.[18]

The first detailed descriptions of the Chinooks and their land came not from the sea-based traders but American explorers trekking overland. In 1803, President Thomas Jefferson sent Meriwether Lewis and William Clark to discover a land route to the Pacific and strengthen U.S. claims to the "Oregon territory." Lewis and Clark were not the first to reach the Northwest by land; Scottish fur trader Alexander MacKenzie had made it through the Canadian Rockies to the Pacific nearly ten years earlier. Lewis and Clark did, however, represent the expansionist aspirations of the young United States.

In 1805, subsisting on a starvation diet of dog and horse meat, the Lewis and Clark expedition straggled down the Columbia River to encounter a different world. Nearing the Pacific, the men entered cool and misty forests of giant evergreen trees, standing over two hundred feet tall. They also found an increasingly dense population of Indians, mostly the Chinookan family of tribes, who shared a common culture and lived off the immense bounty of the river and land around it. On November 4, Clark commented in his diary about one group of Indians: "[T]hey had scarlet & blue blankets, Salor Jackets, overalls, Shirts and hats independant of their usial dress; the most of them had either [*war axes Spears or Bows Sprung with quivers of arrows,*] Muskets or pistols and tin flasks to hold their powder." Later, Lewis would note that many of the tin flasks were "japanned" (the word in those days for lacquered).[19] The men on the expedition had been impressed by the horsemanship of the Plains Indians, but on the Columbia they were impressed by the Indians' canoemanship. As Lewis wrote, another group of Indians, who claimed to have gotten their sailor clothes from "white people," "left us and crossed the river (which is about 5 miles wide at this place) through the highest waves I ever Saw a Small vestles ride. Those Indians are certainly the best Canoe navigators I ever saw."[20] On November 15, about eight miles from Cape Disappointment, Lewis and Clark encountered members of the Chinook Tribe proper, surmising that they numbered over four hundred people, "well armed with fusees." Then, on November 20, Clark wrote, they "found maney of the *Chin nooks* with Capt. Lewis of whome there was 2 Cheifs *Com com mo ly* & *Chil-lar-la-wil* to whome we gave Medals and to one a flag."[21]

Like others before and after them, Lewis and Clark noted how much the

Chinooks differed from other Indians they had met. Instead of teepees, the Chinooks lived in the winter in houses made with boards. Using canoes beautifully hand-hewn out of huge cedar logs up to fifty feet long and five feet across, they fished and hunted, even going whaling along the coast. In battle, Indian warriors wore body armor made of elk skins so tough that a slow musket ball could be warded off (later some of the whites would wear this armor). The Chinooks made and cherished fancy wooden boxes, and sometimes wore elaborately crafted conical hats woven of cedar bark or grass. Most of the time, though, they dressed in little other than a robe, even in the coldest weather, although women usually wore tiny grass skirts. They had short instead of long legs and low instead of high aquiline noses. "Points of resemblance have been noted by many observers between the Chinook and Mongolian physiognomy," Hubert Howe Bancroft would write in his definitive 1886 work on *The Native Races*, "consisting chiefly in the eyes turned obliquely upward at the outer corner. The face is broad and round, the nose flat and fat, with large nostrils."[22]

As mentioned previously, the Chinook proper were also distinguishable by their flattened foreheads, caused by compressing the heads of infants between boards. Such flattened heads were a sign of beauty and aristocracy; slaves, which the Chinooks kept in abundance and traded, had round heads. The flattening affect had no effect on intelligence, as tribe members were regarded as extremely friendly, loquacious, and inquisitive with excellent memories. To Lewis and Clark's astonishment, the Chinook tribes already knew English words such as "musquit, powder, shot, knife, file, damned rascal, sun of a bitch & c." and could recite the names of English-speaking captains of over a dozen sailing ships. One woman had the name of "J. Bowman" tattooed on her arm, and a man they met was "freckled with long duskey red hair . . . and must Certainly be half white at least."[23]

Like other early visitors, Lewis and Clark commented on the lack of clothing and inhibitions among the unmarried women, whose social status, they noted, often seemed higher than in other Indian tribes. Unfortunately, both Lewis and Clark also noted the negative effects on natives from prior interaction with whites; at least one expedition member, unable to resist local charms, soon contracted venereal disease.

More ominously, other signs were evident that Indians near the mouth of the Columbia had already experienced the scourge of small pox and other contagions. Indeed, Clark speculated that the disease may have been responsible for the many deserted villages he saw nearby.

Finding the weather on the north shore of the Columbia miserably damp, Lewis and Clark moved their party to the south shore. A fort was erected in the territory of the Clatsops, another tribe in the Chinookan family, and there the men rested until spring, when they would again set out for the long return journey. Comcomly and the Chinooks proper lived on the river's north side but visited occasionally. Because of their help, in addition to the Clatsops', the Lewis and Clark party survived the winter.

The Ranald MacDonald monument in Astoria, Oregon. A partial replica of Fort Astoria can be seen in the background.

Photo © 1999 Frederik L. Schodt.

Astoria

Astoria is the largest town near the mouth of the Columbia River today. The charming old port on the south side of the river, in Oregon, enjoys a diverse population of nearly ten thousand, including many Norwegians, Swedes, Finns, and some Chinook descendants, too. In recent years, the city's primary industries have begun to shift from fishing and logging to tourism, with an emphasis on history. Six miles southwest of Astoria, the Lewis and Clark winter encampment, Ft. Clatsop, has been reconstructed. On the river itself, a replica of the *Lady Washington*—the ship that helped search for the Columbia and later sailed on to Japan—can occasionally be seen gliding down the river, dwarfed by giant container vessels hauling grain, hops, and wood products to Japan and other nations in Asia.[24]

One of the most imposing landmarks in the city is the Astoria Column, towering dramatically atop Coxcomb Hill, overlooking the Columbia River. A tourist pamphlet declares that the column, built in 1926, "commemorates the westward sweep of discovery and migration which brought settlement and western civilization to the Northwest Territory." This "westward sweep" nearly swept away all indigenous cultures in its path, but in 1961, at the foot of the tower, in what seems to be almost an afterthought, the city added a small memorial to Chief Comcomly of the Chinooks. It is a raised black burial canoe, rendered in concrete, minus his remains. Directly below the hill and monument, on the corner of 15th and Exchange Streets, is a small park, featuring a partial reconstruction of the original Ft. Astoria, with part of a blockhouse and palisade visible. In one corner stands a granite stone memorial to Comcomly's descendant, Ranald MacDonald. Dedicated on May 21, 1988, with funding provided by the Portland Japanese Chamber of Commerce and generous individuals, the MacDonald monument has an inscription in English on one side and in Japanese on the other. The English engraving reads:

> Birthplace of RANALD MacDONALD, 1824–1894. First teacher of English in Japan. The son of the Hudson's Bay Co. manager of Ft. George and Chinook chief Comcomly's daughter, MacDonald theorized that a racial link existed between Indians and Japanese. He determined to enter Japan although it was closed to foreigners for over two hundred years. Sailing in 1848 as a deckhand on an American whaler, he marooned himself on Rishiri Island near Hokkaidō. While waiting his deportation, he was allowed to teach English to 14 Japanese scholars, some of whom became leaders in the modernization of Japan. He spent his active life in Europe, Canada and Australia. He is buried in an Indian cemetery near Curlew, Washington.

The Japanese version on the reverse side is a loose, abbreviated translation of the English, but it adds the information that MacDonald was imprisoned while in Japan.

Bruce Berney, head of the Astoria City Library until 1997, initiated the project to build the monument. He had once taught English in Japan and so had become interested in things Japanese. Like most Americans, however, he had never heard of MacDonald, whose story had been largely forgotten. Around 1970, while weeding out old books in the library, Berney stumbled across the 1923 Eastern Washington State Historical Society's edition of MacDonald's book (the posthumously published *Ranald MacDonald*, containing his *Narrative*, entitled *Japan, Story of Adventure*). Berney found Mac-Donald's story almost too amazing to believe. By coincidence, they both shared the same birthday—February 3—and with this connection in mind, in 1974, Berney put on a "birthday party" for MacDonald. He worked up for the occasion a four-page, printed program, outlining MacDonald's life story. Copies were later sent around the country , and as it happened, one was read by Torao Tomita, then a Japanese Fulbright student studying American history at Yale University. Tomita knew of and was already interested in Mac-Donald, and he therefore traveled to Astoria to meet Berney. Tomita was given an original copy of the 1923 book, which he later translated into Japanese, thus rekindling interest in MacDonald in Japan.

As Berney recalls it today, "[a]fter the "birthday party, I realized not only that MacDonald's story was authentic but that people really were interested in him. As library director in Astoria I also thought the book helped show that literature is important to the community. There were many sailors then coming to Astoria from all over, walking around town without knowing anything about Ranald MacDonald and the fact that he was born here. So I decided there ought to be a monument to him, both in English and in Japanese."[25]

With help from the chamber of commerce, individuals, and especially Mas Tomita, local Japanese head of the Epson Company in Portland, money was raised for a stone memorial. A "Friends of MacDonald" Society was organized as a committee within the Clatsop County Historical Society. A dedication ceremony was carried out under the latter's auspices and attended by local notables, representatives of the British and Japanese consulates, descendants of Comcomly, and relatives of MacDonald from Washington and Montana. Torao Tomita was one of the key speakers.

❈ ❈ ❈

Astoria gets its name from John Jacob Astor, the famous German-born New York merchant. Immortalized in Washington Irving's 1836 classic, *Astoria*, Astor had a remarkably global vision at the dawn of the nineteenth century. He knew some people were making fortunes in land-based fur trade, especially the shareholders of the London-based Hudson's Bay Company, as well as the North West Company, based in Montreal, Canada. Both companies had posts distributed throughout the northeast and central American wilderness; their furs were transported across an elaborate system of rivers and lakes and portages, then shipped across the Atlantic to Europe, whence they could also be shipped to China. The "North Westers" (or Nor' Westers) did a particularly roaring business, and when the company partners showed up in New York they created quite an impression. Irving wrote how they had about them "A gorgeous prodigality, such as was often to be noticed in former times in southern planters and West India creoles, when flush with the profits of their plantations."[26]

When trade became possible between the newly independent United States and British Canada, Astor entered the fur business and soon made a considerable profit. Nonetheless, he foresaw how a trading concern with an outpost on the Columbia River (with other posts inland) would accrue enormous advantages over his rivals. His was truly a bold idea, given the then small size of the United States and its distance from the Pacific. In Astor's thinking, such an outpost could ship furs directly to Canton, China, and even supply Russian forts in Alaska. Such an American outpost would also help to fend off rival trading groups in the area and might help establish a U.S. claim to the region, one upon which the British, Russians, and Spanish had also set their sights.

After receiving President Thomas Jefferson's encouragement, Astor formed the Pacific Fur Company in 1810 and sent two expeditions to the mouth of the Columbia, one by land and one by sea, the latter in the aforementioned doomed ship, the *Tonquin*. In the Hawaiian Islands, the *Tonquin* (like many ships in the fur trade) picked up a group of Hawaiian natives as crew and helpers and then headed for the Columbia. The ship cleared the river's bar at the end of March 1811, losing several men in the process. Shortly thereafter, the survivors built an outpost on the south side of the Columbia, and named it Astoria, after their venture's founder.

Like earlier visitors, the "Astorians"—who included Scotsmen, Iroquois, French Canadians, and Hawaiians—immediately became indebted to Comcomly and the Chinooks. Irving referred to Comcomly in his book as "a shrewd old savage, with but one eye," yet noted that he received the Astorians with great hospitality. Only days after meeting them, Comcomly saved several lives after a boat carrying their de facto leader, Duncan McDougall, capsized in the roiling waters of the Columbia. The Chinooks went on to help the Americans, teaching them to navigate the Columbia and protecting and provisioning them as they struggled to set up their trading operation.

The natives also revealed to the Astorians a remarkable link they had to Asia. As Gabriel Franchère noted in his journal entry for August 11, they brought along a man who—apparently having worked previously for a trading ship—"appeared to be endowed with a good deal of intelligence and knew several English words. He told us that he had been at the Russian trading post at Chitka [Sitka, Alaska], on the California coast, in the Sandwich Islands, and in China."[27]

Comcomly worked particularly hard to cement his relationship with the Astorians. He had several wives, as was the custom among the Chinook aristocracy, and many children, including several attractive daughters. After rescuing the hapless McDougall, who could not swim, from the Columbia, Comcomly took the man and his companions to his village to dry out. As Irving described it, "his wives and daughters endeavored by all the soothing and endearing arts of women, to find favor in their eyes. Some even painted their bodies with red clay and anointed themselves with fish oil to give additional luster to their charms."[28]

The strategy worked. McDougall proposed marriage to one of Comcomly's daughters, and on July 20, 1813, he was united with her in a lavish ceremony. Comcomly sailed to Astoria from his village, a squadron of canoes carrying his royal family. Irving, adding his trademark seriocomic style to the stories and journals of others, observed that the

> [w]orthy sachem landed in princely state, arranged in a bright blue blanket and red breech clout, with an extra quantity of paint and feathers, attended by a train of half-naked warriors and nobles. A horse was in waiting to receive the princess, who was mounted behind one of the clerks, and thus conveyed, coy but compliant, to the fortress. Here she was received with devout, though decent joy, by her expecting bridegroom. . . . From that time forward, Comcomly was a daily visitor at the fort, and was admitted into the most intimate councils of his son-in-law.[29]

The marriage was regarded as a strategic alliance by both Chinooks and whites; among the Astorians, Comcomly was thereafter referred to as a "king" and his children as "princes" or "princesses." (Later, the British would commonly refer to his oldest son and daughter as the "Prince and Princess of Wales.") But Astoria itself proved to be temporarily doomed. The problem was neither the elements, Indians, nor failure of Astor's planning. Indeed, John Jacob Astor's vision steadily turned into reality, with trade initiated between the mouth of the Columbia and Canton, China, via the Hawaiian Islands, as well as the Russian outpost to the north in Sitka. Astoria's real problem proved to be global politics.

The North West Company

The year 1812 found the young United States and Britain again embroiled in war. Although the fighting took place far from Astoria (and for Britain, at least, was really an extension of its wars with Napoleonic France), the area was not unaffected. In October 1813, members of a rival trading company, the North West Company, appeared in Astoria. McDougall—knowing that the men hailed from Canada, which was British-controlled, and fearing British warships would arrive to conquer them at any moment—decided to sell the brand-new fort to the North Westers. The fact that he had formerly been a member of that company—and soon rejoined them after selling the fort—led many subsequent writers to question his basic loyalty to the United States. Like many of the original "Astorians," however, McDougall was not really an American but a Scotsman from British Canada, only chosen by Astor for his prior experience in the fur trade.

The North West Company, formed in 1787, was based in Montreal, Canada, which had itself been wrested from the French by the British in 1763. Like the United States, Canada in 1812 was a fraction of its present size, existing mostly as a strip of land around the St. Lawrence River and the Great Lakes; the region west of the Rockies was still a vast, dimly understood frontier. But as one of the great fur empires of its day, the North West Company rapidly expanded westward. Its partners, or major shareholders, and officers were mainly of Scottish descent. They formed a sort of commercial aristocracy among themselves, many living and working much of the year in the wilderness; their intimate familiarity with the wilderness contributed greatly to the Company's success.

These men had found it nearly impossible to survive without Indian wives, women who knew how to live off the land and could act as friendly intermediaries with local tribes. The result was intermarriage and the birth of a community of mixed-blood children. This was particularly true of the Company's French Catholic employees, the trappers and the tireless canoe paddlers and workers known as *voyageurs*. Far more than Protestant whites, they were, as Irving put it, "prone to intermarry and domesticate themselves among the Indians." They became so acclimated to life in the wilderness that their culture blurred with that of the native. Their dress became a mixture of European and Indian costumes, and their language also became "of the same piebald character, being a French patois, embroidered with Indian and English words and phrases." At a typical gathering of Nor' Westers in Montreal, when the Scotsmen sang and reveled, "their merriment was echoed and prolonged by a mongrel legion of retainers, Canadian voyageurs, half breeds, Indian hunters, and vagabond hangers-on, who feasted sumptuously without on the crumbs that fell from their table, and made the welkin ring with old French ditties, mingled with Indian yelps and yellings."[30]

A few members of the North West Company had visited Astoria right after the Americans built the fort. David Thompson, an official geographer for the Company, made it overland to the area in 1811 and was welcomed by Duncan McDougall, as well as Comcomly and the Chinooks. On July 14, Thompson took his men out to the coast to see the Pacific Ocean for the first time. Although personally thrilled, Thompson would write, "[M]y Men seemed disappointed; they had been accustomed to the boundless horizons of the great Lakes of Canada, and their high rolling waves; from the Ocean they expected a more boundless view, a something beyond the power of their senses which they could not describe; and my informing them, that directly opposite to us, at the distance of five thousand miles was the Empire of Japan added nothing to their ideas, but a Map would."[31]

In November 1813, Astoria's transition to British control became complete when a British warship arrived to take formal possession of the little settlement. Comcomly had difficulty understanding how the "Bostons" could give up without a fight to "King George's men," and reportedly remarked of his son-in-law that his daughter had made a mistake, and "instead of getting a great warrior for a husband, had married herself to a squaw."[32] But like many of the original Astorians who merely changed employers, Comcomly adapted quickly. One witness described his appearance a few months later, wearing "a red coat, New Brunswick Regiment 104th, a Chinese hat, white shirt, cravat, trousers, cotton stockings, and a fine pair of shoes."[33]

British-controlled Astoria was renamed "Fort George," and for a while the settlement prospered, as did Comcomly and his tribe. Still, like the

Astorians, the North West Company's reign was short. Far, far to the north and east, the North West Company's archrival, the Hudson's Bay Company, was steadily expanding its sphere of influence.

The Hudson's Bay Company

In Canada today, the Hudson's Bay Company is best known for its chain of department stores named "The Bay," yet it is also arguably the world's oldest corporation. Chartered in 1670 by the English Crown as "The Company of Adventurers of England trading into Hudson's Bay," its mission was mainly to trade for furs, yet it was also supposed to search for a Northwest Passage that would lead to the riches of the Far East. Functioning much like an independent corporate state, the HBC retained the power to deploy its own armies and navies, make laws, and mint coin. Like Britain's East India Company on the other side of the world, the HBC was also granted monopoly trading rights, in this case, to the entire drainage basin of the Hudson Bay, a vague place called "Rupert's Land," so huge almost no one had any idea how large it really was. For over a century, the Company largely operated around the frigid Hudson Bay, trading blankets and simple manufactures for furs trapped by Indians, and shipping them back to Britain. Initially, its officers were usually English or Scottish, while young men taken from the impoverished Orkney Islands in the North Atlantic formed the main labor source.

Unlike the North West Company, the Hudson's Bay Company long required its employees to submit to an impossible life of bachelorhood, for no white women were brought to the Hudson Bay area, and marriage with Indians was forbidden. But in the wilderness, nature had its way. Like the North Westers later, more and more HBC men developed liaisons with Indian women. Inevitably, as scholar Silvia Van Kirk would come to document in her book, *Many Tender Ties: Women in Fur Trade Society, 1670–1870*, despite HBC policy these liaisons often developed into more permanent marriages that were described as "au façon du pays" (in the custom of the country).

As the Hudson's Bay Company slowly expanded south and west, it began to collide with the newer North West Company, expanding north and west. The two organizations remained arch enemies until 1821, when the North West Company was pushed to merge into the Hudson's Bay Company. The takeover in effect gave the latter a virtual empire of over three million square miles of territory, for Britain gave the HBC not only monopoly trading rights in "Rupert's Land" but sole British trading rights in today's Pacific Northwest, then referred to as "Oregon country." In 1818, a Treaty of Joint Occupation had been signed with the United States over this vast wilderness between Russian Alaska and Spanish California, and it included the Columbia River Basin. Since almost no Americans were then in the region, the HBC wound up with de facto jurisdiction over an area that stretched from the Atlantic to the Pacific.

The Origins of Ranald MacDonald

In 1820, George Simpson was sent out from London to eventually oversee the reorganization of the Company in North America as its "governor." A small but physically tough man, Simpson would so dominate HBC operations in North America for the next few decades that he would be referred to as a little "emperor," in allusion to Napoleon, whom he admired greatly. Simpson would take the Company to its greatest heights of glory and ultimately diversify it beyond furs. But one of his first tasks was to understand and consolidate the assets of the newly enlarged Company. In 1821, he sent a promising young clerk named Archibald McDonald—who would become Ranald MacDonald's father—all the way to the Columbia River and Fort George, the former Astoria, to inventory the Company's new assets.

Like many HBC officials, Archibald McDonald was a Scot. Descended from the famous Donald Clan and a long line of Highland warriors, he was a man of great talent, well educated for his day, with training in mathematics, Latin, English and Gaelic literature, as well as medicine, and other sciences. Jean Murray Cole, a twentieth-century biographer and descendant, notes that he "possessed a joie de vivre, a gift for friendship and loyalty . . . a devotion to family and a delight in children and young people that charmed everyone in his circle throughout his life."[34] According to the *Montreal Gazette*, which ran his obituary in 1853, "His courage, skill, and physical power, as a young man, were extraordinary, and to these were united mental qualifications of no mean order."[35] He had joined the HBC in 1820.

From the beginning, Archibald McDonald was on an elite track. He was a "gentleman" who would become an officer and devote his life to the Company, presiding over large numbers of *voyageurs*, trappers, and laborers. Beneath the governorship was a hierarchy of three grades of officers—chief

OrHi10125. Courtesy Oregon Historical Society. From H.B.C. *Beaver*, Sept., 1945.

George Simpson, in later years, n.d.

factors, chief traders, and clerks—and with diligence and application one could rise through the ranks. As one of Archibald's sons later described it, "The advancement in the Hudson's Bay Company was by promotion, much like the advancement in the army. A clerk would advance to Chief Trader usually after about five to ten years of service and would then be eligible for Chief Factor, if he proved the right mettle, after the expiration of ten years more."[36] The Company was like a military organization in that its officers could expect to be rotated in and out of a variety of assignments and posts.

Around the time Astoria fell under British control, Company policy on marriage to local Indians shifted in favor of it, at least in the Pacific Northwest. George Simpson had a reputation as a scoundrel when it came to Indian women, so much so that he has been referred to as " 'the father of the fur trade' . . . with a nudge and a knowing wink."[37] But even he realized that the highly organized Indian societies at the mouth of the Columbia were different from those inland, writing that "[c]onnubial alliances are the best security we can have of the goodwill of the Natives, I have therefore recommended the Gentlemen to form connections with the principal Families immediately on their arrival, which is no difficult matter as the offer of their Wives & Daughters is the first token of their Friendship & Hospitality."[38] In 1824, when Simpson himself later visited the former Astoria, newly named Fort George, he found himself under great pressure to marry another of Comcomly's daughters. "I . . . have a difficult card to play," he wrote, "being equally desirous to keep clear of the Daughter and continue on good terms with the Mother and by management I hope to succeed in both altho her Ladyship is most pressing & persevering tempting me with fresh offers and inducements every succeeding Day."[39]

Archibald McDonald must have made Simpson very happy, for he had already married another daughter of Comcomly's, variously known as Princess Raven (after her Chinookan name of Koale'xoa) or "Princess Sunday." He was at least the third white man to marry one of the chief's daughters. It is not known if Archibald married for love or simply because of his superior's recommendation and the need for a housekeeper. But he was thirty-three years old, in his physical prime, living in a country where the only white woman ever previously seen had been an English bar girl brought out for a brief stay in 1814. A blue-blood Chinook princess was thus considered an attractive match, despite the vast cultural differences between the two individuals. Many whites criticized the loose morals of single Chinook women, but they thought highly of them as wives. One usually acerbic Astorian wrote, "Many of these women, who have followed a depraved course of life before marriage, become excellent and faithful wives afterwards."[40]

Archibald apparently never discussed his first marriage with his son. In the latter's posthumously published *Narrative*, Ranald MacDonald relates that he only heard about the union from a ship captain at a much later date. Leading up to the wedding site, he was told, covering "about three hundred yards—was a path of golden sheen, of richest *furs*, viz. of prime beaver, otter (sea and land), nothing less! . . . Along this golden path way, as a guard of honor, were three hundred of the slaves, so-called, of the King."[41] In reality, even Ranald had had difficulty believing the story when he first heard it. Jokingly, he once remarked that "that could not be my Father for the H.B.C. had too great veneration of a Beaver skin to make a carpet of it [therefore I thought it] must be Mr. McDougall of the Astor Company [but the captain] said, no, it was MacDonald."[42] About six months after Archibald's marriage, on or about February 3, 1824, Ranald was born. His mother died shortly after the birth and almost nothing is known about her. Ranald was entrusted to the care of her Chinook sister, Car-cumcum, who lived in a lodge next to the fort. He became, according to his own account, "the favorite, the 'Toll, Toll' (Chinook for the Boy! the Boy!) of Gran'pa."[43]

That same year, under Simpson's direction, the Company decided to relocate its Columbia River operations to a place some eighty miles up the river, on the north bank. More convenient for fur collection, this site became Fort Vancouver (in today's Washington State). About a year later in his travels,

OrHi 6599. Courtesy Oregon Historical Society.

Archibald McDonald, in later years, n.d.

Archibald McDonald met and fell in love with Jane Klyne, daughter of Michael Klyne, who worked for the HBC in the Rocky Mountains. Ranald MacDonald's posthumously published autobiography refers to her as a sixteen- or seventeen-year-old "German Swiss" woman, but subsequent research has clearly shown that his stepmother was a French and Indian *Métis* (mixed-blood) woman. The fact is obvious from surviving photographs.

Archibald's union with Jane Klyne proved to be long and happy, producing a total of thirteen children. Jane would grow into her role as wife of a powerful officer in the Hudson's Bay Company, later making a remarkable adaptation to life in a white, civilized world. Glowing reports of her exist in the accounts of early visitors to the West and do reveal hints of her true ancestry. Cushing Eells, an American missionary who visited the McDonalds in 1838 at Fort Colvile, wrote that "[McDonald's] wife was a jewel. A native of the country, she possessed rare excellence. The deportment of her numerous children was living testimony to her maternal efficiency." Mary Walker, wife of another missionary, recorded in 1839 that "Mr. Mdonald is a Scotch Presbyterian, very kind & hospitable has a pleasant wife who is nearly white & speaks good English. Their children appear as well as I think as any I ever saw in N.E. Their mother attends to their instructions having been herself educated by her husband."[44]

Jane Klyne took in Ranald and raised him as her own child, so much so that in his posthumously published Narrative he implies that not until much later in life did he know that his real mother was Comcomly's daughter, a Chinook princess, or even that he was part Chinook. This is highly unlikely, but MacDonald (or his editor) nonetheless write that after learning the real history of his birth, "the disillusionment pained me beyond expression."[45] Exactly what Ranald MacDonald knew about his real ancestry, and when he knew it, is one of the central mysteries all researchers of his story confront, as these facts probably had an influence on his later decision to go to Japan (see Appendix B— "Ranald MacDonald and the Chinooks").

❖ ❖ ❖

Jane Klyne McDonald, in 1865.

OrHi62601. Courtesy Oregon Historical Society.

Questions about MacDonald's knowledge of his true ancestry aside, the fusion of Chinook and Scottish blood that he represented may have helped him in specific ways during his later adventure to Japan. His features did have a slight Asian cast. While this may not have aided his initial landing in Japan—as even returning Japanese castaways were sometimes treated harshly—to his guards, at least, MacDonald may have seemed less threatening than other foreigners. In support of this theory, one of his cousins wrote in 1916, amusingly, that "Ranald's mother, was the daughter of an Indian chief on the Pacific Coast, hence, his complexion was that of Japanese only unusually larger, which I think [was] the true salvation of all the prisoners. No doubt the Japanese Governor, who employed Ranald, possibly thought that Ranald was of his tribe, etc."[46]

Second, while hereditary aspects of personality may be argued, in the end MacDonald was a man of superior intelligence, possessing a phenomenal memory and an absolutely fearless spirit. And like both his father and Chinook grandfather, MacDonald genuinely enjoyed people. In his surviving letters, he displays a wonderful sense of humor. From the letters of those who knew him, and even from Japanese government records, it is clear that he had a rare ability to attract people from broad walks of life, putting them at ease and endearing himself to them.

Finally, and perhaps most importantly in the context of his adventure, Ranald MacDonald inherited an especially healthy constitution, with enormous upper-body strength. He grew to be five feet eight, or nine, inches tall, and at thirty-nine he was described as "very active" and weighing "over 225lb."[47] All indications are that for most of his life he was never ill. He lived to be seventy, which for his lifestyle and era was remarkable, but there was precedent for this among his ancestors. Although his Chinook mother had died in childbirth, his grandfather Comcomly lived into his mid-sixties, as did his father, Archibald. His paternal grandparents lived to be eighty-four and eighty-eight years old, respectively. From his father, young Ranald had inherited a natural immunity to European diseases, but just in case, he was vaccinated against smallpox twice—at a time when inoculations were still a very new medical procedure.

In this context, it is worth noting the subsequent fate of the Chinooks. The Chinooks proper had once been the most powerful and influential tribe in the history of the Pacific Northwest. Their language built the foundation for a nineteenth-century type of "Esperanto"—a native pidgin called "Chinook"or "Chinookwa-wa"—used first by Indians, and then by both Indians and whites, to communicate and trade up and down the Pacific Northwest Coast. The tribe's influence is reflected today in place names in Oregon and Washington and in Chinook helicopters, Chinook salmon, and Chinook winds. A Chinook Indian tribe does survive—headquartered in the little town of Chinook, Washington, set along the banks of the Columbia—but as of 2003 it was still struggling for formal legal recognition on its own land, after a century of legal battles with the federal government and the changing policies of successive administrations.

The Chinooks did not decline in power because of war or conflict. When the Hudson's Bay Company moved its main base of operations from Fort George to Fort Vancouver in 1824, the Chinooks could no longer play their time-honored role of intermediaries between the whites and other tribes upriver. And the Chinook social system had become corrupted by interaction with whites, so that even Comcomly's strict prohibitions against alcohol collapsed. Finally, like indigenous peoples around the world—like the Ainu in Japan and the Polynesians in the Pacific—the Chinooks were nearly destroyed by European germs. In 1806 Lewis and Clark had noticed the debilitating effects of smallpox, but that was only the beginning. Over the years, the Chinooks and other coastal tribes saw their numbers plummet through measles, malaria, and other unknown diseases.

A missionary, the Rev. Samuel Parker, who visited the area in 1835, found relatively few Indians left to convert:

> Since the year 1829 probably seven-eighths, if not . . . nine-tenths, have been swept away by disease, principally by fever and ague. . . . In the burning stage of the fever they plunged themselves into the river, and continued in the water until the heat was allayed, and rarely survived the cold stage which followed. So many and so sudden were the deaths which occurred, that the shores were strewed with the unburied dead. Whole and large villages were depopulated; and some entire tribes have disappeared, the few remaining persons, if there were any, united themselves with other tribes. This great mortality extended not only from the vicinity of the Cascades to the shores of the Pacific, but far north and south.[48]

Ten years later, in 1845, another missionary, the Rev. George Gary, would note in his diary that the Chinooks and Clatsops were "passing away like the dew; there are but four children under one year old in both tribes."[49]

❖ ❖ ❖

If MacDonald's lineage aided him in his adventure to Japan, the geographical location of his birth helped him even more. He gained an easy familiarity with languages, or at least a gift for communicating, through being born into an extremely polyglot environment. Hudson's Bay Company's employees around the Columbia River spoke a myriad of tongues, including French, Cree, Hawaiian, and Iroquois. Yet the area had been a complex linguistic milieu long before the whites arrived, as the Chinooks were used to communicating with other tribes who spoke different languages. After the arrival of the whites, Comcomly learned quite a bit of English, and several of his children became fluent. In 1839 British naval captain Edward Belcher (who would also visit Japan, just before MacDonald) stopped at the mouth of the Columbia and commented on the Chinooks: "As a nation, the first thing that struck us was their facility in picking up words, even to short sentences, and repeating the whole tolerably correctly."[50]

After the young MacDonald began living with his father and stepmother, he was still exposed to a wide variety of languages. His father's native tongue was Gaelic, while that of his stepmother was presumably French, mixed with some Indian. Given that one of MacDonald's stated reasons for going to Japan was to become an interpreter, it is worth noting his own father's acute awareness of the importance of interpreters. In an August 8, 1842, letter to an HBC superior, Archibald noted how hostile Indians had recently rained arrows on him and his men mainly because they had lacked interpreters after a misunderstanding had arisen. Condemning the Company's recent cutbacks in interpreters, he warned headquarters of the long-term consequences, stating flatly: "Interpreters are a necessary evil."[51]

Most important, in terms of MacDonald's adventure to Japan, is the fact that, for their time, people living at the mouth of the Columbia River had a uniquely global perspective and an orientation to Asia. The Astorians traded with China and dreamed of Japan. The Hudson's Bay Company could not sell furs directly to China (then under the jurisdiction of the East India Company), but it did trade with the Russians in Alaska, the Spanish in California, and the independent kingdom of Hawaii. And in an age in which most people spent their entire lives within a radius of a hundred miles, HBC officers such as MacDonald's father were true globetrotters, regularly traveling vast distances across the North American continent and back and forth to Europe. Some, such as HBC Governor George Simpson, were almost constantly on the move, even encircling the globe. To these Company men, Japan, because of its harsh laws, might not have been an immediate place to trade, but it was an object of intense interest. As MacDonald would write in his posthumously published *Narrative*, "Japan was our next neighbor across the way—only the placid sea, the Pacific, between us."[52]

CHAPTER 3

A Fateful Non-Meeting at Fort Vancouver

Ozette lies on a short stretch of Pacific coastline belonging to the Makah Nation, a small Native American Indian tribe living around Cape Flattery, near the northwestern tip of Washington State. Up from the beach, on a slightly elevated grassy area, is an excavation site for an ancient fishing village, where pottery shards from feudal Japan have been found in recent years. This is also where three Japanese sailors are thought to have been rescued in the winter of 1833–34, after drifting across the ocean all the way from Japan in a disabled ship. The same three seamen are often claimed to be one of the reasons Ranald MacDonald decided to journey to Japan.

Led by three Makah guides, on September 29, 1997, nearly one-hundred Japanese men and women—some in their seventies and eighties—hiked in almost four miles from the nearest road toward Ozette, through the lush growth of the Olympic National Forest. From a tiny township called Mihama, on the Chita Peninsula near the modern metropolis of Nagoya, the Japanese had come all the way to Ozette at their own expense for two reasons: to commemorate the souls of the three sailors and their less-lucky crewmates, and to thank the descendants of the people who had rescued the former. Placing sticks of burning incense in the sand next to an impromptu Buddhist altar of flowers and lemon candy, the Japanese recited

Citizens of Mihama Township, praying
at Ozette, 1997.

Photo © 1997 Frederik L. Schodt.

prayers for the now long-dead men. The Makah guides sang traditional songs and beat hand drums. The group then hiked back through the forest to the road, where waiting buses drove them on to Neah Bay, the main town on the Makah Reservation, for more ceremonies.

The Makah are one of the few Native American tribes on the Pacific Coast to have retained much of the land once owned by their forebearers, probably because it was situated in a rainy, stormy spot not coveted by whites. Preserving tradition remains an active goal of the tribal elders, and at the dawn of the twenty-first century, the normally ignored tribe received much media attention when it revived the custom of whaling, arousing the ire of anti-whaling forces. Rather than whaling, though, the real showcase of Makah tradition is an impressive cultural center and museum at Neah Bay, where tribal artifacts—especially items excavated at Ozette—are on display. Traditional Makah culture reveals many parallels with the Chinooks—the use of plank long houses, elaborate hats, an intimacy with the sea, and, though the museum makes little mention of it, trafficking in Indian slaves. One exhibit notes how the Makah also had metal tools long before Europeans arrived on the continent and that the "metal may have been parts of Asian shipwrecks that drifted upon the Makah shores." Because of its geographical location, Makah territory catches a great deal of flotsam and jetsam that drifts in on the North Pacific or the "Japan" Current.

The three Japanese sailors who washed up on Makah territory were part of a fourteen-man crew on the *Hōjunmaru*, which left the port of Toba in the Owari District of Japan on December 2, 1832. Encountering a violent storm on the way to Edo (today's Tōkyō), the rice and pottery-laden ship became disabled and drifted for over a year all the way to the Northwest Coast of America. For the three survivors (known today as the "three kichis" because of their names—Otokichi, Iwakichi, and Kyūkichi), the catastrophe was only the beginning of an extraordinary odyssey. From Makah territory, the rescued men were taken to the Hudson's Bay Company outpost at Fort Vancouver on the Columbia River, and then sent around the world on British and American ships via Hawaii, London, and China, eventually arriving in waters off the coast of Japan in 1837. There, near Edo and Kagoshima, the men encountered Japan's Seclusion Laws at their cruelest and ultimately had to abandon all hope of ever returning home. They all eventually died abroad.

The "Three-Kichi" Movement

In Japan, the "three kichis"—especially Otokichi, who in 1834 was only fifteen years old—are far better known than Ranald MacDonald. But like him, they have gradually emerged from the margins of history with the help of a strong grassroots movement. Their story is always intertwined with his.

The beginnings of the "Three-Kichi" Movement, as it relates to the township of Mihama, can be traced back to 1960, when the Japan Bible Society began trying to confirm the origins of the three men. While it might seem odd that this organization would take a leading role in the effort, as less than one percent of all Japanese are Christian today, the Bible Society in fact had good reason to do so. One of the first translations of the Bible into Japanese was done by a German missionary in Macao named Dr. Karl (Charles) Gutzlaff, with the help of Japanese castaways including the "three kichis." It is one of the most curious Bible translations in existence. Gutzlaff's specialty was really Chinese and the "three kichis" themselves were barely literate fishermen from a vicinity of Japan known for its peculiarly strong dialect—one sometimes made fun of by modern Japanese comedians.

After much searching, Bible Society members made the remarkable discovery that there was a gravestone with the names of all the crew of the Hōjunmaru in Ryōsanji, a Buddhist temple in Onoura, in today's Mihama Township. No bodies lie in the grave, of course, since in 1832 family members and friends presumed the entire crew to have been lost at sea. In 1961, however, confirmation of the "tombstone" enabled construction of a substantial monument in Onoura to the three men, commemorating, among other things, their contribution to Christianity. The monument, in turn, helped gain the three castaways recognition beyond a few academics and specialists.

In 1979, historian Akira Haruna published a book chronicling the men's odyssey. Titled *Nippon Otokichi Hyōryūki* [The story of castaway Nippon Otokichi], it was highly readable, meticulously researched, and won several awards for non-fiction. Because the story of Otokichi is always linked to Ranald MacDonald—and because Torao Tomita was then in the process of translating MacDonald's posthumously published autobiography—Haruna was able to consult with Tomita. Based on Tomita's careful reading of Mac-Donald's text, Haruna informed his readers that, while the Japanese men undoubtedly influenced MacDonald's decision to go to Japan, there is in fact no hard evidence that they actually met him. To declare this in writing at that time was quite rare; in both Japan and North America the presumed meeting had become something of a historical orthodoxy.

In his posthumously published *Narrative*, MacDonald is rather vague about his relationship to the "three kichis." In explaining his decision to go to Japan, he describes the possibility of death for visiting foreigners, and even returning Japanese. "This fact was well known to us of the Hudson's Bay Company in the Columbia," he says. "On one or two, if not more occasions, the Company had to deal with Japanese cast, in shipwreck, upon their shores, there and northwards, they had been carried thither by the periodically prevailing winds . . . and by the great 'Gulf Stream,' Kuro Siwo (the Great Black River, in Japanese nomenclature) of the Northern Pacific." He then tells the story of the "three kichis," from the time of their arrival on "Queen Charlotte Island" (believing it to be the site of their actual landing) to their attempt to reenter Japan on the U.S. ship *Morrison* in 1837. Cryptically, he adds, "I must admit, that when I started on my own mission, I had not heard, nor knew of this *Morrison* episode: but of the Queen Charlotte Island waifs I did know, being in the country at the time."[1] It is the last part of this sentence that has left the door wide open in both North America and Japan to much romantic speculation.

In 1978, a year before the publication of Haruna's book, a well-known Japanese Christian novelist named Ayako Miura had begun serializing the story about the odyssey of the "three kichis" in the weekly *Asahi* magazine. By 1983 Miura's work had been published in a three-volume set titled *Kairei* [Undersea ridge]. Her writing was well researched, but the novelistic structure also allowed Miura to imagine how the three castaways might have felt when they first encountered, for example, the Makah people and the Europeans and were alternately befuddled and shocked by such exotic items as shoes and trousers, glass windows, the eating of red meat (generally prohibited in Japan), and the worship of the Christian god (punishable by death at home).

Like most popular writers on the subject, Miura was unable to resist the temptation of showing the three Japanese meeting Ranald MacDonald at Fort Vancouver, where they were taken after being retrieved from the Makah by the Hudson's Bay Company in 1834. In her story, a ten-year-old Ranald runs up to the three Japanese at the fort to proclaim: "How great you are, to have spent months crossing the ocean in a wrecked ship, rocked by the waves, with no food or water. You are true heroes. . . . I hope we can be friends because I want to grow up to be strong and brave like you. Someday I, too, will cross the Pacific and go to Japan!" Upon parting, Ranald throws his arm around Otokichi and—in what would have been an utterly shocking gesture to Japanese at the time—kisses him on the cheek in admiration. In a historical aside, Miura then describes MacDonald's background, his later adventure to Japan, and the fact that "the Japanese language he learned from the three castaways is said to have aided him greatly."[2]

Miura's work was such a popular success that one month after her book came out a feature film version of the same title was released. It was quite inspirational, as befits the novel's religious theme, and for the time it was a fairly international work, being filmed on location not only in Japan but also Canada, Hong Kong, and Macao. The "three kichis" were played by fairly big-name Japanese actors. John McLoughlin—chief factor at the Hudson's Bay Company's Fort Vancouver, who arranged for the three Japanese to be ransomed from the Makah and sent to England—was played by born-again Christian, singer-songwriter Johnny Cash. Critics were not overly kind to the film, but the ending was dramatic, focusing on a historical incident of the "three kichis" landing on the shores of Japan's coastline, only to be bombarded with cannon balls by Shogunate forces.

With this sort of publicity, at the end of the 1980s the citizens of Mihama Township started to actively promote their three hometown "kichis." They initiated exchanges with fellow groups in the state of Washington, including eventually, the Makah Nation. By 1992 township officials were using business cards imprinted with Otokichi's picture and staging the first "Nippon Otokichi Triathalon" event to commemorate the spirit of Oto-

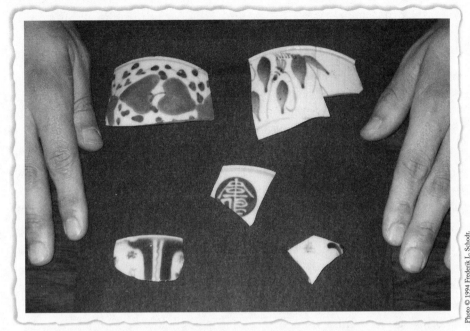

Shards of pottery from Ozette. On loan to Mihama Township; shown by Yasuo Takeuchi.

kichi, who had withstood so many hardships. In 1993, a musical, "The Story of Nippon Otokichi," was produced, with many citizens of Mihama taking part on stage; later the program was also performed in Singapore, the site of Otokichi's death in 1867. In 1995, CBC-TV, based in nearby Nagoya, made an award-winning documentary on Otokichi with a title that translates as "Nippon Otokichi, the castaway who yearned to return home but became a victim of the Seclusion Laws." In 1996, the Mihama Township borrowed from the Makah Nation various shards of Japanese pottery found at Ozette, displaying them like religious relics to awed visitors.

To the citizens of Mihama, the "three kichis" are understandably a source of enormous local pride. In part this is because so many citizens are deeply rooted in the area, and they thus identify closely with the events of nearly two hundred years ago. The overwhelming focus in Japan has been on Otokichi, because he is the best-documented survivor. But locals have links to other participants in the story, too. The Yamato Inn in Mihama, for example, is operated by direct descendants of the captain of the ship on which the "three kichis" first sailed.

Mihama Mayor Kōichi Saitō led the 1997 tour to Washington State.

One of the chief Otokichi boosters in Japan, he has tirelessly fostered contacts with not only the Makah and citizens of Washington but also Singapore, Germany, England, and China, all places with which Otokichi had connections. As Saitō explains, the Mihama region once flourished during Japan's feudal era partly because of its shipping industry, but in more modern times it has been somewhat left behind. As a former farmer and history buff, when he first read Akira Haruna's non-fiction work about Otokichi, he had become enthralled with the story's local connection and global nature. Honoring the memory of the "three kichis" thus became both a personal mission and a civic cause, one that could bolster Mihama's declining prospects in an era when its farming and fishing were declining in importance.

"Otokichi was left out of history," Saitō explains, "mainly because he never returned to Japan. We want to make sure that he's known and that there's enough information on him to get into textbooks, and we want to publicize Mihama in the process. We also hope someday to build a museum in Mihama to commemorate the role of castaways."[3]

Castaways and Drifters

"Castaways" is an imperfect translation of *hyōryūsha*, which literally means "drifters." In the context of Japan's Seclusion Era, the term refers to sailors—like the "three kichis"—whose ships became disabled in storms and drifted helplessly into the wide Pacific. This was largely a Japanese phenomenon and the result of a cruel policy implemented by the Shogunate. Before the Seclusion era, Japanese ships plied the waters throughout Southeast Asia and had been fully capable of sailing on the open seas. Early in the 1600s, however, the government, in its attempt to seal off the nation from foreign influences, prohibited the construction of large ships for the open seas. The decision was made despite the fact that, as Japan's cities developed economically, more and more goods had to be transported along coastal routes.

On Japan's eastern seaboard—particularly between the fertile area around Ise Bay, then known as Owari, and Edo—much of the cargo was carried in what were popularly called *sengoku-bune*, sailing ships that could carry a thousand *koku* (bales of rice), roughly equivalent to 150 tons. These ships were of sturdy construction but became greatly disadvantaged if swept too far out to sea. Single masted, sailed by a visual point-to-point system of coastal

navigation, they had high sterns with huge rudders—designed to prevent lat-
eral drift and be raised, if necessary, to allow passage into shallow waters. For
flexibility the rudders were often attached to the ship's hull by ropes.

When *sengoku-bune* were caught in storms and unable to make land, the
crews trimmed the sails and hoped for the best. But in truly rough conditions, the rudders were often lost. In that event, the next step was to cut
down the mast and start throwing cargo overboard to stabilize the ship. If
that failed, the crew would begin praying and drifting, helplessly. Usually
they drifted into oblivion, but sometimes, driven by winds and currents in
the Pacific, they might drift to land. Many fishing boats also became disabled, but the *sengoku-bune* always drifted out to sea the farthest. With huge
cargoes of rice aboard, crews could survive a long time by eating the supply,
fishing, and drinking rainwater (or distilling fresh water with a device called
a *ranbiki*, normally used to brew sake). Some ships drifted north to the
Kurile Islands, to Kamchatka, to the Aleutians, or even to the Northwest
Coast of America. Others, caught in different currents, drifted to Hawaii
and Mexico.

As Ayako Miura, the popular chronicler of the "three kichis," writes, in
the impassioned afterword of her book,

> Once these ships ran into storms and were blown into the open sea,
> what percentage of their crews were ever able to return? In the vast-
> ness of the Pacific, it is easy to imagine how few ever met up with
> another ship. And the odds of landing on an island somewhere were
> infinitesimal. . . . All those who died on the ocean, or expired on
> some distant island, all their deaths were a crime, committed by the
> Shogunate.[4]

❖ ❖ ❖

A few drifters survived mind-boggling hardships and hapless journeys of
thousands of miles and then were able to return to Japan—especially if their
rescuers returned them when the Seclusion Laws were not being so rigorous-
ly enforced. Several crews, who drifted north to Russian territory, were returned by the Russians. Others, who drifted much farther, with luck and
timing also made it back, often after being picked up by American whalers.
Between 1806 and 1852, over thirty-four Japanese are documented as having

drifted to American territory or having been picked up by American ships in the Pacific, and this is only a partial listing. Many of these castaways did eventually return to Japan, either through the Northern Territories or via Canton or Batavia, where Chinese or Dutch ships were found that would be allowed to take them to Nagasaki.[5]

One of the first documented cases of a Japanese reaching North American soil was Jūkichi Oguri. His ship, the *Tokujōmaru*, was blown off course in 1813 en route to Edo and disabled. After drifting for sixteen months, the fourteen-man crew dying slowly of starvation and scurvy, Jūkichi and two other survivors arrived near the coast of Santa Barbara, California, thinking they were landing in Nagasaki. As luck would have it, the men were rescued by the *Forester*. Although flying under an English flag, this ship was really chartered by John Jacob Astor; the War of 1812 had made it too dangerous then to fly American colors in the area. Astor had ordered the *Forester* to sell rum and linen to the Russians at Sitka, Alaska, and, mission accomplished, its captain had been exploring the Pacific coastline on the way back. From California, the *Forester* took the men back to Sitka, then across the Pacific to Kamchatka. Finally, with the help of a Russian ship, the two remaining Japanese seamen were able to enter into Japan via the southern Kuriles. After being jailed and interrogated, they were at last allowed to return home in 1817.[6]

Some of the "drifters" became quite famous. Hikozō Hamada was saved by an American sailing ship in 1850 and taken to the United States, where he was baptized and given the Christian name "Joseph Heco." He became a naturalized U.S. citizen (the first Japanese American) and served his new country well as an interpreter and civil servant when relations were eventually established with Japan. Favored by many in high positions, he met with Presidents Buchanan and Lincoln.[7]

The most famous castaway of all is Manjirō Nakahama, known simply as "Manjirō." Marooned as a teenager on a Pacific island in 1839, he was rescued by an American whaling ship and sent to Massachusetts. He went on to study English, mathematics, surveying, and navigation, and took the name of John Mung. One of the first Japanese to learn English fluently and gain a good knowledge of the United States, he boldly returned to Japan in 1850 via Okinawa; after intensive interrogation, he was allowed to stay. Curious officials carefully recorded his comments on American life and his observation that the United States was not a land of barbarians but in many ways more advanced than Japan. Manjirō was never completely trusted by the Shogunate, yet, after the feudal government collapsed, he proved to be of great service to his country as a navigator, teacher, and translator.[8] His story is the subject of books, plays, and films, and his name graces the neon signs of several bars in Japan.

While not as well known as Heco or Manjirō, the "three kichis" do have a special cachet. They were ordinary sailors, dealt a harsh hand by fate, who survived against all odds, but their own government most cruelly prevented them from returning home. Within Japan their story even provided ammunition for some more daring intellectuals to criticize the government's Seclusion Laws.

MacDonald on Stage

In Japan, public awareness of the "three kichis" has been greatly hindered until recently by the fact that the men were unable to return home. Nonetheless, the extraordinarily global aspect of their experience now makes them an ideal promotional vehicle for international relations. In the fall of 1997, when the Mihama townspeople visited Washington, their trip was billed as "Mihama Town's First Grassroots Exchange Project between Japan and the United States." They brought with them an ultimate stamp of recognition—a translated message straight from then Prime Minister of Japan Ryūtarō Hashimoto:

> [T]he three men who, through the kindness of the local people, had lived on were, regrettably, unable to return home, unlike Nakahama Manjirō (also known as John Manjirō), but were to spend the rest of their lives in foreign lands. As a bridge between Japan and foreign countries, they contributed to the curtain-raiser for Japan's internationalization.
>
> Also, Canadian Ranald MacDonald, who was influenced by the three men and had learned from the Japanese, felt he would like to teach if he could. So, he made his way to Japan and, while being detained at the seaport of Nagasaki, taught English to the Japanese studying Dutch there. One of these was Moriyama Einosuke, who later was chief interpreter for the Japanese when Commodore Perry first arrived in Japan.

In this way, Iwakichi, Kyūkichi and Otokichi—the so-called "three kichis," as they were referred to—performed a great service in opening doors to Japanese-American relations.[9]

The prime minister's remarks were read aloud by Mayor Saitō at the October 1 performance of "The Tale of Otokichi: A Musical Play & Friendship Gift from the Town of Mihama, Aichi, Japan," held in Bellevue, Washington. This was the same production previously staged in Japan and Singapore, supported by powerful corporate underwriters.

Long and melodramatic, the performance ended with scarcely a dry eye in the audience. Professional Japanese actors participated, of course, but Mihama citizens played the parts of the villagers in Otokichi's town of Onoura; Makah Indians played the Makah; and local Bellevue children enacted the children of Fort Vancouver. Ranald MacDonald was played by Rob Edmunds, an English teacher and actor then living in Japan. Although not half-Indian, his British accent lent a touch of realism, as MacDonald presumably had a Scottish lilt to his speech.

The play opened with the three starving sailors landing at Ozette and being saved by the Makah (dressed in traditional tribal garb, speaking authentic Makah). In a flashback to the start of the voyage, the *Hōjunmaru* is depicted being lashed by storms and—after the crew chops down the main mast—drifting on the Pacific for fourteen months, its men dying one by one of scurvy and starvation. After sojourning with the Indians, the three sailors enter the custody of Hudson's Bay Company officials, who enroll them in school at Fort Vancouver to learn English. Here, an adult Ranald MacDonald makes an appearance as an interlocutor, stating: "The first school in Oregon opened at Fort Vancouver . . . on November 17, 1832, and was named the Ball School, after John Ball. . . . [W]hen I heard about the three Japanese sailors who had been shipwrecked, I was strangely impressed, especially when I thought that Japan is in fact our neighboring nation across the Pacific ocean, even though far from here. . . . Before I entered the Red River academy, and while I was still at Ball's School, they enrolled in it as students. . . . Whenever I heard those three castaways tell me their story about their country, it always aroused in me a curiosity to go there."

The "three kichis" are next shown being sent by the Hudson's Bay Company half-way around the world, becoming the first Japanese ever to visit London in 1835. From there they are sent to Macao, and taken under the wing of Gutzlaff, who learns Japanese from them and employs the sailors, along with four other Japanese castaways, to translate the Bible. In 1837, Gutzlaff and two American missionaries did try to repatriate the Japanese to their homes on the *Morrison*, but the ship was shelled near Uraga, in today's Tōkyō Bay, and repulsed again near Kagoshima, on Kyūshū Island. In the play, the actors depict the distraught Japanese sailors attempting to commit suicide on the decks of the *Morrison* but being dissuaded. A furious Otokichi cuts off his hair in a ritual act of renunciation and abandons all intention of ever returning to Japan.

Weaving in much factual information on the "three kichis," the play also introduced MacDonald's Japan adventure. In describing his landing in Japan in 1848, the interlocutor noted the ironic difference between the "three kichis" and MacDonald. Whereas they had drifted to America against their will and were not allowed back into Japan, MacDonald *tried* to infiltrate Japan, pretending to be a castaway, only to be deported. In the play, he is por-trayed being interrogated by the authorities, trying to communicate with the Japanese, fumbling with chopsticks, and—after being sent to Nagasaki and incarcerated—teaching fourteen "Dutch interpreters" desperate to learn English. One of them, Einosuke Moriyama, becomes his favorite pupil and fast friend. MacDonald is also shown dramatically refusing to bow to the authorities and holding his gaze, thus impressing the Japanese, who announce, *Nanto kimottama no futoi yatsu da!* [What a gutsy fellow!].

The musical's last scene in which MacDonald is mentioned (but does not appear) took place long after he actually left Japan. It is the final, most romantic link in the curious Ranald MacDonald–Otokichi saga and may well have occurred, although not exactly as depicted.

In 1862, only a few years after America forced Japan to end its isolation, Einosuke Moriyama was to follow the first Japanese diplomatic mission to Europe. On February 17, the entourage stopped at Singapore and was astounded to find a Japanese there—none other than a middle-aged Oto-kichi, by then a successful businessman fluent in English. This encounter was documented by Yukichi Fukuzawa, a famous Japanese intellectual who was on the mission. In the 1997 play, however, Moriyama is depicted as having a conversation with Otokichi in which the castaway explains how he came to live in Singapore, how he was shipwrecked in North America, and how he had learned English while attending the Ball School at Fort Vancouver. When Moriyama confesses that he himself had learned English at Nagasaki from a North American named Ranald MacDonald—who had been inspired to go to Japan by three shipwrecked Japanese sailors he had met at the Ball School in Oregon—the two men reel in astonishment at the coincidence.

❖ ❖ ❖

The fact that modern tribal members of the Makah Nation participated in the Bellevue production of "The Tale of Otokichi" was testimony to the adroit diplomacy of Mayor Kōichi Saitō and local coordinator Ken Nakano, a Japanese American active in the Friends of MacDonald society. The Japanese constantly stressed that the "three kichis" had been "rescued" by the Makah, while aware that most of the records also indicate the castaways were enslaved after being rescued.

That this is a delicate subject with the modern Makah should come as no surprise. Like most Native American tribes, the Makah have received rather shabby treatment in recent history, and the last thing they need is any negative attention. In a contemporary North American context, the word "slavery" is weighted with so many negative connotations that it is easy to forget that in 1833–34 slavery was still legal in the United States and had only just been abolished in the British Empire.

As historians Robert H. Ruby and John A. Brown document in their book, *Indian Slavery in the Pacific Northwest*, slavery was commonplace among coastal tribes. In the early days of the fur trade, even white ship captains dabbled in it. One notorious American captain kidnapped several Makah tribe members around 1810 and abandoned them as far south as California. The Russians were involved in both sides of the business. In 1808, when the *Nicholai* became wrecked on the coast, some of its crew and passengers, including a woman, were enslaved by local Indians, who traded them to the Makah. Two years later, in a prelude to the case of the "three kichis," the Russians were ransomed by a captain Thomas Brown. The rescued Russian woman, apparently having fallen in love with one of her captors, committed suicide.[10]

In the context of discussing Pacific Coast slavery, Ruby and Brown also mention the case of the "three kichis." But they make a claim no one else does, that MacDonald's father, "Hudson's Bay Company clerk Archibald McDonald . . . ransomed and brought them to the Ft. Vancouver school for native women, orphaned children (usually child slaves freed by the Company), and those of half-blood employees." Further, in a footnote, the historians also state: "Befriending the freed Japanese slaves, who also attended the Ft. Vancouver school, Ranald McDonald, son of Archibald and Comcomly's daughter Princess Sunday, learned of the slaves' account [and] he sailed to Japan, feigning shipwreck to be admitted there, even before Commodore Matthew Perry entered it."[11]

Ruby and Brown are renowned experts on the Old Northwest and the Chinooks, so if they can make such a mistake, it is easy to understand how so many others in Japan and America have, too. The historical vectors of Ranald MacDonald and his father, and that of the "three kichis," come so close to intersecting that it is almost hard to imagine how they did *not* meet. Yet a close inspection of the actual historical record reveals that the lines never completely converge, at least not in North America.

The Historical Record

As previously described, around 1825 the baby Ranald MacDonald joined his father and stepmother at Fort Vancouver, the new headquarters of the Hudson's Bay Company on the Columbia River. Yet his father was still a young clerk with the Company, so it was a life of considerable motion, with the fort serving as a base. Except for particularly dangerous expeditions or furloughs back east—when Ranald would be left behind at Fort Vancouver—the boy accompanied his family from trade post to trade post throughout the Pacific Northwest. He later wrote how

> [in 1826] our family also left in the fall for old Fort Colville, which was then built, from there we went to Kamloops now in British Columbia by way of Okanagan. From there we went back to Fort Okanagan where we remained a short time, from there back to Colville. I think in 1828 again left Fort Colville for Vancouver. . . . [O]thers generously left their families at Vancouver for a season while away, but somehow we were always on the move. Our journey to Vancouver was by bateau but to the interior on horseback my brother in one basket & me in the other.[12]

Fort Vancouver rapidly prospered in its role as the Hudson's Bay Company's central outpost in its "Columbia Department," an area spanning today's British Columbia, Washington, Oregon, and Idaho. Far more than a fur emporium, the outpost also had its own farms and workshops, and, in a sense, was the capital of the limited civilization then existing in the Pacific Northwest. And from Fort Vancouver, Chief Factor John McLoughlin reigned over the area like a monarch.

McLoughlin is sometimes referred to by Americans as the "Father of Oregon" because he helped American settlers when they later began swarming into Oregon, and thus helped to strengthen the United States' claim to the area. For this he greatly displeased his employers, who felt that the chief factor's real job was first to manage Company affairs in the Northwest, monopolize the fur trade (keeping out U.S. fur traders), and wring as much profit as possible from the land. Rather than encourage white settlement, McLoughlin was supposed to help maintain a permanent peace among the many Indian tribes. They were to be encouraged to collect more furs and bring them in to Company posts throughout the Northwest. From there the furs were collected at Fort Vancouver and then shipped halfway around the world for sale in Europe.

Originally from Quebec and a Catholic by faith, McLoughlin had been trained as a physician. In copious letters written to him by other Company officials in the Northwest, including MacDonald's father, he was always referred to as "the Doctor." Six-feet-four-inches tall, sporting long white hair that earned him the nickname of "White Eagle" among Indians, he cut an imposing, almost regal figure and easily garnered respect, if not fear.

McLoughlin's wife, Margaret, was a mixed-blood woman and the widow of Alexander McKay, a prominent member of the original batch of Astorians (who had been massacred along with the rest of the crew of the *Tonquin* in 1811). Like most white men in the Northwest at the time, McLoughlin had married Margaret in the extra-legal "custom of the country," yet he was devoted to her and to their mixed-blood children. For both the Indians with whom he had to deal, and the white men over whom he presided (most of whom had Indian wives and mixed-race children), he helped make Fort Vancouver society a progressive oasis, for he did not like racial or religious bigotry. In 1838 a dogmatic Church of England missionary named Herbert Beaver received orders to go to Fort Vancouver, and while there he made known his opposition to unsanctioned and mixed marriages. In one famous incident, McLoughlin, who felt that his wife had been slandered, grabbed the man's cane and physically assaulted him with it.

In the somewhat caustic "Character Book" kept by George Simpson, governor-in-chief of the Hudson's Bay Company's empire in North America, McLoughlin is described thus:

> [He] has a good deal of influence with the Indians and speaks Saulteaux tolerably well. Very Zealous in the discharge of his public duties and a man of strict honour and integrity but a great stickler for rights and privileges and sets himself up for a righter of Wrongs. . . . Altogether a disagreeable man to do business with as it is impossible to go with him in all things and a difference of opinion almost amounts to a declaration of hostilities, yet a good-hearted man a pleasant companion.[13]

❖ ❖ ❖

When the three Japanese castaways washed up on the Makah territory, they entered the realm of John McLoughlin and the Hudson's Bay Company, and the increasingly global perspective of Fort Vancouver. The fort was at the center of a communications and intelligence web stretching from Russia's Sitka, Alaska, in the north; to Yerba Buena (today's San Francisco) and even Chile's Valparaiso in the south; to Hawaii in the west; and far away to the eastern part of today's Canada. Ships sailed off regularly to Hawaii and London; steamers eddied up to Fort Langley and to visit Sitka; and a regular system of "expresses" plied their way by *bateaux* or pony to posts such as Fort Colvile, deep in the interior of the continent, moving on from there to Montreal. By 1832, there were over ten forts scattered throughout the HBC's huge Columbia Department. Most, like Fort Vancouver, were constructed of wooden palisades and blockhouses surrounding storehouses and living quarters.

Among his assignments, Archibald McDonald spent several years with his growing family at Fort Langley, in today's British Columbia. Like many Company officers, he was intent on educating his family and did much home schooling. In 1831 he noted in a letter how under his tutelage his young wife had "become an excellent scholar" and that (using Ranald's Chinook nickname) "Tool is a stout chap—reads his new testament and began his copy the other day as he got out of his 7th year." In an 1832 letter to a fellow trader, Archibald mentioned Ranald again: "[M]y Chinook now reads pretty well &

has commenced ciphering." Then in the next year, the proud father wrote another letter, noting "Jenny has now her 4th Boy, so that with herself & Tool at the head of the class I am in a fair way to having a thriving school." When Archibald was assigned to Fort Colvile, because of all the moving about, he decided it was time to enroll Ranald in school at Fort Vancouver for the winter of 1833–34.[14]

A year earlier, at the end of 1832, an American named John Ball had established the first school in Oregon. One of Chief Factor John McLoughlin's older sons, John, Jr., had been sent to eastern Canada and then Paris to study, but the boy was having problems; a younger son, David, was still at Fort Vancouver. Concerned that his own children, as well as those of Company employees, should be better educated, McLoughlin had requested Ball to form a school at the fort. As Ball, who agreed, describes it:

So [Dr. McLoughlin] sent the boys to my room to be instructed, all half-breed boys of course, for there was not then a white woman in Oregon. The doctor's wife was a Chippewa woman from Lake Superior, and the lightest woman, a Mrs. Douglas, a half-breed woman from Hudson Bay. Well, I found the boys docile and attentive and making good progress, for they are precocious and generally better boys than men. And the old doctor used to come in to see the school and seemed much pleased and well satisfied.[15]

Like the population at the fort, Ball's students were a polyglot, polyracial group, and early teachers had difficulty getting them to speak English. Ranald MacDonald would later write, "I attended the school to learn my ABC & English. The big boys had medals put over their neck if caught speaking French or chinook & when school was out had to remain and learn a task. I made no progress."[16]

While young Ranald MacDonald was at the school, McLoughlin received word of a mysterious wreck far to the north. He at first believed the seafarers to be Chinese and, in a later letter to London, dated May 28, 1834, wrote,

Last winter the Indians informed us that a vessel had been wrecked somewhere about Cape Flattery . . . a few days ago I received through the Indians a letter written in Chinese characters. . . . [F]rom the

Indians I am informed that only three of them are alive and that forty of them are either dead of desease or have been drowned—the Indians say the Vessel was loaded with China wares.[17]

To say that a wrecked Chinese or Japanese ship was shocking news in the Pacific Northwest would be a gross understatement. In modern terms, the event would be equivalent to the Martians landing. Whether the ship hailed from Japan or China, it was nearly five thousand miles off course, from a place unknown to Indians and many whites.

On March 23, McLoughlin ordered Thomas McKay to command an overland expedition to rescue the surviving crew members. McKay was to take what he needed from Fort Nisqually, on the Nisqually River by Puget Sound, near today's Tacoma, Washington. Ranald MacDonald's father, Archibald, had created the fort only the previous year with the help of Canadians, Indians, and Hawaiians (then known as "Kanakas" or "Owhyees"), who worked for the Company. But Archibald himself had gone back to Fort Vancouver on June 21, 1833, and then moved to Fort Colvile.[18]

McKay actually was John McLoughlin's stepson. Already in his early forties, he was a veteran Company employee, reportedly married, like Archibald McDonald, to one of the many daughters of Chinook Chief Comcomly. This therefore made McKay Ranald MacDonald's uncle by marriage. HBC Governor Simpson described McKay in his "Character Book" as

a half breed of the Salteaux Tribe . . . one of the best Shots in the Country and very cool and resolute among Indians. Has always been employed on the most desperate service in the Columbia and the more desperate it is the better he likes it. He is known to every Indian in that Department and his name alone is a host of Strength carrying terror with it as he has sent many of them to their "long home" . . . possesses little judgment and a confirmed Liar, but a necessary evil at such a place as Vancouver; has not a particle of feeling or humanity in his composition.[19]

McKay was assigned the rescue task because of his experience, not because any attack on the Indians was contemplated; as noted earlier, the Indians were the Company's prime customers and force was to be used against them only in defense or if retribution was deemed absolutely necessary.

Nonetheless, McKay was stymied by rough terrain and harsh weather conditions.

On May 16, McLoughlin therefore ordered William H. McNeil, an American captain of the Company's brig, the *Lama*, to try to retrieve the young men. He was to sail up to Nisqually and Fort Langley on regular business and "stop both going and coming at Cape Flattery trade with the Natives at the rate of three Skins for two and a half point Blanket and do your utmost to Recover the unfortunate people said to be wrecked in the Vicinity of that place."[20] Four days later, McLoughlin also ordered McNeil that "on your return will take them on Board and their property and you will reward the Indians for their trouble so as to induce them (if any should be so unfortunate as to be wrecked on their Shores) to treat them with kindness."[21] In July, hearing that McNeil had been successful in his mission, McLoughlin wrote, "I am happy to find that you have been so successful in procuring the poor Chinese whom it seems the natives were much inclined to keep in slavery. You will please come up with your vessel as soon as possible."[22]

By late summer, mention of the "three kichis" appeared in the writings of two Methodist missionaries sent overland to Fort Vancouver from the East Coast of the United States—Cyrus Shepard and Jason Lee. On Sunday, the 28th of September, less than two weeks after arriving, Lee wrote the following entry in his journal:

> Assayed to preach to a mixed congregation English French scotch Irish Indians Americans Half Breeds Japanese &c. some of whom did not understand 5 words of english. Found it extremely difficult to collect my thoughts or find language to express them but am thankful that I have been permitted to plead the cause of God on this side the Ry. Mountains where the banners of Christ were never before unfurled.[23]

Shepard was engaged to teach the school founded by John Ball, who had earlier left. In a report filed at the end of 1834 to his supervisors back East, Shepard explained what it was like:

> My daily employment, at present, is with about thirty half-breed youth, instructing them in the sciences, and giving them such religious instruction as I hope may be, by the blessing of God, a lasting

benefit to their souls. In addition to the day school, I have two young men and eight boys in the evening. Besides these, I have been teaching three Japanese, named E-wa-ketch, Ke-o-chi-cha, and O-too, who were wrecked on the coast, some time last season, and taken by the Indians, and held in slavery until released by the humanity of Governor M'Laughlin, and brought to this place. . . . While at school, they made rapid improvement, and were remarkably studious and docile, and learned to repeat the Lord's prayer and some portions of the Scriptures. God, who ever delights to work by small instrumentalities, to attain the most astonishing ends for the good of the world, thereby shaming the unbelief of his people, may, by these poor children, carry the gospel to their neglected countrymen."[24]

It is doubtful whether the missionaries realized the full implications of the "three kichis" carrying the gospel back to Japan—where they might be executed if found to be Christian. But the Americans were more concerned with spreading the word of God than the well-being of their pupils. As almost always happened, the Japanese castaways had already become pawns in a larger game, one in which the missionaries were not the only players.

In mid-November, McLoughlin ordered the Japanese taken to England on the Company's brig, *Eagle*, via Honolulu and the Straits of Magellan. On November 18, he wrote to his superiors in London, explaining his action. Referring to the "three kichis" as Japanese for the first time, he quite accurately recounted their story. The ship, he noted,

was from Yahongari and bound to Yiddo the capital of Japan with a cargo of Rice nankeens and porcelain ware. They were first driven from their course by a Typhoon and subsequently a sea unshipped their Rudder or broke their rudder Irons, when the vessel became unmanageable, and that they were about a year from the date they left their home when they were wrecked, at which time they had plenty of Rice and water yet on board but that a sickness carried off all except these three. A little after the Vessel grounded and before the natives could get any thing worth while out of her a storm arose and broke her up.[25]

The chief factor then cut to the core. Revealing that he could have sent the castaways to Hawaii and left them on their own to find a way home to Japan, he added,

> [A]s I believe they are the first Japanese who have been in the power of the British Nation I thought the British Government would gladly avail itself of this opportunity to endeavour to open a communication with the Japanese government and that by these men going to Great Britain they would have an opportunity of being instructed and convey to their countrymen a respectable idea of the grandeur and power of the British nation.[26]

McLoughlin's superiors approved of his humane treatment of the Japanese but criticized the expense of his roundabout idea for repatriation. In 1834–35, Britain was too involved in China to think much about Japan. Thus, the Japanese, upon arriving in London, were sent the rest of the way around the world, to Canton, and there abandoned, "His Majesty's Government not being disposed to open a communication with the Japanese government thro the medium of three shipwrecked Seamen." McLoughlin was reprimanded with the words, "[I]t would have been far better to have sent them no farther than the Sandwich Islands, from whence the Agent Mr. George Pelly could have easily procured them a passage to China by some one of the frequent opportunities that occur of communicating from thence."[27]

Creation of a Myth

Fort Vancouver today is a designated National Historic Site. A sizable portion of the fort has been reconstructed, with blockhouses and palisades, buildings within and gardens without. Once an island of civilization in a sea of wilderness, it now is an oasis of green in the urban sprawl of Vancouver, Washington, with Portland, Oregon, in sight right across the Columbia River. Still, it is easy to imagine the fort, once bustling with Indians of many tribes, French Canadian trappers, British employees, scores of Hawaiians, and children such as Ranald MacDonald. In the recreated Chief Factor's House, where John McLoughlin resided and the "gentlemen" of the company always dined together (without their wives), Archibald McDonald would feel right at home.

Portion of reconstructed Fort Vancouver.

There is no monument to Ranald MacDonald on the site, but next to the Visitor's Center is an upright, two-ton stone slab, engraved with the image of the "three kichis." A stopping point for many Japanese tourists, the memorial was unveiled in August 1, 1989, and donated by a Japanese Boy Scout troop from Hyōgo Prefecture, with the assistance of the 1989 Washington Centennial Commission, the National Park Service, and the Japanese American Citizens League. The only English words are on a small copper plaque on the slab's reverse side; they recount the story of the sailors (but mistakenly identify them as the "first Japanese to arrive on the continent of North America"). The larger block of Japanese text on the front of the stone is engraved, and under the bold, oft-used ideograms for *yūkō shinzen* (goodwill and friendship) it, too, tells the story of the sailors. Luckily, most people cannot read the Japanese text, for it represents a miniature hijacking of history. By far the most prominent name engraved on the slab is not that of one of the castaway sailors, but the head of the Hyōgo Prefecture Boy Scout troop. Then also the governor of Hyōgo Prefecture, he was clearly looking for more publicity.

❖ ❖ ❖

The true history of Ranald MacDonald has also been subject to some sub-version in the Vancouver–Portland area. Here, in nearby Oregon City, Eva Emery Dye in 1906 wrote the first published biography of Ranald MacDonald, and firmly planted the myth that MacDonald met the "three kichis."

Dye had a romantic fascination with pioneers and a gift for popular writing. In 1900 she published her first book, a biography of John McLoughlin that depicted him heroically, from the vantage point of the U.S. settlers who later benefited from his kindness. Titled *McLoughlin and Old Oregon*, in format it was quite accurate but entertaining, and almost entirely dialogue-based. An imagined 1832 interchange between McLoughlin and an American trader sets up the story and contrasts the philosophies of the Hudson's Bay Company and the Americans: "Your servants," the American says, "have intermarried with the tribes to hold the trade. Our policies are diametrically opposed. Yours is to perpetuate savagism, to keep Oregon as a game preserve, a great English hunting park. Mine would be to fill it with a civilized people."[28]

The book was extremely popular among readers who identified with American pioneers, and by 1913 it had appeared in eight editions. It contains no mention of Ranald MacDonald, but Dye later wrote that she had stumbled across him while writing the manuscript: "I then intended to call [it] 'The King of the Columbia.' I was referred by all the old Hudson's Bay men to McDonald, who claimed the title. 'I am the King of the Columbia,' said McDonald, but he knew all about McLoughlin and gave me many picturesque points in that book." Dye's correspondence with MacDonald before his death survives in letters held in the archives of the Oregon Historical Society, located across the river from Fort Vancouver. She later described him as "the strangest, most romantic and picturesque character of Northwest annals."[29]

Dye's book on MacDonald himself—*McDonald of Oregon: A Tale of Two Shores*—appeared in 1906, twelve years after his death. Written in a chatty style, it included the story of the "three kichis." From her prior work on McLoughlin, Dye knew that the Hudson's Bay Company had directly aided the three Japanese sailors. She also had access to a draft of MacDonald's manuscript (where he obliquely mentioned them) and she had read a book on the voyage of the *Morrison*. But Dye's real focus was on her trademark theme of Anglo-Saxon conquest of the West, onto which was grafted the story of the "three kichis" and MacDonald's Japan adventure. One reviewer commented that her biography was about "nothing less than the meeting on the Columbia and in Japan of the vanguard representatives of the eastward-moving and the westward-moving races. . . . Incidents in the great westward streaming of the English-speaking peoples and in the interflow of the races reaching even to the shores of Japan constitute the bulk of the volume."[30]

Dye's biography generally adheres to the historical record regarding the rescue of the "three kichis" until the moment they arrive at Fort Vancouver on the Columbia. There, she has Dr. McLoughlin prescribing medicine and bouillon and fruit, so that "in a short time the lively little brown men began to recover."[31] But at that point, Dye begins to embroider the facts. She has McLoughlin turning to Ranald MacDonald and the son of Thomas McKay, Billy (William) McKay, ordering the boys "to look after those Japanese at the hospital. You are to wait upon them, bring them food, and act as a sort of bodyguard until they get well."[32] Dye continues,

> Never more delighted lads undertook a task, running in and out in their soft moccasins all day long, eager to anticipate every wish and fulfill every desire. With the quick ears of youth some Japanese words were speedily treasured, and the strangers themselves soon showed an equal facility in Chinook, so that in a few weeks more details of their shipwreck came to light.[33]

> Before McLoughlin repatriates the three Japanese, Dye has the fifteen-year-old Otokichi making friends with young Chinooks, "almost surpassing them in use of the jargon." She also depicts the arrival of the Japanese as the subject of enormous speculation at the fort.[34]

❖ ❖ ❖

Regrettably, Dye's version of Ranald's "encounter" with the "three kichis" settled like sludge into the historical record, and subsequent writers have found it hard to free themselves from it, even in Japan, where her book was translated in 1989. As Friends of MacDonald society's Bruce Berney once wrote, Dye became "a thorn in our side."[35] In 1923, when MacDonald's *Narrative* was posthumously published by the Eastern Washington State

Historical Society, the carefully researched annotations of its editors also did little to help set the record straight, partly because MacDonald had employed such ambiguous phrasing. Furthermore, certain critical dates are in error, apparently the result of a flawed transcription; for example, MacDonald is listed in the book as having left Fort Vancouver in 1838, whereas in a draft it clearly states that he left in April 1834.[36]

The next American biography of MacDonald appeared in 1940, when Marie Leona Nichols—also from around Portland, Oregon—wrote *Ranald MacDonald, Adventurer.* Her book was more accessible

" The little brown men had thrown themselves on the floor."

The "three kichis" meet John McLoughlin
at Fort Vancouver.

than MacDonald's own *Narrative* and written in a style more up-to-date than Dye's book. While presumably targeting young readers, she nonetheless footnoted quotations, and her bibliography indicates effort at serious research, citing an 1857 draft of MacDonald's manuscript held in the British Columbia Archives. Yet, Nichols's book is also marred by innumerable errors of fact, and her frequent use of the word "redskins" grates on the modern ear. When first issued the reaction was not altogether positive. As one reviewer wrote in 1941, "One wonders . . . just what Mrs. Nichols' object was in writing this story. In spite of numerous citations and footnotes it is no contribution to historical research."[37] Of the "three kichis," Nichols brashly claimed,

> While Ranald was still at Fort Vancouver in 1834 and 1835 he made the acquaintance of these Japanese fishermen. This young lad was now ten years of age and he listened eagerly to every word that his Oriental friends told him. At one time when one of them was ill in

the hospital, Ranald volunteered to act as his nurse. His imagination was fired with the tales of adventure that came from the lips of these castaways, and he says himself, in telling the story of his life, that the early acquaintance which he formed while attending school at Fort Vancouver had much to do toward spurring him on to seek adventure in the alluring Orient.[38]

Nichols's footnote to this claim indicates that the information derived from the papers of MacDonald's editor/friend Malcolm McLeod, held in the British Columbia Provincial Archives, but no one else has ever found it. Instead of the Makah Indians, she has the Japanese rescued by the "Clay-oquots" at Point Grenville, an area over sixty miles south of Ozette, on today's Quinalt Indian Reservation in Washington. At Fort Vancouver, Nichols says of the "three kichis" that "the kindliness of the fur traders won their hearts and converted them to the Christian religion. They were so zeal-ous in this new-found consolation that they were anxious to return home and become missionaries."[39] As the men would have faced probable execution for such beliefs, this latter statement by Nichols again shows considerable igno-rance of the harsh reality in which they were placed.

Correcting a Myth

For fifty years after 1940, no further books on Ranald MacDonald were pub-lished. The Dye and Nichols biographies—as well as the 1923 version of MacDonald's own *Narrative*—went into a hiatus, out of print. When writers did mention MacDonald in articles, they usually repeated the by-now-famil-iar myth of his having met the "three kichis."

In North America, information demonstrating the improbability of a meeting between Ranald MacDonald and the "three kichis" only became widely available in 1990. It was made possible largely through the efforts of the founders of the FOM society, especially a Japanese gentleman living in the Portland area of Oregon named Masakatsu Tomita, otherwise known simply as "Mas." In 1972 Mas had joined what is now known as the Seiko Corporation in Japan, and in 1983 he had been transferred to Epson Ameri-ca, Inc., where he steadily rose in the ranks. Based primarily on his efforts, Epson built its first computer printer manufacturing plant outside of Port-land, and Mas eventually became its president.

There was considerable trade tension between Japan and the United States at the time, and Mas believed that Epson needed to involve itself in the local community, to help alleviate some of it. As a history buff, in the late 1980s he had read Akira Yoshimura's *Umi no sairei* [Festival of the sea], a popular book describing MacDonald's adventure in the context of the opening of Japan. Mas was captivated by MacDonald's story, but like many people was confused by all the place names in it. Even Americans confuse Vancouver, Washington, with the Vancouver of today's British Columbia, but Mas also did not realize that Fort George (where Ranald was born in 1824) was the Hudson's Bay Company's name for Astoria—only ninety miles away. In February 1988, Mas heard that Bruce Berney was fundraising for a Ranald MacDonald memorial in Astoria. After contacting Berney, Mas helped obtain funding from his company for the project. The more he realized how connected MacDonald's story was to the area, the more enthusiastic he became.

That same year—along with Berney and Stephen Kohl, a Japan specialist at the University of Oregon—Mas helped form the Friends of MacDonald society and was promptly nominated chairman. This proved to be fortuitous, as MacDonald's story fit in perfectly with Mas's interest in history and need to cultivate good community relations. But MacDonald's story also resonated with him on an even more personal level. Mas had a congenitally transmitted form of Hepatitis C, and in 1993 would receive a liver transplant from an American donor. His condition thus bound him emotionally and physically to America, as liver transplants were not then done in Japan, and he could never hope to return to Japan save for short visits. The transplant kept him alive until 1996, but his precarious health seemed only to fire his determination to proselytize MacDonald's story. As his widow describes it, "he became a missionary." Up until his death at age forty-seven, Mas kept at the ready a bag of materials on MacDonald, which he used to give talks and educate anyone interested.

As often happens with volunteer organizations, one man's enthusiasm proved infectious. For a brief period, there was an explosion of interest in MacDonald's story. Membership in the society mushroomed to over two hundred people, and members soon wrote in with ideas and information. This was at least in part because Mas could utilize the resources of his company under the pretext of its "being good for business." In 1990, Mas helped obtain Epson funding for the republication of the 1923 Eastern Washington Historical Society's edition of MacDonald's *Narrative*.

As part of this movement, on May 6, 1989, the Friends of MacDonald sponsored a seminar in Portland, with Jean Murray Cole invited to give a speech on MacDonald's early years. A meticulous historian and author of a biography on MacDonald's father, Cole shocked some in the audience by disputing several assumptions about MacDonald, in particular the popular orthodoxy that he had met the "three kichis." By carefully tracing timelines, as established for the "three kichis" and as indicated in Archibald McDonald's letters, she clearly demonstrated that Ranald had left Fort Vancouver before the castaways arrived. As she commented much later, "I knew when he arrived at Fort Colvile and also when he went east, and I knew when the Japanese were at Fort Vancouver. So often people don't look at the dates!"[40] Her paper, "Ranald MacDonald: His Ancestry and Early Years," was excerpted in the fall 1989 issue of the FOM newsletter. In 1990, it also became the basis for an updated afterword when the 1923 edition of MacDonald's *Narrative* was finally republished.

North American writers at long last had reason to pause before connecting the dots between MacDonald and the "three kichis," but the desire to do so dies hard. In 1994, for example, Evelyn Iritani wrote a lyrical book, *An Ocean Between Us*, about the relationship between Japan and the United States. She included a section on recent contacts between the Makah Nation and Japan, as well as the story of "the three kichis." Sure enough, of MacDonald she writes, "the young boy became fascinated with the Japanese sailors, convinced that their ethnicity was in some way linked to his own background. He befriended the Japanese sailors and traded English lessons for schooling in Japanese."[41]

In 1997, when Jo Ann Roe wrote the third biography of Ranald, *Ranald MacDonald: Pacific Rim Adventurer*, she was able to clearly state that by the time of the "three kichis'" arrival, "Young Ranald had already left Fort Vancouver in March to rejoin his father at Fort Colvile and proceed to the Red River settlement." Still, a few sentences later, she could not help adding in parentheses, "(It is possible that, much later in his wanderings, Ranald could have met Otokichi, who eventually lived in Macao, a stopping place for whalers)."[42]

In popular writing, it is always Otokichi whom MacDonald is thought to have met. But real history is often odder than assumed, and there is a stronger possibility that MacDonald later did meet, not Otokichi, but Kyū-kichi, one of the lesser known of the three Japanese castaways. If not face-to-face, the two men came within a stone's throw of each other. On May 23, 1849, after being retrieved from Japan by a U.S. warship, MacDonald was briefly in Hong Kong, where he was personally interviewed by the missionary-linguist Gutzlaff. Then working as the "Chinese Secretary" for the British government, Gutzlaff employed Kyūkichi—now married and settled in Hong Kong—and regarded him as an able and discreet assistant.[43]

❈ ❈ ❈

In 1834, MacDonald did not meet the "three kichis" at Fort Vancouver, but he soon heard of them, for they generated extraordinary interest throughout the territories of the Hudson's Bay Company. On February 12, 1835, not long after the "three kichis" departed Fort Vancouver, one of his father's fellow officers excitedly wrote a mutual friend way up in Fort York, on the Hudson Bay:

> A vessel from a port in Japan was likewise wrecked a little to the northward of Ft. Vancouver. She was loaded with porcelain pieces which is to be had in great abundance now from the Indians on this coast—beautiful vases & flower pots are applied to uses for which they were never intended—three Japanese the only survivors of the crew were purchased from the Indians and sent home to England by Dr. McLoughlin, making the impression that through them the Government may be able to open an intercourse with their nation.[44]

And among those living on the Pacific Coast, the shipwrecked Japanese also stirred debate on the origin of Native Americans, suggesting a connection to Asia. Even MacDonald is reported to have said later in life that he believed Indians had come from Japan, and that Japan was the "land of his ancestors."[45] Whether he actually believed this before going to Japan is debatable, but that the presence of the "three kichis" planted such thoughts in the minds of many, is not.

One of MacDonald's cousins later wrote of McNeil, the captain who had picked up the "three kichis:" "From wrecks of Chinese junks discovered by him and found years ago, he had no doubt of the discovery in ages gone of this continent by the Chinese and Japanese. The features of both nations are indelibly fixed in the physiognomy of the Alaskan Indians."[46] Rev. Parker, who toured in the Columbia vicinity around 1835 and met Captain McNeil, also considered this theory. After noting then-prevailing theories on the origin of Indians—including the notion that they were descendants of the lost tribes of Israel—he observed:

> It is not very uncommon that junks and other craft have been found by whale ships in the great Pacific Ocean, in a state of starvation, without the nautical instruments and skill of mariners necessary to enable them to find their way to any port of safety. Undoubtedly many are entirely lost, while others drift to unknown shores. . . . May not such facts throw light upon the original peopling of America, which has engaged the attention of men for a long period[?][47]

Eva Emery Dye, who helped foster the myth that MacDonald met the "three kichis" at Fort Vancouver, also was convinced that Native Americans "were descendants of Asiatic races through stray shiploads stranded on these shores and had retrograded from higher planes of civilization."[48] She was both condescending and romantic, but she may not have been far off track, after all, when she let her imagination wander and wrote,

> Eagerly, in the Summer evenings, Ranald McDonald listened to the theories of his elders as to other wrecks, reported from time to time. The Kanakas of the kitchen, too, inflamed his imagination with tales of junks off the shores of Hawaii. Soon after, Captain McNeil returned from the Islands with a report of eighteen more rescued Japanese at Honolulu, relics of the same terrific wave-sweep that had sent these three across the ocean to Oregon. . . . The impressionable children of Ft. Vancouver treasured these talks of their elders, and wondered about the land across the sea, but none more than Ranald McDonald. In his little bunk-bed in the night-time he dreamed of his friends . . . and longed to visit them in their own country. What was it like? How would they receive him? Was it as beautiful as they said,—a kingdom of temples and flowers?[49]

CHAPTER 4

Education at Red River

Like many Hudson's Bay Company officers, Archibald McDonald worried greatly about the future of his half-Indian son. He knew that for Ranald to one day live in the civilized world, rather than the world of his late mother, he would require an education beyond anything the little school at Fort Vancouver could offer. As early as February 20, 1833, when Ranald had just turned nine years old, Archibald therefore wrote to a friend about his plans to enroll all of his older sons in "the Red River new Academy."[1]

Red River was the name of the only true settlement in the Hudson's Bay Company's vast territories. It was an artificial community, which Archibald McDonald had himself helped establish, in the middle of the North American land mass. It offered a semblance of civilized life, with churches and new schools—real schools—including some just for the children of officers. Getting to this community from the Pacific Coast, however, required crossing over the Rocky Mountains on a winding and arduous journey of nearly three thousand miles.

From the writings of Ranald MacDonald and others, we know that he traveled east in the spring of 1834 with Chief Factor Duncan Finlayson, on the Company's regular Express. He was not with the Express when it left Fort Vancouver on March 19, however, for Finlayson's businesslike journal

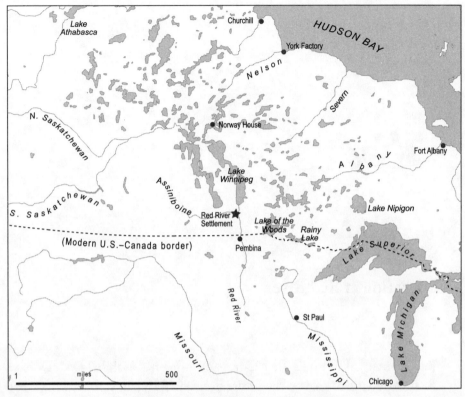

The Red River settlement (today's Winnipeg).

entry that day describes three boats, each manned by nine men, going up the Columbia; the only child passenger listed is young Ranald's classmate at Fort Vancouver—Chief Factor John McLoughlin's thirteen-year-old, mixed-blood son, David, who was to be schooled in Montreal, then Paris.

The Express arrived at Fort Colvile on April 11 and remained there until the 20th. It was here that young Ranald apparently joined the Express, having preceded it. Archibald McDonald had been newly placed in charge of the fort, but he was scheduled to travel to London for a brief furlough; he had therefore decided to send his entire family to Red River to stay there during his absence and to enroll his older sons in the local schools. It was not uncommon then for people to travel with HBC brigades in an unofficial, unlisted capacity, since it was the only means of traveling safely in the West. This may explain why almost no reference is made to Ranald in Finlayson's journal beyond an oblique and cryptic mention on May 5 of a "Mr. McDonald and his 2 boys" when crossing the Rockies. It was a harrowing and unforgettable journey for a ten-year-old boy, requiring travel in typical Hudson's Bay Company style—by horse, boat, canoe, and foot, utilizing rivers and lakes wherever possible. At the Athabasca Pass, the snow was eight-feet deep. The family did not reach the Red River settlement until mid-June.[2]

For the next five years—his most formative ones—Ranald MacDonald would live and study at Red River. It was a place far removed from Asia or Japan, and the center of a new Euro-Indian hybrid culture. This culture would briefly flower and ultimately be crushed, but for many of the youths of mixed heritage who lived in its midst, it fostered a special sense of pride and entitlement. In the case of MacDonald, it may also have encouraged a desire to accomplish great things.

❖ ❖ ❖

Today, the site of the Red River settlement is covered over by Winnipeg—a modern metropolis that spills across the junction of the Assiniboine and Red Rivers, in what is now Manitoba, Canada. The land was formerly a vast untilled prairie, dotted with lakes and crossed by rivers, home to millions of buffalo.

Except for a few rebuilt churches and a refurbished HBC fort north of the city, few physical artifacts survive from the 1830s. Most of the ethnic groups now in the area are new, too, as Winnipeg is currently one of Canada's more diverse cities, with a high percentage of immigrants—from the United Kingdom and its former colonies, China, Eastern Europe, and Iceland—almost all of whom have arrived in the past one hundred years.

Among the groups with ties to MacDonald's era are the people of the "First Nations," or the original inhabitants, especially the Cree, Assiniboine, and the Ojibwa. Also present are the descendants of the fur trade people, both Indian and European, who refer to themselves with the French word, "Métis," similar to the Spanish "Mestizo." Métis is a somewhat confusing term because its usage has shifted over the centuries. In MacDonald's day, it usually (but not always) meant Catholic descendants of French and Indians; Protestant children of Anglo and Indian descent were called "half-breeds" or "country-born" and sometimes *bois brulés* (French for "burned-wood," mainly indicating those of French-Indian descent). In modern Canada, however, "Métis" has become a comprehensive term that refers to both groups. Along with the Inuit and the First Nation tribes, the Métis are granted aboriginal

Photo © 1999 Frederik L. Schodt.

Stone bastion at the Hudson's Bay Company's Lower Fort Garry
near modern Winnipeg. Now designated a National Historic Site of Canada.

rights in the Canadian Constitution of 1982. In a modern Canadian context, Ranald MacDonald is considered a Métis.

Winnipeg today is a center for research into both the fur trade and the Métis, and it has the added cachet of being the historical epicenter of the short-lived Métis Nation—the last independent nation declared in North America. In case anyone should forget, standing proudly behind the local Manitoba Legislative Building is the imposing statue of the most famous Métis leader of all, Louis Riel. Some thirty years after MacDonald left the region, the Hudson's Bay Company sold its vast territory to British-controlled Canada, and the Métis way of life was threatened. Riel, a prophetic figure who dreamed of creating a giant confederacy of mixed-bloods and Indian tribes, led Métis communities in insurrections locally in 1869–70, and in neighboring Saskatchewan in 1884–85. The latter revolt was crushed by British and Canadian troops using Gatling guns; Riel was execut-ed, and the Métis Nation was destroyed as a political force, its members dispersed in a diaspora across the Canadian West and down into the U.S. territories of Montana and North Dakota.

Ranald MacDonald was not a particularly political man, and what he thought of the Métis social or political movement is unknown. Later in life, he would have read much about it, however, for he had Métis relations in Red River and his younger half-brother, Allan, participated as a soldier in the suppression of

Hudson's Bay Company coat of arms, circa 1800.

the 1870 rebellion. As a teenager and an elite "half-breed" youth at Red River, MacDonald was also present during a flowering of Métis consciousness. As a result, he likely would have felt empathy for Métis aspirations, while identifying with the powerful Hudson's Bay Company of his father.

In that regard, modern Winnipeg has yet another direct link to the past. The Hudson's Bay Company Archives was donated to the province of Manitoba in 1994 and is now administered locally. It is a vast treasure house of information dating back to 1670 on the HBC, the fur trade, the Red River Settlement, and the Métis. Original documents include ledgers authored at Astoria in 1821 by MacDonald's father, in his precise penmanship.

Only a block from the Archives is "The Bay," Winnipeg's largest department store, still run by MacDonald's father's company. And not too far away is the headquarters of the HBC's once-sworn enemy, The North West Company. Both companies incorporate beavers into their coat of arms. The HBC's design, until updated in 2002, also crowned the motto: *Pro Pelle Cutem*, roughly meaning "For Pelts, We Risk Our Skins."

Origins of the Red River Settlement

Ranald MacDonald's father, Archibald, came to North America from Scotland in August 1813, at the age of twenty-three, in the employ of Lord Selkirk. He was to serve as the nobleman's personal representative at the new

Red River settlement, independent of the HBC, and be capable of performing a wide range of roles, from overseer to accountant to physician.

Selkirk, a wealthy philanthropist, believed the impoverished peasants of the Scottish highlands could only be helped by emigration. He chose to establish a colony for them at Red River based on information he had about the area's prospects (and cost). It has also been suggested that he chose such a northern clime because of an antipathy toward the United States to the south. In 1778, when Selkirk was a young boy, John Paul Jones, the American Revolutionary War hero, had raided his home.[3]

In 1810, Selkirk became a major shareholder in the London-based Hudson's Bay Company. A year later, for the nominal sum of ten shillings, he obtained title to a tract of its land in the Red River area. Called Assiniboia, it was only a small part of "Rupert's Land" but it was 116,000 square miles and roughly four times the size of Scotland, stretching from Lake Winnipeg in the north all the way down into today's North Dakota and Minnesota. Among the London public, Selkirk's idea of plopping a colony down in the middle of the wilderness met bitter criticism, one source complaining, "By God, Sir, if you are bent on doing something futile . . . why do you not plough the deserts of the Sahara, which is so much nearer?"[4]

As noted previously, for over a century the Hudson's Bay Company had remained active mainly around the Hudson Bay. This focus, however, had enabled the emergence of a rival, the more aggressive North West Company, which had expanded into HBC territories and successfully captured much of the fur trade in the western plains and the Northwest. For the Hudson's Bay Company, Selkirk's plan to build a colony in Company territory therefore represented an opportunity. It would not only help the Company reassert its charter rights, but also help it resist the North West Company and develop a base of labor and a means for supplying inland posts with provisions. A colony could also offer an attractive place for employees who wanted to retire in the country with their native wives and children.

On a local level, however, the fur trade and colonization were incompatible, as agricultural settlements destroy the very environment on which fur trade depends. A clash of cultures also became inevitable for other reasons. Selkirk's proposed colony, for example, cut across the routes that the North West Company used to access the fur-bearing territories of the West. And a culture had already grown up in the area, consisting not only of trappers and traders and *voyageurs* of Anglo or French descent but offspring from their unions with native women. These Métis and half-breeds lived off not just agriculture but the buffalo hunt, like the Indians. And whether of French or Anglo descent, many were increasingly beginning to think of themselves as a separate, unique people—a new nation.

By the time Ranald MacDonald's father arrived in the Red River area in 1814, the bitter rivalry between the Hudson's Bay Company and the North West Company was reaching a crescendo. Nothing could have prepared the young Archibald for what he encountered.

Companies at War

The members of the North West Company at first planned to sit back and wait for Selkirk's fledgling colony to fail. But on January 8, when its appointed governor issued the so-called "Pemmican Proclamation," the Nor' Westers' attitude changed. To help the struggling new settlers and prevent starvation, the governor banned taking any provisions—including pemmican—out of the colony. Yet pemmican was the lifeblood of the fur trade. Made from dried buffalo or caribou meat, mixed with melted fat and berries in a process learned from the Indians, the high-calorie food sustained trappers and *voyageurs* on their trips into the interior. And it provided an important industry for the Métis population. The Nor' Westers thus began to harass the settlers and to incite both local Indians and Métis against the colonists. The Indians were largely immune to this incitement, but not the Métis. Many of the latter were the Nor' Westers' own sons. It was easy to persuade them that their lifestyle was at stake and that they had an intrinsic right to the land through their Indian heritage. Métis sentiment was further inflamed by the fact that—unlike the settlers—they normally hunted buffalo on horseback, Indian-style, and the governor had banned "running" buffalo near the settlement.

By 1815, armed clashes had begun. As Archibald McDonald described it in his journal, scare tactics with war whoops and cattle raids gradually escalated, until several of the settlers were wounded in attacks, one mortally. "The enemy consisted of about 40 & I believe the composition was of all nations, viz. natives, half bloods, Scotch, Irish, English & Canadians. . . . In consequence of the havoc they made our men are willing to surrender."[5] By June, the colony had been largely abandoned. Efforts were made to reestablish it, but in the interim Archibald temporarily returned to England.

Meanwhile, back in Red River, open warfare broke out, climaxing in June of 1816 in the famous Battle of Seven Oaks.[6] Accompanied by over two dozen men, a new governor of the colony, Robert Semple, marched out to meet a band of heavily armed and mounted Nor' Westers laden with pemmican after a raid on an HBC post. The latter group, made up of Canadians, Indians, and especially Métis, was led by a charismatic, mixed-blood young man named Cuthbert Grant, with whom Archibald McDonald had had an armed confrontation a year earlier. Grant had been educated in Montreal (some say Scotland) and was a skilled leader. His men fought Indian style behind their horses and suffered only one casualty, while Semple and twenty of his men, surrounded, were mercilessly killed. To the horror of HBC officials and many Europeans, the dead were stripped, dismembered, and mutilated or scalped, their corpses left to rot on the plains.[7]

Lord Selkirk later restored order in the settlement with mercenary soldier-settlers brought in from Switzerland. But his dream of a self-sufficient agricultural community was doomed. Floods and locusts, wolves and winter, and desertions, all plagued the colony. Fighting off lawsuits and ill health, Selkirk died prematurely in 1820. That same year, Archibald McDonald decided to join the Hudson's Bay Company.

The British government was appalled at the disarray in its territories, but matters were not resolved until the North West Company was folded (under pressure) into the Hudson's Bay Company in 1821. The merger consolidated personnel and forts throughout the fur country, and resulted in Archibald McDonald being sent to Fort George (Astoria), where he sired Ranald. Selkirk's land was bought back by the Hudson's Bay Company, and instead of a colony for the displaced poor of Britain, Red River became primarily a haven for former laborers, *voyageurs,* and other employees of the defunct North West Company, as well as those of a vastly expanded Hudson's Bay Company. These men were used to the ways of the wilderness and had Indian or mixed wives and children; it was easier for them to settle in Red River than to try to integrate back into civilization in faraway Canada.

Life in the Red River Settlement

When ten-year old Ranald MacDonald arrived in the young Red River Settlement in mid-June 1834, it was a mosaic of communities united by a shared environment and residence on Hudson's Bay Company land. The wife of

Duncan Finlayson (who took Ranald across the Rockies, and would later become the governor of Assiniboia) described the settlement in 1840 as being about five thousand people, mainly "Scotch settlers, Canadians, and half-breeds, the latter forming by far the largest portion of the population."[8] The reality of the situation, however, was even more complex, there being groups of English and Scottish settlers, Orkney Islanders, a few Swiss, communities of mixed Anglo-Indian descent, and communities of French Canadians and mixed French-Indian descent, villages of Indian tribes, Indians who worked at the Company forts, and Indians who came to visit and trade. Among the non-Indian population there were also deep divisions of language, class, Protestant-Catholic religion, and lifestyle. Like Fort Vancouver, the Red River settlement was extremely polyglot in nature, so much so that church ministers regularly used interpreters. Many of the Métis population (especially in the traditional sense, meaning those of Indian and French blood) had a truly hybrid Euro-Indian culture. They had their own style of dress and speech—a mixture of French and Cree called Michif—and an ability to understand English and Ojibwa, too. An American who later encountered the people of Red River in 1858, in St. Paul, Minnesota, described them in highly romantic terms:

> [They wore] dark, coarse blue coats, glittering with a savage profusion of enormous buttons of polished brass; their long, waving sashes of the brightest red, and jaunty little caps, half Tartar and half French; even their loose trowsers of English corduroy or some dark woolen stuff, if not of elk or bison skin, down to the quaint and dingy moccasins wherewith they cloth their feet, savor of the wild, wondrous, and romantic. . . . The various hues of their complexion, from that of the dusky Indian with his arrowy raven hair, up through all the intervening tints of dingy browns, to the ruddy cheek and blue eyes of the fair-haired Gael, proclaim the intermingling of the Caucasian with the blood of the aborigines. Within the circle of their camp, you may hear French, Gaelic, English, Cree, and Ojibewa, with all the wild and adventurous life incident to the savage; while to the blood of their fathers can be traced those demi-social habits and inclinations which they evince although entirely shut out from contact with enlightened society by their remote geographical position.[9]

Although the Red River settlement was created on some of the world's most fertile land, with the technology of the day its residents constantly struggled to achieve self-sufficiency. Temperatures ranged from 105°F in summer to −45°F in winter, and the short growing season was often interrupted by flooding in spring and prairie fires in summer, when "the air is filled with mosquitoes, and flies, which never cease tormenting you day or night."[10] Over the years, various schemes were floated to develop export industries. A Buffalo Wool Company was formed, using bison hair for wool. A Tallow Company produced hides and tallow from cattle herds. And there were attempts to grow flax and raise sheep for real wool, too. But it was hard to overcome the settlement's sheer isolation. In 1856, another American (with a somewhat exaggerated perspective), wrote of the area, saying,

> There is a spot on this continent which travelers do not visit, and from which civilization seems in a measure shut out . . . no railroads, or steamers, or telegraph wires, or lines of stages make their way thither. . . . It sends forth neither newspapers, nor books, nor correspondents' letters . . . it is not even marked on the maps or mentioned in the gazetteers.[11]

A large portion of the Red River population, especially the mixed-bloods, depended on the buffalo hunt. Usually twice a year, men and their families would gather with horses and guns and two-wheeled, squeaky contraptions called "Red River carts" (made of wood and leather); they would then elect a captain and officials of the hunt and move out to the plains. Rules were strict, a priest was taken along, and no hunting was allowed on Sundays. When a buffalo herd was sighted, as many as four hundred men would charge, dashing into the herd,

> firing as they go at the fattest cattle; ride on and on, through and through the close ranks of the buffalo, until there are but a few stragglers—the leanest brutes—alive. Each man has his mouth full of balls, and loads and fires at full gallop. . . . Though the hunt seldom lasts over an hour or so, a good hunter will kill his ten or twelve buffaloes.[12]

The mixed-blood and Métis attachment to the hunt was a rational one, given the environment in which they lived, but to many Hudson's Bay Company officials, missionaries, and clergymen, the hunt seemed to prevent the settlement's residents from becoming fully successful farmers, in short, from becoming "civilized people." As Alexander Ross, the main historian of the settlement (and a long-term resident) described it, the attachment to the spring hunt created a burst of commercial activity and borrowing to obtain supplies before the hunt, all in hopes of making a quick fortune:

> The practical result of all this may be stated in a few words. After the expedition starts, there is not a manservant or maid-servant to be found in the colony. At any season but seed time and harvest time, the settlement is literally swarming with idlers; but at these urgent periods, money cannot procure them. This alone is most injurious to the agricultural class.[13]

Hudson's Bay Company officials had a particularly conflicted attitude toward the Métis hunters. On the one hand, the hunters provided much needed pemmican. On the other hand, as free agents, they also were potential competitors in the fur trade. Conversely, many Métis distrusted the HBC and chafed at the constraints it imposed upon them. They were, after all, living under a benevolent corporate dictatorship, and they had been forbidden to trade on their own, on land they increasingly considered their own because of their long residency and Indian ancestry. In 1824 George Simpson, the otherwise brilliant governor of the Hudson's Bay Company in North America, had revealed his own biases and fears about these matters in a letter comparing the various ethnic groups in Red River. Of the "half-breeds," he wrote,

> they are fond of dress show and liquor, which they cannot then procure, they are accustomed to an erratic life, and cannot immediately be brought to agricultural pursuits, they possess all the savage ferocity of the Indian with all the cunning and knowledge of the whites, so that unless early means are taken to bring them round to industrious habits and withdraw them from the plains, I do most seriously apprehend that they will in due time be the destruction of the colony. They never inter-marry with the whites, but on the contrary all the best looking women among them are picked up by the whites, and this produces everlasting jealousies . . . there is every prospect that they will become a

most alarming banditti who will have recourse to acts of violence and barbarity in order to gratify their love of plunder and revenge.[14]

"Civilizing" Influences

If the Red River settlement had untamed aspects, it also quickly developed many attributes of civilization and could be surprisingly cosmopolitan. In part because of its location on the main HBC trade routes, the settlement was regularly visited by *voyageurs* and trappers, as well as educated HBC officers, who brought information from their constant travels around the world. The same American who wrote of Red River's extreme isolation in the 1850s also noted that by then it was "profusely supplied with clergy," had a "citadel of formidable strength and large size," mills, and many model farms. As an "oasis in the great North American zahara," he marveled that it offered "more than one good library," and that

> a man may dine there according to Soyer, drive a two-forty nag in a dashing cariole over the crisp snow, dance the last Celarius polka redowa with ladies of any shade of color from the pure bronze to the mere white, discuss the principles of human society and the theory of popular governments as learnedly as the thing could be done at Washington or Cincinnati.[15]

Key to the "civilizing process" was the settlement's schools, which developed under the aegis of missionaries. One for Roman Catholics appeared first; then an Anglican mission school was founded in 1820 by Rev. John West, the first officially appointed chaplain of the Hudson's Bay Company. West was also a missionary from the London-based Church Missionary Society and soon would demonstrate that the goals of the Company and its appointed clergy were not always compatible.[16]

West's instructions were to "afford religious instruction and consolation to the servants in the active employment of the Hudson's Bay Company, as well as to the Company's retired servants, and other inhabitants of the settlement." But at the outset, he dreamed of opening a school for Indians, too, and spreading Christianity throughout the Northwest. Whereupon, as he wrote, "It was now hinted to me, that the interest I was taking in the education of the native children, had already excited the fears of some of the chief factors and traders, as to the extent to which it might be carried."[17]

The Hudson's Bay Company was first and foremost a commercial enterprise centered around the collection of wild animal furs. In a May 20, 1822, letter to his superior in London, the Company's ever-blunt North American governor, George Simpson, commented that West's plans

> in my humble opinion will be attended with little other good than filling the pockets and bellies of some hungry missionaries and schoolmasters and rearing the Indians in habits of indolence; they are already too much enlightened by the late opposition and more of it would in my opinion do harm instead of good to the Fur Trade. I have always remarked that an enlightened Indian is good for nothing . . . even the half Breeds of the Country who have been educated in Canada are blackguards of the very worst description, they not only pick up the vices of the Whites upon which they improve but retain those of the Indian in their utmost extent.[18]

At the same time, the Company was the nominal ruler over a vast territory. Associated with its charter, it had a vague responsibility to the British Crown to spread Christianity, and it generally did realize the stabilizing influence of religion. Furthermore, when it came to education, especially of "half-breeds," the attitude of Company officers was complicated by the fact that many of their own progeny and those of their closest friends were affected. Most, including Simpson, had children from liaisons with women who were either Indian or of mixed heritage. Some officers, such as the governor, would later abandon their native companions in favor of white wives from England, but many of the true "gentlemen" did not. And those who did not wanted desperately to provide the best for their children, that they might succeed in the civilized world.

In the 1830s, some HBC officers sent their children to Canada or even Europe for education. But as Jennifer S. H. Brown—one of Canada's premier researchers on the Métis—notes, those with big families could ill afford to do so for all of their children, so the result could be educated and uneducated siblings in one family. Indeed, as the Scottish wife of one Company officer lamented in 1840, "The state of society seems shocking. Some people educate & make gentlemen of part of their family & leave the other savages. . . . Dr. MacLoughlen, one of our grandees at a great expense gave 2 of his

Photo © 1999 Frederik L. Schodt.

Parish church of St. Andrew, known as the "Lower Church," first established in 1828 as the diocese of Rupert's Land, on the banks of the Red River. MacDonald attended services here, while living briefly in Rev. William Cockran's nearby rectory. Cockran is buried in the church's cemetery, as are several officers of the Hudson's Bay Company from MacDonald's era. The present structure dates from 1845.

sons a regular education in England & keeps the 3rd a common Indian."[19] The schools at Red River were thus a low-cost alternative to Canada or Europe, but the remoteness of the settlement meant they could provide only a poor facsimile of the education available there.

❖ ❖ ❖

Ranald MacDonald's family maintained a particularly strong connection to two clergymen at Red River—the Rev. David T. Jones, the Company's new chief chaplain, and the Rev. William Cockran, the assistant chaplain. Both men played key roles in helping to quickly "civilize" the family upon its arrival in 1834.

During the time that Archibald McDonald was on furlough in England in 1834–35, his wife and children boarded with Cockran. Baptism was considered a critical weapon in the war against heathenism, and records show that on November 2, 1834, Ranald, his stepmother Jane Klyne, and his half-siblings Angus, Archibald, Alexander, Allan, and Mary Anne were all baptized by the assistant chaplain "in the territory of the Hudson's Bay Company." Ranald is clearly listed as the son of "Arch-d Mcdonald & an Indian Woman."[20] Yet on the day Cockran baptized the McDonald family, even the reverend realized the practice had its limitations, observing in his journal that "[t]he present year is adding greatly to the Church of Christ; but I begin to apprehend that baptism is more a matter of custom than of conscience; therefore the increase, though encouraging in the first instance, will eventually carry with it a share of disappointment."[21]

Sketch of the Rev. William Cockran, n.d.

Image N9817. Courtesy Provincial Archives of Manitoba.

Cockran looms large in Red River history, and he has been depicted by writers as being everything from a near-saint to an over-zealous fanatic, helping British imperialism subdue indigenous peoples.[22] He was powerfully motivated to convert Indians to Christianity (specifically Anglicanism) and to teach them the settled ways of agriculture and British-style "civilization." Yet as the Company's assistant chaplain, he was charged first and foremost with serving the larger half-breed and European population of Protestants, which included the McDonald family. It proved hard for anyone—whether Indians, mix-bloods, or Company officers—to live up to the reverend's standards. One man wrote of his sermons in 1835, that "Cockran spins out his long yarns as usual, murdering the Kings English most unmercifully in his flights of Pulpit eloquence—and railing occasionally at the immoral habits of the Gentlemen of the Fur Trade."[23]

Cockran and other clergy were often critical of fur traders who had not formalized their marriages to native women. Sometimes, though, this failure to formalize was simply the result of there having been no ministers at the remote posts where the traders lived. Ranald MacDonald's parents, for example, had already been living together for nearly a decade "in the custom of the country" before their marriage. Still, the notation on his stepmother's 1834 baptismal record states that she was the "lawful wife of Arch-d McDonald of the Hudson's Bay Company's service."[24]

After returning from England in 1835, Archibald McDonald made up his mind to do things properly. On June 9, he and Jane Klyne were officially married, with Ranald and his half-siblings presumably present. The union is recorded as one of "mutual consent," with Jane listed as "a Half Caste Native." The ceremony was performed by Cockran, the "2nd Chaplain to the Hon-ble Hudson's Bay Company," in his house and witnessed by Chief Chaplain Jones and Alexander Christie and Duncan Finlayson, chief factors of the HBC.[25]

Both Cockran and Jones mentioned the marriage ceremony in their journals. Cockran, always filled with religious fervor and little time for gossip, had had to get up at 3:00 A.M. that day and travel to help a parishioner with a terrible nosebleed, then return home, where, he matter-of-factly wrote, he "baptized an infant, married a couple and attended the meeting."[26] Jones was far more involved in the secular world, and of the formal marriage he approvingly noted in his journal that "this laudable practice is now becoming general." Then he commented on the great sacrifice Archibald and Jane were making, adding,

> I mean parting with the children for an indefinite period in order to procure them moral & religious improvement; this gentleman is an instance in point; he is to embark immediately for the western side of the Rocky Mountains, taking with him his wife and two small children, leaving four others with us whom he cannot expect to see in less than five years time! May he find a recompense in the benefits secured them![27]

On July 14, 1835, Archibald and Jane Klyne finally left for Fort Colvile on their "long & arduous journey to the westward of the Rocky Mountains," taking the two smallest children and leaving Ranald and three younger half-brothers behind at Red River.[28] It would be the last time Archibald would ever see his eldest son.

Red River Schools

Nearly sixty years later, Ranald MacDonald wrote to a friend that "in the year 1836 [I] was at Richard Mortimer Pritchard's school & from that to the Revd David Thomas Jones' High School."[29] He understandably had difficulty recalling details that far back, but a more contemporary letter that his father wrote on April 1, 1836, survives. In it, Archibald wrote of his children that "[t]hree of them are at present at the Red River Academy. Ranald, or if you will have it Toole, was removed there from Pritchards last summer & now costs me £30 a year."[30] From both of these letters, it is clear that in the school year of 1834–35, before entering the Red River Academy, Ranald was educated by, and probably boarded with, John Pritchard, a man with a particularly colorful past.

In 1805, while a member of the North West Company, Pritchard had been lost on the prairie for forty days without gun, knife, clothing, or food, saved only by the grace of local Indians. In the spring of 1814, he had offered little resistance when Lord Selkirk's men seized pemmican at a North West Company fort; afterward, labeled a "coward" by a superior, he had left the Company and settled in Red River. In 1816 Pritchard had witnessed the Seven Oaks massacre and was briefly been taken prisoner by Métis forces. In 1819 he had journeyed to London, and presented a petition to Parliament for protection of the Red River settlement from the North West Company; while there, he searched unsuccessfully for a schoolmaster for the colony. After returning in 1820, he farmed and became deeply involved in various disastrous business ventures for the HBC.[31] Most historical references to Pritchard are laudatory, but his failed business dealings led the ever-caustic Governor Simpson to once call him "a poor little Drunken Sot" and "a wild visionary speculative creature without a particle of solidity and but a moderate share of judgment."[32]

Pritchard may have been physically small, but he was religious and apparently had a big heart. He established Sunday schools and day schools for children of both sexes, "whose parents cannot afford to pay for their instruction" and he was paid £25 per annum by the HBC to support his "benevolence."[33] Around 1832 he began teaching at a school called The Elm at Frog Plain, near the site of the Seven Oaks battle. In the summer of 1835, Cockran and Jones filed a report on Red River schools for the London Church Missionary Society. Of Pritchard and The Elm, they declared,

Mr. Pritchard having undertaken the work of educating a limited number of children belonging to the officers in the Hudson's Bay Company's service, found that he could afford his energies a wider scope by opening his door for the reception of the settlers' children; and during the period above named he has with zeal and perseverance prosecuted his disinterested labours in affording them for the most part gratuitous instructions. At present this school contains the following numbers; 12 private boarders, all halfbreeds; 33 European children, almost entirely of Highland Scotch extraction.

The system of tuition here embraces reading, writing, arithmetic, grammar, and book-keeping. The progress of the scholars generally is no less creditable to the master than satisfactory to the parents and friends of the children.[34]

Pritchard had several children of his own, one from a former liaison with an Indian woman. Indeed, one of the few times the word "Japan" appears in documents related to Red River is in a letter circa 1814, referring to him as "little Pritchard . . . eager to go to Red River; he is full of love and enthusiasm and has a japan Lady who he admires."[35] Since there were no Japanese women in all of North America then, this presumably meant a dark-skinned (as in "lacquer-colored") native woman. The *Red River Settlement Census* from the years between 1827 and 1840 shows that Pritchard lived on Lot 753 and had a son, also named John Pritchard, who was a "native protestant . . . who lives with his father." In 1835 Pritchard is listed as fifty-five years old, with five sons and four daughters, one manservant, two women servants, and twelve Protestant boy pupils, eleven of whom were under the age of sixteen.[36] One of them was presumably Ranald MacDonald.

❖ ❖ ❖

In the context of North American history, the Red River settlement was unusual. A later historian described the place as being "[a] compromise between civilization and barbarism, between a sedentary and a nomadic economy, and, be it said, between Christianity and paganism."[37] But according to the 1835 report filed by Cockran and Jones, the Red River community was also quite idyllic around the time Ranald arrived, one of the few places in North America where whites, "half-breeds," and settled and nomadic Indians lived in harmony and health. In the "Upper Church," where both chaplains regularly preached to the Protestant population (including Ranald), the congregation consisted of three hundred mostly Scottish, English, and Orkneymen, and "460 half-castes and 70 native Indians." People in the area did not need to lock their doors, and there had been "but two instances of theft in the course of twelve years and the perpetrators were persons unconnected with the settlement." Of the many still nomadic local Indians, even those passing through "in a state of starvation . . . commit no depredations on the property of the settlers [although] they might with almost certainty of impunity, slaughter our cattle, and destroy our crops." But in an exception to this otherwise happy report, the two chaplains mentioned: "It is, however, painful to state that among the Halfbreeds a spirit of insubordination to a considerable extent manifested itself in January last."[38]

One of the reasons for the unrest was that the Company, in a twisted attempt to finance enforcement of its own monopoly, had levied a heavy tariff on imports and exports, seized the furs of several residents, and arrested them. These acts inflamed the French Canadian population, in particular, but also the French and even English-speaking half-breeds. As Cockran explained in an October 1835 letter to his London superiors,

> A spirit of discontent had been raging amongst the [Roman Catholic half-breeds] for several months; it was now ready to burst forth into open resistance. They wanted only the sanction of the Protestant Half-breeds to carry their threats into execution. . . . As soon as a coalition was affected, and the parties understood each other; they began to resist the Governor's authority; dispute the territorial rights of the Hudson's Bay Company; their exclusive right to trade and determined to settle the matter by scalping the Governor and electing a representative of their own.[39]

In yet another letter, Cockran noted that the half-breeds had "threatened . . . to drive the whites out of the country."[40]

The "half-breed" population in Red River was normally divided into those with Anglo-Protestant fathers and those with French-Catholic fathers. But the community and language barriers this different paternity caused could be bridged both by the Cree language of the half-breeds' mothers, and by the culture of the hunt. The English-speaking progeny of HBC officers (such as young Ranald MacDonald) were social elites in the internal hierarchy of the mixed-blood populations, and thus in a separate category, but even they occasionally sided with the larger Métis community.

Around the time of the discontent that Cockran mentioned, these young elites, too, had reason to be inflamed. As Ross, the settlement historian, described it, an English half-breed fell in love with and proposed to an HBC officer's daughter at a local boarding school. The girl was also half-Indian, but her father preferred another suitor, a Scottish lad. The father summoned the half-breed boy and reprimanded him for acting above his station in life, deeply wounding the young man's pride. As Ross next observed,

> [t]he young man, without saying a word, put on his hat and walked out of the room; but being a leading man among his countrymen, the whole fraternity took fire at the insult. "This is the way," said they, "that we half-breeds are despised and treated." From that moment they clubbed together, in high dudgeon, and joined the French malcontents against their rulers; so that for years afterwards this spirit of combination and hatred gave rise to plots, plans, and unlawful meetings among them, which threatened . . . the peace and tranquility of the settlement.[41]

❖ ❖ ❖

There were schools in Red River for children of Catholic French Canadians, Anglo-Protestants, and Indians, but there was only one boarding school of the type Ross mentioned, for the older offspring of HBC "gentlemen." That was Rev. David Jones's Academy, also called the "Red River Academy," which Ranald MacDonald entered in the summer of 1835. It "exclusively provided for the children of Governors, Deputy-Governors, and chief Factors, the great nabobs of the fur trade."[42]

Early in 1832, Jones had proposed to Governor Simpson "a respectable Seminary on a large scale in this Settlement for the moral improvement, religious instruction and general education of Boys; the sons of Gentlemen belonging to the Fur Trade." It was a proposal tailored to please the frugal Simpson, as the Academy was to be both self-supporting (sustained by annual fees of £30 for tuition, room, and board) and ostensibly independent of the

Church Missionary Society. The pupils, moreover, were to be "habited uniformly as in all public schools" and, because Jones felt that there were altogether too many unfavorable influences in the Settlement, isolated as well, "entirely apart from the natives of this country . . . [with] no opportunity of speaking other than the English language and . . . such children as may have relatives at the settlement may have but very limited intercourse with them." Almost immediately upon the opening of the new school, the officers, or "gentlemen" of the Company, began sending in their children, of both sexes, from remote fur trade posts to attend the academy.[43]

A tutor, John Macallum, and a governess arrived in the fall of 1833. By the next summer, Governor Simpson reported back to London that "the boarding school, under the direction of Mr. & Mrs. Jones is attended by forty boys and girls, and seems to be well managed; the tutor and governess affording entire satisfaction."[44] It was hard to keep tutors, as they were inclined to leave to join the more lucrative fur trade, but Macallum stayed (and later took over the school after Jones left). Around the time that young Ranald entered, the Academy's enrollment consisted of "25 young ladies and 30 gentlemen." To help support them all, the establishment required fifteen servants, three houses, livestock, and thirty-six acres under cultivation.[45]

Although Jones wanted to isolate and protect his young charges, there were limits to what he could do. One of his biggest fears was that one of the children might become ill or die so far from home. Sure enough, just a few weeks before Ranald's parents left him at Red River, influenza struck the settlement so badly that church attendance plummeted and teaching had to be temporarily suspended. On September 15, Jones recorded that a young "Miss M," the daughter of "Chief Factor M.," died, her Indian mother by her side. A month later, the girl's brother and one other student followed. From surviving letters, it would appear that the young woman may have been Sophie McDonell, daughter of Chief Factor Allan McDonell—the same girl whose suitors had nearly caused a riot in the settlement earlier.[46]

Given that there were almost no opportunities for formal education on the North American frontier at that time (especially for non-whites), the Academy curriculum was rather ambitious. Jones and Cockran described it in their 1835 report as follows:

The course of education for the young ladies' school embraces reading, writing, arithmetic, geography, the use of globes, history and catechical information. In the young gentlemen's school progress is made in reading, writing, arithmetic, bookkeeping, algebra, mathematics, Latin, Greek, &c. The younger ones read *Delectus* and study grammar, history, etc., while the newcomers are in the New Testament and Catechisms of various sorts.[47]

It was the Red River Academy that Ranald MacDonald was clearly referring to in his 1891 interview with Elizabeth Custer, when he said his father had sent him there so he could obtain " 'a No. 1' education. . . . I knew something of Romanism, but those Episcopalians at that church school knocked the spots out of the Catholics with their doctrines. We used to have pemmican for our luncheon, and it was something of which a little goes a long ways."[48]

The culture of the Red River Academy helps explain much about MacDonald's adult personality, including the old-fashioned patterns of speech Custer later noted in him, his slightly archaic spelling habits, and his knowledge of the classics. The school also probably influenced the religious bent he had as a young man, his teetotaling, and even his curiosity about the outside world. Children happily received letters from their elite officer fathers, many of whom would stop in at the settlement to give first-hand accounts of their travels in the western wilderness, Europe, or the Pacific. The tutor Macallum ordered newspapers brought in from Montreal. Jones and Cockran likewise were intimately connected to the global network of missionaries who corresponded with one another about local and world events. In one February 24, 1837, journal entry, Jones even mentions receiving copies of some of the first newspapers published in the Hawaiian Islands, where MacDonald would later prepare his adventure to Japan.[49]

At the Red River Academy, MacDonald became truly literate, in the advanced sense of the word. In his posthumously published autobiography, he attributes his later survival in Japan partly to the fact that he "was not a man of learning, but always a lover of books . . . in fact, it was *that* that saved me: for seeing me ever reading, a man of books, they drew to me: the books magnetized them: and *they* (books and Japanese) *made me their teacher!* "[50]

✳ ✳ ✳

Yet all was not well at the Academy. The Company paid Jones an annual subsidy of £100, but the school was never a financial success. And it proved extremely difficult to secure qualified female governesses, for they tended to give up and return to England, get married, or prove incompetent. As George Simpson wrote Jones on June 24, 1836, "[Y]ou will find required that the lady they wished to fill that situation should be qualified to teach not only the useful but ornamental branches of education, such as music, drawing &c which they find Miss Armstrong is not qualified to do."[51] Miss Armstrong may not be to blame, but years later, when asked to draw simple pictures related to his Japan adventure, MacDonald replied, "I don't think that I ever attempted anything of the kind before. . . . I tell you before hand it will be the rudest kind . . . I am afraid you cannot make any use of them after it is done."[52]

Macallum, the first tutor and later headmaster, also had overly high expectations. He had a Master of Arts degree from his native Scotland, and he began his service, noting of his charges that

They may now, if so disposed, acquire such a measure of useful knowledge, such an acquaintance with the arts & sciences, with whatever dignifies the mind, refines the taste, & adornes the character, as will suffice to raise them far above the condition of their maternal ancestors, & render them at once useful & respectable members of society. But will they improve their privilege? Will they pursue that line of conduct which reason & interest point out? I know not.[53]

When Macallum took over the Academy from Jones in 1838, his goal was to make it as good or better than the best schools in England. His method was implement "a new system of discipline," which

invigorates both the body and the mind of the Pupil, & implants & cherishes habits which will be of special service in active life. It was the want of such a system, that amongst other things, proved so detrimental to the reputation of the establishment while it was under the superintendence of Mr. Jones—the main sources of individual comfort in after life, carefulness, neatness, cleanliness, regularity, & politeness, were entirely overlooked.[54]

Many graduates of Red River Academy would become quite successful later in life, a few finding employment in the Hudson's Bay Company, others even entering government service. But as one historian notes, in many cases "the more advanced subjects—Latin, Greek, Euclid, English Literature, and Geography—were neither interesting nor useful to the teen-aged youngsters of mixed blood."[55]

As time went by, Macallum also became a rather cruel taskmaster. By 1843, only a few years after Ranald MacDonald had left, conditions were so bad that the gossipy wife of one HBC trader wrote,

> They say the Mr MacCallums school is going to wreck. Children who have had duck geese & venison 3 times a day are supposed to suffer from breakfasts of milk & water with dry bread, severe floggings, confinement after any fault & the total want of the following meal. The boys & girls are constantly fainting but MacCallum won't change his system. Many girls have got ill, and as he makes them strip off their Indian stockings & adopt English fashion it is not surprising. They must take a certain walk every day, plunging thro' the freezing snow. They wear Indian shoes, but without the cloth stockings or leggings over them the snow gets in. . . . Then if the mothers are not legally married they are not allowed to see their children. This may be all very right, but it is fearfully cruel for the poor unfortunate mothers did not know that there was any distinction & it is only within the last few years that any one was so married. Of course had all the fathers refused, every one woman in the country [would] have been no better than those that are represented to their own children as discreditable.[56]

* * *

Back in Fort Colvile, Archibald McDonald took pride in the accounts he received of his son 's progress at Red River, but he worried terribly that some undisciplined "Indian" part of the boy's nature might assert itself. On January 25, 1837, writing to a friend, Edward Ermatinger, about his "young Chinook," Archibald confided,

I heard very favorable accounts of him this fall from Mr. Jones, &

who knows but he may turn out a rare exception to the race. I tell them to keep him at a Jointer plane or Beauvet's Sledge hammer when the younger Boys are at play; & he will in reality be turned to one or the other should we unfortunately discover a leaning to unsettled habits . . . at all events if we cannot make Gentlemen of them I trust we shall always have the wherewith to set them up as humble unpretending farmers.[57]

A year later, on February 1, 1839, when Ranald was nearly fifteen years old, Archibald wrote again about his son, that "he has a high character for application & good behavior from Mr. Macallum." Then of all his sons, the father wrote, "It will go very hard with me if I let any of them loose in this vile country, tho' that nevertheless seems to be the lot of the entire rising generation."[58] In his next communication, on March 10, 1839, he quoted a letter from Cockran from the previous fall that said, "I preached at the upper Church last Sunday & saw the boys—they were all well then. Angus (the little white headed chap you [saw] crawling about at Okanagan house) still takes the lead; but Ranald has *certain indescribable qualities* which leads me to imagine that he will make the man that is best adapted for the world." Despite the praise, Archibald felt compelled to confess, "So far, good; still I cannot divest myself of *certain indescribable fears* which you can conceive as well as I can."[59]

The Dickson Filibuster

The mid-1830s were a time of rising tensions in the Red River settlement. In 1836 the crops failed because of a terrible frost, and anticipated supplies did not come through on boats from Hudson Bay. "Thus we are shut up," wrote Jones, "for a whole winter without letters—without publications—without School-books and various other items on which much of our case depends."[60] That October, Jones's wife, who taught the girls at the Academy, died of illness, leaving him miserable. In November, the settlement was visited by a large band of Sioux Indians, showing surprising military discipline, who had just returned from raids on United States soil.[61]

Social problems, prevalent at the best of times, were fanned by conflicts brewing far to the east. In Lower and Upper Canada (today's Quebec and Ontario, respectively), armed rebellions were soon to erupt, the one in Lower

Canada led by French Canadian Louis Joseph Papineau. According to Settlement historian Ross, "The Canadians of Red River sighed for the success of their brethren's cause. Patriotic songs were chanted on every side in praise of Papineau. In the plains, the half-breeds made a flag, called the Papineau standard, which was waved in triumph for years, and the rebel's deeds extolled to the skies."[62] It took all the diplomatic skills and wily cunning of HBC officials to keep the lid on this volatile mix.

And around this time, one of the more curious events in North American history occurred. On February 10, 1837, Jones recorded in his journal that he had been summoned to the HBC fort in the settlement to attend

> at a conversation with a person calling himself General Dickson, who came here with about a dozen adventurers in the month of November last. His professed object was to beat up for recruits among the half breeds & Indians to go & take Sta. Fe from the Spaniards on the Rio Bravo del Norte, seize a deposit of dollars amounting to 25 millions, & then take Mexico & establish himself an independent Sovereign. No doubt the real object was expecting to find here a bandill of half breeds & others who would join him in plundering the Company's Stores. The man is certainly insane, & his friends in London, who seem respectable, ought to get hold of him & confine him.[63]

Were it not for the fact that this so-called "Dickson Filibuster" involved several mixed-blood sons of prominent HBC officers, the episode would have had little relation to Ranald MacDonald and be merely another bizarre footnote in the annals of North American history. As it was, however, the Dickson Filibuster would reinforce in the minds of Archibald McDonald and other HBC officers their worst fears for their own male progeny. At the center of the controversy was John McLoughlin, Jr., upon whom Dickson had bestowed the rank of Major of the Cavalry. As mentioned previously, John, Jr. was the son of Dr. John McLoughlin, chief factor at Fort Vancouver and head of the entire Columbia territory. He was also the older brother of David McLoughlin, with whom Ranald MacDonald had gone to school in Fort Vancouver and traveled over the Rocky Mountains.

In 1821 Dr. McLoughlin had left his beloved eldest son, John, Jr., then nine, with a relative in Montreal, hoping to further his education. Intelligent and promising, the poor boy desperately wanted to be with his father in the West and soon exhibited an undisciplined streak and (like his father) a temper. The elderly guardian in Montreal began to despair of him. He felt the boy could never become the doctor his physician father so fervently desired, and that he was best suited to be an Indian fur trader. But the guardian also knew the HBC was reluctant to hire mixed-race sons of officers. In an April 20, 1827, letter he therefore recommended to the father that he purchase a commission in the military for his son. As for becoming a physician, the guardian condescendingly wrote, "[T]hese boys are remarkable for want of steadiness and application, tho by no means deficient in understanding."[64]

McLoughlin, Sr. nonetheless sent his son to Paris, at great expense, to study medicine there with an uncle. But instead of taking advantage of this opportunity, the young man squandered money and misbehaved. In 1835, when Archibald McDonald was on furlough in Europe (having left his family safely at Red River), he visited John, Jr.'s boarding house, hoping to find him in, in the evening, at an hour "[w]hen Young Men who study ought to be at home." But he was told that "John did nothing but go about and Neglected his Studies."[65] Later, John, Jr. committed some breach of good behavior for which his uncle could not forgive him, and he was packed off, back to Canada. Out of money, he applied to the HBC but was rejected. It was then that he signed up with the Dickson Filibuster.

"General" James Dickson has been variously described by historians as an educated Englishman or half-Sioux Indian. He first appeared, handsomely dressed in military uniform, in early 1836 in cities in the American northeast. According to a report later filed by Governor Simpson, his face was "covered with huge Whiskers and Mustachios, and seamed with sabre wounds." Dickson variously called himself "General Dickson of the Indian Liberating Army" or "Montezuma the Second."[66]

Dickson was secretive and told different people different things, so his true goal remains obscure. In one surviving letter, he claimed that he planned to march to Red River to enlist "the English half breeds & Indians of the quarter with the purpose of falling upon Santa Fe and California and thus create a powerful diversion in favour of Texas." A fur trader, who interviewed him, wrote that Dickson's ultimate goal was to capture then Mexican-controlled California and make it an independent nation for Indian tribes about to be displaced from the eastern United States. At Red River he was to enlist the half-breeds, proceed to Santa Fe and overthrow the Mexicans there, then cross the Rockies to California, where he would be joined by a force of Cherokees and others. "That with their aid, they mean to endeavour obtaining possession of that Country for the Indian Tribes, and locate them there under a Military Government, preventing all except those of Indian blood, from possessing an acre of land. All Whites only to be received as Officers of the Govt."[67]

In the Hudson's Bay Company, which controlled Red River, such news set off a near panic. First, Governor Simpson believed that Dickson's true intent in going to Red River was to

> excite dissatisfaction in the minds of the different Indian Tribes and half breeds under the plea of encroachments on their territory by the British and United States Governments, to point out to them the practicability of terminating those evils and improving their condition by electing Dickson as their King and his half breed Leaders as their Chiefs, and thereby forming themselves into a great and independent nation. . . . Should the party make their appearance in Red River settlement, where there is a population of several thousand ignorant half-breeds and Indians, I am apprehensive of danger to the White population & to the Fur trading establishments in its vicinity.[68]

While some people found Dickson to be a lunatic, he had enough charisma to raise a force of some sixty followers, and with them he left in August of 1836 from Buffalo, New York, for Red River. Most unsettling to the HBC was that for his top officers he had recruited several mixed-blood sons of prominent fur trade officials, such as John McLoughlin, Jr., and John George Mckenzie. The latter, in particular, was thought to have influence with the young men of Red River, and he was regarded with special suspicion. Mckenzie's father had once been a prominent member of the North West Company during its days of bitter confrontation with the HBC.[69]

Yet from the start the expedition proved to be a comedy of errors, the worst of which were the choice in route taken and time of departure. Plagued by desertions and problems, the band did not get past Lake Superior until too late in the season. Eventually, on December 20, only Dickson and ten men straggled into the Red River Settlement, nearly dead from cold, exhaustion, and starvation.

By and large, the expedition's "officers" were young and inexperienced.

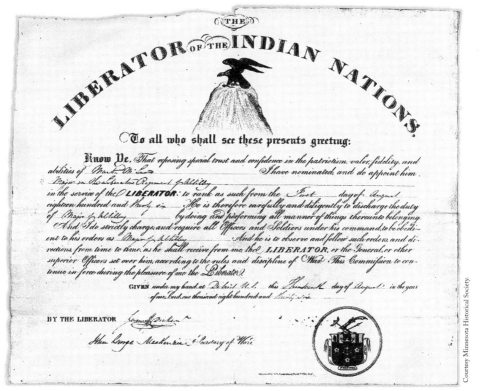

1836 commission of Martin McLeod as "Major of Artillery," signed by General James Dickson, "the Liberator."

One, Martin McLeod, was a fan of the romantic poet Byron.[70] Letters of John McLoughlin, Jr., show him expressing more concern about obtaining a fancy military uniform than his duties as an officer, and threatening to break the bones of his men for their poor attitude.[71] In this context, Governor Simpson's method of dealing with the filibuster threat was brilliant. He worked to make sure that none of the officers' drafts for money would be honored and that all support would be withheld in Rupert's Land. To break up the group itself, he began offering jobs to the young men whom he personally knew, such as John McLoughlin, Jr.

At Red River, the filibuster force was finished and snowbound. Along with two other sons of Company officers, young McLoughlin later accepted a job. James Dickson stayed the winter with Cuthbert Grant, the head of the Métis, and, after bequeathing his sword to him in the spring, vanished into the mists of history.[72]

❖ ❖ ❖

Exactly what teenage Ranald MacDonald thought about the Dickson Fili-buster is not known, yet given the small community of sons and daughters of HBC officers it would be naive to think that he was not affected. At the very least the Filibuster meant that he would be forever viewed by his father and his father's contemporaries through the framework of what John McLough-lin, Jr., and his friends did. In a letter to Edward Ermatinger at the beginning of 1838, Archibald McDonald referred directly to the expedition:

> While on the subject of *Bois Brules*, the late adventures of three of them below in '36 recurs to me, namely the sons of Factors Mc-Loughlin, McBean and McLeod. If you did not hear of the young Captains themselves individually I think you must have heard of their General Dickson & the motley army he embarked with at Buf-falo that Summer for the conquest of Texas. . . . [B]y different routes the wreck of this extraordinary army *!!* reached R.R. where the Artillery, Cavalry & Lancers &c &c &c were to be procured, & here indeed the glory of this division of the heroes of Mexico. . . . What think ye now of all that! and the melancholy satisfaction parents have on this way.[73]

❖ ❖ ❖

By virtue of his father's position, Ranald MacDonald belonged to a social elite at Red River. At the settlement's schools and churches he was, for the most part, indoctrinated in the values of a civilization he had not yet experi-enced. Yet at the same time, he was present during a period of rising Métis consciousness and pride, which fostered a special sense of destiny among many of mixed parentage. And he was about to enter a white world where his parents hoped he would succeed and feared he would fail, and where many close to him expected him to accomplish nothing at all. It is hard to imagine a place more unrelated to Japan than the Red River settlement of the 1830s, but it provided an explosive mix of influences that would help propel Ranald MacDonald on a trajectory his father could never have foreseen.

CHAPTER 5

A "Trial in Business" at St. Thomas

On April 1, 1836, Archibald McDonald wrote his old friend Edward Ermatinger—living in far-off St. Thomas in today's Ontario, Canada—about the plans he had for his son Ranald, then still at Red River. He bemoaned the fact that fur traders often amassed the money to educate their children and then turned them loose on the world "brimful of [their] own importance," with the "melancholy examples resulting from this blind practice . . . but too common." He believed it was better to bring up children "in habits of industry, economy and morality, than aspire at all this visionary greatness for them," stressing that all "the wealth of Rupert's land will not make a *half-breed* either a good parson, a shining lawyer or an able physician, if left to his own discretion while young."[1] In the same letter Archibald then made a proposal:

[B]y '38 I think he ought to be qualified enough to begin the world for himself. Will you then do me the favour to take him in hand—without flattery I feel confident he cannot be under a better guardian—you know their facility with the pen & indeed their aptness altogether while young. He will not at the time I am speaking of be a learned lad, but with the help of what he can pick up with you will have knowledge enough to develop what may be in him as a man.[2]

Alluding to Ranald's ancestry, and his own high hopes for him, Archibald added,

Bear in mind he is of a particular race, & who knows but a kinsman of King Comcomlie is ordained to make a great figure in the new world—as yet he bears an excellent character—Unless he takes it after his father and *prince Cassacas* (I do not mention the princess) he won't have an itching for *Rum*—Be good enough next spring to write me your sentiments about him and suggest the best way of getting him on in Summer '38 from the Sault St Maries by way of the Lakes.[3]

From Fort Colvile, Archibald McDonald usually sent his letters to Edward Ermatinger on the Company's annual, east-bound, spring Express. A priceless link to the outside world, each letter was conveyed on foot and horseback over the Rockies, through forests, across plains, and by canoe and boat on countless lakes and rivers. But the writers had to take into account a year or more time-lag in communications. While few of Ermatinger's letters survive (despite the fact that he was a voluminous correspondent), Ermatinger kept many that he received from his lonely friends, and they are filled with gossip and requests for information about politics and social life. Like hearing half of a conversation and figuring out the rest, the broad outlines of young Ranald's experience in St. Thomas can be deduced from these letters.

The next year, on January 25, 1837, Archibald alluded to having received a positive (but probably guarded) response from Ermatinger about his son. Using the cross-hatched writing technique favored by fur trade men to save paper and precious space in canoes and packs, he filled one side of the page with tiny handwriting and turned it ninety degrees. Then he wrote again on top of the existing text. He reaffirmed his intention to send his "young Chinook," saying, "I have expressed myself still more serious as regards him—indeed my mind is made up to send him down in '38 if your letter of '37 will not absolutely prevent it."[4]

When 1838 rolled around, his son was still at Red River, but Archibald

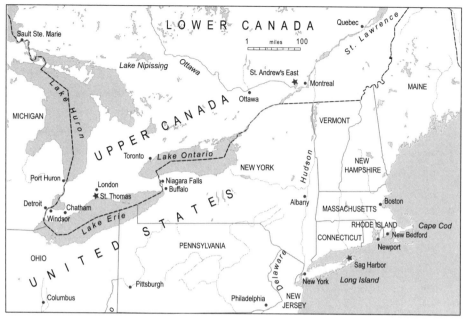

North America, showing St. Thomas, St. Andrews East, and Sag Harbor.

by then had received more encouraging news from Edward. On February 2, amid gossip about shared acquaintances, politics, the Dickson Filibuster, and "the rage for Railroads all over the world now," he wrote,

> I am exceedingly obliged to you for the readiness with which you came into my views respecting my own Boy. If [your brother] Frank goes down he is to take him, but if not, I will for a year or two yet leave him at Mr. Jones', which must finish all the education I intend for him. Were I certain of the time I can get down myself, I could with more ease say how I would like to have him begin the world.[5]

On March 10, 1839, Archibald reaffirmed his determination to have Ranald move to St. Thomas that spring. Confessing that he had not seen his son for over four years, he said,

> Before he went to Red River in '34, I had him myself pretty well advanced in Arithmetic, so that one would suppose he is now something of a scholar; yet I am aware boys of his age leaving school, not

unfrequently are very deficient, & that a little practical learning about that time brushes them up amazingly. . . . I should like to give him a trial in the way of business, & with this view have him bound to yourself, Sir, as an apprentice. By the spring of '40 you will be able to judge of his conduct & capacity, when I shall trouble you for a full expose of all you think about him. My reply to that letter you will have in the fall of '41, which will either confirm all our plans of making a Gentleman *tout de bon* of him, or have him enter on a new apprenticeship at any trade he may select for himself.[6]

At the same time, Archibald confided,

You know the Rock on which is split all the hopes & fortunes of almost all the youth of the Indian Country. Ranald I hope will have none of those fatal notions. His success in the world must solely depend on his own good conduct & exertions. He has a few letters his father & mother lately addressed to him, with the very best advice we could give situated as we are; which you will have the goodness to see that, the better to impress their import on his mind, he will frequently peruse. Above all let him be a constant attendant at church.[7]

In accordance with his father's wishes, in 1839 fifteen-year-old Ranald MacDonald journeyed over 1,500 miles from the Red River settlement to St. Thomas, in trademark HBC fashion. He left, as later he recalled it, in a brigade of four birch bark canoes in the charge of a "Rodrick McLeod" (presumably HBC officer Alexander Roderick McLeod, whose son had joined up with the Dickson Filibuster but later been hired on by the Company). They crossed Lake Winnipeg, then navigated the Lake of the Woods, Rainy Lake, and crossed Lake Superior to Sault Ste. Marie. Here, Ranald was handed over to an agent of the American Fur Company on the other side of the channel, and for the first time saw an African American, an American soldier, and a steamship. He traveled by steamship across Lake Huron to the Detroit area, and impressed the American passengers when they discovered he was originally from famous Astoria. From Detroit he journeyed to Windsor by Canadian steamer, then went by land to Chatham and made the last leg of his trip from the town of London to St. Thomas by stagecoach.

Whether steamers or soldiers or stages, the sights of civilization surely fascinated the teenager from the wilderness.

St. Thomas and the Ermatingers

St. Thomas lies in Elgin County in today's Ontario Province. One of the southernmost towns in Canada, it is sandwiched between London to the immediate north and Port Stanley—the first deep water port on Lake Erie—to the south. Despite a population today of over 20,000, St. Thomas has been overshadowed by neighboring London and eclipsed in importance by

St. Thomas Church.

Photo © 1999 Frederik L. Schodt

Toronto to the immediate east, but at different times in the past it has served as a regional hub for agriculture and for railways. Today tourist brochures highlight the town's contributions to the two World Wars, its bygone railroad era, and a life-size statue of "Jumbo," a 13,000-pound Barnum and Bailey Circus elephant killed by a locomotive in 1885.

Sightseers are also directed to a picturesque older part of town near the Jumbo statue, where wooden houses dating back to the 1830s and 1840s can be seen. There, on Walnut Street, is the St. Thomas Anglican Church, built in 1824, in which young Ranald worshipped. Its interior is still dominated by a raised pulpit that presides sternly over box-style pews (once rented by prominent local families on an annual basis). Ranald's guardian, Edward Ermatinger, was deeply involved in factional squabbling that erupted among the congregation over, among other things, the seating arrangements in these pews. He lived, with his family and boarders, only a short stroll away at 59 Walnut Street, and his bones today rest in the graveyard immediately surrounding the church, along with those of his brother, Francis, and daughter,

Maria. Ranald regarded the birth of Maria, which occurred on November 21, 1841 (while he was still living with the Ermatingers), as particularly propitious, writing to his father that Maria was born only a few hours apart from Queen Victoria's first daughter, the Princess Royal.[8] But history did not prove kind to Maria. A persistent local legend has it that she was a witch, probably because her oddly shaped tomb is the only black one in the graveyard.

❖ ❖ ❖

When Archibald McDonald first considered sending his son to St. Thomas, the town appeared to have an unlimited future. Only two years earlier, the wife of a local official had penned one of the best descriptions of it:

> St. Thomas is situated on a high eminence. . . . The view from it over a fertile, well-settled country, is very beautiful and cheering . . . it is rising fast into importance. The climate, from its high position, is delicious and healthful; and the winters in this part of the province are milder by several degrees than elsewhere. . . . [At nearby Port Stanley] steamboats and schooners land their passengers and merchandise, or load with grain, flour and lumber. The roads are good all round. . . . The population of St. Thomas is at present rated at seven hundred, and it has doubled within two years. There are three churches, one of which is very neat, and three taverns. Two newspapers are published here, one violently tory, the other as violently radical. . . . I was very much struck with this beautiful and cheerful little town, more, I think, than with any place I have yet seen.[9]

Like many Hudson's Bay Company officers, Archibald yearned for the intellectual communion that accompanies civilization, and he hoped one day himself to retire in St. Thomas. His letters to Edward Ermatinger were filled with his dreams of building a house and with requests for news of the area. Ermatinger, once a fur trader himself, was a highly regarded member of the St. Thomas community. Among many lonely fur traders, he was envied, and his friendship was cherished.

For his time, Edward Ermatinger had an unusually international background. He knew English, French, Italian, and some Latin. His grandfather, an early Montreal fur speculator, was of German-Swiss extraction. His father had joined the British army and married an Italian woman in Europe. Edward was born on the Island of Elba in 1797, and his brother Francis, or "Frank," was born a year later in Lisbon, Portugal. The mother died shortly thereafter, so the boys were educated in boarding schools in England under difficult circumstances. On becoming adults, the father arranged for the two of them to join the Hudson's Bay Company, and in 1818 both had signed five-year contracts, starting as apprentice clerks. On the ship to North America, they met up with young Archibald McDonald, then still in the employ of Lord Selkirk, and the three young men became lifelong friends.

Despite similarities in age and upbringing, and affection for one other, the Ermatinger brothers had utterly different personalities. Edward was intellectual, fond of books, musical, and religious, yet subject to what he later in life called "intense depressions of spirit" and "violent transports of rage." He spent ten years with the Company, mainly as an accountant, traveling as far west as Fort Vancouver and developing life-long friendships with many HBC officers.

But the life of a fur trader in remote regions did not suit him, and, after resigning in 1828, he journeyed east to St. Thomas, where he settled and married a white woman of considerable status. He became a businessman, property owner, postmaster, banker, justice of the peace, and—after Ranald MacDonald left—a newspaper publisher and a politician. Throughout his life, Edward remained extraordinarily generous to his old friends in the fur trade.[10]

Francis, on the other hand, was outgoing, boisterous, fond of drink and women, and lived hard. He stayed on with the Company until 1853 and was on the move constantly between posts. He often worked in close association with Archibald McDonald and frequently mentioned the McDonald family (including Ranald) in his gossipy letters. Had it not been for a change in schedule, Francis would have been the one to take Ranald to St. Thomas in 1839. Like Archibald, Francis regularly wrote his brother for news, and yearned to emulate his success and retire to St. Thomas.

A Politically Charged Environment

As it turned out, Ranald arrived in St. Thomas during a time of considerable turmoil. The town was no stranger to conflict, having been burned at least once by invading U.S. forces in the War of 1812, but in 1839 it was also just beginning to recover from a mini-civil war.

Like Red River, Upper Canada—the English-speaking part of British Canada—suffered from what some of its citizens perceived as a lack of representative democracy. It was then controlled by an oligarchy of conservatives called the "Family Compact." Staunch loyalists favoring the British Crown and its traditions, these men were economically progressive but against the more free-wheeling, American-style of popular democracy. In reaction, a reform movement emerged, advocating the establishment of a more representative, elected legislative assembly. The movement stressed the interests of independent farmers, and one of its most radical leaders—William Lyon Mackenzie—had been highly influenced by the Jacksonian democracy of the neighboring United States.

In December 1837, Mackenzie led an armed rebellion into nearby Toronto. Mackenzie's forces were routed by Loyalist troops, but he fled to the United States with many of his men, and from there, along with American sympathizers, he continued to make raids on southern Canada throughout 1838 and even into 1839. The rebellion and raids largely coincided with an even more violent and passionate revolt on the part of French-speaking Canadians in Lower Canada, in today's Quebec.

Because of its proximity to the United States, St. Thomas was deeply affected. British troops were garrisoned in the town, and a local militia was raised to help defend the area, many of its members seeing action against the rebels. In December 1838, a force of Canadians and Americans crossed over from Detroit into the Windsor area (approximately one hundred miles east of St. Thomas), only to meet defeat at the hands of British troops (and in an act of great controversy in St. Thomas, at least four of the prisoners were summarily executed). Even six months later, when Ranald traveled through the same area to arrive in St. Thomas, action was still taking place nearby. According to a son of Edward Ermatinger who later wrote a local history, "marauding parties crossed the Niagara and St. Clair rivers during the summer and committed serious depredations before they retreated or were captured."[11]

Young Ranald thus entered an environment far more politically charged than his father could have envisioned. The rebellion had serious consequences for St. Thomas residents, especially if they were of American origin, or had sided with the reform movement, many becoming the "victims of prosecutions and petty persecutions." The local liberal paper was suppressed, and many residents were arrested or forced to flee to the United States. At least one man was exiled around the world to the British penal colony in Van Diemen's land, known today as the island of Tasmania.[12]

Edward Ermatinger had little time for his young boarder, as he was far too involved in local politics, on the side of the loyalist Tories, fighting what he called the "hydra head of democracy." He already had become something of a local authority figure. Just before the rebellion, he had been appointed deputy postmaster of the town. Toward the end of the conflict, he was tasked with not just delivering the mails but communicating to the government "any important information that may reach you either publicly or privately" to protect the country.[13] He had a patriotic duty, of course, but in a small town it could not have been easy to inform on neighbors or watch what happened to them.

The postmaster at the time, Bela Shaw (described by Edward's son later as an "inoffensive merchant"), was an American, and his store had been a meeting place for reformers, so he had reluctantly become associated with their cause. After the rebellion, the authorities unsuccessfully tried to imprison Shaw, but he sold out and moved to America.[14] Yet Shaw's bad luck became Edward Ermatinger's good fortune, for his departure made it possible for Edward to become postmaster. Edward also bought Shaw's store and property on 55 Walnut Street (presumably at quite a bargain), and it was into this house that Ranald MacDonald moved a year later.

If this complicated arrangement ever troubled Edward Ermatinger, there is no indication of it, for he excelled in murky situations where he could apply a type of moral absolutism. He was a man of impeccable English, and he wrote hundreds of letters to local newspapers about politics and gave frequent speeches during the time Ranald boarded with him. The prospectus of the St. Thomas *Standard*, a newspaper he formed in 1844, two years after Ranald's departure, gives an idea of Edward Ermatinger's personality. The paper's chief object was to

> uphold and maintain British Connexion, the sure guarantee of Civil and Religious Liberty, and to aid in rescuing the [local] London District from the political degradation, in which it has so long been sunk, owing to the combined efforts of our anti-British republican faction, regardless of all consequences, save those which may result in

gratifying their own inordinate ambition, and thirst for place and power.

If this was not enough, the *Standard* was also to

point out the errors of its friends, as well as to expose the crimes of its enemies.[15]

❖ ❖ ❖

In his posthumously published Narrative, Ranald MacDonald says little about St. Thomas, as his focus is on Japan. He describes being installed "in the comfortable mansion house of my father's old friend, of the Columbia, Mr. Edward Ermatinger," but MacDonald was an extremely generous person, and he always described people with the highest regard. Of Ermatinger he has nothing but effusive praise, writing that his father's friend was a

gentleman of fine culture and high public spirit, with a practical ability in his special line of work and study, viz: finance. . . . [H]e was, by habit, unselfish and unobtrusive in his ambition. . . . In his private life, and domestic, I ever found him most estimable. To me he was ever considerately kind: and in the manner of his kindness—marked, ever, by a gentle reserve—there was nothing to hurt my feelings in any way.[16]

Yet there is ample indication that Ranald's time in St. Thomas was not as happy as this passage indicates. If Ermatinger's Tory politics did not affect the young teenager, there were plenty of other factors that would have made life even more difficult for him.

Problems of the Country-born

About a year after his son's arrival in St. Thomas, Archibald McDonald wrote to Governor Simpson, commenting that "Mr. E. Ermatinger speaks very well indeed of his temper, good behaviour, and close application but does not say quite so much of his education or aptitude for business in that part of the world."[17]

Ranald MacDonald was highly intelligent and far better educated than most people living in the mid-nineteenth century. Still, his education may not have been enough for the world of "gentlemen" that his father hoped he would enter. In the British colony of Canada in the 1840s, entering that world would have required knowing social niceties and conventions tightly linked to British concepts of class, and knowing how to "walk the walk and talk the talk." It would have been quite a leap for a biracial lad from the frontier, who possessed a different set of skills and interests, and a different body of knowledge.

Portrait of Edward Ermatinger in later years, n.d.

Several years later, Edward Ermatinger's brother Francis bluntly noted some of the problems children from Red River had. Referring to one young man from there—with whom he was working—as a "mere automaton," Francis wrote that it was

> as good as we can expect from the limited knowledge any one can acquire at a Red River school. Fathers who think that twenty or even forty pounds worth of mechanical reading or writing, obtained at a secluded place, where practice or even thought is out of the question, is enough for the children to commence business with; do not do them justice, I know that they require something more.[18]

Shortly after arriving in Red River, even Ranald's teacher at the elite Academy there, John Macallum, had alluded to similar problems, writing to a friend that the "juvenile mind here is in a great melancholy state of vacancy" with "none of that wrap of general information which an English Child, properly educated, has accumulated by the time it has reached its fourth year."[19]

* * *

Ranald MacDonald was not the first or only "country-born" boarder at the Ermatinger mansion. Later in life, Edward would complain how he himself "had the reputation of being rich and fond of money," whereas in reality he had "never been able to extricate [himself] from debt."[20] His perceived success nonetheless meant that people constantly applied to him for work, or wanted to place their sons with him as boarders or apprentices to advance their places in society. This was particularly true of the officers in the fur trade, who romanticized Edward's life. While Ranald MacDonald was at St. Thomas, other boarders included Alfred J. Allworth and Lawrence Ermatinger. Of Allworth, little is known except that he went on to manage a loan society in St. Thomas. Of Lawrence, quite a bit is known, as he was the mixed-blood son of Edward's brother, Francis, still working far away in the HBC's Columbia district. The way Francis reacted to his son's problems says much about the context in which Ranald found himself.

No one romanticized Edward Ermatinger's life more than Francis, who put his own nine-year-old son, Lawrence, in his older brother's care in 1837. Like Archibald McDonald, Francis hoped life in St. Thomas under the aegis of Edward would help his son integrate into the civilized world. Yet Lawrence hardly paved the way for Ranald, as he had even more trouble adapting, and his misfortunes only deepened the misgivings many in and outside the fur trade already had about mixed-blood children.

Lawrence was a child of misfortune, the product of Francis's alliance with a native woman named Cleo. Early on, Francis had caused controversy in the fur trade community when, after an Indian suitor eloped with Cleo, Francis had exacted Indian-style revenge by having the man's ears cut off. Cleo would eventually hang herself, but before that Francis sent their child, Lawrence, to be schooled at Fort Vancouver, as Ranald had briefly been. John McLoughlin, the ever-kindly chief factor there, took responsibility for Lawrence. But in a February 1, 1836, letter to Edward Ermatinger, McLoughlin acknowledged some of the problems: "the Boy had so much misery in his Youth and has Been so sickly that he makes but slow progress he has also an infirmity he is a little Deaf—however it is wearing off—and I hope—he will be cured of it."[21]

In letters to Edward, Francis talked optimistically of sending Lawrence to board with him, in hopes the boy might gain the means to earn a living, but in reality the father was increasingly frustrated with his son's problems. On June 1, 1837, Francis noted that the McLoughlins had fed the poor boy well, "but they have so many of them about them, of all tribes, that they cannot pay the attention to them that children require." Lawrence, he complained, had also acquired the habit of "piddling in his bed," and his ears had "been neglected. They are equal to those of my mule, and I doubt whether, even with care, they can be brought to a reasonable compass." "Give them a trial and let him wear hats," he recommended to his brother, "for with caps we can never succeed." He railed against the Fort Vancouver school, which he felt had corrupted his son. The schoolmaster, he wrote, was a child abuser, who took advantage of his female pupils and had been publicly flogged twice, but "ought to have been shot."[22]

Francis at first had planned to have Lawrence live with the McDonald family at Fort Colvile before sending him on to his brother's. But in the summer of 1837 he instead sent Lawrence straight to St. Thomas with an American missionary, William Henry Gray, through St. Louis rather than the normal northern HBC route. If the nine-year-old had been traumatized by life before, the trip could hardly have reassured him. In what became the talk of the fur trade country, the party was attacked by Blackfeet Indians and nearly massacred. Even Archibald, in a letter to Edward wrote, "We have had marvelous acc'ts in the Columbia of the many hair breadth escapes he and. his guardian Gray had in passing through *Blckfeet* Country."[23]

At St. Thomas, Lawrence showed some improvement, but it was only temporary. Few details of what happened are clear, but Francis's letters, reacting to Edward's reports, bear uncanny similarities to those of Archibald, responding to reports about Ranald.

On February 6, 1840, Francis wrote from Fort Vancouver, "I have no idea of making him a gentleman. Neither would I wish to see him come to this country, but my utmost desire is to make him a moral, industrious farmer or tradesman after a few years education."[24] On March 15, he added, along with a remedy he thought might cure his son's bed-wetting problem, "[O]ne thing I should like to give the boy a chance to make a good and decent man."[25] The next year he would again stress, "I hope Lawrence will do well, but bear in mind, that I cannot make a gentleman of him. He must not be brought up with high notions, but be taught to work, and all I can do is give him a tolerable education and start."[26]

Francis's confusion over what to do with his son was long standing. On July 12, 1838, he had written, half-jokingly, "If Lawrence does not turn out well we must make a sailor of him."[27] Half a year later, on February 26, 1839, he added, "[L]ct him have every chance to show his disposition, when, if he is found to be hopeless, I will bring him back here and make an Indian of him."[28] Four years later, in the spring of 1843, he wrote, "With respect to poor Lawrence, we seem to understand each other. If he turns out as I see many of the young fellows of this country do, I shall be distressed indeed." But he did send his love to the boy and asked that he write.[29]

By 1844, now sixteen-year-old Lawrence's situation had worsened, and on April 4 Francis wrote, "With respect to Lawrence, I am at a loss what to advise. I wish him to have a chance to gain a living; but if he is worthless, it will be impossible. To send him here would I think cut off all hope, but perhaps he could be apprenticed to trade in the States, where if he does well, and I am able, I will assist him."[30] Then, on March 23, 1845, the father added, "If we find that he will not do any good for himself, he must come here. To try to make a gentleman of him would be folly, indeed for nothing gentlemanly can come of the tribe. Yet if they can be made useful something will be accomplished."[31] By the end of 1847, when Ranald was already headed toward Japan as a sailor, Lawrence had developed a habit of taking off and wandering, and Francis was ready to cut him off. "I cannot support him in idleness," he would write. "Let him go to the States, to Oregon, engage as a voyager, sailor, or in fact do anything honest, to gain his livelihood. . . . If he is determined to be a vagabond the sooner that he proves himself the better and let us have an end to it."[32]

On a visit to Montreal in 1846, Archibald McDonald would later meet the young man, who was by then a lost cause. Lawrence was dressed in the cast-off clothes of the local chief magistrate, before whom he had appeared, and he did not remember Archibald, though he did remember Ranald, from St. Thomas. Archibald wrote Edward that Lawrence had been found, "in a woeful plight . . . in tatters . . . his appearance and manners exceedingly sloven and unprepossessing. . . . He does not like to work . . . in short he is a miserable wretch." Archibald's advice was "to have him bundled off to Oregon" as soon as possible.[33]

❖ ❖ ❖

Ranald MacDonald was entirely different from Lawrence Ermatinger. No one doubted his intelligence, or his enormous potential. And his relationship with his father was entirely different. While desperately wishing the best for his son, Archibald feared Ranald would develop the same problems he saw in other mixed-blood children. In a sense, Ranald's biggest problem may have been simply that his father's ambitions for him were set too high, rather than too low, and did not fully take into account the formidable obstacles he faced.

Unlike Lawrence, Ranald had been raised in a loving household, at least until sent to Red River at the age of ten. His father arranged further to provide for his future, and, in 1834, before parting with him at Red River, specifically wrote him into his will, listing Ranald as his "Natural Son" (a code term for "illegitimate") but still bequeathing him the considerable sum of £300. A codicil, added a year later, stipulated the request, that if he (Archibald) died, his wife and children should be "removed to the neighborhood of a good school in the Civilised World," where the children could be educated. Because of changed family circumstances, Ranald's inheritance would be reduced to £100, but he was allowed to share in the remainder of the estate with his half-brothers if one of them died before coming of age (which four did).[34]

Ranald had also been treated by his stepmother, Jane Klyne, as one of her own. And Jane, a mixed-blood woman in her own right, was well treated by her husband and unlikely to have passed on any inferiority complex or resentment to her stepson. After the 1830s, fur traders were increasingly encouraged to marry white or mostly white women, especially by Governor Simpson (who, after years of advocating marrying into Indian tribes, cast off his own half-Indian companion to marry a Scottish cousin of good birth). A bias was building up in some HBC officers' circles against native or part-native women, but all the evidence shows that Archibald loved his wife deeply and never regretted marrying her.

Francis Ermatinger, on the other hand, was notorious for his poor treatment of Indian women. His letters reveal that he was married "in the fashion of the country" to several, whom he subsequently cast off, sometimes with children, and that he was always hoping to achieve an alliance with a white woman who would help him integrate back into civilization. In this context, his native wives and mixed-blood children were burdens. When Archibald

McDonald formally married Jane in Red River in 1835, it was Francis to whom he had referred in a letter to Edward, saying of fur traders with native companions that

> it is my full conviction few of them can do better—the great mistake is in flattering themselves with a different notion too long. . . . Some there are, as you know, who even do worse—despise, maltreat & neglect their partners when at the same time they cannot bring themselves to part with them. You are aware of your brother's *penchant* towards a connection of this kind.[35]

In 1836, dreaming of one day living in St. Thomas, Francis wrote his brother to complain about a Thomas Dears, another former fur trader who had relocated there with his native wife: "He, poor fellow, I am for having near us, but it is his wife. I should like to form a little neighborhood in your quarter by and bye, and would not like to see anyone in it with whom we could not freely associate; with her it is impossible to do so."[36] By 1843, Francis did formally marry Catherine Sinclair, a schoolmate of Ranald's from Red River and the granddaughter of his superior, Dr. John McLoughlin, but still Francis could not refrain from making an issue out of the limited Indian blood she possessed. When Edward complained that his business in St. Thomas was not doing well, Francis wrote back jokingly,

> If it is a novelty you require, I will bring down Mrs. E. who with Mrs. Dears in a cheenook petticoat and one with a skin shirt garnished with scalps and bear grease, and thus supported I think we will, with the aid of a little vermilion, draw folks to your store. You say that you think a new face would do something. If that is all you want, I will soon bring you one with plenty of brass in it.[37]

In 1837 Francis had nakedly revealed his true feelings about both mixed-blood wives and mixed-blood children. Expressing his envy of his brother, who had successfully left the fur trade and married a white woman, he wrote,

> You have a respectable home and family with whom you are happy. Different indeed would have been your lot, had you remained under the most favourable circumstances. Subject often to the whims of

some empty fellow, and always of course under control, and if you had married in the country, had the additional mortification to have found yourself with offspring, the subjects of derision and contempt.[38]

But in truth, Edward regarded his own marriage as a miserable failure, and the state of affairs between him and his wife must have made life miserable for his young boarders, too. Years later, Edward confessed in his memoirs that he and his wife had an "incompatibility of temper," and that while she was "cruel" toward him, toward her his "acts of violence or ill conduct were never premeditaded or conceived in a spirit of settled hatred."[39] When Francis finally retired to St. Thomas in 1853, even he finally realized the truth, commenting of their "eternal bickerings," that "[i]t is really too bad, that a family with everything to make them happy, should mar it. Mrs. E. does not appear to have one feeling in common with her husband and no matter who is by, at dinner or otherwise employed she takes every opportunity to show that she has not. God help them."[40]

Negative Reports

Despite having been raised in a loving family as a small boy, there were deep tensions between Ranald MacDonald and his father. Toward the end of his life, Ranald wrote that his father and Dr. John McLoughlin were the only two persons he was in any fear of, despite the fact that both had kindly dispositions, adding, "why I should fear them was always a mystery to me."[41]

In St. Thomas, both Ranald and Lawrence Ermatinger were viewed as representatives of all mixed-blood youth from west of the Rockies, or "westsidians" as they were called. Shortly before his own son arrived in St. Thomas, Archibald had heard from Edward Ermatinger of some of Lawrence's problems, and had responded, "I am sorry to hear the good folk of St. Thomas have such a bad specimen of us in the person of poor Lawrence."[42] In the spring of 1840, after Ranald had arrived, Archibald heard that Lawrence was improving and replied, "I am glad to hear the young nephew is likely to turn out better than was at one time expected. With them both it rests to develop the character of the *west sidians*, & God sent it may be a creditable one."[43]

Archibald's original plan had been for his son to be apprenticed to

Edward to learn the ways of business, and assist Edward at his store or bank. But around a year after Ranald arrived, the plans started to go awry. Sometime in 1840, Edward apparently sent negative reports on Ranald, not only to his father but also to his other correspondents in the fur trade. One of them, John Tod, stationed in Fort Alexandria on the upper Assiniboine River, in a gossipy letter dated March 1, 1841, wrote back:

> Often do I fancy I see Mrs. Ermatinger at her hortician amusements in her new garden . . . sometimes too I think . . . in her management of that poor but intractable Chinook would not be the worse of Your humble Servant at her elbo—I do not much like this part of Your arrangement—the office, I conceive, would have better suited one of less equanimity of temper than Mrs. Ermatinger.[44]

Archibald MacDonald, in his annual letter, on March 5, wrote Edward back (sounding much like Francis Ermatinger later would):

> About my son, I am truly at a loss what to say. . . . I fear much the stupid fellow takes no right view of his new situation—he is now approaching the age of manhood, & he must be given to understand that I cannot afford to make a Gentleman of him, nay, to put him even in the way of gaining a decent livelihood for himself without the proper exertion on his own part.[45]

Then revealing, to his consternation, that Ranald was apparently been thinking of joining the military, Archibald continued,

> What in the universe could have put the "Army" in the head of the baby—does he forsooth think that I am going to buy a commission for him? Please have the goodness [to] tell him I am exceedingly displeased at his notions, & that the sooner he drops them the better, otherwise, tho' it galls me to say it, he must speedily shift for himself. My wife, too, is much concerned to hear of the little satisfaction he is likely to afford us.[46]

In a subsequent postscript dated April 21, Archibald then mentioned how James, the mixed-blood son of HBC officer John Tod, would also be soon joining Edward in St. Thomas. After praising this boy's "sedateness, & correctness of conduct," Archibald further compared him to Ranald, by saying,

> [This one] will not pester you for a commission in Her Majesty's army. Whether Ranald leaves you immediately on receipt of this or hang about you 'till Spring, have the goodness to drive out of his head his new notions of greatness. Even for the few months he was with you I can see he very much improved in his hand of & business appearance altogether.[47]

✳ ✳ ✳

In his own writings, Ranald MacDonald never mentions his desire to join the army, but it is easy to understand why the idea might have been appealing. The military were hard to ignore in St. Thomas. The Victorian Age had begun and British power was at the height of its glory. Because of the 1837–38 Rebellion, British troops, complete with military band, had been garrisoned in the little town. And St. Thomas itself had raised a cavalry troop that saw considerable action against the rebels. The Ermatinger family, for that matter, had a long and proud history of military service. Edward's father had been with the British army in Europe. One uncle had fought in Spain. Another, Charles Oakes Ermatinger (Sr.), had fought in the War of 1812, and two of his sons (Edward's cousins) had helped to put down the rebellion. One, Charles Oakes, Jr., had been in command of a detachment of Montreal cavalry when the rebellion erupted and had been wounded when the first shot was fired. The other, James, like Ranald had been sent to St. Thomas to learn business, and during the conflict he had organized and commanded the locally raised St. Thomas cavalry troop.

If Ranald intended to join the military, it was surely in part because he was such a physically active person, having been involved in adventures almost from the day he was born, traveling in canoes, riding horses, and covering vast distances. Even at the Red River settlement, the hallmark of a truly useful man had been an ability to hunt or farm. The image of Ranald as a teenager, at the peak of health, cooped up in a dimly lit store or a bank, copying numbers and handling money all day long, is indeed pathetic.

Compounding Ranald's misery was his inability to satisfy his father's ambitions for him. As he describes it in his published *Narrative*, he hated being "put on a Bank stool," writing that it "was done kindly and from motives I was bound to respect.... There was nothing better, before me; that I could ask for; and I submitted to the ordeal as best as I could." He also worried about being a burden to his "kind father, whose large and increasing family—most of them in costly educational institutions—had better claims on him." He adds that "banking, or dealing with money in any way, was *not* to my taste: I hated the—to me—'dirty thing'! I had no ambition for riches." As for becoming a learned professional of some sort, "I had no inclination ... in that way ... in fact, had no inclination for any particular mode of life—for bread."[48]

Ranald did not fit in with the Ermatingers. In an early draft of his *Narrative*, he writes, "Naturally social, I made friends all about me & I believe had no enemies. All about me was made as pleasant time as possible. But in me there was ever that strain for utmost liberty of action & thought; which chafed at such restraint; while, at the same time I could not—did not even try—to acquire the tastes, habits, ambitions (petty & personal) of the people—good & worthy in every way though they were—amongst whom my lot there seem to be cast. Of this *malaise* I said nothing to any one: not even to my father, towards whom my feelings were always wholly loving."[49]

In supplementary material included in MacDonald's posthumously published autobiography, yet another reason for his unhappiness is given. According to one woman who talked with him late in life, MacDonald decided to go to Japan while in St. Thomas also because his heart had been broken. In this account, he used to attend fine parties and dances at St. Thomas and fell in love with a pretty young girl whom he hoped to marry. It was then that he supposedly learned for the first time that Jane Klyne McDonald was not his real mother, that he was part Indian, and that his Indian blood put him at such a disadvantage. And it was then that he began planning to go to Japan, the "land of his ancestors," and to make something of himself.[50]

Unfortunately, this story cannot be taken completely at face value. It is suspiciously similar to the tragic mixed-blood romance that had happened back in Red River. And it is highly unlikely that MacDonald, dark complexioned and broad featured, first learned of his Indian heritage only at St. Thomas.

Race

It is tempting to think of Ranald MacDonald as the sole, non-white young man in a bastion of refined, white, English-speaking citizens—a sort of polar opposite to the comfortable Métis culture of Red River. But the real situation at St. Thomas was far more complex. Indians still lived in the area, as well as numerous free blacks who had escaped from their masters in slave-holding states in America. While not as many as in Montreal, there were also families in St. Thomas that had relocated from Red River, and there were several mixed-bloods in the town.

They included Lawrence Ermatinger, who preceded Ranald, as well as James, the son of John Tod, who arrived in 1841. The wife of Thomas Dears, who lived nearby and to whom Francis Ermatinger had objected so strongly, was an Indian and had children. And Edward Ermatinger, by virtue of his long years with the HBC, was hardly a stranger to either Indian ways or the Métis culture of Red River (later in life he would attempt to write a history of the settlement). His uncle, Charles Oakes Ermatinger, had married the daughter of a famous Indian chief, and Charles's son James (Edward's cousin)—the respected captain of the St. Thomas cavalry during the rebellion—was, like Ranald, a "half-breed."

Yet, at the same time, the town's limited diversity did not guarantee lack of prejudice, and at times may have amplified it. As noted fur trade scholar Jennifer S. H. Brown observes, children of officials who were sent to Britain to be educated were often "few enough and sufficiently dispersed that they did not suffer distinction as a racial category . . . they could gain acceptance both in their formal qualifications and in their social behaviour as members of the British middle class, despite some difficulties of adjustment." Mixed-blood children who relocated to older communities in Canada—especially Montreal, with its large population of Catholic French Canadians and retired fur traders with Indian wives and mixed-blood children—were also regarded as a normal presence. But in St. Thomas, they may well have seemed conspicuous and strange to many of the local populace.[51]

St. Thomas was newer, a predominantly Anglo-Canadian community. It had a strong British tradition, and English Protestants tended to frown on interracial marriages. Moreover, right across Lake Erie was the United States, where, unlike Canada, relations with native peoples had been characterized by almost constant, bloody warfare. The closer one got to the United States in the years leading up to the Civil War, the more people's attitudes became con-taminated by American thinking on race, color, and miscegenation.

❖ ❖ ❖

In a 1980 article on "Scientific Attitudes toward Indian Mixed-Bloods in Early Nineteenth Century America," scholar Robert Bieder points out that after Europeans arrived in North America, a great debate arose between "monogenists"—who saw mankind as one species—and "polygenists"—who saw the various races as separate species and acts of creation. In this context, in the New World mixed-bloods or "hybrids" became a focus of intense interest.

Early in United States history, attitudes toward Indians and mixed-bloods were quite positive. But by the 1830s, when the government began to forcibly remove Indians to the west of the Mississippi, these attitudes "shift-ed from a positive belief in their capabilities and potential for civilization to one of reservation and finally to discouragement over their lack of progress." Instead of believing that mixed-bloods would assimilate into larger society and possibly help civilize the Indians and contribute to humanity, polygenists increasingly warned that "mixed-bloods often failed to adapt to civilization and sometimes even proved a detriment to Indian advancement, having seemingly accepted the vices of both races and the virtues of neither." More-over, with the rise of more Victorian ideas of propriety, mixed-bloods were increasingly regarded as Indians:[52]

> As with Blacks, so also with mixed-bloods: if a person possessed some Indian blood, he was an Indian. Blood not only gave a person his identity but served to shape the public's expectations of his des-tiny. . . . Not only were the mixed-bloods considered "faulty stock" who seemed unable to advance, but they were believed to prefer Indi-an life and to have cast their lot with the Indian. Like the Indian, the mixed-blood was viewed as headed for extermination.[53]

Given the acceptance of multiculturalism and multiracialism in the Unit-ed States today, it is hard to imagine how poisoned attitudes were in the late nineteenth century. However, one need look no further than the writings of Hubert Howe Bancroft, one of the most respected historians on the American West and Native Americans. In his 1884 opus, *History of the Pacific States of North America*, under the subheading of "The Fur-Traders' Curse," Bancroft condemned the "native" predilections of HBC officers (leaving out Archibald McDonald's name only by accident):

> I never could understand how such men as John McLoughlin, James Douglas, Ogden, Finlayson, Work, Tolmie, and the rest could endure the thought of having their name and honors descend to a degenerate posterity. Surely they were possessed of sufficient intelligence to know that by giving their children Indian or half-breed mothers, their own old Scotch, Irish, or English blood would in them be greatly debased, and hence that they were doing all concerned a great wrong. Perish all the Hudson's Bay Company thrice over, I would say, sooner than bring upon my own offspring such foul corruption, sooner than bring into being offspring subject to such a curse.[54]

Even fur traders with mixed-blood children themselves were not immune to such attitudes. As noted previously, Archibald McDonald's superior, Governor Simpson, largely subscribed to them, referring to the mixed-blood children educated in Canada as "blackguards of the worst description."[55] It was in fact this same bias that made Simpson and the HBC often reluctant to hire children of the Company's fur traders.

For someone young, intelligent, educated, and proud like Ranald MacDonald, the effect of such racial attitudes would have been amplified many times over in St. Thomas. He was the eldest son of a Hudson's Bay Company chief factor, brought up in privilege—if not materially, at least in the sense that he had a special status due to the fact that his father wielded great power over a vast territory. And he had also just come from Red River, where a unique hybrid culture was in ascendancy and where—as an Anglo-Protestant, half-Indian child—he had been part of the local elite. Moreover, he had been raised by a father who wanted to subscribe to the older view of Indians and mixed-bloods, who wanted to believe that his son, precisely because of his royal Indian background, was destined for a special role in life.

As for Edward Ermatinger, we have no way of knowing exactly what he thought of mixed-bloods, or even young Ranald, but he was not immune to the prejudices of his day. Despite being the surrogate parent of numerous children of his fur-trader friends, he apparently did not consider them a very important part of his life. He rarely mentions them in his memoirs or his surviving letters. And when he does, he reveals an acute awareness of their mixed-race and "Indian-ness," referring to Ranald as a "Chinook" in letters, and criticizing the son of a different HBC officer as having "too much of the Bois Brule."[56]

Years later, in 1858, when the Hudson's Bay Company came under attack in Britain for its stewardship of its vast lands, Edward Ermatinger defended the Company in a series of published letters. He disparaged the Métis of Red River who complained of the Company's treatment as being self-serving, not "true" British subjects, and a "difficult people to deal with." Of the Indians on the Canadian frontier, he depicted them as "a poor besotted race, rapidly diminishing in numbers . . . a living illustration of the inability of the red man to adopt the habits and ideas of the whites, or to live in contact with them."[57]

As often happened with Edward Ermatinger, his dogmatic letters struck a raw nerve among some of his readers. Peter C. Pambrun, the mixed-blood son of a well-known former HBC official, wrote a ringing defense of what he called "the half Caste," hinting at their frustration and at the violence that was to erupt in Red River in the future:

> To those of a better class and who have received a better education [the Company] do not even award a much better position. And if entered into the Service, upon a lower rank and Salary than Europeans. . . . Their education is as good and conduct as correct, but conduct which in a European is overlooked, is in a native punished, and has always been the case since ever a Bois Bruille was entered the Service.[58]

Escape from St. Thomas

Stung by Edward Ermatinger's negative reports about his son, Archibald McDonald felt that he "was placed in a very awkward situation so much so, that with the view of relieving my anxiety at once about him, I have resolved on trying the Indian country again."[59] Reversing his former opinion about the best place for his son, in the spring of 1841 Archibald pulled all the strings he could pull in his capacity as an HBC officer and desperately tried to find Ranald employment in the organization. He wrote both Governor

Simpson and Duncan Finlayson about Ranald, reporting to the former, with some embarrassment, that his son in Canada was

> still unsettled in the world & as I foresee that sort of thing cannot be even attempted without much outlay in the first place, & doubtful success after all when so far removed from the eyes of the parent, I have resolved in relinquishing all projects on his behalf in that quarter. . . . I therefore take upon myself to recommend him for a tryal in the Indian Country on the footing you may consider he deserves. He will be 18, February '42.[60]

In making his application in 1841, Archibald was influenced by what had happened to John McLoughlin, Jr., the "enfant terrible" of the fur trade and the son of his immediate superior. After his disastrous participation in General Dickson's "Indian Liberating Army," John, Jr., had been hired into the Company and sent west. Although disparaged as the "scape-grace from Paris, and the would-be hero of California" by the Company chaplain at Fort Vancouver, under the watchful eye of his powerful father—Dr. John McLoughlin—the young man had made a remarkable turnabout and showed himself to be an at-least-satisfactory employee.[61] His case seemed to illustrate that educated, mixed-blood children, who might have problems in the civilized world, could in fact flourish in the West and help the Company. John, Jr., had also been joined by his younger brother (and Ranald's friend), David, as well as what Archibald described as "a host of half-breed apprentices" from the Red River Academy.[62]

The next year, on March 30, 1842, Archibald again wrote Edward, telling him his application for Ranald had been forwarded by Governor Simpson to Company headquarters in London. To be doubly sure, Archibald had also sent an application to the secretary of the Hudson's Bay Company in London, by ship via Cape Horn. This way, he explained, Ranald would have a chance of being "placed on the footing of apprentice *Clerk*, instead of *apprentice*, as is the case with all those relieved into the Service from the country."[63] The secretary later replied personally to Archibald, noting that Ranald's name had indeed been placed on an official list of applicants for apprenticeships, with the promise that "if any appointment can be given him, communication will be made to the youth at St. Thomas."[64] But to Edward, Archibald added, "You will however my dear Sir . . . have the goodness to continue your kind offices to him, & keep him about you till you hear from London conformably to my wish." And in a postscript, he pleaded, "For God's sake don't lose sight of him until he is fairly embarked in that course which I believe is the most suitable for every mother's son of them, bad as it has proved for many."[65]

But in the interim, Ranald's situation at the Ermatingers had already deteriorated. On March 4, 1843, Francis wrote his brother, amid queries about his own son, to ask, "Why do you trouble yourself about Ranald? If he will not do any good, write to his father to take him back, and while you wait the opportunity, put him out to board and make the father pay for it. You had better refuse any more."[66]

Because of the time lag in communications, Francis did not know that the now nineteen-year-old Ranald had already moved out of Ermatinger's house the previous year. When Archibald heard the same news, he became enraged and wrote his son a scathing letter, the contents of which are unknown. Then, on March 15, Archibald, too, wrote Edward Ermatinger. In a line that has tricked many researchers into thinking that Ranald was already in the capital of England and not the town of the same name next to St. Thomas, he noted,

From Master Ranald himself I also heard by a few lines dated in March from London. As matters have now turned out, I am not at all sorry that the young buck is made to look more to himself; but I fear from what you say of his thoughtless & indolent disposition that Mr. John Clair's store has too many tempting cordials in it to be a fit nursery for the young Gents of the far west.[67]

Archibald's use of the word "buck" has been interpreted by Japanese historians, such as Torao Tomita, as a racial slur, but it was and is a word also applied to undisciplined, head-strong youth of any background. Exactly what Ranald did is unknown, but the misdeed could not have been too bad because Ermatinger later agreed to take on one of his younger half-brothers as a bank apprentice (and praised him highly). As Archibald's letter implies, it may have involved tippling at John Clair's store, or it may simply have been a case of his son not doing exactly as his father wanted him to do. Yet Archibald's despair was real. He had just been promoted to the powerful position of chief factor, he had many other children to worry about (at least one of whom was gravely ill), and his own health was starting to fail. He had, moreover, pulled many strings with his superiors to get his problem son hired into the Hudson's Bay Company on a preferential basis. If he had been embarrassed when he first submitted the application, he was furious now, and confided to Edward,

> Never mind, my friend, we have done our duty, & things must now be allowed to take their course. If he can only keep out of egregious acts of impropriety till we can once more have him back to the Indian country I shall consider it a great point gained that the experiment with him was made & tested so early in life. Here, for all I shall ever do for him again, he may just crawl thro' life as the Black Bear does—lick[ing] his paws.[68]

✷ ✷ ✷

Part of Archibald's despair was related to what had happened to John McLoughlin, Jr., in the previous year. After returning to the West, John Jr. had been placed in charge of Fort Stikine, which the HBC then leased from the Russian America Company in today's British Columbia. It was exceedingly rare for a mixed-blood son of an officer to be given such authority, and the experiment proved disastrous, as John, Jr., was shot to death by his own men one April night in 1842. The men, a mutinous mix of Indians, Hawaiians, Canadians, and mixed-bloods, claimed they had been grievously abused by a violent and drunken John, Jr. Because of earlier, negative experiences with the errant young man, Governor Simpson seemed to sympathize with the mutineers. This enraged Chief Factor Dr. John McLoughlin, who uncovered evidence his son had been performing admirably. The heart-broken father became convinced his son had been murdered in cold blood and was being maligned in death. The Stikine incident shocked the employees of the HBC, and the ensuing ill will between Dr. McLoughlin and George Simpson nearly split the organization in two. Writing the governor on April 27, 1843, Archibald noted how "the unfortunate occurrence at Stikine of itself has caused more writing and botheration than all our other doings put together." But he sided with Simpson against McLoughlin, who he felt was a blind parent, unable to realize that his own son had *not* been a "good and correct man."[69]

The tragedy of John McLoughlin, Jr., profoundly affected the way all mixed-blood sons of Company officers, including Ranald MacDonald, were thereafter viewed, even by their own fathers. As Archibald lamented in his March 15, 1843 letter, "Edward, we are all most unfortunate parents. Instance the awful shock of mind our old friend the Dr. has lately experienced from the irregular and inveterate habits of his unhappy son John, after spending £2000 on his education in foreign lands, too."[70]

Others in the fur trade chimed in. In a letter dated March 20, John Tod thanked Edward for looking out for his own mixed-blood son, James, but complained, "he thinks, am told, he has been treated with cruelty, because he has not been made a gentleman!" Then, reflecting his increasingly crackpot obsession with race and physical characteristics (an obsession criticized by his fellow traders), Tod stated,

I was sorry to learn that Mr. McDonald's Son had conducted himself so badly, truly Mrs. Ermatinger & Yourself have had Your hands full with the *bois brulies*. Well have You observed that all attempts to make gentlemen of them, have hitherto proved a failure—the fact is that there is something radically wrong with them all as is evidently shown from Mental Science alone I mean Phrenology, the truths of which I have lately convinced myself from personal observation.[71]

✳ ✳ ✳

Sometime in the beginning of 1842, Ranald had already put his long-simmering plan into action. As he writes in his published *Narrative*, "In the monomania of the project I had sagacity enough to keep it to myself. I had resolved upon it; that was enough. For means to carry it out, I simply, with grip sack in hand, walked forth into the darkness of an unsympathetic world; alone, telling no one; with barely scrip for the hour."[72]

The next time Archibald heard from his son, he was at sea. In a letter written in the spring of 1844 to Governor Simpson, the father confessed, "I reproach myself in some measure for having used language to the young man after I heard of his having left Ermatinger that very likely led to the step he eventually took."[73] To Edward Ermatinger, he resignedly wrote,

The case of unfortunate Ranald certainly gave me great pain. As it is clear however that the bent of his inclination was anything but what we could wish, perhaps the step he has taken is the very best that could have happened. As for the service, in the case of these chaps, I never looked upon it but as a mere apology to keep them out of harm's way; & that in all probability is as effectually done on the wide ocean as in the most obscure corner of the Indian country; & all I hope is that he may stick to the ship "Tuskeny." His miserable scrawl does not enable us to say whence he sailed, but that is immaterial—it is enough that we know he was yet in existence, contrary to the rumours that reached the country from Canada.[74]

Like many sons, Ranald MacDonald did not turn out the way his father anticipated. He was determined to follow his own dreams, in his own way.

CHAPTER 6

Sag Harbor's Japan Connection

On March 21, 1843, a year after his son suddenly left St. Thomas, Archibald McDonald wrote a gossipy letter to a fellow Hudson's Bay Company officer, complaining of the difficulty in collecting furs, especially beaver. "I find you all throw cold water on every other laudable exertion we make to find you substitutes for Beaver," he wrote, "& yet the universal Cry is that the old HB gold dust is gone for ever—What say you to the whalefishery?"[1]

The fur industry was dying from overtrapping and changes in fashion; in the 1840s it was whales that were sought after by ambitious men, just as gold and then oil would be later. Archibald may not have known it yet, but his son had already signed on as a crewman on a whaling ship based in Sag Harbor, a port on the northeastern tip of Long Island, in the state of New York.

Missing Years

Contradictions in the timeline of Ranald MacDonald's published *Narrative* abound, especially between 1842 and 1845, and they have obscured the role that Sag Harbor played in his Japan adventure. In one account, MacDonald claims that he left St. Thomas in 1845; in another, he says that in the same year he "shipped before the mast" from "New York."[2] Since he is known to have left St. Thomas in 1842, these dates fail to account for nearly three years of his life.

In the same book, MacDonald mentions dropping out of his bank clerk job in St. Thomas, going west to the Mississippi, and then working as a boat hand on a palace steamer before making his way to New York. In an unpublished draft (filtered through the florid pen of his editor friend Malcolm McLeod) he notes that the Mississippi was

> an attractive field for American youth. Needless to state the hardships of the rude life I there encountered. Suffice it to say its novelty passed; it pleased me not. . . . I longed for still freer action in the battle of life: something more ennobling than mere sufferance in social elements antagonistic to my best feelings."[3]

It was during this period (and not when in St. Thomas), he says, that the idea of "trying Japan came across my mind . . . with all the force of an inspiration." He had, he writes in the same draft, known of Japan and its policy of exclusion from

> information obtained by my people from Japanese castaways on the Pacific Coast and in the Sandwich Islands, with which the Hudson's Bay Company had regular commercial communication. . . . [T]he idea was not a mere passing fancy; not the idle dream of a disordered brain; nor the desperation of misfortune or trouble of any kind. . . . I was, in every sense, myself . . . with no fear of aught from man; and with but the magnetic sense of a higher "mission" in a sphere where for over two hundred years under laws of Draconic force, the Christian civilization had ever been and was still under mortal ban.[4]

The 1923 published edition of MacDonald's *Narrative* made his activities in this period even murkier, for his new editors occasionally added confusing footnotes. One such note indicates that MacDonald sailed in 1842 to London, England, when in reality he was still in the town of "London," Canada. Furthermore, the same book includes reminiscences of people who had known him in his old age but who were themselves recalling things he had said many years before, which they may have misunderstood or which

MacDonald was himself recalling from half a century earlier. One of the stories, for which no corroborating evidence has been found, asserts that MacDonald had worked on a slave ship off the west coast of Africa, and watched in horror when the ship dumped its live cargo in the sea after being chased down by a British man-o'-war. Another account has him visiting California's Yerba Buena (today's San Francisco), on a secret smuggling mission via London and Calcutta in late 1842.[5]

The surviving letters of Archibald McDonald are one of the most reliable means to ascertain his son's whereabouts, and they indicate Ranald MacDonald was still in Canada at the beginning of 1842, and that by 1843, at least, he was at sea in the "Tuskeny." The *Tuscany* was a whaling ship that did sail from Sag Harbor on October 7, 1842, under the command of a Captain James Godbee. No log book survives, but the *Tuscany* is recorded as having returned from its voyage on February 26, 1845. This would have given MacDonald ample time before shipping again in a better-documented whaler, the *Plymouth*, which left Sag Harbor in December that year, headed for the Pacific and the waters near Japan.

The *Tuscany*'s formally listed destination was the whaling ground near the Crozet island group, due south of Madagascar in the Indian Ocean, which would have taken it near Africa. Sag Harbor whaling ships of that era did occasionally participate in the highly illegal traffic in slaves, known as "black diamonds," yet from contemporary sources we know that the *Tuscany* spent most of its time in the Pacific. Moreover, the *Tuscany*'s voyage was recorded as being extremely successful, yielding a rich cargo of sperm whale oil and bone. It is unlikely to have been involved in such different activities on different sides of the earth within such a short time frame. On the other hand, it is possible that MacDonald never mentions the ship later in life, either in his *Narrative* or his surviving letters, because it was involved in some sort of illegal activity.

Hawaiian newspapers, and especially the authoritative New Bedford *Whalemen's Shipping List* (published only a short distance from Sag Harbor), clearly show that the *Tuscany* did *not* head out to its listed destination of the Crozets. On December 26, 1842, it was recorded as being in the Atlantic, east of southern Brazil. Much of the Tuscany's voyage is unknown, but newspaper records confirm that on December 26, 1842, it was in the Atlantic, east of southern Brazil. On February 12, 1843, it was in the Pacific, at Valparaiso in southern Chile, and by April 8 it was in the Hawaiian Islands. On June 13,

Northern view of Sagg Harbor, Long Island.

From *Early Woodcut Views of New York and New Jersey*, by John W. Barber and Henry Howe. New York: Dover Publications, 1975.

Sag Harbor, 1840.

it was in the Pacific Northwest, and from September to October it was in San Francisco, California. The records do not show when the *Tuscany* returned to the Hawaiian islands, but they do show it left Maui on August 25, 1844, and arrived back in Sag Harbor on February 26 the next year.[6]

Letters from MacDonald near the end of his life do firmly place him in the Pacific in this period. Although his memory is off by a year, in one letter he writes, "I had been at San Francisco in 1842 but never thought it would outstride Astoria. It had some 20 or 25 adobe dwellings besides the HBCo post."[7] A much earlier letter, written to his father in 1848, on the eve of his adventure to Japan, further establishes that he had been in the Pacific between 1842 and 1845. When he wrote the 1848 letter he was a crewman on the *Plymouth*, which had left Sag Harbor at the end of 1845, but in it he describes himself as being on "*another* Cape Horn voyage" [italics added].[8]

From Archibald McDonald's letters we also know that in 1845, after returning to Sag Harbor on the *Tuscany*, his son briefly visited Buffalo, New York. By then, Archibald had decided to retire to the East and in an October 7 letter from St. Thomas, addressed to his superior, Governor Simpson, he wrote, "On 4th I came up here from Port Stanley to see Mr. Ermatinger about my son that was off round Cape Horn & the North Pacific for the last three years, & who I understand was back to Buffalo the other day."[9]

In that same letter, Archibald further implies that he was hoping to see his son in Buffalo. He may have had a serious purpose in doing so. At that time, the United States and Britain were about to resolve ownership of the "Oregon country" and fix the border at the 49th parallel. According to one theory, the father may have thought Ranald would be eligible for some sort of compensation in the negotiations as a direct descendant of Chinook chief Comcomly. It was something that Ranald MacDonald himself only learned of much later, and deepens the mystery of when he knew of his origins, for as he wrote his friend (and family lawyer) Malcolm McLeod in 1889, fairly blurry on the dates and facts,

> I have a faint knowledge that about 1844 my father and Mr. Duncan Finlayson followed me to New York with the object of catching me, I suppose, and bring me home, but also there were certain claims pending the Oregon dispute connected with it. Whither I learned this from yourself, my Mother or someone else, I cannot now recollect, because it was so vaguely intimated at the time that even now I cannot understand it.[10]

MacDonald's exact movements between 1842 and 1845 may never be known, but prior to leaving on the *Plymouth* in 1845 it is clear that he was already a veteran sailor and had spent considerable time in the port of Sag Harbor. For a young man from the West, it was an exciting place to be, and one of the few spots in all of North America from which an individual could attempt an adventure to Japan.

A Window on the World

Today's Sag Harbor is a sleepy Long Island resort town, but modern tourists seek out its colorful past as one of America's busiest whaling ports. Scores of buildings from the mid-nineteenth century are carefully preserved, including churches where sailors worshipped and lavish mansions where investors in lucky voyages once lived in splendor. Tombstones in a nearby cemetery show how dangerous whaling was for the crews; one famous marble memorial in the shape of a broken mast is dedicated to local ship masters who died at sea, including a man, who, while whaling in the Pacific, "lost his life in an encounter with a Sperm Whale, in the 28th year of his age." Few local people in today's Sag Harbor have heard of Ranald Mac-Donald, but on May 12, 1849, the Sag Harbor *Corrector* was one of the first East Coast newspapers to report his attempt to infiltrate Japan. And in a 1931 history of *The Whale Fishery on Long Island*, MacDonald rates a full paragraph—in the context of Sag Harbor's early connections to Japan.

To most North Americans in the 1840s, Japan was a land on the other side of the earth, shrouded in mystery—but not to whalemen. Hundreds of whaling ships from New England and Long Island ports—such as Sag Harbor—had begun to ply the waters around northern Japan. As writer Herman Melville's alter-ego Ishmael correctly prophesied in the classic 1851 novel *Moby-Dick*, "If that double-bolted land, Japan, is ever to become hospitable, it is the whale-ship alone to whom the credit will be due; for already she is on the threshold."[11]

Old Whalers' Church (First Presbyterian Church), Sag Harbor. Dedicated in 1844, the church was one of the most imposing structures in the area at the time, and visited by most sailors, presumably including MacDonald. The soaring steeple was blown off in a hurricane in 1938.

Photo © 1999 Frederik L. Schodt.

* * *

In the mid-nineteenth century, whale baleen (often called "bone") was used in the manufacture of buggy whips, corsets, and umbrellas. But more than anything else, it was whale oil and especially the spermacetti, or oil from the sperm whale, that was in demand. Before natural gas and petroleum-based products were developed, whale oil was by far the most efficient fuel for lighting; unlike other fatty animal oils, it was prized for its waxy nature and the bright and clean way it burned.

As demand for whale products soared, American ships scoured the world's seas for diminishing populations of whales. In the process they sailed farther and farther from home through often unexplored territory. In 1820, after rounding South America's Cape Horn and entering the Pacific Ocean, they discovered the rich "Japan Grounds" off the coast of Japan. The vast majority of the world's whaling ships then were American, from New England and Long Island ports. In 1845—the year MacDonald left Sag Harbor on the *Plymouth*—Sag Harbor was the busiest port next to New Bedford, Nantucket, and New London, its fleet peaking at sixty-three vessels, bringing in a catch worth $675,000 dollars. But by then, voyages had lengthened to over three years in duration.[12]

Whaling was a dangerous and gruesomely dirty job, yet crews shared both in the profits of the voyage (in a system called "lays") and in the excitement of a global chase for fortune. For young men curious to see the world, the industry was a magnet. It may not have been what Archibald had in mind in the way of a "finishing school" for his son, but whaling became so for many bright men of MacDonald's age. Melville, who left us some of the best descriptions of New England whaling ports, went to sea himself in the 1840s, and in *Moby-Dick* wrote, "a whale-ship was my Yale College and my Harvard." And the industry attracted dreamers as well: "For nowadays, the whale-fishery furnishes an asylum for many romantic, melancholy, and absent-minded young men, disgusted with the carking cares of earth, and seeking sentiment in tar and blubber."[13]

Melville also noted how applicants for berths on whaling ships were swelled by many rank amateurs known as "hay-seeds." In New Bedford, only a short ways up the coast from Sag Harbor, he observed,

> There weekly arrive in this town scores of green Vermonters and New Hampshire men, all athirst for gain and glory in the fishery. . . . Many are as green as the Green Mountains whence they came. . . . Look there! that chap strutting round the corner. He wears a beaver hat and swallow-tailed coat, girdled with a sailor-belt and sheath-knife. Here comes another with a sou'-wester and a bombazine cloak.[14]

Indeed, on his first whaling voyage out of Sag Harbor MacDonald himself may have appeared something of a "hayseed." According to one account, he "applied for a berth . . . deliberately dressed rough and looking more like a hunter than a sailor," sporting "a buckskin shirt trimmed with fringe, heavy wool trousers tucked into his fur-trimmed leggings and a fur cap, with a tail at the back of it, on his head."[15]

One of the best depictions of 1840s Sag Harbor comes not from Melville, but from the memoirs of Howard C. Gardiner, a native of the town, who wrote mainly about his experiences in the California gold fields. Gold was discovered in California in 1848, while MacDonald was in Japan, and the Sag Harbor whaling industry nearly collapsed as a result. Most of the port's able-bodied men—including Gardiner and later even the captain of MacDonald's own ship, the *Plymouth*—took off in the whaling fleet (which was then largely abandoned in San Francisco, the men heading for the hills).

But before the Gold Rush began, Sag Harbor was itself a true boom town, what Gardiner describes as "an amphibious" community, where every boy wanted to go to sea, and where the business of whaling formed an integral part of the community fabric, not to mention a constant daily topic. As Gardiner writes,

> In the palmy days of the whale fishing, there were about sixty ships hailing from our village, and as nearly everybody was either a stockholder, or had some friend or relation on board, news from the fleet was a matter of paramount interest. . . . The latitude and longitude of each ship when last reported, and the quantity of oil and bone on board was an index, telling them when to expect her return; hence every available means was resorted to get the latest reports.[16]

Men in the town, moreover, found that their whaling skills determined their worth among their peers, and among women. "Every officer was graded according to his ability to throw a harpoon, or to wield a lance; no matter what other qualifications he lacked or possessed, his dexterity as a harpooner was the main consideration."[17] And the men in the fleet were particularly international and multiracial, a group in which young MacDonald would have blended in easily. Melville describes nearby New Bedford as being thronged with "Feegeeans, Tongatabooans, Erromanggoans, Pannangians, and Brighggians."[18] Gardiner, in plainer language, describes Sag Harbor similarly:

> [D]uring the summer the village streets were thronged with a miscel-
> laneous multitude of sailors of almost every hue and nationality. Por-
> tuguese from the Azores, Spaniards from South America, Maoris
> from New Zealand, Kanakas from the Sandwich Islands, convicts
> who had stolen on board while the vessel was at anchor in some har-
> bor of Van Dieman's Land, and even cannibals from the Fijis were
> included in the incongruous collection.[19]

In his memoirs, Gardiner refers to Sag Harbor as the place of his upbringing and includes the story of Ranald MacDonald's adventure to Japan, to demonstrate to "what extent a man will sometimes go in order to gratify his taste for adventure." He spells MacDonald's name completely wrong, listing him as "Alexander McDonald," but in describing him as a sailor on the *Plymouth* leaves no doubt about to whom he is referring. While some of his information may have derived from articles read later, some of it also appears to be from firsthand knowledge. In Sag Harbor, Gardiner says, MacDonald was known as

> an expert boatsteerer; hence the desire to secure his services excited
> much competition between the shipmasters. He finally decided to
> join the *Plymouth*, and signed the shipping articles under the follow-
> ing conditions: [he] was to stay with the ship until her cargo was
> completed and she was ready to leave the "whaling grounds" on her
> homeward passage, after which time he was to receive his discharge,
> at any time he might desire. It was also agreed that the captain would
> furnish at a fair price, a boat and whatever provisions he might
> require.[20]

The Plymouth

The *Plymouth* was a new ship, bought in Boston in 1845, by Cook and Green for $14,500. Yet it was only through sheer luck that the ship went anywhere at all, for on the night of November 13, 1845, a fire started in a furniture store on Sag Harbor's Main street and turned into a conflagration. The flames nearly destroyed the entire town, burning over seventy-two buildings and causing over a hundred casualties. In the harbor, the *Xenophon* caught fire and burned, and so did the *Konohassett* and the *Plymouth*. The *Plymouth* was saved only because it was towed out into open waters.[21]

Damage to the *Plymouth* was slight, however, and on December 2 the ship set sail via Cape Horn for the Pacific Ocean, the Hawaiian Islands, and eventually the Japan whaling grounds. It would not return until April 30, 1849, and then without Ranald MacDonald, but the voyage was at the time the most successful in American whaling history, yielding a total of 4,873 barrels of whale oil and 29,000 pounds of whale bone.[22]

Few details are known about the *Plymouth* or its crew, for, like the *Tuscany*, the log book for MacDonald's voyage has been lost. It was a large ship for the time, however, of 425 tons, crewed by around thirty people of different nationalities and races. The captain, Lawrence B. Edwards, was one of the better-known Long Island whaling skippers and a veteran. Prior to the *Plymouth*, he had made multiple voyages on another Sag Harbor whaler called the *Columbia*, and spent considerable time in the Pacific. He may have been a god-fearing man as well. An 1843 letter to the evangelical *Sailor's Magazine* shows that, after returning from New Zealand and a two-year whaling voyage, he and his crew donated $17 to the Sag Harbor Temperance Society, with a note thanking the society for religious reading materials.[23] Still, Edwards may have put profit before crew; as we shall see later, while in command of the *Plymouth* he would lose a high number of his crew to disease and scurvy—and lose MacDonald's respect.

Looking East

Statements in MacDonald's *Narrative* aside, it is not entirely clear whether he really had a concrete plan or merely a vague idea of going to Japan when he first arrived in Sag Harbor. But if he was seeking more information on the little-known land, he had come to the right place.

In the 1840s—before radios, televisions, widely usable telegraphs, and transcontinental railways—information flowed around the world far faster on sailing ships than it did on land. It usually took much longer, for example, for MacDonald's father to send a letter from Fort Colvile to St. Thomas, Canada, than it took to send a letter from Canton, China, to Sag Harbor, New York. Whalers, by virtue of their extreme mobility, had access to more intelligence about foreign lands than almost anyone else in North America, and they were particularly knowledgeable about Japan.

Since the time of Columbus, businessmen and explorers had dreamed of accessing Japan's presumed (yet phantom) riches. But to whaling crews in the 1840s, Japan was a source of intense interest for a very practical reason; there were precious whales off Japan's northern shores, and more and more of ships were running into difficulty or being wrecked near Japan in the course of pursuing them. In ports around the world, whaling crews therefore exchanged information. They swapped stories of Russian, European, and American attempts to open Japan to trade, and of Japan's strange policy of secluding itself from the world.

Whaling voyages were long and arduous, and reprovisioning was always a problem, so around this time British and American whaling ships had also begun making surreptitious landings on Japanese soil to collect firewood and fresh water. Such actions were highly dangerous, and could result in sailors becoming imprisoned or worse, but the Japanese could not detect all the landings that might occur on their long and unguarded coastlines. One Sag Harbor whaleman writes in his memoirs of an 1843 voyage on a ship called the *Citizen*. It was, he says, altogether a voyage of "chasing delerium and death around the world," with the captain intending to winter "in one of the harbors of Japan to be ready to engage early in the spring in the capture of whales in the Japan Sea." The crew were extraordinarily lucky that bad weather thwarted the captain's plans, for he had intended to harbor "in the straits between Kyūshū and Honshū"—one of the more populous areas of Japan that would certainly have resulted in their apprehension and imprisonment.[24]

Sailors from Sag Harbor and other eastern seaboard ports also had a growing interest in the fate of their Japanese counterparts. There is a certain bond between sailors on the open sea, and Americans were particularly interested in stories of Japanese sailors in distress. Little was known about Japan, and Japan's laws were thought to cruelly forbid its own citizens from returning home. To most inhabitants of the civilized world in the mid-nineteenth century, and especially to American sailors, the policy was appalling, and absolutely baffling.

Manjirō

As it happened, during the period that MacDonald sailed in and out of Sag Harbor there was only one Japanese person in the entire United States. That was Manjirō Nakahama, today the most famous of all Japanese ship-wrecked sailors. Only three years younger than MacDonald, on January 5, 1841, at the age of fourteen, Manjirō had sailed on a tiny fishing boat from a village on the southern island of Kyūshū. The boat, with a crew of five men, had been caught in a terrible storm. After losing both mast and rudder, it began drifting helplessly into the Pacific, on January 14 eventually reaching Torishima (Bird Island), where the crew was marooned for six months. In June, the men were picked up by the *John Howland*, a New Bedford whaling ship, captained by William H. Whitfield, and taken to Honolulu, in the Hawaiian Islands. Whitfield was so impressed with young Manjirō's intelligence and character that he decided to take the boy home with him to Fairhaven, Massachusetts.

Manjirō, late in life, n.d.

Courtesy The Millicent Library, Fairhaven, MA.

The *John Howland* arrived in New Bedford on May 17, 1843, whereupon the young Japanese became "the center of attention."[25] As noted previously, he was given the name John Mung and enrolled in school, studying English, mathematics, surveying, and navigation. In an adventure that rivals that of Ranald MacDonald, Manjirō later worked as a whaler, participated in the 1849 Gold Rush in California, and—after picking up some of his former crewmates in Hawaii—snuck back into Japan with the aid of another American ship.

Between 1843 and 1846, however, Manjirō lived in the area of Fairhaven, on Buzzard's Bay opposite New Bedford, and from April to

October 1845, he worked as an apprentice cooper, or ship's barrel maker, in New Bedford itself. No record exists of Manjirō ever meeting Ranald Mac-Donald, nor, conversely, does MacDonald ever mention Manjirō in any of his surviving writings. But if MacDonald were considering an adventure to Japan while in and out of Sag Harbor between 1842 and 1845, it is hard to imagine that he had not at least heard of Manjirō. In 1845 the two young men were only around eighty nautical miles apart, and both connected to a community of whalers for whom travel among the local ports was common-place.

The Manhattan

Sag Harbor also had other connections to Japan. After MacDonald returned on the *Tuscany*, another ship from the port shocked the world by making direct contact with Japanese authorities. The *Manhattan*, a 440-ton ship, had departed Sag Harbor on November 8, 1843, for the "Pacific Ocean," captained by a Long Island veteran named Mercator Cooper. Taking a route common in those days, it sailed across the Atlantic, rounded Africa's Cape Hope, caught some whales near the Crozet Islands, cruised through the Indian Ocean, and then journeyed north past the west side of the Australian Continent. After wending its way through the islands of Indonesia, the ship passed the east coast of Japan and then headed for the rich whaling grounds off northern Japan. On the long voyage it was necessary to obtain provisions, so the ship occasionally stopped at islands along the way, the crew well aware they would be unable to reprovision around Japan proper.

In the summer of 1844, in time for the whaling season, the *Manhattan* finally arrived in the waters off Hokkaidō—then part of Japan's poorly chart-ed and lightly defended northern frontier. The *Manhattan* was hardly the only Sag Harbor or New England whaler in the area, since the whale-rich waters were a mecca for Americans, attracting as many as three hundred ships in a season. As was common among whalers in those days, when the *Manhattan*'s holds were full with whale oil and bone, it sailed on to the Sandwich Islands, or Hawaii. There, it sent home part of its cargo and, while waiting for the next season, underwent reprovisioning and repairs.

On January 7, 1845, the *Manhattan* left Hawaii and headed for the Bonin Islands (today, technically under the jurisdiction of metropolitan Tōkyō). It stayed a month, reprovisioning and waiting for the whaling season to start, and left on March 12, arriving three days later at Torishima, a barren, uninhabited volcanic island known to Americans as "St. Peters," about 375 miles south of Tōkyō—the same island on which Manjirō and his companions had been marooned. Hoping to find turtles for food for his crew, Cooper explored the island and instead came across eleven shipwrecked Japanese sailors, who prostrated themselves on the ground before him. A man of great kindness and courage, Cooper then made the astounding decision to interrupt his whaling voyage and return the sailors to Edo, the capital of Japan.

As a veteran whaling ship captain, Cooper knew of Japan's centuries-old Seclusion Laws; he knew only Dutch and Chinese (and occasionally Korean) ships were allowed to visit Japan, and then only in the southernmost port of Nagasaki. He would also have known of failed Russian attempts to trade with Japan in the north, and of abortive attempts by other European nations to establish contact in the south. He most certainly would have heard of the 1837 voyage of the U.S. ship *Morrison*, which—in attempting to return some Japanese castaways—had been fired upon by Japanese batteries near Edo and nearly sunk. Cooper likely did not know, however, that only a few years earlier, in 1842, the Japanese government had changed its policy toward foreign ships. Instead of unconditionally repelling them with force, the Shogunate had decided to provide them with water, wood, and even food, if necessary, before demanding a speedy departure.

As Cooper later recounted to a friend, he determined to set sail to Edo for two reasons. "The first was to restore the shipwrecked sailors to their homes. The second was to make a strong and favorable impression on the government, in respect to the civilization of the United States, and its friendly disposition to the Emperor and people of Japan."[26]

As luck would have it, on the way to Edo Bay the Manhattan came across even more shipwrecked Japanese men, their disabled vessel drifting helplessly at sea after an earlier storm. Cooper writes in his log: "We fell in with a Japanese Junk with her stern stove in and 11 Men on board we took the men and their clothing and rice out and some riging and then set it on fire and left it."[27] The Manhattan was now jammed, packed with nearly as many shipwrecked Japanese as American crewmen. Reaching Japan somewhat north of Edo Bay, Cooper landed a boat in two spots, where he was warmly welcomed by local inhabitants, and he tried to get them to convey his peaceful intentions to the authorities in Edo. Finally, on April 18, 1845, "about three hundred Japanese boats with about 15 men in each took

Portrait of Captain Mercator Cooper, n.d.

AR#1983.45.1 Courtesy New Bedford Whaling Museum.

the ship in tow and towed us at the rate of three knots per hour ... they towed us into a bay little below Yeddo and there formed their boats around the ship with a guard of about three thou men they took all of our arms out to keep till we left they were severel of the nobillity came on board to see the ship they appear very friendly."[28]

The Japanese probably allowed the ship to enter the bay because of the large number of Japanese sailors being returned, the obvious lack of armaments on the whaling ship, and the extraordinary nature of the situation. The *Manhattan* was kept at anchor in the Bay for four days, surrounded by hundreds of guard boats decorated with banners and spears, and visited by people of all ranks, "from the Governor of Jeddo and the high officers attached to the person of the Emperor, arrayed in golden and gorgeous tunics, to the lowest menials of the government, clothed in rags. All were filled with an insatiable curiosity to see the strangers and inspect the thousand novelties presented to their view."[29]

The shipwrecked Japanese sailors were eventually accepted by the Japanese government, and the *Manhattan* was graciously supplied. Cooper, with his always-bad spelling, recorded that "they sent the watter on board latter part they sent us 20 sacks of rice 20 sacks of wheat and one box of flour 11 sacks of sweet potatoes 50 fowl 2 cords of wood large quantity of redishes and 10 lbs of tea."[30] The Japanese accepted no payment for this service, but they never allowed the Americans to disembark from their ship, or to land. One of the first people to greet the Americans had been "a native interpreter who had been taught Dutch, and who could speak a few words of English, but who could talk still more intelligibly by signs." He informed them that should they leave their ship, they would be put to death, this fact "communicated to [us] by the very significant symbol of drawing a naked sward across the throat." Then, before leaving, the men on the *Manhattan* were told to never come to Japan again. When Cooper inquired what they should do if they came across other helpless or shipwrecked Japanese, he was made to understand that "it would please the Emperor more for them to be left, than for strangers to visit his dominions." When a horrified Cooper protested, it was suggested that he "carry them to some Dutch port, but never come to Japan again."[31] The *Manhattan* thus left Edo Bay and proceeded on its original mission of whaling in the north.

The Sag Harbor whaler thus became the first ship to officially fly the American flag in Edo Bay and to enter into negotiations with Japanese authorities—eight years before Commodore Perry arrived with a U.S. Navy fleet of warships and once and for all forced Japan to end its isolation. In addition, in an act that could have resulted in their execution, the shipwrecked Japanese sailors accidentally left a detailed map of Japan on board the *Manhattan*. The map was taken back to the United States and became an object of intense interest; today it hangs on a wall of the whaling museum in the town of New Bedford. The interpreter with whom the *Manhattan* crew dealt in Edo Bay—the man who issued the Shogunate's warnings in such eloquent sign language—would later become Ranald MacDonald's star pupil in Nagasaki.

❖ ❖ ❖

Did MacDonald know of the *Manhattan*'s voyage? He leaves almost no record of his actions or thoughts between 1842 and 1845 (when he was in and out of Sag Harbor), and the *Manhattan* did not return to its home port until October 14, 1846, ten months after he had already left on the *Plymouth*. In the eight-month interval between the *Manhattan*'s Japan visit and MacDonald's departure on the *Plymouth* in December 1845, it is technically possible that another ship brought word of the *Manhattan*'s daring visit. Yet it is far more likely that he heard about it after leaving port, while at sea.

On the vast oceans of the world, American whaleships competed—and cooperated. Within the community of whalemen, the special bond between men hailing from the same ports was especially intense. In addition to socializing and trading information at ports of call, sailors also routinely conveyed information while out on the high seas. Whaling ships sometimes sailed in pairs, and, in a lonely world, they regularly met with other ships on the sea, in a practice called "gamming." Priceless letters from home were exchanged, along with reports on sailing conditions and news of foreign lands. For land-based investors in whaling voyages, any news of ships was highly sought after, so whenever ships were met or sighted at sea, the news was conveyed from ship to ship as fast as possible back to home ports. There, it was printed along with reports of ships' positions and their catch of whale oil and bone. In local newspapers, such as the *Sag Harbor Corrector*, this information usually appeared in a column under the heading of "Spoken." The log of the *Manhattan* does not show her having spoken to the *Plymouth*, but shortly after leaving Edo Bay, in July, alone, she "spoke" to five other Sag Harbor whalers. On the voyage out, MacDonald's ship, the *Plymouth*, probably heard the news of the *Manhattan*'s visit to Edo Bay. It was astounding news for everyone, but for someone contemplating an adventure to Japan, the report of the visit would have been especially encouraging, for it showed the Japanese government to be far less hostile to foreigners than generally believed.

❧ ❧ ❧

The *Plymouth* left Sag Harbor on December 2, 1845, and headed for the Pacific Ocean via the southern tip of South America. If MacDonald did not along the way directly learn of the *Manhattan*'s adventure, he was about to, for he was headed toward the independent kingdom of Hawaii. It was the hub of the entire whaling industry in the Pacific, and a center of information on Japan.

CHAPTER 7

A "Staging Ground" in the Hawaiian Islands

For a mid-nineteenth-century whaler, the *Plymouth*, with MacDonald aboard, made the trip from Sag Harbor to the Hawaiian Islands in good time. Records show it arrived in Lahaina, Maui, on May 17, 1846, after a journey of five-and-a-half months, equaling the average time of a man-o'-war. It had cleared the treacherous Cape Horn in the southern hemisphere's summer and then crossed over to the Hawaiian Islands after pulling up the West Coast of South America, arriving "clean," with no cargo of whale oil or bone. At Lahaina the *Plymouth* was by no means alone. That year an estimated 429 ships docked, the vast majority from the East Coast of the United States, many either headed to or returning from the whaling grounds around Japan.[1]

* * *

In 1846 the Hawaiian Islands were an independent kingdom, "discovered" only sixty-eight years earlier by Captain Cook. King Kamehameha I and his descendants had followed a remarkably progressive path of trying to bring the kingdom into the modern world, welcoming visitors, importing Western technology and advisors, and sending young Hawaiians abroad to learn for-

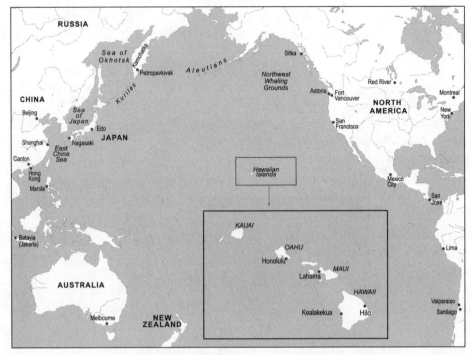

The Pacific Ocean and the Hawaiian Islands.

eign ways, often as crewmen on American whaling ships. This open-door policy, however, would have unintended and tragic consequences, for—as typically happened with aboriginal peoples throughout the world—new ideas eroded traditional beliefs, and new diseases caused the population to drop precipitously. The British and French jockeyed for control of the islands, but by the 1840s much of Hawaii's independence had already been usurped by American businessmen and Christian missionaries, who had installed themselves as advisors and officials at the highest levels of government.

American involvement with the Hawaiian Islands began shortly after their discovery. Ships in the sea otter and tea trade found the islands a convenient place to stop on long voyages from East Coast ports to the Pacific Northwest, China, and then back home. After sea otters were nearly exterminated, Hawaiian sandalwood was found to be a prize commodity in China, and U.S. ships began taking it to barter. When sandalwood resources were exhausted, the Pacific whaling grounds were discovered, and the islands began to depend on income from the whaling ships that swarmed into the

Pacific. Because whaling ships stayed out on the open ocean far longer than either merchant vessels or warships, the islands became an essential place for them to reprovision and repair, for crews to rest and recuperate, and for captains to find replacements for men who had deserted or died.

The Hawaiian Islands thus came to function as a hub for transportation and commerce in the Pacific, and with this flowed information on Japan. Most early explorers of the North Pacific and the waters around Japan had stopped by the islands. Civilian and military vessels from France, Britain, Denmark, Russia, and the United States regularly visited, often coming from Canton, where Chinese junks returning from Japan could be found, or Batavia (today's Jakarta, Indonesia), where Dutch ships docked on the way back from Nagasaki. And whaling ships returning from the hunting grounds off Japan's northern coasts brought information, too. In the 1840s, the Hawaiian kingdom lacked any direct, official contact with Japan, which still maintained its strict Seclusion policy, but information on Japan was turning into a mini-flood. To most residents of America in the 1840s, MacDonald's death-defying infiltration of Japan may have seemed like the act of a madman, but in the Hawaiian Islands the logic of his adventure and the forces that helped shape it become crystal clear.

Preparing for the Adventure

In MacDonald's posthumously published *Narrative,* he never mentions that he had spent considerable time in the Hawaiian Islands on the *Tuscany* before arriving on the *Plymouth.* He merely writes that the place was of "special interest" to him because, during his boyhood, the Hudson's Bay Company had had intimate trade relations with the islands. Rather obliquely, he also adds that a childhood acquaintance, the famous botanist David Douglas, had died there—gored by a bull in 1834. Only in what almost seems to be an afterthought, does he cryptically mention that "the place had also been always an objective point with me for immediate preparation for my contact with Japan."[2]

In Hawaii, MacDonald says he "looked out for a Whaler bound for the northern seas of Japan." At Lahaina, on Maui, "after a sojourn of a few days throughout the group," he "accidentally" ran into his "old Captain of the 'Plymouth,' which had lain over in Kalakakna Bay to repair." And it was here, he says, that he applied for "reshipment, again before the mast, on the ordinary partnership terms of whalers—of payment on share profit—but with the special stipulation on my part, that I was to be free to leave the ship off the coast of Japan wherever and whenever I should desire, when the ship would be full, or be on the eve of returning or going elsewhere." It was also here, he writes, that he made a bargain with the captain to be taught how to navigate, using a Hadley's quadrant and nautical almanac "acquired for the purpose." The captain reluctantly agreed, apparently thinking he would never be able to carry out his plan.[3]

MacDonald's *Narrative* makes it sound as though he left the *Plymouth* upon arriving in the Hawaiian Islands and signed up again with it later, yet this is highly misleading—as is the preposterous idea that he applied for reshipment "after a sojourn of a few days throughout the group." In local Hawaiian newspapers of the time, the *Plymouth* is recorded as arriving in Lahaina on May 17, 1846, and not departing for the Japan seas until November 11, 1847, the next year. In the interim, the ship was out whaling in the Pacific and the Northwest, and regularly laying over in Hawaii. Was MacDonald on the ship or not? One article in the December 1, 1848, edition of the Honolulu newspaper, *The Friend*, suggests he was. The paper's editor, who interviewed MacDonald's crewmates, unambiguously describes him as being on board: "After remaining in the vessel two years, while at Lahaina in the fall of 1847, he requested his discharge, unless Capt. Edwards would consent to leave him the next season *somewhere* upon the coast of Japan."[4]

From this account, two things are clear—that between 1845 and 1848 MacDonald was with the *Plymouth* and that he also spent considerable time in the islands. Local newspaper records are frustratingly incomplete but they show the *Plymouth* docking not only at Lahaina on Maui, but also Hilo, on the big island of Hawaii, and at Honolulu, on Oahu, throughout 1846 and 1847. Usually the ship is described as returning to port with a large cargo of whale oil, hinting at the success for which it would later become renowned.

Although MacDonald never specifically mentions it, it is also clear that he spent considerable time in Hawaii preparing for his adventure, gathering information, books, and the gear he would need, for his adventure was hardly planned overnight. In a letter written toward the end of his life, he states that "from the time I made the bargain [with Captain Edwards], I considered I was fairly launched in the enterprise altho I also had brooded over the matter for years."[5] The 1848 article in the *The Friend* further reinforces this, for the impressed editor wrote of MacDonald's plans that while they were not "upon so gigantic a scale, as those which might emanate from a 'Board of Admiralty' or a 'Naval Bureau,' yet to answer his purpose, they certainly indicate some 'head' work."[6]

Lahaina, Whaling Port of the Pacific

Of all the places MacDonald visited in Hawaii, Lahaina figures the largest. It is the port from which the Plymouth left for the Japan whaling grounds and the only port he specifically mentions visiting. A quiet little resort town today, Lahaina now consists mainly of shops stretching out from a picturesque yacht harbor, selling curios and beach wear to milling tourists. Its basic layout is not too different from that of 1846, except that the shops then were mostly thatched huts selling grog and women to sailors. Like Sag Harbor, the town is well preserved (a designated National Historical Landmark), so it is far easier to walk down the streets by the harbor and imagine what they were like in 1846 than it would be in, say, the sprawling metropolis of modern Honolulu.

Until 1843, when King Kamehameha III moved the seat of government to Honolulu, Lahaina was the capital of the Hawaiian kingdom and the site of the royal palace. By 1846, when MacDonald arrived on the *Plymouth*, Lahaina had lost much of its political, but not its economic, power, mainly because of the whaling industry. A forest of masts covered the harbor, and over a hundred ships might be in port at the same time, waiting for the winter storms in the North Pacific to subside. It was not uncommon for ten thousand men from around the world to visit the seaport a year, and eight hundred to be on shore on liberty at a time.[7]

Despite the huge number of visitors, an 1846 census revealed the town had a permanent population of 523 dogs and 3,557 people, of which only 112 were foreigners, "not including seamen of the hospital and others on the hands of the consuls." There were, in addition, "882 grass houses, 155 adobie houses, and 59 of stone or wood." Most of the shops were run by Americans or Europeans, but a list in the newspaper the same year shows, among the proprietors, a "Shiek Mahomet" and "Achow (Chinaman)."[8]

❉ ❉ ❉

Today, a popular history walking tour through Lahaina passes by at least three stone structures that survive from the 1840s. They tell much of the story of Lahaina and, indirectly, how it came to be a clearinghouse for information on Japan.

The first structure, in the center of town, is a small corner of what used to be a fort, with thick walls made of coral stone. Erected in 1831, it symbolizes the permanent state of tension that existed then in Lahaina between seamen (and the merchants who supported them) and local authorities, allied with the missionaries.

For sailors, Hawaii was a type of paradise, and under the slogan of "No God West of the Horn," they wanted to enjoy their time on shore. After being cooped up in ships at sea for months on end, the men cavorted with women and raced through the streets on rented horses, not infrequently so drunk they could barely stay in the saddle. Fights were common, and as one English visitor noted, the sailors' salty influence resulted in the native population "speaking our vulgar tongue, in its grossest and most offensive terms, with great fluency."[9] One sailor reminisced later that "the place was anything but 'The Paradise of the Pacific.' It was then more correctly termed 'The Brothel of the Pacific'."[10]

The fort had been built partly in response to incidents that had occurred in the 1820s, when American missionaries tried to prevent young Hawaiian women from visiting whaling ships and prostituting themselves. These attempts succeeded mainly in arousing the wrath of the sailors and their captains, and in 1825 one ship's crew attacked the home of a local missionary and threatened the lives of his family. Two years later, another ship's crew fired their cannon on the man's home.

By 1846, the local authorities, with the encouragement of the missionaries, had the situation almost too well under control. The fort, which had always served a mostly symbolic purpose, was used as a prison for deserters and drunken sailors, regularly rounded up on the town streets. In 1844 twenty-one ship's masters addressed a sarcastic petition to the authorities, complaining that "[i]t is hard that peaceable men cannot walk through your streets without having their lives endangered by stones thrown, or clubs wielded, by the authority of the police, to quell a disturbance originating with a few drunken men, made so at your LICENSED GROG SHOPS."[11]

MacDonald never recorded his impressions of the prison, but a fellow sailor did. Jotham Newton was a young crewman on the *Uncas*—a New Bedford whaling ship that followed a course similar to the *Plymouth* and later played a minor role in MacDonald's adventure. Around 1847–48, Newton visited the fort-prison. Noting that the Hawaiian king's cabinet members were mainly Americans, he wrote, "[I]t is a shame to those who legislate for that country that they do not provide more decent place for the reception of even murderers. Were the legislators heathen heathenish laws and management would be expected but where such barbarism is visible under men who profess to be enlightened, bred in [an] enlightened country, [it] appears strange and preposterous."[12]

For the local missionaries, who were allied with the authorities, Lahaina was also a paradise of sorts. Natives could be converted to Christianity and helped to adapt to the "civilized world." And lapsed-Christian sailors could be reintroduced to their faith and led away from the paths of intoxication and fornication. Sailors, in particular, were ripe for proselytization because of their loneliness and the treacherous nature of their work. In the mid-nineteenth century, up to a thousand young men are estimated to have lost their lives annually in the whaling industry. Newton spoke for every sailor when he wrote at the end of his "long and monotonous voyage," of his good fortune in surviving storms and encounters with whales, "expecting every moment to be my last," and in miraculously escaping "the many contagious diseases [to] which we were unfortunately exposed."[13]

The Lahaina missionaries often ministered to sailors directly on board ships, at the invitation of their captains.[14] But the local hospital proved to be an even more fertile ground for evangelizing. Unscrupulous whaling ship captains found the islands a convenient place to dump sick or injured seamen, who were the last thing they needed on a profit-based voyage. So many sailors were abandoned in Lahaina that in 1843 the U.S. government helped establish a U.S. Seamen's Hospital, where they could be taken care of with the rudimentary medical skills of the day and ministered to by the local missionaries. Restored, the hospital is another popular attraction on the walking history tour of modern Lahaina.

Along with his captain, Newton visited sick crewmates at the hospital and attended a religious service there. He remarked at the men's good care but grieved over their plight, so far from home and family: "Most of the inmates of this hospital are young men and in the prime of life. Some have broken limbs others consumption and other calamities which befall mankind. It is here where . . . the messenger of death is actively engaged in ushering spirits into the eternal world."[15]

There is no record of MacDonald having been injured or sick on his voyage, but he had many friends who were. Indeed, in the spring of 1846, the *Plymouth* may have arrived in such good time with an empty hold precisely because the crew was too weakened to do much whaling along the way. As the newspapers then reported, fifteen men—nearly half the crew—were stricken with typhus on the way out, two crewmen dying before the ship reached Brazil's Rio de Janeiro, and another expiring shortly thereafter. "Capt. Edwards, thinking the fever originated with the potatoes and onions he brought from home, cast overboard what remained." After arriving in Lahaina on May 17, 1846, and recuperating, the *Plymouth* went whaling in the Northwest. It returned briefly to Hawaii on November 23, with 1,000 barrels of whale oil, but local papers show that on June 18, while catching the first whale, Charles Isaac, a young cabin boy, and Manuel Lewis, a seaman from the Azores, had drowned. On July 31, yet another man, Daniel Reeves, of Long Island, had been lost.[16]

From Lahaina's harbor today, it is only a short stroll to one of the town's most popular attractions—the restored house of Dr. Dwight Baldwin, a renowned missionary physician who arrived in 1835. Made with thick walls of coral, as well as stone and wood, it is Lahaina's oldest standing building. It is also impossible to ignore, as it is physically and metaphorically in the center of town. In the 1840s, Baldwin, in addition to serving as a practicing physician and local postmaster, was host to ship captains and diplomatic personnel, as well as weary travelers. As he later wrote, "You can . . . ask the scores of ship-masters at New Bedford, Nantucket, N. London, and Sag Harbor, who have been at Lahaina, time without number, a fortnight at a time, who have been at our house and sat at our table."[17]

Modern writers tend to view the Lahaina missionaries much like those of Red River, as either saintly apostles of Christ or agents of destruction of native culture and prudish scolds. Yet, in an age before established mail services, men like Baldwin (and their wives) in remote spots functioned in a supra-religious context as the providers of information and promoters of knowledge. Baldwin served for a while as one of Lahaina's two chaplains for seamen, and he was interested in educating men's minds as well as saving their souls. The mid-nineteenth century was a time of evangelism among U.S. sailors, led by the New York–based American Seamen's Friend Society, for next to slaves the ordinary sailor was regarded as one of the most abused, downtrodden species of humanity, tempted by liquor and women when ashore, and subject to flogging and other cruel punishments by ship masters when at sea. Missionaries serving the whaling community therefore commonly established places for sailors to read, not only to help keep them out of trouble but also to educate them. Next to the Baldwin House there were special reading rooms for ship's officers and regular seamen, where they could peruse newspapers and books and, it was hoped, Bibles and religious tracts, too.

Whaling voyages were often long periods of monotony punctuated by moments of hair-raising terror, so many sailors hungrily sought out reading material to help pass their idle moments. The American Seamen's Friend Society sent Baldwin a box of books shortly after his seaman's chapel was built, but before long, he wrote back: "Fifty more hymn books would be acceptable—the fifty spelling books are nearly all gone, owing to the number on board whale ships who cannot read. The seamen's library of 400 vols. which has been gathering here, is now nearly all floating on different parts of the ocean. I hope such a box will be sent every year. Religious and other papers in files are read with avidity. Late papers are very desirable for reading rooms."[18] In another letter, the missionary asked for a map to put up on a wall and for copies of the *Sailor's Magazine*, published by the Society as part of the Temperance Movement. In addition to evangelical stories, the magazine ran news about Japan and, in 1850, even featured the tale of MacDonald's own adventure.[19]

Books on travel and exploration were especially popular among sailors, and it is safe to assume that the Lahaina reading room had some, authored by early explorers of the North Pacific and containing information on both Hawaii and Japan. In response to reader queries, the July 13, 1844, issue of the Honolulu-based newspaper *The Polynesian* featured a list of locally popular works that, it said, "relate to, or treat of, the Hawaiian Islands." The list included works by British explorer W. R. Broughton, the German G. H. von Langsdorff, and the Russian captain I. F. Kruzenshtern, books which were all widely available in English and dealt with Japan in considerable detail.[20] Particularly striking in the context of MacDonald's adventure, these books all contain descriptions of then little-known northern Japan, and the coordinates of the remote island where he eventually chose to land.

But local newspapers were even better sources of information on Japan than books. In the 1840s, three English-language newspapers were published in Honolulu, on Oahu, and distributed in Lahaina. Two of them—*The*

The Baldwin House, Lahaina.

Friend and *The Polynesian*—frequently featured articles on Japan, and some of the best articles in the latter were written by none other than missionary Dwight Baldwin, who can, in fact, be thought of as the first American "Japanologist." While part of the Protestant evangelical tradition resurgent in the mid-nineteenth century, Baldwin also was intensely curious about the mysterious Asian nation across the Pacific.

Geopolitical Shifts

In the 1840s, the world was undergoing major convulsions, driven by technology and politics. Even though Hawaii was far removed from Europe, America, and even Asia, its local newspapers tried to describe some of the changes to readers, in particular the global political changes, for they directly affected the fortunes of captains and crews of whaling ships, as well as missionaries.

To the west of Hawaii, in South and Southeast Asia, Europeans had long been conducting business and establishing colonies. But China remained independent and, like Japan, tried to regulate trade with foreigners, limiting them mainly to the port of Canton. Then, in 1839, capitalizing on the weakness of the Chinese central government, the British used Chinese refusal to buy opium as a pretext to start the so-called Opium War. This resulted, in 1842, in four more ports being opened to trade with foreigners, the ceding of Hong Kong to Britain, and the eventual carving up of China into spheres of influence by European imperial powers.

By the time MacDonald embarked on his adventure, Japan was one of the last nations still to ban most Europeans and to prohibit them from trading or promoting Christianity within its borders. As a result, so little was known about Japan that as late as March 1853, a major U.S. magazine would repeat myths dating back to the time of Marco Polo and write that "[t]he productions of Japan are gold, which is so plentiful that the roofs of palaces and the ceilings of rooms are of pure gold. 'Niphon' [in the language of the article] 'is a great gold mine.'"[21] Most people in Hawaii assumed Japan would eventually be forced to open its ports to wider trade and that the British, with their aggressive and powerful navy, would probably be the ones to do it. But Britain was preoccupied with its possessions in India and in carving up China, and the balance of power in the Pacific thus began to change.

The shift was accelerated by a major redrawing of the territorial map of the United States in 1846. The land of Ranald MacDonald's birth—the entire Pacific Northwest of today's United States—had been under joint control of the United States and Britain, but that year the border was finally fixed at the 49th parallel, giving the United States sole control. That same year, war also broke out between the United States and Mexico, and it became obvious that the entire Southwest and California would fall into U.S. hands, making it for the first time a true Pacific power. Not only would the United States directly face Japan across the ocean; the shortest sailing distance to Japan would be reduced from twenty-two thousand to six thousand miles. Not surprisingly, the newspapers in the Hawaiian Islands were filled with articles about the war.

Until the 1840s, few high-placed Americans had been seriously interested in the Pacific or Japan. John Quincy Adams, who served as secretary of state from 1817–1825 and president from 1825–1829, was one exception. He forcefully advocated keeping Hawaii within the U.S. sphere of influence and out of the hands of the European powers. But at the same time, he was also against the right of any nation to refuse to trade, or to be isolated, and he thus supported Britain against China in the disgraceful Opium War. Extrapolating from this, Adams's convoluted and frightening position vis-à-vis Japan, as later described, was that it was "the right, and even the duty, of Christian nations to open the ports of Japan, and the duty of Japan to assent on the ground that no nation has a right more than any man has to withdraw its private contribution to the welfare of the whole."[22]

By 1846 many more Americans were thinking the same thing. As citizens of a muscular young Pacific power, many were swept up in the notion of a "manifest destiny"—a passionate, almost religious belief in the right to expand their civilization westward (a belief that coincided with a revival of zealous Protestant evangelism). For politicians of the new "Pacific nation," relations with Japan came to be viewed in a geopolitical context, as part of America's rivalry with Britain and France. For businessmen, Japan represented imaginary riches. For missionaries (to whom Japan had long presented only the possibility of martyrdom), proselytizing one day in the mysterious locked empire became the equivalent of the Holy Grail.

Lahaina Links to Japan

Four years after arriving in Lahaina, the Reverend Dwight Baldwin had found himself host to several Japanese shipwrecked sailors. As he wrote in an extensive report published on August 1, 1840, in *The Polynesian*, the men had been saved by an American whale ship, the *James Loper*. Their ten-man Japanese junk, the *Chōjamaru*, had been engaged in Japan's coastal trade, but was blown out into the Pacific during a violent storm. Disabled but still afloat, the ship had drifted helplessly, three of the crew over the months slowly dying of starvation and disease. After rescuing the survivors and their effects, the American captain set fire to their wrecked junk and then returned to Hawaii, where one more crewman later succumbed. Baldwin wrote,

> I had never before seen a Japanese. Such was the case with most who were present. Of course the sight of these men awakened no little curiosity. We wished to know what strange events had befallen them; and to learn some thing about their country from which the people of all other nations were effectively excluded.[23]

Several of the castaways stayed with Baldwin at his house for several weeks, and during that time the missionary did his best to communicate with them. They spoke a language that no one in Hawaii then understood, but Baldwin discovered that a local "Chinaman" could communicate with them to a limited extent through writing. Baldwin tried to learn something of their language and teach them his. He was mightily impressed with their desperate resolve to somehow return to their families in Japan, despite the known prohibitions, and did his best to help, hoping to at least demonstrate that not all Christians were bad, as they had been taught. "I tried every expedient to interest them in the Christian religion," he wrote, "but probably without much success."[24]

Baldwin's first letter to *The Polynesian* described for curious readers the Japanese and their ordeal. And from information gained from the castaways, he described the islands of Japan, including the northernmost island of today's Hokkaidō, then known as Ezo (or Ezochi), where MacDonald would later spend time. Baldwin pleaded for any merchant or warship in Hawaii to take the Japanese to Canton or Kamchatka, from where they might attempt to return to their homes. The end of his letter included a detailed list of all the effects of one sailor, with Japanese prices converted into dollars.

On October 17, the missionary followed with a long article about the Japanese numbering system. The subject fascinated him, and he filled the entire front page of *The Polynesian* with information gleaned from his visitors, including Japanese names for numbers, which—like MacDonald later—he had to figure out how to render in the English alphabet. In the same issue, readers could learn that the Japanese sailors had been in fact returned by a British ship to Kamchatka, Russia's Pacific territory north of Japan, and were now in the hands of the local Russian governor, awaiting an opportunity to somehow return to their homeland. The paper had noted earlier, however, that the American ship, *Morrison,* had tried to return shipwrecked Japanese sailors in 1837 and been fired upon, so that "it must be confessed that . . . there is but little chance of a friendly welcome for this party."[25]

❖ ❖ ❖

In Lahaina, it was not necessary to meet Dwight Baldwin to hear about Japan or the Japanese. With so many whaling ships returning from the seas off northern Japan, sailors regularly traded information on the mysterious locked land; some had had interaction with Japanese sailors off the coast of Japan, or had aided Japanese castaways, or had even landed on Japanese soil surreptitiously to collect water and firewood. If MacDonald had not yet heard of the story of Mercator Cooper—who in 1845 on the *Manhattan* brazenly sailed into Edo Bay—in Lahaina he could hardly have missed it.

On February 2, 1846, only two months before the *Plymouth* arrived in Lahaina, *The Friend* used four entire pages to feature a detailed account of the *Manhattan*'s voyage. The same article was picked up and subsequently reprinted by newspapers throughout North America, even running in the June edition of the New York–based *Sailor's Magazine*, which, along with *The Friend*, was regularly carried in the seamen's reading room in Lahaina. The author was none other than C. F. Winslow, a physician who lived in Lahaina and worked with Dr. Baldwin; Winslow had heard the story directly from Cooper in Hawaii. News of the *Manhattan*'s voyage was hugely exciting to both missionaries and businessmen in Hawaii because it represented the most friendly and successful encounter to date between Americans and Japanese. As the editor of *The Friend* wrote in a preface to the article, "Although a most rigid policy of non-intercourse with foreign nations has long been exercised by the Japanese government, yet the period is probably now rapidly hastening, when the interior of that Empire will be exposed to the gaze of the civilized world."[26]

Honolulu, The Pacific Northwest, and Japan

If Lahaina was the whaling center of the Hawaiian Islands in the 1840s, Honolulu, on the neighboring island of Oahu, was the commercial center, and it, too, played a central role in MacDonald's adventure to Japan. MacDonald had been in Honolulu on the *Tuscany* in 1844, if not before, and he was there when the *Plymouth* docked in December 29, 1846, and also November 14, 1847. Like Lahaina, Honolulu had many links to Japan, with the added twist of long-standing connections to the Pacific Northwest and sites of MacDonald's early childhood, too.

George Vancouver, who explored the coast of the Pacific Northwest in the 1790s as a young midshipman, had visited Hawaii with Captain Cook on his fateful visit; Vancouver also had functioned as a type of advisor to King Kamehameha I and introduced cattle to the islands. His lieutenant, William Broughton, who early on explored the Columbia River, also visited the

Honolulu area and explored the waters around northern Japan and the island on which MacDonald would later land.

In the early years of the sea-otter trade, American ships regularly ferried furs from the Columbia River area via Hawaii to Canton, which brought them in proximity to Japan. This is what had led American sea captain John Kendrick—who helped "discover" the Columbia River—to become one of the first to fly the American flag in Japan, on the *Lady Washington* in 1791. Kendrick, also said to have started the sandalwood trade between Hawaii and China, was accidentally killed in Honolulu in 1794 by a misdirected gun salute from a British ship.

Americans encountered Japanese on Oahu only a few years after Kendrick's death. Amasa Delano, a New England sea captain and friend of Kendrick, in his memoirs describes how he personally met and aided eight Japanese sailors in the islands in 1806. Disabled at sea, their ship had drifted helplessly, the starving men drawing lots and (according to Delano) cannibalizing fellow crewmates to survive. The survivors were rescued by another American sea captain who worked for John Jacob Astor, "bound from China across the Pacific ocean to the coast of America." Delano took great pity on the men and transported them all the way to Canton on his ship, in hopes that they might find their way home from there. The Japanese then were sent to Batavia on a Chinese ship and made their way home to Nagasaki on an American vessel chartered by the Dutch. In the year-and-a half-odyssey, six died of disease, and one committed suicide in Nagasaki after interrogations. Only one man managed to return to his home.[27]

John Jacob Astor never met any Japanese, but in 1811 he permanently linked the mouth of the Columbia to Hawaii and, indirectly, to Japan, when he formed Astoria (where MacDonald was born). He used Hawaiians as laborers, and both the North West Company and later the Hudson's Bay Company continued his example. For the always cost-conscious Hudson's Bay Company, Hawaiians (or "Kanakas") were a bargain, and it used them throughout its Pacific Northwest forts after 1821. The Hawaiians were excellent swimmers, boatmen, trappers, and hunters, and they were loyal men to have on hand during trouble with Indians. Their contribution to the Pacific Northwest lives on today in place names such as the Owyhee River. Until MacDonald departed for school at Red River at the age of ten, he had Hawaiians around him all the time.

After 1821, the link between the Columbia River and Asia via Hawaii was broken, because Britain's East India Company had monopoly trade rights in China. Yet the HBC presence in Honolulu became increasingly important. Company ships left Oregon's Fort Vancouver with furs to head for England via Hawaii and Cape Horn. And the Company began doing business in Honolulu, in 1834 establishing a permanent office under its agent, George C. Pelly, who remained in that position while MacDonald sailed in and out of the islands. The Company office, on Fort Street near the waterfront in 1846, regularly ran ads in local newspapers, advertising goods for sale such as

> carpenters adzes, shell augers, brad awls, earthen ware, basins, ewers and soap draminers; Day & Martins liquid blacking, hessian Wellington and Clarence boots; sugar bowls and slop bowls; india rubber braces . . . velvet wine corks, striped shirting cottons, navy blue prints, cambric for ladies dresses, cruet stands . . . with a variety of articles not listed here.[28]

The manufactured goods brought from London on Company ships were sold in Honolulu to Europeans, Americans, and Hawaiians, for by the mid-1840s, Honolulu far surpassed Lahaina in population. The ships then loaded up with Hawaiian sugar, molasses, salt, rice, and coffee, which was hauled to Fort Vancouver for the use of Company employees throughout the Northwest. When the ships returned, they carried furs destined for London, but for local Hawaiian consumption they carried flour, salted salmon, lumber, and even wool from farms established at Fort Nisqually (by MacDonald's father) and Fort Cowlitz.[29] Other Company ships sailed to Monterey or Yerba Buena (today's San Francisco, where the Company had an office) and up to Sitka to trade with Russian America.

In his writings Ranald MacDonald never mentions visiting the Company offices in Honolulu to pay his respects to George Pelly, but Pelly knew of him. When queried in 1848 by the editor of the Honolulu paper *The Friend*, right after the *Plymouth* left for the Japan grounds, Pelly replied that "this young man received a good education but instead of pursuing a mercantile life on shore, betook himself to the sea."[30]

❖   ❖   ❖

As a boy, MacDonald had heard a great deal about Honolulu from Hudson's Bay Company employees, for a remarkable number of his father's fellow officers traveled through the town.[31] And through the visits of these men to Honolulu, yet another web of links between MacDonald's world and Japan becomes apparent.

In 1833, around the time Ranald MacDonald attended school at Fort Vancouver, the Hudson's Bay Company hired two physicians—William Fraser Tolmie and Meredith Gairdner—and brought them from London to Fort Vancouver via Honolulu. Tolmie later

Meredith Gairdner's grave in Honolulu.

became one of Archibald McDonald's closest friends and helped him found Fort Nisqually. Gairdner—who dug up the grave of MacDonald's grandfather, Comcomly, near Fort Vancouver—later wound up back in Honolulu permanently. He died of tuberculosis there in the spring of 1837 and is buried in the cemetery by Kawaiahao Church, only a block or so from where the Company offices were located. Tolmie's journals show that he was studying Japanese history on his way out from London. Although he does not mention it, there were Japanese in the Honolulu area when he arrived.

In December 1832, a year before the Company's Honolulu office was established, a disabled Japanese junk had washed up in Waialua, on Oahu, after drifting for ten or eleven months. Four men out of an original crew of nine were still alive, despite thirst, starvation, and scurvy, and they were later moved to Honolulu. An article about them, which appeared in the local *Hawaiian Spectator,* is of particular interest because the author gave readers a rare report of the ship's construction. Without knowing that Japanese authorities *required* ship designs unsuitable for open sea navigation, the

writer noted the vessel's top-heaviness, difficulty in handling, rude compass-
es, and a helm, worked by a long pole, "such as I should suppose would have
been used in the infancy of the arts."[32] The Japanese sailors stayed in Honolulu for eighteen months, until being forwarded to Russian-held Kamchatka; from there, they tried entering Japan through her northern territories.

John Ball, the founder and teacher of the first elementary school Mac-
Donald attended at Fort Vancouver, encountered these men on his way
home. On December 22, 1833, Ball sailed into the Honolulu harbor, where,
as he later wrote,

> There were strangely here, too, four Japanese, and in this way. A
> strange looking craft was seen off the harbor, and it was found to be a
> Japanese junk or vessel with but four men alive on board. They were
> brought in and were kept by a Mr. French, an American merchant,
> and when they had so far learned English that they could talk with
> them, they said they got lost, had been out so many moons, that
> being their way of reckoning time; that the rest had perished for want
> of food. They had been there about a year when I saw them. When
> the merchant proposed to take them home, for they thought they
> could use them to open a trade with that exclusive people, they
> declined to go, and for why? They answered that they would be exe-
> cuted for having been in a foreign land, and so would not consent to
> go.[33]

As soon as these Japanese left Honolulu, more arrived. In 1834, Chief
Factor John McLoughlin sent the shipwrecked Otokichi and his two crewmates from Fort Vancouver to London via Honolulu and then on to Asia, in
hopes of establishing relations with Japan. The ship that had rescued them in
the Northwest was the *Lama*, captained by an American who had been hired
by Company officer Duncan Finlayson in Honolulu. And it was Finlayson
who had taken MacDonald to Red River in 1834 and later become governor
of all of the Assiniboia region.

In the spring of 1842, George Simpson—governor-in-chief of the Hudson's Bay Company in North America and MacDonald's father's boss—
spent about a month in the Hawaiian Islands. He was on a whirlwind tour of
the world that would take him through Red River, Fort Vancouver, Sitka (in
Russian America), and then across the Pacific to Kamchatka, and—via

Siberia—St. Petersburg, and London. Before arriving in Honolulu, he stayed with Archibald and Jane McDonald at Fort Colvile. In Sitka he had arrived immediately after the murder of John McLoughlin, Jr., and become deeply involved in the dispute over who was to blame. In the Hawaiian Islands he met with European and local elites. In Lahaina he spent time with the king and queen, listened to a sermon given by Dr. Baldwin at the seamen's bethel (a chapel for seafarers), and had a personal visit with him. But he spent most of his time and let his thoughts roam most freely in Honolulu.

Simpson's account of his trip was published in 1847, and it shows how he pondered Hawaii's position in the world. Meditating on the west-east direction of the trade winds, he concluded that the Hawaiian islanders probably were from between the "southern extremity of Malacca and the northern limits of Japan." Extrapolating, he concluded that the New World had been populated by Asian peoples who not only came over the Bering Strait but migrated along several routes, including through the Kurile and Aleutian Island chains. He believed that "in a word, America and Polynesia appear to have been chiefly, if not solely, colonized from one and the same general region of eastern Asia."[34]

To support his theories, Simpson discussed the four Japanese survivors who had drifted to Oahu in December 1832 and the "three kichis" rescued by the Hudson's Bay Company in 1834. But he also mentions a more recent Japanese crew, retrieved from a disabled ship and brought to Honolulu in 1839. These men had already left before he arrived, but Simpson met up with them later in the Russian town of Okhotsk, in Kamchatka, just north of the Japanese territories:

> They were maintained at the expense of the government and were waiting an opportunity to return home. Whatever the chapter of accidents might ultimately disclose, there was then no definite prospect that the unhappy exiles would ever reach the shores of Japan, or that even if they should get that length, they would be allowed to land.[35]

Although Simpson does not mention it in his book, four other Japanese castaways were living in the Honolulu area when he was there. Late in 1841, the captain of the whaler *John Howland* had rescued five Japanese sailors marooned on an island and brought them to Honolulu. As described previously, the captain had taken the youngest—Manjirō—with him back to Fairhaven, Massachusetts, but he had left the older, less-literate crewmates in Honolulu. Around the time Simpson arrived, these men were still partially under the care of a famous missionary-doctor and politician named Gerrit P. Judd, who had finagled a role as one of the most powerful officials in the Hawaiian kingdom.[36] It is to these men that a popular 1844 history of the Hawaiian Islands refers, when it describes a typical Saturday afternoon at the races in Honolulu as being attended by

> people of all tongues and nations—English, Scotch and Irish—Russans, Americans, and Frenchmen—Spaniards, Danes, and Swedes— Portuguese, Japanese, and Chinese—Lascar and Arabian—the Kakaued Marquesian, the Tahitian, Samoan, and forbidding Nw Zealander, besides many others whose origin seems to be a combination of every variety.[37]

In his own book, Simpson mentions visiting Judd and discussing tax issues but he makes no specific reference to the Japanese in Judd's care. Even so, from what Simpson learned in Hawaii and later saw in Okhotsk, he was able to comment at length about Japan and about the future of the Pacific. The Japanese, he observed, were very different from the Chinese, of whom there were already over forty happily settled in the islands, actively engaged in various occupations. The Japanese refused to be Christianized, and "[n]otwithstanding all the kindness that they experienced, particularly from the missionaries . . . [they] pined for their own islands, the young as well as the old, the single as well as the married."[38]

Simpson furthermore realized that the Hawaiian Islands—especially Honolulu—could become the transportation epicenter of the Pacific, connecting not only China and Japan, but North and South America, and the islands of the North Pacific. Using what was for the time very "modernspeak," he wrote that, "[i]n effect, the group is a kind of station-house, where two railroads cross one another, each with parallel lines for opposite trains." Eventually, he foresaw that there would be the equivalent of a Panama Canal and that Japan's isolation would end:

> When the ports of Japan are opened, and the two oceans are connected by means of a navigable canal, so as to place the group in the

direct route between Europe and the United States on the one hand, and the whole of Eastern Asia on the other, then will the trade in question expand in amount and variety, till it has rendered Whoahoo the emporium of at least the Pacific Ocean, for the products natural and artificial, of every corner of the globe.[39]

Honolulu Newspapers and Japan

Two English-language newspapers in Honolulu helped drive interest in Japan during the 1840s and stimulate the belief that its isolation would soon end. One, *The Polynesian*, a weekly edited by an American named James Jackson Jarves, became the "Official Journal of the Hawaiian Government." The other was *The Friend*, a semimonthly religious newspaper, published for seamen by a Congregational missionary named Samuel C. Damon, dedicated to "Temperance, Marine, and General Intelligence." Jarves and Damon competed to demonstrate interest in Japan, but they also shared articles, so in Honolulu the same news on Japan frequently appeared twice.

The Friend, which began publication in 1843, was widely read among whaling ship crews. Damon was the Honolulu seamen's chaplain, and he used his publication as a weapon in the movement to get sailors to renounce the most popular drug of the day—alcohol. News from around the globe was thus interspersed with testimonials about the evils of drink, and philosophical questions such as, "Is it Right to Take Whales on the Sabbath?" But Damon's own influence extended far beyond his newspaper because, like Baldwin of Lahaina, he ran the local bethel for seamen, as well as a reading room (only a short distance from the Hudson's Bay Company store), and preached to sailors. As one of his fans noted,

His audience is frequently composed of English lords and knights, consuls and consul generals, admirals and rear admirals, the king of the islands and his suite, the ardent votaries of wealth in the character of merchants and sea captains, naval officers of different nations, common seamen and Kanakas. . . . About four hundred seamen annual visit him at his study, to receive religious instruction and advice.[40]

In 1846 Damon wrote that he never allowed his visitors to leave "without

Temperance Advocate,
AND SEAMEN'S FRIEND.

| VOL. I. | HONOLULU, OAHU, SANDWICH ISLANDS, SEPT. 16, 1843. | No. IX. |

SEAMEN'S CHAPEL, Honolulu, Oahu.

Front page of the September 16, 1843 edition of what later became simply *The Friend*, showing Samuel C. Damon's Seamen's Chapel in Honolulu.

carrying away a package, which usually consists of a bundle of tracts, some late copies of the Friend, perhaps a Bible and such other reading-matter as I am able to furnish him." But he also actively visited arriving ships, hospitals, and proselytized on the street, boasting of his paper that, "I find the Friend an invaluable ancillary to my usefulness among seamen. More than 1000 copies of each number are distributed gratuitous here, and at Lahaina."[41]

It was Damon who, on February 2, 1846, had first printed a detailed account of Mercator Cooper's visit to Japan. And in the months leading up to MacDonald's Japan adventure, his interest in Japan intensified. He and his paper increasingly scooped news about attempts to visit to Japan, shipwrecked American sailors in Japan, and shipwrecked Japanese sailors picked up by American ships. It was Damon who, in a December 1848 article widely reprinted throughout North America, would be the first to report Mac-Donald's infiltration into Japan. And while there is no record of Damon having met MacDonald, he was one of the first people MacDonald wrote after leaving Japan in 1849. He also personally befriended Japanese castaways in Honolulu and did everything he could to help the famous Manjirō and two surviving shipmates return to Japan in 1852.

Damon hoped Japan would someday be open to evangelization, but he knew it had to be opened for trade first. As he wrote on December 1, 1848, "There is a growing conviction throughout the civilized world, that the time is rapidly approaching when the exclusive policy of the Japanese will be done away with, and a commercial intercourse be opened between that and other nations of the earth, besides the Chinese and Dutch."[42] By 1849, Damon and *The Friend* were so widely known as a source of information on Japan that he would write, "Of late we have had persons make inquiries respecting Japan.—Should any desire additional information, they may find articles relating to that country in the following numbers of *The Friend*." And he then provided a list of all the relevant back number issues[43]

❋ ❋ ❋

Over at *The Polynesian*, editor Jarves matched, if not exceeded, Damon's interest in Japan. A free-thinker and something of a renaissance man, Jarves much later became an art critic and authored one of the first books on Japanese art. While in Honolulu, MacDonald may well have picked up Jarves's two books on Hawaiian history, as they were widely available and heavily promoted in *The Polynesian*. One of them, *Scenes and Scenery in the Sandwich Islands*, first published in 1844, reprinted Baldwin's article on shipwrecked Japanese sailors and their method of counting, and prefaced it with Jarves's comment that "Honolulu is quite a resort for the Japanese, who have either been wrecked on the shores of Oahu, or picked up at sea by vessels of other nations, after having been for months exposed to the casualties of the ocean, in their imperfect and rude barks."[44]

Jarves did not have Damon's network of contacts with whalemen, but as editor of the Hawaiian government's official paper he could present information in more of a geopolitical context, without a religious agenda. While MacDonald was in and out of the area, *The Polynesian*, too, ran more and more articles on Japan.

On May 27, 1846, *The Polynesian* reprinted a long column of news and rumors from the *Singapore Free Press*. It mentioned (in addition to reports of a huge fire in Edo) failed attempts by the French and Danish navies to initiate communication and trade with the Japanese, visits by European ships to the Japanese-controlled Ryūkyū Islands, and a whaling ship that had foundered near there and been helped by Japanese. It also reported that a British surgeon (presumably a missionary doctor named Bettelheim) had determined to stay on one of the Ryūkyū Islands with his wife and children and a Chinese interpreter, despite the refusal of the local people to have him.[45]

By fall, articles on Japan in *The Polynesian* had begun to explode in number. The trigger was the visit to Honolulu, in September, of a U.S. Navy warship, the U.S.S. *Columbus*. With one-hundred guns, the *Columbus* was the largest ship ever to dock in the islands. For three weeks, Honolulu hosted its commander, Commodore James Biddle, of the U.S. East India Squadron, and a large crew of sailors, all of whom had just returned from an extraordinary visit to Japan in late July.

Biddle had tried to deliver an official letter from the U.S. government to the emperor, requesting relations. Like the whaling ship, the *Manhattan*, the U.S.S. *Columbus* (along with the *Vincennes*, which did not stop in Honolulu) had sailed to the entrance of the bay leading up to Japan's capital, Edo. Biddle had just been in China, where—in the wake of the humiliating defeat inflicted on China by the British—the United States had been able to conclude a treaty. His orders were therefore to see if Japan might also have opened its ports, and to ascertain whether a trade treaty could be negotiated with Japan, too. He had been instructed to avoid creating a sense of hostility or distrust toward the United States, and to proceed with extreme caution. Luckily for him, his visit came at a time when the Japanese government had relaxed its Seclusion Laws, and coastal batteries were no longer required to automatically fire on foreign visitors.

Japanese officials came out to meet Biddle at the entrance to Edo Bay. They had an interpreter with them named Tatsunosuke Horii, but there were then no interpreters in all of Japan with a good grasp of English, and Horii had a terrible time translating the American requests. Days were spent trying to figure out what Biddle wanted. When asked, the Japanese supplied the waiting U.S. ships with food and water and firewood, at no charge. Eventually, however, they informed Biddle that foreign ships were only allowed to visit at Nagasaki and that even there it was useless to ask for permission to trade, because Japan's ancestral laws forbade it. Finally, the officials told the commander to go away and never come back. But just before the U.S. ships were towed out to sea an unfortunate incident occurred. In the process of stepping aboard a Japanese boat to receive a communication, Commodore Biddle was shoved by a Japanese guard, who reportedly drew his sword. Only profuse apologies from Japanese officials averted a major disaster.[46]

The Polynesian ran the first report of Biddle's exciting visit to Japan on September 12. This article was reprinted in *The Friend* and later in newspapers throughout North America. On September 19, *The Polynesian* ran another article on Biddle's visit, noting that a French frigate had been expected to try the same approach to opening Japan even before Biddle, but had abandoned the effort. The reason, the newspaper implied, was that

> The Japanese officers, instead of killing their enemies have an awkward practice of ripping themselves up when unable to fulfill the mandates of their Emperor. To force a landing under such circumstances would result therefore in the voluntary death of innocent parties. Humanity recoils at the idea and desires of intercourse become powerless before opposition of such a character.[47]

On October 30, 1847, after weeks of reporting on the U.S. war with Mexico, *The Polynesian* ran a copy of Biddle's official report to the secretary of the navy on his visit to Japan. Written on board the U.S.S. *Columbus* off the coast of Japan, the report was already a year old, but it contained a detailed, first-hand account of what had happened, with new information. Biddle explained that the Japanese had refused to look at the copies of treaties with China that had been brought to show them; that Japan still refused all foreign ships, except those of the Dutch at Nagasaki in the south; and that the Dutch monopoly with Japan was unprofitable and probably being maintained for symbolic value. He further emphasized that, while the Japanese had not let the Americans land or send boats to shore, they had generously supplied the U.S. ships with the large amounts of fresh water they required.

In a day when personal and national honor were paramount, Biddle feared the American government and public might think negatively of his mild response to the rogue Japanese guard. While personally outraged at the man's behavior, he stressed that the Japanese officials had convinced him it was all due to a misunderstanding, "owing to bad interpretation," and that they had apologized and tried "in every way to appease me." He would not have communicated the matter, he concluded, "except to guard against any incorrect statement that may appear in the public prints."[48]

The next issue of *The Polynesian*, on November 6, 1847, contained a reprint of another long account of the U.S.S. *Columbus*'s visit, this time by a ship's officer. Unlike Biddle's official report, this article included a description of Japan. The writer was severely constrained in his understanding, because, like all foreigners, he could neither read nor speak Japanese, and he had never been allowed off ship. Nonetheless, he reported with relative accuracy on Japan's feudal system, religions, arts and crafts, military outfits, education, writing system, and traditional fear of foreigners and Christianity. Like most Americans fascinated by the samurai system of ritual suicide to avoid dishonor, he grossly misunderstood what he heard (through interpreters or sign language or rumor), writing that "In case of earthquakes or storms, from which the Islands suffer every few months, the authorities order numbers of the people to appease the offended deity, and the order is at once obeyed." His conclusion, at the end of his report, was that "[t]aken altogether, the Japanese are a plain, simple, unostentatious people, and whether the other nations will succeed in opening intercourse with them, remains to be seen. A French fleet was to visit Jeddo after us, to be followed by an English fleet, which latter will probably batter down their walls."[49]

Of all the accounts on Japan published in Hawaiian newspapers in 1847, those regarding Biddle's visit on the U.S.S. *Columbus* are especially intriguing because, in his surviving writings, MacDonald specifically mentions having read them. On June 4, 1891, near the end of his life, he wrote an old friend, straining to explain his long-ago adventure to Japan. The letter contains errors in spelling, names, and events, but it reveals that he had gained information from *The Polynesian* before leaving for Japan, and that after leaving Japan he had read Damon's article on him in the December 1848 edition of *The Friend*. The latter reported on MacDonald's attempt to enter Japan in a little lifeboat, dubbed "The Young *Plymouth*," and compared his efforts and those of Mercator Cooper on the *Manhattan* to the heavily financed and state-sponsored efforts of Biddle on the U.S.S. *Columbus*. In MacDonald's words:

> You mentioned the failure of Commodore Briddle in the Columbus Seventy-four to open a commercial treaty with Japan. . . . Having read an Account of the failure of the expedition & of the repulse &

the Commodore personally insulted, it was a surprise to many that he did not open his batteries & give the Japanese a taste of shot-shell & canister however the press at the time commended his policy of moderation. This circumstance was one of my rasons for adopting the plan I did, going all alone. As one of the Sandwich Island papers puts it, the young "Plymouth" "the name he called my Boat" accomplished what the Columbus failed to do, or words to that effect.[50]

❖ ❖ ❖

Exactly what date MacDonald left the Hawaiian Islands on the *Plymouth* for Hong Kong and thence the seas around Japan is not clear. Judging from records in Honolulu and Hong Kong papers it was sometime in the latter half of November 1847. According to *The Friend*, right before leaving Hawaii the *Plymouth* docked at Honolulu on November 14 along with the *David Paddock*, a Nantucket whaling ship with which it traveled. It was a time when local interest in Japan was reaching a fever pitch.

The day before, on November 13, *The Polynesian* had reported that the king of Holland had "strongly recommended the Emperor of Japan to throw open his country to Europeans so as not to run the risk of being bombarded into civilization like the Chinese."[51] The next issue, on November 20, ran an article on Captain Jackson, of the whaling ship *Inez*, who in the spring of that year had landed on the shores of Japan, in the straits between Hokkaidō and Honshū Islands. While the *Inez* laid at anchor for three days, Jackson had visited a local temple and unsuccessfully tried to trade. He had been met by a large force of armed samurai and asked to leave, but he had been well treated and provided with food and water.[52] The following issue of *The Polynesian*, on November 27, reported that in the spring yet another disabled and drifting Japanese junk had been picked up in the Pacific, this time by a German whaling ship, the *Otaheite*. The starving crew of nine men had been kept on board for four weeks and then transferred to a Japanese junk, found in the straits between Honshū and Hokkaidō. But the *Otaheite* had brought the junk's cargo back to Honolulu, where it was sold at an enormously popular auction for several thousand dollars.[53] Around the same time, the newspaper reported, the *Frances Henrietta* (a New Bedford whaler) had also come across a disabled Japanese junk, adrift for seven months, its crew reduced from seventeen to four through starvation and perhaps cannibalism. After transferring the Japanese survivors to another junk in the area, the *Frances Henrietta* also had brought back the junk's cargo to Honolulu, where the goods soon "scattered among our residents."[54]

"We begin to feel ourselves as near neighbors to Japan," the editor of *The Polynesian* wrote. "We think . . . the signs of the times are threatening to the barrier of exclusion the Japanese government would so rigidly maintain. England, France and the United States ardently desire to effect a breach in this policy. They perhaps have too high a sense of national honor to do this by mere force of arms, but circumstances now appear to be preparing the way for their intervention in some shape." After saying that he believed the whaling fleet was destined "to do something in this cause," the editor went on to point out that hundreds of whalers were now prowling the coasts of Japan in search of prey, and that they would inevitably be tempted to land for wood, water, and provisions, or be forced ashore by bad weather or emergencies. Since whaling ships would also be encountering more and more disabled Japanese junks, he advised the whaling ship masters to carry the survivors and their cargo to Japan, and further make a good impression on the Japanese.[55]

In its December 13 issue *The Polynesian* outdid itself, devoting many thousands of words to Japan, summarizing in a remarkably accurate fashion nearly everything that was then known about the "tabooed country"—from information brought back by whalers and from books written by those who had actually visited the land with the Dutch (and presumably knew what they were talking about). It was a special feature that would have been priceless to anyone contemplating going to Japan. As *The Polynesian*'s editor had written a year earlier, after the failed visit of the U.S.S. *Columbus*, "How long Japan will be enabled to maintain herself as a *terra incognita*, is a problem of great interest to us lovers of something new. In the present age it is almost the only country there would be any excitement in visiting, or that could furnish a taking book."[56]

CHAPTER 8

Rishiri Island: The Adventure Begins

Against the strong and earnest remonstrances of the Captain and crew, I stepped into my boat. . . . My comrades refused to unloose the knot which bound me to them. . . . Myself, with averted face, had to cut the rope by which I hung to all of them. I felt in the cord the strong electric sympathy bursting from the true friendly hearts of my comrades. With a quivering "God bless you, Mac!" they bade me a long, and, as they thought, a last adieu![1]

Off the coast of Hokkaidō, on June 27, 1848, MacDonald made his rendezvous with history. His published *Narrative* contains many inconsistencies, but from this point on, until leaving Japan in the spring of 1849, it becomes far more detailed, and accurate, for the first two months in Japan are based on a section of his original journal that survives. His story can also be verified through a process of historical triangulation, using Japanese and other contemporary records. The basic facts are indisputable. MacDonald was a twenty-four-year-old crewman on the *Plymouth*. He had arranged nearly a year earlier with the captain to be taught navigation and to be let off the coast of Japan in a small boat with a sail. He was about to enter the unknown, or what his crewmates considered certain death. For this priv-

East Asia and Japan.

ilege, he had given up a small fortune in wages, traveled immense distances, and already survived extraordinary dangers.

Another account of the same moment survives from a crewmate with the initials "E. P. F.," who provided it, five months after the fact, to *The Friend* in Honolulu. It was nine o'clock on a beautiful morning, the man recalled, and the *Plymouth* stood off an island visible in the distance that was shrouded in a light mist. MacDonald had been given his choice of the ship's boats, with a sail attached; it was "a center-board-boat, partly decked over and very strong for one of her kind." The crew lowered the little boat, and put his effects into it. These consisted of "a quadrant, 'epitomy,' two pistols, two small kegs of water, keg of meat, barrel of bread, anchor, 35 fathoms of tow line, and oars. His own chest was nearly full of books of various kinds." MacDonald set foot in the boat, the *Plymouth* towed it behind briefly, and then he

let go the line and was clear from us forever. His little vessel dashed over the waves like an arrow. All hands had gathered aft to see the last of the bold adventurer. He took off his hat and waved it, but in silence. . . . He was watched from the masthead until he was gone from our sight forever. . . . The last we saw of the little vessel she was standing in for a small bay on the north side of the island. . . . Every man on board felt sad to see a shipmate leave the ship under such circumstances.[2]

The crewmate described MacDonald as "a man of about five feet seven inches, thick set, straight hair and dark complexion," and "a good sailor, well educated, a firm mind, well calculated for the adventure upon which he had embarked. . . . No one can blame Capt. Edwards for leaving the man in such a manner, for he advised him until his boat was launched over the side not to go on such a hazardous voyage, but no, his mind was not to be changed."[3]

After returning to Sag Harbor in the *Plymouth* in 1849, Edwards was quoted as saying the ship had been homeward bound, "[W]hen one morning McDonald came aft and demanded his discharge. . . . Of course, I was taken all aback at his request, as I had supposed that he would leave us at the Sandwich Islands where we were to touch on our

Hokkaidō, formerly known as "Ezo."

way. He asked for a boat and provisions, and reminded me of our agreement, stating that he had performed his part in accordance with its terms, and insisted on a strict fulfillment on my part."[4]

Edwards claimed it was "a wild and fool-hardy expedition" but that since MacDonald would not pay him any heed he had been forced to outfit the boat and make "other arrangements for his safety as my experience suggested," which included giving him provisions and water for at least a month's consumption. In addition to guns and ammunition and fishing line, the captain made sure MacDonald had a "tub of sand," cooking utensils, and firewood in the boat so that he could cook.[5]

On an ominous note, the article in *The Friend* mentioned that several days after MacDonald left the *Plymouth*, another American whaler, the *Uncas*, had been "cruising in the region [and] picked up the rudder of his tiny craft. . . . Whether she reached the shore or was swamped in the surf remains a profound mystery."[6] This final report, combined with the fact that no word was heard of MacDonald for nearly a year, led many to assume he might have been lost at sea.

From Hawaii to the Sea of Japan

It had taken MacDonald a long time to get into position for his adventure. After leaving the Hawaiian Islands in late November 1847, the *Plymouth* and *David Paddock* had sailed west, stopping at the Mariana Islands, sailing past the Bonins, then stopping again in the Batanes (south of today's Taiwan) and catching many sperm whales in the area. After encountering fierce gales in the China Seas, the two ships finally docked in Hong Kong on January 15, 1848, and stayed for three weeks, refitting the ships and readying for a cruise in the Sea of Japan. The *Plymouth* hired four new Filipino crewmen.[7]

In Hong Kong, too, the talk had been of Japan. On February 3, an article appeared in the local *China Mail* discounting a rumor flying about port to the effect that "the English, French, and Americans, have all brought their ships of war to China, really because they wish to go to Japan to revenge themselves for their soldiers who were formerly killed there." As the editor pointed out, this was the third or fourth time that the same rumor had emerged among the Chinese population, and the nations mentioned had neither soldiers to be killed in Japan nor warships collected in Hong Kong intent on revenge.[8]

Finally, on February 9, the two ships departed for the Sea of Japan. They first sailed to Bataan to get fresh vegetables but, in a portent of problems to come, arrived too early in the season. Then they proceeded north, past the Ryūkyū Islands, which were loosely controlled by Japan, and spent considerable time whaling around today's Cheju (then called "Quelpart") Island, immediately south of the Korean Peninsula. MacDonald found Cheju beautiful, but he was intrigued most of all by its strategic possibilities. Given the island's location, he was puzzled that the British had not occupied it and turned it into a Pacific version of Malta, their fortified island in the Mediterranean. In his journal, he would write, "I saw that in not a very distant day a brisk trade would [be] carried on from Oregon & California if not from the whole of the United States. I saw no reason why the Whitny plan could not be put in execution, that of establishing a Railroad to Oregon. And in the event of Japan opening her ports, Quelperts Island would then command both empires of China and Japan."[9]

At last, on March 26 the two ships entered the Sea of Japan, where they would spend over three months whaling. On a map, the sea looks like a giant lake. Its western boundary is formed by the Asian continent, by Russia,

China, and the Korean Peninsula; to the east is the Japanese archipelago and Sakhalin Island, effectively shielding the sea from the Pacific Ocean. The Japan Sea is relatively shallow and calm, and because a branch of the Japan Current flows through it, the northernmost reaches are considerably warmer than otherwise. At the time, the Sea of Japan was famous for its right whales, which swim slowly and are relatively easy to catch—unlike deep-diving, open-sea sperm whales, which require great skill and courage to capture. As MacDonald writes, during three months in the Sea of Japan, "[W]e had invariably calms or very light breezes scarcely to fill our top sails. The whales were numerous. We had no occasion to chase them with our ship, nothing to do but lower our boats, harpoon them and bring them alongside, where the usual process takes place of stripping the blubber from them."[10]

By May 19, the *Plymouth* already had 3,800 barrels of oil and was well on its way to the nearly 5,000 barrels with which it would end up.[11] As the season progressed, the ship moved north up into the narrow Tartary Straits, where the Japan Sea is almost pinched shut between Sakhalin and the Asian mainland and barely exits into the Sea of Okhotsk. The *Plymouth* then turned south toward Japan again, capturing more whales. There were more and more thick fogs.

The *Plymouth* and *David Paddock* were hardly alone. American whaling newspapers were filled with reports of ships being "spoken" in the Sea of Japan. In the last whaling ground, MacDonald writes, that "during the day there were about 25 to 30 ships in sight," and that some of the whales caught had New Bedford irons stuck in them.[12] But Americans were not the only ones spotting American ships; Japanese guards manning the northernmost outpost of Sōya—facing Sakhalin across the narrow straits where the Japan Sea leaks out into the Pacific—were also observing scores of foreign ships, and they were becoming increasingly alarmed but powerless to do anything. Jotham Newton, the sailor on the *Uncas* in the same area at the same time as MacDonald, noted in his journal how one night his ship accidentally ran into a Japanese fishing boat; some of his crewmates went on board the boat to make sure the Japanese were okay, and then the *Uncas* continued on its way.[13]

The Risk

In 1848, most American whaling ship crews knew it was illegal and dangerous to land on Japanese soil, but they did not know the reasons Japan's Seclusion Laws had been enacted in the first place. Between 1543—when the Portuguese first arrived—and 1636, there had been European traders and missionaries in Japan, and in the south many Japanese had converted to Christianity. The Japanese had, in their own right, once been aggressive traders, pirates, and settlers throughout Southeast Asia. In fact, in 1612 one mission of 183 merchants and samurai had even traveled to Mexico, some members crossing overland and going all the way to Spain, while others remained in Acapulco and Mexico City for as long as six years.[14]

But this internationalist period had ended around 1635 when the Shogunate—fearing European (particularly, Portuguese and Spanish) encroachment and the subversive influence of Christianity—enacted its Seclusion Edicts. Practicing Christianity was made punishable by death. Contact with the outside world was limited to a tiny amount of trade conducted at the southern port of Nagasaki with the Dutch and Chinese, and occasional communication with Korea and the Ryūkyū Islands. Otherwise, foreigners were no longer allowed into Japan, and Japanese were no longer allowed out.

The Seclusion Edicts were interpreted in a variety of ways during the nearly two and a half centuries they were in effect. In 1640, when the Portuguese sent a ship to Japan, to beg that the ban on contact be lifted, the ship was burned and most of the crew executed.[15] In 1825, in response to increasing encroachments on its territory, the Shogunate issued its notorious *uchiharai* (expulsion) decree, whereby all foreign ships approaching Japanese soil, even in distress, were to be automatically fired upon. As noted previously, only a decade before MacDonald's arrival, in 1837, the *Morrison* had tried to repatriate some Japanese castaways (including the "three kichis") and been fired upon in Edo Bay, a cannon ball ripping through its upper deck. MacDonald claimed never to have heard of this incident, but among foreigners it contributed greatly to the general mythology of Japan as a forbidden, dangerous place.

By 1848 the *uchiharai* policy had been revoked, but foreign ships still were forbidden to land. If anything, the Japanese authorities were even more afraid of the outside world—the British, after all, were expanding into southern Asia, the Russians were pushing into the north, and American whaling ships were swarming by the hundreds into neighboring seas. Nonetheless, with the relaxation of the law, when shipwrecks or other emergencies did bring whaling ship crews onto Japanese soil, they could now be given food and water and quickly sent away or, if that was impossible, arrested and sent to the southern port of Nagasaki. There, the hapless sailors would be interrogated, forced to step on a Christian religious image, and deported on the annual Dutch trading ship.

By 1848, exaggerated tales of cruelty to shipwrecked American crewmen were common among the sailing community and in newspapers in the United States, leading to calls for the American government to do something. In one particularly notorious incident in 1846, sailors from the whaler *Lawrence* were wrecked off the coast of Japan's northern frontier. One of the men—it was reported—was mortally wounded by a Japanese guard while trying to escape from prison. MacDonald had heard of this event while in Hong Kong, but as he wrote in typical style in his *Narrative*, "it did not frighten me."[16]

Reasons for the Adventure

Knowing the dangers, why did MacDonald choose to leave the *Plymouth* as he did? And what was his true goal? Surviving records give varied and elusive answers to these most central questions and suggest that he may have had multiple reasons.

MacDonald had an innate sense of curiosity, and later in life he specifically stated that "My principal motive in this was, it must be confessed, the mere gratification of a love of adventure."[17] This is supported by many documents from the time that describe him as an "adventurer," as well as by an interview of May 23, 1849, conducted in Hong Kong, in which he is described as having been "anxious to explore Japan."[18] The New Bedford *Whalemen's Shipping List*, on August 14 of the same year, was even more explicit, reporting that "[h]e intended to explore Japan, and then write an account of his observations."[19]

In a letter addressed to his father before leaving the *Plymouth*, MacDonald says he had considered being discharged on the Spanish *Main*, leaving open the intriguing possibility that at one point he may not even have been fixated on going to Japan for his adventure at all.[20] But of his stated reasons for choosing Japan, specifically, one of the clearest explanations appears in an 1850s draft of his *Narrative*:

The mysterious veil of mystery which then hung, as it still hangs, over that strange realm, unaccountably attracted my roving mind, and at any risk, I determined to solve it. Having heard that which I thought might induce them to engage me as an instructor on history, geography, commerce, and modern art, and the Bible: this I did in expectation of being engaged by them as a teacher.[21]

MacDonald also implies that his adventure might have been hastened by conditions on board the *Plymouth*. On May 24, 1849, while in Hong Kong immediately after leaving Japan, he dashed off a rough letter to Samuel C. Damon, publisher of *The Friend* in Honolulu, saying,

> It is very improbable that I should ever visit Japan had I not been actuated by curiosity and other causes. You probably remember when the first ships arrived from the Japan Sea, how they reported that sea to be full of whale.
>
> I saw the inconvenience which must arise among the shipping, so you are perfectly aware that Captains are very loath to leave the whaling ground when they have an opportunity of killing even at the expense of men. It must be still fresh in your memory—how on the year 1847 ships arriving at the Island were infected with the scurvy.[22]

By the mid-nineteenth century, scurvy was becoming less common, as captains had generally learned to prevent it by replenishing their stock of fruits and vegetables. But whaling ships tended to stay out on the open sea for months to fish, and around Japan—where whales were plentiful and landing was dangerous—greed entered into the equation. As one newspaper put it in 1847, scurvy was on the rise among whaling ships, caused by "the flattering prospects of the fishery in the sea of Okhotsk [near Japan], having kept them out so long."[23] Not coincidentally, scurvy broke out on the *Plymouth* right after MacDonald was left off, and all four Filipino crewmen hired in Hong Kong died. On returning to Honolulu, Captain Edwards reported to *The Friend* that on the voyage he had slaughtered a hog and ordered "the sick men to be bathed in the blood, and the inwards to be bound on warm, not knowing what else to do for them, which I testify is a great relief in cases of scurvy."[24]

In MacDonald's rough letter to Damon, it is scurvy that he alludes to when he gives his deeply encompassing explanation for his adventure:

To remove in a measure this inconvenience, encouraged also by my dark complection and my near resemblance to the Japanese in features, I should certainly would not let the opportunity pass of learning the language and the country.[25]

"E.P.F.," the fellow crewmate who submitted a report to *The Friend* in December 1848, gave a more fleshed-out explanation of MacDonald's motive in being let off near Rishiri Island, saying,

His intentions were to stay at this island and learn some of the Japanese language, and from there go down to Jeddo the principal city of Nepon, and if the English or Americans ever open a trade with the Japanese, he would find employment as an interpreter. He had other intentions which I never heard him mention only in a secret manner.[26]

What were these secret intentions? There are two possibilities. Early drafts of MacDonald's *Narrative* imply that he had a missionary urge because of his upbringing, for as his long-time editor friend McLeod once wrote, as a young man MacDonald "was ever of deep religious life."[27] This may help explain why—despite knowing the extreme danger—MacDonald took a Bible along with him in his little boat, as well as a Church of England prayer book. As a Protestant and perpetual optimist, MacDonald reasoned, as he later wrote, that the Japanese "condemnation of Christianity was more particularly of that form of it known as Roman Catholic"—the missionary efforts of which had caused Japan to enact its policy of isolation in the first place.[28] The second possibility, alluded to in a draft of his manuscript, also rings true. It is, furthermore, an explanation that he indeed might not have wanted to be made public at the time: "Early in life I mapped out a career for myself which would be not unlike that of the autocratic fur trader, who in reality was a power ruler in his own petty kingdom. I thought the Japanese to be much the same as the Indians."[29]

Alone at Sea

To accomplish his goal, MacDonald had to devise a plan of action that would allay Japanese suspicions that he was an infiltrator. In an extraordinary leap of faith, he was convinced that if he could pretend to be a shipwrecked sailor they would take pity upon him: "With all their reputed cruelty to foreigners, I assumed or half believed, that even Japanese would have some compassion on such of their fellow men as storm or uncontrollable circumstances should cast upon their shores."[30]

According to Captain Edwards's account, MacDonald came to remind him of their deal when the ship was on its way home, at 35° North and 160° East of Japan, coordinates in the Pacific considerably to the east of Japan and south of Hokkaidō Island.[31] If true, this meant the *Plymouth* backtracked into the Sea of Japan, for MacDonald was finally let off south of Rishiri Island, near the western end of La Perouse or Sōya Strait, which runs between Hokkaidō and Sakhalin islands. In his *Narrative*, MacDonald writes that the sea was foggy, with "no land in view." The *Plymouth* "went one way and I the other. She hoisted the stars & stripes dipping it several times which I answered by dipping a little white flag which I had provided."[32]

MacDonald began sailing northeast in his little boat, in a light wind, but exactly what course he took is subject to some debate, as there are contradictions in the 1849 deposition he gave to the U.S. Navy (after his release from Japan) as well as in the descriptions he wrote much later and in the map he provided for his *Narrative*. In any case, he came across two small islands. He narrowly averted rocks and surf near one—probably today's Teuri—and fell in with a herd of *todo*, or twelve-foot-long Steller's "sea lions," grunting "wo! wo!" and sounding like the "compound bark of a large deep-mouthed dog and the bellow of a bull." To test out his pistol he shot one of the sea lions. Then he landed in the bay of the other small island, which he had been told by his captain was inhabited, but he could find no people. He spent two days there, sleeping inside his boat, experiencing what he calls a "Robinson Crusoe life," plotting and refining his "plan of invasion." By lying low for a while, he hoped to make it more difficult for any Japanese he might later meet to connect him with the *Plymouth*, and to assume he was deliberately trying to enter their empire.[33]

The first island on which MacDonald landed, Yagishiri, is only 3.3 miles square, and separated by only 2.5 miles from Teuri, its tiny neighboring twin. Easily visible from the western coast of Hokkaidō, Japan's northernmost main island, Yagishiri was actually inhabited at the time, for on the other side, where MacDonald apparently never explored, was a small outpost of Japanese. In fact, Yagishiri, or "Yangeshiri" as it was then known, had one of the older outposts in the area, dating back to 1746 and dedicated mainly to fishing, especially herring.

From Yagishiri, MacDonald spotted another island almost due north, with a "snow-capped mountain, rising as if from the centre of the Island."[34] This was Rishiri, near which he had originally asked be to let off. It appeared to him to be about ten miles away, and he resolved to head toward it, but why he did so is today something of a mystery. Rishiri is actually over forty-five miles north of Yagishiri, and it was then an island well known to Westerners, MacDonald in fact referring to it as "Timoshee," the same name used by early English explorers. Yet had MacDonald's goal truly been to infiltrate Japanese territory unobserved, it would have made more sense to head, not north to Rishiri, but directly east to the shore of Hokkaidō. Not only is mainland Hokkaidō far closer—in contrast to the 3.3-square-mile Yagishiri or the 114-square-mile Rishiri, it is a whopping 30,130 square miles, nearly the same size as South Carolina. MacDonald could have landed in a depopulated area and been able to plan his next course of action without being detected.

People living on Rishiri today and visitors from abroad have speculated that fog banks may have influenced MacDonald's course, that he may have feared Hokkaidō was governed too tightly by government forces, or that he went north simply because sea currents and the winds flow in that direction. Some have even surmised that he was subconsciously drawn to Rishiri's snow-capped mountain because it is one of the most striking landmarks in the area and resembles Mt. Hood in the land of his birth.[35] On the other hand, he had been told that people were present on Rishiri, and for his purposes he probably did not want to land where there was no one at all; if his goal had really been to live off the land for a while he would have taken a long gun instead of two pistols.

Be that as it may, during the day of June 30 MacDonald practiced overturning his boat in the open water, so that he could pretend to be in distress (or, as he put it, "destitute") before actually landing. Then he spent another night on Yagishiri, and on July 1 he sailed north for Rishiri. At ten in the morning, five or six miles from Rishiri (a considerable ways out), he claims he deliberately overturned his boat by turning out the reef in his sail. Because he had forgotten to lock his sea chest, however, he also accidentally lost much of his clothing, one pistol, some books, his bailer, and even his rudder (later retrieved by the *Uncas*). Undaunted, he says he "unstepped my mast, righted my boat, restepped my mast, set my sail and stood towards the land."[36] After once more righting his boat closer in, he nearly met disaster because he fell overboard and barely managed to swim back to his boat. That night he waited off shore, staying put in the boat. If he were trying to appear destitute, at this point it would not have been difficult. Captain Edwards claimed to have given him his pick of the boats on the Plymouth, but after leaving Japan MacDonald would bitterly complain that he had given over his wages to the captain in exchange for "a nearly condemned boat and very little apparatus."[37]

At dawn, on July 2, MacDonald glimpsed smoke on Rishiri, and watched as men came toward him in a large skiff from a little village. He pulled the plug on his own boat and let it fill partially with water to affect an emergency, then tried to induce the men to assist him in bailing his boat and towing it to shore. When these people reached him, he says that they bowed and "salaam"-ed, and "continued in their mode of salutation which was to run both hands and stroke their beards down then stretch both forward with the palms up moved them up and down uttering a guttural sound. I became impatient, for this piece of novelty had continued from the time they hove up without any intermission by either one or the other and sometimes, by all hands, to make them desist."[38]

Instead of Japanese, MacDonald had been met by the indigenous people of northern Japan, the Ainu. They finally helped him move toward shore, where he could see what appeared to be a village surrounded by beautifully green fields. Here, he imagined himself being taken in and protected by their wealthy master, "[h]aving heard and read of the very advanced state of civilization which the Japanese had acquired." But on shore he was again met by more Ainu, who saluted him as their compatriots in the boat had done. Showing considerable deference, they placed sandals on his feet and, taking him "gently by each wrist," helped him ascend "the steep and rocky bank."[39]

"I was greatly surprised to see before me a barren waste," MacDonald writes. "What I took at a distance for fields of wheat corn and other grain was nothing more than course [sic] rank grass, and fern. In crossing one of these fields my feet several times came in contact with stumps of brush wood and not being used to walking in sandals I often stumbled." The Ainu led him to a village, which consisted of "a large wooden house surrounded by a few miserable huts." He had arrived in the village of Notsuka, on the northeastern coast of Rishiri, and here he met his first Japanese. The man seemed to be a "person of consequence," who "had the front part of his head shaved and all the hair taken up and tied into a top knot with the que leaning forward, his dress . . . a long cotton garment kept round the body by a wide belt, and a pair of sandals, the sleeves on his robe were very much like those on the gown of Episcopal ministers; from this appearance I thought that he might be the priest." After being led to the main house and told to take off his sandals, MacDonald was shown to a room, given a gown to wear instead of his wet clothes, and fed a breakfast of boiled rice, roasted fish, shellfish, and pickles. He would spend ten days here, at Notsuka.[40]

The Ainu

In 1848, Rishiri was part of Japan's northern frontier, known as "Ezochi," which included all of Hokkaidō, the southern Kuriles, and even part of Sakhalin. In many ways it was a mirror image of the land of MacDonald's birth (in 1848, a new U.S. frontier). Rishiri lies just above the 45th parallel, only a tad south of the latitude of Astoria. The Ainu, the indigenous people in the area, had many parallels with the Indians of the Northwest coast of America. For centuries they had subsisted by hunting, gathering, and fishing; living close to nature, they enjoyed a rich animistic tradition and a highly developed mythology and sense of design. They were very different from the Japanese, not only in physique, hairiness, and demeanor, but also in the tattoos on their mouths and bodies and the striking, abstract patterns on their clothing.

MacDonald was one of the first North Americans to have contact with the Ainu, and in his posthumously published *Narrative* he speculates as to their origins. In early drafts, however, his comments on the Ainu were quite pithy, for at the time of his adventure he was more interested in the Japanese; he only added the Ainu sections forty-odd years later, after prodding by his friend McLeod (who, like many educated men of the late nineteenth century, was fascinated with the concept of "race" and had his own theories about racial origins that veered from the biblical to the crackpot). MacDonald's after-the-fact impressions are not altogether flattering. He thought the Ainu probably came from mainland Asia, or perhaps Sakhalin, "the Tartar country." "When I got among them," he says, "first my feeling was that I had got into a nest of pirates or Tartars, with their heavy beards, uncombed long hair, and unwashed faces; they looked uncouth and wild, both in person and in

"A Man and Woman of Volcano Bay." Ainu in happier times, as viewed by Europeans, ca. 1804. From an account of William Robert Broughton's 1796 voyage to Japan.

dress, comparing very unfavorably in this respect, with the clean, refined, and cultivated Japanese." Physically, they reminded him of some tribes along the coast of British Columbia, such as the Bella Coolas or Hydras, although he notes that the Hydras were far more fierce and warlike, and "will bend to no man."[41]

Because of the Ainu's hairiness, round eyes, and large bones, many popular writers in the West until recently distinguished them from the Japanese by calling them "Caucasians." It was a romantic notion, exaggerating the "mirror-image" analogy to North America, where the "Caucasians" subjugated the Native Americans, who were often said to be of "Asiatic" origin. Today, the real origin of the Ainu is unclear, but MacDonald's speculations may not have been too far off the mark. The Tartars are actually a Turkic-speaking people from Russia and Central Asia, a once-nomadic tribe that had intermixed with the Mongols under Genghis Khan. Most anthropologists today consider the Ainu to be descendants of proto-Caucasoids, or descendants of a Paleolithic people from mainland East Asia mixed with other unknown groups. Recent theories also indicate that some early Native Americans may have represented "an unspecialized early Caucasoid form related to the Ainu of Japan."[42] The true origins of the Ainu aside, MacDonald wrote of them that "I shall ever gratefully remember their Samaritan kindness," and he described them as being extremely gentle, simple, meek, and deferential. He understood quickly, however, that they were "a subject race," firmly under the control of the Japanese.[43]

Like many North American Indian tribes, the Ainu were once proud hunters, fishermen, and fierce warriors. Formerly the rulers of Hokkaidō, and even some of the northern part of Japan's central island, Honshū, they were an essentially Stone Age people, lacking a writing system and a unifying political structure. As such, they were unable to compete with the more organized and technologically sophisticated Japanese, or *wajin*, who over the centuries had moved up from the south.

Friction and mistrust were common between Japanese traders and the Ainu, and clashes often erupted over trading disputes and perceived ill-treatment, especially when Japanese gold miners entered the area and (as in North America) disease ravaged the Ainu population. The last major Ainu uprising—Japan's version of Little Big Horn—took place around June 20, 1669, sparked partly by rumors that Japanese were poisoning the Ainu. A charismatic chief named Shakushain led a combined force of Ainu groups for two months against the Japanese Matsumae Domain in southern Hokkaidō, and around three hundred people were killed. At a peace parley between the two forces, however, Shakushain and his top lieutenants were murdered.[44]

From then on, Ainu civilization steadily declined, from demoralization, further disease, and loss of territory; in one seventy-year period between 1804 and the end of Japan's feudal government, the population is said to have dropped seventy percent.[45] By the time MacDonald arrived in 1848, Ainu throughout the Hokkaidō area had been reduced to complete subservience to the Japanese, and to the Matsumae Domain. Today, although there has been a great revival of interest in Ainu culture and ethnic pride among those who consider themselves Ainu, so much intermarriage and cultural assimilation have taken place with Japanese that in 1997 the *Encyclopedia Brittanica* referred to traditional Ainu culture as "virtually extinct."[46]

Under Guard

At Notsuka, on Rishiri Island, MacDonald was well treated. He was always watched but allowed to go outside, and he had "the privilege of rambling in the immediate vicinity."[47] There were books in the room in which he was lodged, and his own effects were brought in from his boat and dried. On the second day, he met two Japanese overseers of the island, whom he understood to be named "Kemon" and "Kechinza" (or "Kehenga"). They inventoried his possessions in excruciating detail, and were particularly fascinated by an English book with its alphabet letters, which they would look at "one way then reverse it and talk over it." Of his meat-filled keg, they were appalled, for Japanese in those days generally followed the Buddhist precept of not eating animal flesh. Like any good budding interpreter, MacDonald began writing down Ainu words he heard on a slate that he had brought with him, but otherwise he communicated by sign language.[48]

On the third day, Kechinza told MacDonald that he was going to report his presence to the closest official Japanese outpost at Sōya, on the tip of Hokkaidō, some thirty miles away by boat. In the interim, MacDonald became friends with another Japanese, whom he remembered as "Tangaro," who seemed fascinated by English words.[49] MacDonald tried to teach Tangaro English in exchange for Japanese and, amazingly, made a quill pen from a crow feather and used it to begin constructing a vocabulary list. "It was contrary to rule and desire for me to do so," he writes, alluding to Japanese prohibitions on foreigners learning their language. "Still, I managed to keep up my notes, and the habit."[50] He got Tangaro to trust him to an extraordinary degree, for while still at Notsuka he was taken aside into a nearby field and secretly shown a map of Japan, an act that normally would have resulted in extreme punishment, if not death, for a Japanese guard.

On the sixth day after his arrival, two Japanese junks anchored some ways from Notsuka, and several officers came to where MacDonald was staying. The next day, he was visited by half a dozen officers and some soldiers, and he was interrogated (apparently in sign language) as to where he had come from and why he had left his ship. He replied that he had had a disagreement with the captain. All his effects, including the contents of his chest, were "minutely examined" again and carefully inventoried. The men were particularly fascinated by his woolens, which were unknown to Japanese, who then kept no sheep. MacDonald himself was also measured. "Being five feet eight inches in height, and very broad shouldered and large chested—even stout in proportion, and muscular, I was something of a giant amongst them, their average height being, I would say, about five feet four inches or even less."[51]

On the eighth day after his arrival, MacDonald was marched between two officers and two lines of Ainu to the village of what he called Tootoomari (today's Hontomari), stopping along the way occasionally to smoke with everyone, apparently in a very friendly fashion. Near the village, ceremonial cotton-cloth curtains decorated with stripes and insignia hung on either side of the long line of the march. Symbolically, they ended his last semblance of freedom in Japan, as henceforth he would be a true prisoner, whatever he saw and observed highly circumscribed. At Hontomari, he was confined to a barred room in a house. It was clean, about twelve-foot square. Reflecting his always optimistic and accommodating nature, he writes, "Being well fed, kindly attended, and amply supplied with all conveniences, with the luxuries of tea and tobacco *ad libitum*, I had no reason to complain of my quarters."[52]

From this point on, MacDonald's posthumously published *Narrative* reflects the sudden change from the drama and excitement of his arrival on Rishiri to what must have been a monotonous life of confinement. The events of the first eleven or so days are described in great detail in sixteen pages, while the next thirty, until departure from Rishiri, are compressed into a simple paragraph. He simply mentions being guarded by Tangaro and another samurai, kept in his room, and allowed out only three times to take a bath in the house.

Searching for MacDonald on Rishiri, 1992

I first visited Rishiri Island on June 14, 1992, but even then it was not an easy place to reach. Getting to Tōkyō from overseas was no problem; it was the trip within Japan that took time. I opted for the land route, which meant overnight express trains headed north. Between Honshū and Hokkaidō islands—once a rough and sometimes treacherous ferry ride across the Tsugaru Straits—the first train zipped through the brand-new, thirty-four-mile-long undersea Seikan Tunnel. At the central Hokkaidō city of Sapporo, I rested briefly and then took another, much slower and rather grueling over-nighter—the "Rishiri Express"—to the end of the line at Japan's northernmost town, Wakkanai. Arriving shortly after dawn and feeling rather bleary-eyed, I staggered to the ferry terminal and boarded the 7:30 A.M. boat for the one-and-a-half-hour sea voyage west to Rishiri Island.

It was a nippy and overcast day, and as the massive steel-hulled car ferry churned through huge swells, it began to drizzle. I kept thinking of young MacDonald alone in his twenty-seven-foot wooden boat, being tossed on the rolling open sea, sailing forty-five miles from Yagishiri to Rishiri, soaked to the bone much of the time. Even at the end of June, the water and the wind can be bitterly cold.

Modern ferry docking,
Oshidomari, on Rishiri Island.

Photo © 1992 Frederik L. Schodt.

About an hour out of Wakkanai, Rishiri Island finally floated faintly into sight, and when a few rays of the sun made it through the clouds it was a spectacular sight. The island itself is formed by a towering, conical but dormant volcano that pushes straight out of the sea to 5,646 feet. Because the peak resembles the icon of all Japanese mountains—the beautiful but more southern Mt. Fuji—it is referred to as Rishiri-Fuji. With a cap of snow, it quickly dominated the field of view from the ferry as we neared.

The ferry docks in the little port town of Oshidomari, which lies nearly halfway between the spot where MacDonald landed on Rishiri, and where he finally left for Sōya. A climb to the top of the hill by the harbor affords a stunning view of not only the volcano (visible from nearly everywhere), but also, in summer, the flower-bedecked, nearly flat Rebun Island further to the north. Together, the islands form Japan's northernmost national park.

On a map, Rishiri looks tiny, but it takes about two hours to drive around it, and fourteen hours to walk. Almost everyone lives on the narrow coast, as the rest of the island is a giant mountain. Before the Japanese, Rishiri was populated by Ainu, and before the Ainu by the Okhotsk peoples. In MacDonald's time, Rishiri had less than a hundred people on it, most of whom were Ainu overseen by a few Japanese; records from 1822 reveal that Rishiri then had a population of only 116, but this figure may have included the population on neighboring Rebun, as well.[53] After World War II, Rishiri's population boomed to over 20,000, when refugees poured in from nearby Sakhalin, but today the population is only 6,422. The Ainu are all gone (or have melted into the Japanese population), and the island has a hard time retaining its young people, as life for humans on the island remains rough in the cold, snowy, and blustery winter months. Once in a while, the local harbor is closed by ice flows, and then the only contact with the Hokkaidō mainland is by small aircraft. The island's main industry is fishing, and has been so for centuries, but the growth industry today is tourism, especially in summertime. During August, when the average temperature climbs to a pleasantly warm 68°F, tourists flock to the island for the mountain climbing and the flowers.

Rishiri is also the first stop for all those seriously interested in Ranald MacDonald's story. On my first day there, I visited the island's main museum in Honchō and was thrilled to see an exhibit on MacDonald, with a display of both English and Japanese printed materials on him. It was the first place in Japan I had seen anything commemorating MacDonald. The exhibit's curator, Eiji Nishiya, seemed as excited by my visit and interest in MacDonald as I was to meet him. He gave me copies of all the information in his files, and drove me the rest of the way around the island. Along the way he showed me, among other things, Hontomari, the former site of the Japanese outpost on the island where MacDonald had been taken and, nearby, hidden in a grassy area, a shrine with a Shinto *torii* gateway dating back to around 1840 or so, which MacDonald may have described in his *Narrative*. Nishiya also told me about a memorial to MacDonald, where he had landed at Notsuka.

The next morning, I walked a few miles along the sole highway circling the island, from Oshidomari to Notsuka, moving fast to keep warm in the chilly, overcast weather. Notsuka today is a simple cluster of houses with a road through it, with a few fishing boats hauled up on land. When MacDonald approached from a distance, with its snow-capped mountain, forests, and lush greenery, Rishiri looked like an oasis, but as he describes in his journal, the spot at which he landed is indeed bleak. The beach, if it can be called that, is covered with dark volcanic rocks and boulders and rises steeply up to the grassy covered slopes that ring the island. It is a formidable-looking place to dock a small boat. Nonetheless, in 1992 there was a little plaque in English in the ground overlooking the shore and a carved wooden, totem-pole-esque sign in Japanese next to it, marking the spot. The plaque said:

In 1848 ("Kaei" 1), Ranald MacDonald born in Oregon, reached "Notsuka" pretending to be a shipwrecked sailor. He felt deep racial connections with Japan across the Pacific, although he knew of her total seclusion from the outside world. Inevitably he was arrested and sent to Nagasaki via Sōya and Matsumae. During his imprisonment in Japan he did his best for mutual understanding and friendship between two peoples, transcending language barriers. Five years later, when Commodore Perry came to force open the closed doors of Japan, MacDonald's former students at Nagasaki, Einosuke Moriyama and others, played an important role as official interpreters. Thus Ranald enjoys the honor of being the first formal teacher of English and indirectly a father of modernizing Japan.

Return to Rishiri, 1998

In September 1998, a time when I was far more involved in MacDonald's saga, I returned to Rishiri again, as part of a tiny delegation from the American Friends of MacDonald society. Five of us—all Japanese-Americans except me—had come to commemorate the 150th anniversary of MacDonald's landing in Japan.

North American fans of MacDonald's story often identify with his complex background and feel he was denied the recognition he was due. Often, they, too, have experienced what it is like to be an outsider. On the 1998 trip, our members included Massie Tomita and May Namba, two women from the Seattle Japanese-American community and World War II camp survivors, formerly involved in the Redress Movement. Atsumi Tsukimori, from Spokane, was one of the first persons to teach Japanese by satellite to Americans in eastern Washington; she saw her role in American society as almost a mirror image of MacDonald's in Japan, as he was one of the first teachers of English there. The leader of our group, Ken Nakano, had a background as dramatic as MacDonald himself. Born a U.S. citizen in the Seattle area, Nakano had moved with his adopted family to Hiroshima just before World War II. During the atomic bombing of 1945, he lost his mother and many schoolmates and was severely burned. On recovering, and after Japan's surrender, he joined the U.S. Army and served in Korea. Returning to America, he had a long career as an engineer and then became involved in a wide variety of causes, including veterans' issues, redress for Japanese-Americans incarcerated in World War II, and the "Down-Winder" Movement among residents near the Hanford nuclear facility in eastern Washington. A highly charismatic man and winner of the prestigious Jefferson Award for Public Service, Nakano was also an amateur history buff. His interest and identification with Japanese castaways—especially Otokichi, who drifted all the way from Japan to the Pacific Northwest in 1834—had led him to the story of Ranald MacDonald, whose adventures had taken him in the reverse direction.

Wherever we went on Rishiri, our little group was feted by the local people and officials. MacDonald, for that matter, seemed far better known in 1998 than he had been six years earlier. In Japan, as in North America, MacDonald is a niche figure, and interest in him comes in cycles, often stretched out over generations; that year the interest on Rishiri was especially strong because it was the 150th anniversary of his landing.

The charming little wooden memorial at Notsuka, first erected in 1987, was gone, blown away by a gale—and replaced by something far more grand and permanent. The old English-language plaque was now incorporated into a standing stone structure facing Mt. Rishiri. Next to it, overlooking the beach (with the modern port of Oshidomari in the distant background), was now another large stone monument, its face cut and polished to appear like two pages of an open book. The right side had a quotation from Akira Yoshimura's *Umi no sairei* [Festival of the sea]—an historical novel that is one of the main ways ordinary people in Japan learn of MacDonald today— and it lyrically described MacDonald's arrival on Rishiri. The left-hand side had another, special inscription by Yoshimura, topped by a circular bas-relief image of a young MacDonald. This inscription generally follows the text of the 1987 English plaque, but highlights a different aspect of MacDonald's contribution. Translated from the Japanese, it reads:

Ranald MacDonald, an American fascinated by Japan, left his whaling ship and landed alone on this shore on July 2, 1848. He was sent under guard to Nagasaki, where he became the first person to teach English conversation to Japanese. Those of his students who mastered English conversation were subsequently able to contribute to the diplomatic negotiations that took place between Japan and the world powers of the day, and thus to save Japan from the threat of destruction. As a result, this site where MacDonald landed on Rishiri Island is of great historical significance.

❖ ❖ ❖

Stone, typhoon-resistant monuments to long-gone persons usually require money, sponsoring organizations, and individuals who can act as local champions. In Ranald MacDonald's case, in both Japan and America the individuals who have served as his local champions have sometimes found it hard to put his accomplishments into a national and historical context. As a result, it has often been hard to enlist the help of organizations.

South of Rishiri, on tiny Yagishiri Island where MacDonald first landed, Hiroshi Ishikawa learned of him in the 1990s, when reading records of the island's early history. As a native of the island and a social studies teacher at its junior school, Ishikawa was shocked that he had never heard of MacDonald before. In doing further research, he realized MacDonald was a man "who encountered a variety of difficulties in his life, yet possessed a powerful dream and a global vision, and managed to overcome the handicaps he confronted." With his students, he therefore initiated a project to carve two Northwest American, Indian-style totem poles and erect them to commemorate MacDonald's landing.[54]

On Rishiri Island itself, Kyōji Furukawa was one of the very first residents to become fascinated by MacDonald. In 1966, while working for the local government, he visited the town of Haporo, on the coast of Hokkaidō directly opposite Yagishiri Island. Like Ishikawa would later, while reading about the local history, Furukawa came across a reference to a young American "castaway" having been on Yagishiri in 1848. Faintly recalling a similar reference to a young American "castaway" on Rishiri in the same time frame, he wondered if the two foreigners might not be the same person. Upon further research he confirmed it was the same man, but realized the foreigner had not been a castaway, but Ranald MacDonald, who had of his own volition landed first on Yagishiri and then Rishiri. As a Rishiri resident, Furukawa was bothered that he knew so little about such an interesting man. He later contacted the Prefectural Library in Nagasaki—the port far to the south where most foreign castaways had been sent in the old days and where many old records are still kept. "I still remember it," Furukawa says of his excitement in making the first call, "I was sweating nervously, and my female coworkers in the office were giggling at me."[55] Sure enough, the library sent him a copy of their official records on MacDonald.

From then on, Furukawa adopted Ranald MacDonald as a cause—not as

Friends of MacDonald at the Rishiri Island monument to MacDonald, on a windy day.

a historian but as a Rishiri resident who had made an important discovery about the island's history. When MacDonald's posthumously published *Narrative* was translated into Japanese by Torao Tomita in 1979, and when Akira Yoshimura authored his 1986 novel featuring MacDonald, Furukawa became one of their main contacts for information on Rishiri. And he worked to spread word of MacDonald to the island's young people and to support construction of a local monument. The Rishiri islander brings his own perspective to the MacDonald story, and to this day he finds it incredible that MacDonald could have deliberately capsized his twenty-seven-foot wooden boat before landing on Rishiri, and then been able to right it again. With experience in fishing and plenty of fishermen friends, he declares, "no ordinary man could have done it alone."

Subsequently, other individuals on Rishiri have become champions for MacDonald, too. By 1998, Eiji Nishiya, head of the Rishiri Town Museum, was actively trying to make the museum a repository of information on MacDonald and had even issued a Rishiri-based newsletter for the Japanese "Friends of MacDonald" society. In 2003, he also coordinated the publication of a new book in Japanese on MacDonald, with contributions by Japa-

From Lewis and Murakami's 1923 *Ranald MacDonald*. Daguerreotype originally in the possession of A. T. MacDonald, Great Falls, Montana.

Ranald MacDonald daguerreotype, ca.1853.

nese researchers (and FOM society members). For Nishiya, too, MacDonald became a personal interest and—under the slogan "From Rishiri You Can See the World"—a way to publicize the unique role that the tiny island has played in Japanese and world history.

When enlisting the help of organizations to promote a historical figure, the issue of "appropriateness" always comes up. Akira Yoshimura likes to tell the story of how the editor of his novel at first wondered why the book was going to be about a famous hamburger chain, for in Japan (as in North America), it is the primary association most people have with the name. Luckily—for those who dread a hijacking of MacDonald's name—there are no fast food restaurants on Rishiri Island yet, and it was instead the local Rotary Club that sponsored the first wooden monument to him, in 1987. The Club has formed links with its sister organization in Nagasaki, which has also been actively promoting MacDonald's story, and in 1988 it contributed to the construction of a monument to MacDonald, this time in the town of his birth, in Astoria, Oregon. In 1996, the same club helped complete the more permanent stone monument on Rishiri itself, sharing part of the estimated $70,000 construction costs with the local government. As Masaki Takahashi, the chairman that year (and major booster of MacDonald's story in the region), explained, "We hope that it will become a new sightseeing spot for as many tourists as possible."[56]

The bas-relief portrait of Ranald MacDonald on Rishiri's stone monument is intriguing, because only three contemporary portraits of MacDonald survive, and all artists drawing his likeness today reference one of them. The earliest is a daguerreotype made around 1853, another is a drawing of him descending a river on a raft on Vancouver Island in 1864, and the third is a photograph taken on July 5, 1891, around the time of his interview with Mrs. Custer. The Rishiri monument image is based on the 1853 daguerreotype, showing MacDonald's head tilted slightly to his right, his face in half-shadow, looking uncomfortable in a jacket, vest, starched high-collared white shirt, and cravat. Either consciously or unconsciously, the Japanese artist has highlighted some details that are not so immediately apparent in the original image. Close inspection shows that MacDonald has long mutton chops growing out from under his clean-shaven chin, in the style of the day. And his face looks a little broader, a little more Asian, with a flatter nose and smaller eyes.

CHAPTER 9

On Japan's Northern Frontier

Around ten in the morning, in early August 1848, two junks left Rishiri Island for the lonely samurai outpost at Cape Sōya, on the northernmost tip of Hokkaidō. The first junk carried a guard and MacDonald, for he was a prisoner. The other carried all of his possessions, including the little whaleboat in which he had landed on Rishiri.

MacDonald was a sailor, and he carefully observed the voyage. His junk used sails when there was wind and oars when there was not. The crew consisted of an *oyakata*, or supervisor, from Sōya; an Ainu headman wearing a faded silk frock ("trimmed with gold to distinguish him from the rest"); and nineteen other men, twelve of whom rowed with their oars in front of them, Western-style, and six men aft, two to each oar, who sculled. MacDonald was surprised to hear the men singing back and forth in choruses, as American sailors did. The Ainu crew ate lunch at 1 P.M., and he observed, as he had on Rishiri, that before eating they dipped their chopsticks into sake and sprinkled it in four directions as an offering to the gods. The Japanese officers ate their meal an hour later and shared with him their boiled rice, fish, and pickles. Everything, he noted, "was served in beautifully Japan'd wooden bowls on wooden trays which was also Japan'd."[1]

By ferry today, the journey from Rishiri to the Sōya area takes under two hours, but the junks took over eight, arriving around six in the evening. During the voyage, MacDonald was asked to stay in the covered part of his junk, but he found it so small he could barely sit up, and he "suffered a great deal of pain" until he was let out on deck to eat with the officers.[2] As was true for foreign sailors captured in Japan, the cramped quarters and spaces to which the smaller Japanese were accustomed could prove torturous, even when not intended to be so.

At Sōya, MacDonald was escorted by troops through curtained-off streets, past a group of Ainu, to a government building. He was still accompanied by "Tangaro," his friend from Rishiri Island who served as his "interpreter," but he had now entered the hierarchical world of officials and the military, where samurai officers carried two swords and plain soldiers one, and where average people, especially Ainu who lined the road, were compelled to show extreme deference to their superiors. Not wishing to genuflect in such an extreme fashion as the others, MacDonald merely touched his hat, but when told to take it off, he did so.

As MacDonald understood it, there were one hundred soldiers and five cannon at the Sōya outpost, with more soldiers available on call. The post was strategically positioned, guarding Japan's northern frontier for the Shogunate; to the east was the Sea of Okhotsk and—once past the Kurile Island chain that stretches north to the Kamchatka Peninsula—the vast Pacific Ocean. To the west was the Sea of Japan, extending to the Asian mainland. Due north, a mere twenty-eight miles across the Sōya Strait—or what English maps often list as the "La Perouse Strait," after the French explorer who sailed through it in 1787—was Sakhalin Island.

MacDonald was led to a barred prison that appeared to be "very slightly put together as if it was built in a hurry." He protested that "a prison was not good for me, that I would not make compliments to any body with the bars & gratings between us," but he was placed in two rooms, one about 12' x 8' for him, and one for the guard, both with clean *tatami* mats. The officers escorting him, rather than being rough, were solicitous. They warned him not to drink the water and, aware that foreigners were not used to sitting Japanese-style on grass mats, provided him with a bench. When he complained of the tiny space and poor ventilation, he was given access to the other room as well and told that the windows would be opened in the evening. He would be held here for over two weeks, waiting for a junk to transport him south, but he had little to complain about. From the officers, he notes, "I received every atten-

Photo © 1992 Frederik L. Schodt.

Sōya monument to "The Most Northern Point in Japan."

tion; tea, sugar, pipe, tobacco was supplied by them."[3]

A discrepancy exists between the surviving scraps of MacDonald's journal and his deposition (taken by the U.S. Navy on April 30, 1849), for the latter indicates that the prison that bothered him was the one located on Rishiri Island and not at Sōya. Yet regardless of location, in requesting and receiving better treatment instead of punishment MacDonald demonstrated a trait that would characterize his entire stay in Japan: a remarkable ability to avoid conflict and to accept his situation, but, when necessary, to win over others through his charisma and powers of persuasion. When he finally left Sōya, all the samurai officers came by to say farewell, and—despite the fact that Japanese had no such custom—he writes that "each shook hands with me."[4]

Modern Sōya-Wakkanai

Today, the old samurai outpost on Sōya is gone, and one of the few remnants of the time is a nearby cemetery with the graves of many soldiers who once manned it. Sōya was one of the worst assignments in Japan, bitterly cold with daily blizzards in winter and ice floes in spring. So many soldiers died from a scurvy-like condition then called dropsy that today there is a huge stone monument at Sōya, in the shape of a coffee bean. The authorities eventually discovered that coffee helped the troops; guards at Sōya thus became some of the first coffee drinkers in Japan.

There are no monuments to MacDonald around Sōya, and few people have heard of him, yet he has not been completely ignored. In 1996 the March edition of *NL 45° Sōya*, a magazine put out by the Wakkanai department of the Hokkaidō Development Agency, contained a six-page *manga*, or comic strip, introduction of MacDonald's life. Designed to boost local industry and tourism, the magazine's cover featured a photo of blonde young Russian girls. While the inclusion of a comic strip in such a publication might seem incongruous, with over thirty percent of all published books and magazines in Japan taking the form of comics, it is difficult to reach a broad audience without *manga* today.

The magazine's artist, Satoru Matsumura, relied on materials supplied by the Rishiri Town Museum and struggled to fit MacDonald's

Excerpt from "Ranald MacDonald, Japan's First English Teacher," by Satoru Matsumura, *NL 45° Sōya*, March 1996. Courtesy of Wakkanai Kaihatsu Kensetsubu.

"The islanders were kind and considerate to me, as if it were the most natural thing in the world, but I shall never forget it. . . . And Tangaro (or Tajirō) gave me the precious gift of true friendship."

complex story into only six pages. He shows young MacDonald in typical *manga* style, with large eyes and soft features; when MacDonald signs on a whaling ship, he is dressed not in buckskin but in a fashionable but slightly-out-of-period waistcoat, knickers, and black leather shoes, his hair in a ponytail.

The story, told as a soliloquy, begins with MacDonald saying, "I am not a famous person who went down in history. I'm often called 'Japan's first English teacher,' but I only became so by accident." In a flashback, he recalls being a little boy, listening to his Chinook chief grandfather (depicted as a Plains Indian in full headdress) recount a tribal legend of their ancestors coming from a place far to the west across the sea, called "Japan." This makes him yearn to go to Japan someday, and as he grows older the yearning only increases. "Racial discrimination was virulent in America then," MacDonald recollects, "and there was no place for me. . . . As a half-Indian, in both occupation and in marriage possibilities America was the land of disappointment."

The strip then quite faithfully shows MacDonald leaving the *Plymouth* off the coast of Rishiri, being saved by Ainu, and spending ten days in greatly enjoyed freedom on the island, where he makes friends with the Ainu and Tangaro. Then he is sent south to Nagasaki, where he becomes an English teacher. The final scene shows him on his deathbed in the state of Washington, mentally saying good-bye to a vision of his old friend Tangaro, explaining that the friendship he experienced in Japan was worth far more than any fame he might have gained. His last utterance is "Sayonara."

For a story in a magazine with "Sōya" in the title, it might seem odd that there is no mention at all of Sōya, the place. Yet since the artist had to tell a complex story in a limited number of pages, he presumably chose to concentrate on the more romantic locales in MacDonald's saga. Rishiri is the place of his dramatic arrival. Nagasaki is where he spent most of his time and made his biggest contribution to Japan. At Sōya he was present only for a relatively short time until a ship could take him south, and his stay there was subsumed by even more dramatic events in the area.

* * *

Wakkanai, which now has jurisdiction over the old Sōya site, is the main population center in northern Hokkaidō today. It is a typical Japanese town of around 47,000, with the usual cluster of pachinko parlors, gift shops, and ramen noodle eateries near the train station. Yet it takes only a few minutes to realize that something is quite different about the area. It is not just a sense of remoteness, of being at the abrupt end of all train lines and, as a sign in the station purposefully notes, "3,134.8 kilometers" from the central capital of Tōkyō.

Many street signs are written not only in Japanese and English but Russian. Out at Cape Sōya, weather permitting, Russia, in the form of Sakhalin Island, is easily visible across the straits. In addition to a monument to modern "Japan's northernmost spot," there is a special "Peace" Monument, and a giant soaring crane-like structure commemorating the victims of a Korean Airlines crash, many of whom washed up on the shore when their 747 jet was shot down by a Soviet MiG in 1983. With the collapse of the Soviet Union in 1991, relations with Russia have improved greatly, but in many ways, mainland North America—over six thousand miles removed—seems much closer than Russia, which is only twenty-eight miles away. This is an area where there historically has been great tension between Russia and Japan.

The local history museum's displays illustrate this. In 1998 exhibits showed how, from 1706, the southern Matsumae Domain was granted control over the Sōya area; how explorer Rinzō Mamiya surveyed the poorly understood region in 1808–9 and helped confirm that Sakhalin was an island (and not a peninsula); and how trade flourished early in the Sea of Japan along the west side of Hokkaidō. Visitors to the museum could even gaze at a photo of the "last Ainu" woman in the area and push a button to hear her recite a *Yukar*, or traditional Ainu poem. But there was also a special exhibit prominently featuring the famous "nine maidens" of Karafuto, the Japanese name for lower Sakhalin prior to the end of World War II. Sakhalin was a long-disputed territory, with Russians moving south and Japanese moving north, and both displacing the local Ainu. For a while, its status resembled the confused British-American joint occupancy of the Oregon country. After the Russo-Japanese war of 1904–5, however, Sakhalin was formally partitioned into two zones, Japan gaining the southern half. Then, in 1945, in the waning days of the war, the Soviets suddenly attacked and took over Japan's portion. The "nine maidens" refer to the young female telephone operators there who chose suicide over surrender.

Japan relinquished its claims to Sakhalin after it was annexed by the Soviets at the end of World War II, but relations with Russia have been slow to improve, mainly because agreement has never been reached on the disposition of four Kurile Islands lying off the northeastern coast of Hokkaidō. Like Sakhalin, these were also taken over by the Russians, but Japanese still consider them their "Northern Territory." Over half a century later, demonstrations are regularly staged throughout the nation to demand their return, and Japan and Russia have yet to formalize a peace treaty.

When MacDonald arrived in Japan in 1848, he chose to land in a sparsely populated, frontier region. That he was caught by the authorities so quickly, and handled in such a systematic fashion was partly due to the fact that—even at that time—Japan already had had a long history of problems with its nearest northern neighbor. Without intending to do so, MacDonald had stepped into another complex web of history, one joining not only Japan and Russia but also the Pacific Northwest of his birth. To understand what happened to MacDonald requires a little detour, to introduce this history.

Russia, America, and Japan's Northern Frontier

In the rain-drenched winter of 1805–6, the Lewis and Clark party waited patiently near the mouth of the Columbia River. They fervently hoped an

American ship would come by to trade with the Indians along the Pacific Coast; because if so they would be able to obtain a ride home instead of trekking thousands of miles by land through dangerous and often hostile territory. To their dismay, no ship came, and on March 23, 1806, the explorers left.

Unbeknown to Lewis and Clark—while they were leaving—a Russian ship called the *Juno* was struggling mightily to cross the bar to enter the Columbia River. Its crewmen, many from the Russian America Company fort at Sitka, in southern Alaska, were badly weakened, some near death from malnutrition and scurvy. Only four years earlier, the settlement had nearly been wiped out in an attack by local natives. The leader of the Russian expedition—a nobleman named Nicholai Petrovich Rezanov—was hoping to relocate the Sitka fort to the Columbia River, for he had heard it was a far more favorable place, but storms and the notorious river entrance thwarted him, and he gave up, sailing south to San Francisco, in the Spanish colony of California, instead. Had he succeeded, Oregon and Washington today might belong to Russia.

Of greater relevance to MacDonald's adventure is the fact that, just before sailing across the Pacific to Alaska and the West Coast of America, Rezanov had spent nearly six months in the supposedly "locked" country of Japan, in Nagasaki, and he had even sailed by Rishiri Island and visited Sōya. On board the *Juno* was a Russian-Japanese dictionary and grammar that Rezanov compiled in Nagasaki, and one of the earliest descriptions by Europeans of the Ainu, their habits, and language.[5] And it was largely due to subsequent actions by Rezanov that the Japanese outpost at Sōya would later become so heavily fortified.

❋ ❋ ❋

Long before Lewis and Clark explored the American continent to the Pacific Ocean, the Russians, spearheaded by Cossack explorers and fur trappers, had expanded east, across Siberia to the Pacific. By the beginning of the eighteenth century, they had taken possession of the coast of the Sea of Okhotsk and the Kamchatka Peninsula, putting Russian borders in close proximity to Japan. By the middle of the century, Russians had landed on the Alaskan coast and the North Pacific had been opened for Russian adventurers, traders, and hunters.

By the end of the eighteenth century, the Russians had established a colony in North America and formed the Russian America Company. Like the Hudson's Bay Company, it was granted a monopoly, in this case to develop and exploit the Aleutian Islands, the Kuriles, and anything in North America above the 55th parallel (or below, provided it was unclaimed). Almost an independent state, the Company was allowed to maintain military and naval forces, occupy new territories, and trade with foreign nations. By 1810 there were over a dozen Russian settlements between Kodiak and Sitka, and—before Russia's Alaska territories were sold to the United States in 1867—even a colony ninety miles north of San Francisco, at Fort Ross.[6]

The Russians were also interested in Japan, and given the new proximity of the two nations it was inevitable that their peoples would come into contact, despite the Shogunate's policy of isolation. Hokkaidō and Sakhalin Islands and the southern Kuriles were a frontier thinly populated, mainly by Ainu, whose movements the Japanese could not control. Limited, unofficial contacts thus first emerged between Japanese and the Russians in the far north, often with the Ainu acting as intermediaries.

And just as some disabled Japanese ships drifted helplessly eastward in the Pacific, so, too, did many drift north. In 1695 one such ship drifted for twenty-eight weeks north to Kamchatka. One of the surviving crew members, Denbei, an Osaka merchant, was taken across Siberia to the Russian capital, where he met Czar Peter the Great, near Moscow in 1702. A farsighted ruler, Peter knew if Russia were ever to have any sort of dealings with Japan it would need interpreters. Denbei was therefore taught Russian, and a Japanese-language school was created in St. Petersburg, where he—and other Japanese castaways who later arrived—served as teachers and interpreters.

The more the Russians learned of Japan, the more their interest intensified. Like the Europeans and Americans, the Russians too presumed it to be rich, but in their case, it was also their close neighbor. Until U.S. warships arrived in Edo Bay in 1853, no nation tried harder than Russia to open relations with Japan.

In 1783, another Japanese ship was blown off course and wrecked on one of the Aleutian Islands. The surviving crew made it to Kamchatka, and six of them were eventually taken back to St. Petersburg by Eric Laxman, a Finnish-born scientist interested in Japan. He came up with a plan for a mission to Japan, using the return of castaways as a pretext to open negotiations.

It was a ploy that nearly every nation would subsequently use in trying to enter Japan, up until and including the Americans in 1853.

In 1792 Laxman's son, Adam, was placed in charge of the expedition to Japan. He was ordered by Catherine the Great to return the castaways and deliver a message from the governor of Siberia expressing a desire for trade. In a clear recognition of Japanese attitudes toward Christianity, expedition members were given specific cautions against any displays of "crosses, images, prayer-books and everything that only portrays Christianity, or bears the sign of the cross."[7]

Laxman and his men arrived at Nemuro on the northeastern coast of Hokkaidō in October. They announced their presence to members of the local Japanese outpost, who relayed news of their arrival to the Matsumae Domain in southernmost Hokkaidō, from where news was sent on to the Shogunate at Edo, on Honshū. Because of the onset of winter and the primitive communications of the day, Laxman had to wait a long time for an official response. To survive the severe winter, he and his men therefore built lodging on shore near the Japanese outpost and holed up. Remarkably, the two peoples got along quite well, even exchanging information on geography, maps, and their respective cultures.[8] At this point in Japanese history, the Seclusion Edicts had been in existence for so long that they had become "ancestral laws," with a bureaucratic momentum and logic of their own; for many individual Japanese, far away from central authorities, the novelty of meeting a foreigner outweighed whatever laws were on the books.

As for the Japanese castaways Laxman had brought along, under strictly controlled circumstances the Shogunate sometimes permitted the return of such unfortunates, providing those returning them did not attempt to initiate trade or spread Christianity, in which case they might be refused.[9] Official policy was that castaways should be returned on Dutch or Chinese ships to Nagasaki, or on Korean ships to Tsushima, and that any attempt at negotiation should also be carried out at Nagasaki. Laxman, however, had arrived in the far north from a hitherto unfamiliar nation, with apparently friendly intentions. After much bureaucratic confusion and debate, officials broke with tradition and allowed him to return the castaways at Matsumae, in southern Hokkaidō.[10]

Laxman thus arrived in Matsumae in June 1793 and there had several meetings with Shogunate representatives, who came all the way up from Edo. The castaways were accepted, and Laxman was told no trade issues could be discussed or any of his gifts accepted. He was ordered to leave but given a special permit that would allow him to return once, to visit Nagasaki in the future. As usual, the language barrier created huge misunderstandings. The Russians interpreted the pass as something that would allow them to travel to Nagasaki to initiate trade negotiations. The Japanese intended it to allow the Russians to return to Japan one time, to repatriate any additional Japanese who might have been left behind in Russia.

Over a decade later, in 1804, Czar Alexander I decided to send Nikolai Petrovich Rezanov as his official ambassador to Japan, with the permit. Rezanov was a majority stockholder in the newly formed Russian America Company and a man with a vision for Russian control of the entire North Pacific. He carried with him an official letter from the czar to the emperor of Japan, expressing a desire for relations and trade. He brought expensive gifts, some shareholders of the Russian America Company, and, of course, castaways. Conveniently, more Japanese sailors had been found in the Aleutian Islands in 1794 and brought back to Russia, where they lived at Irkutsk, which became another site for instruction in the Japanese language. Many became Christians and remained in Russia, but five chose to return to Japan with Rezanov, thus becoming the first Japanese to circumnavigate the globe.[11]

Rezanov thought on a truly grand scale for his day. The Russian America Company, of which he was a leader, was in desperate need of a place for ships to shelter in the winter and a source of supplies, and he hoped that access to northern Japan might provide both. In the late eighteenth century, Russian outposts in the Kuriles, Aleutians, and Alaska were often unable to grow enough food, as the climate was harsh, and the abused native populations often staged uprisings. If supplies could be brought in from Japan instead of Siberia, Rezanov reasoned, the Company would be helped enormously.

On September 7, 1804, after arriving at Kamchatka from the Baltic Sea via the Atlantic, the Straits of Magellan, and Hawaii, Rezanov confidently headed south for Nagasaki on the *Nadezdha*, a Russian man-o'-war. After much confusion on the part of the Japanese—who at first did not know what nation he was from (and could not understand why he had a decade-old permit—on October 7, Rezanov was finally admitted into Nagasaki Harbor. There, he discovered to his horror, his pass did nothing more than admit him. Stranded, disarmed, and under a type of house arrest on a tiny space of land on shore, he found himself caught within a morass of Japanese bureau-

Courtesy Bancroft Library, University of California.

Nicholai Petrovich Rezanov visits Nagasaki, October 1804. Uncredited and undated woodblock print.

cracy, receiving overly polite treatment, accompanied by deliberate obfuscation, procrastination, and avoidance of decision-making, compounded by the problem that Edo, the capital, where ultimate decisions were made, was two weeks removed from Nagasaki by courier. Even simple answers could require over a month. Georg Langsdorff, the German physician who accompanied Rezanov, huffily wrote, "We were not, as we had hoped, treated as friends, not even as foreigners of distinction and importance, but rather as criminals or state prisoners locked up in a spot, at the most, a hundred square spaces in size for an undetermined length of time and guarded from all sides. That was hard and unjust."[12]

Japan's particularly complicated system of government made matters worse. A Shogun, or hereditary military commander, resided in Edo and wielded absolute power, ruling in the name of the emperor, who had been reduced to a figurehead. Local power rested in warlords who controlled large domains throughout Japan, but the Shogunate held them in check by heavy taxes and requirements that they spend vast sums of money and time traveling with retainers to the capital every other year, where they spent months as hostage-guests. Throughout Japan, control was further enforced by an elaborate, institutionalized system of informants and spying. As Langsdorff noted, during visits by the Japanese there were always one or more new people involved, acting as checks on the interpreters and others to make sure no secret business agreements were taking place, "the government's mistrust . . . mainly at fault."[13]

During the nearly six months that the Russian mission remained in Nagasaki Harbor waiting for an official answer, Rezanov's frustration steadily grew. In the end, the Japanese officials finally gave him his reply. Contact was only allowed with the Dutch, Chinese, Ryūkyūans, and the Koreans; contact with other nations was impossible because it would entail an unequal, and dangerous, relationship. Rezanov's presents could not be accepted because that would entail reciprocating with items of equal value and sending an ambassador to Russia, which Japanese laws prohibited. Finally, the officials told the Russians, Japan had no great wants or needs and therefore did not desire trade, especially when it would "occasion frequent intercourse between the common people and the foreign sailors; and this is a thing strictly prohibited."[14] The castaways, however, were accepted, and after long interrogations and imprisonment eventually allowed to return home.

Enraged by what he perceived as humiliations, Rezanov left Nagasaki on April 18, 1805, and sailed north through the Japan Sea, heading for Petropavlovsk, on the Kamchatka Peninsula. Despite having been strictly warned to avoid Japan's coasts and not to land, his ship did quite a bit of exploring on the way. In books later published, both Langsdorff and the ship's captain, Ivan Fedorovich Kruzenshtern, give coordinates for and correctly name Teuri and Yagishiri islands. Langsdorff mentions, on the morning of May 10, Rishiri, "a conical snow-clad mountain visible from a great distance," but he calls it "Mount de Langle," after the name given to it by La Perouse in 1787. He notes that it is an island separate from Hokkaidō, and in footnotes gives the correct Japanese name, "Rii-siire."[15]

On May 11, the *Nadezdha* landed at Cape Sōya, which Kruzenshtern named Cape Romanzoff. Again, both his book and Langsdorff's provide the correct Japanese name and coordinates, and describe being met first by a group of Ainu, who came on board and invited the Russians to visit their homes on shore. The Russians noted the Ainu's appearance, dwellings, the use of poison arrows for hunting, the practice of keeping young bears in their huts, and their general subjugation by the Japanese. The Russians also met several groups of Japanese, and one group, either fishermen or traders, was so uninhibited and different from Nagasaki bureaucrats that Langsdorff could not resist writing, "[I]t all seemed strange to us." These men tried to sell the Russians various Japanese manufactures, including "books with obscene woodcuts, which the Japanese are forbidden to sell to foreigners on pain of death but are rather well known in Europe as Chinese bibles."[16] A Japanese civilian officer in charge of "guarding" the coast threatened to report the Russians to the central government unless they left immediately, but he provided them with considerable information on local geography and was familiar with a place called "America."[17]

On June 5, traveling via Sakhalin, the *Nadezdha* arrived at Petropavlosk, on the Kamchatka Peninsula, and the Russians learned for the first time that Napoleon had been named emperor of France. Rezanov was still fuming over his treatment at the hands of the Japanese and vowing revenge, but he received orders to tend to his job as head of the Russian America Company. He therefore sailed to inspect the Aleutian Islands and Russian possessions on the Northwest Pacific coast of America.

Arriving in Sitka, Alaska, Rezanov found the Russian outpost in appalling condition, its men starving and suffering from scurvy. It was then that he purchased the American ship, *Juno* (with its provisions), and in the spring of 1806 set out on a foraging and relocating mission to the Columbia River. Unable to cross the bar into the river, he sailed south to San Francisco, hoping to form a treaty whereby the Russian territories could be supplied with food. He also considered the possibility of a Russian expansion into California, where Spanish control was weakening.[18]

While at the Presidio in San Francisco, Rezanov had a love affair with—and became betrothed to—the commandante's beautiful sixteen-year-old daughter. As fate would have it, however, Rezanov was Greek Orthodox and the woman Catholic, so any marriage had to be approved by Rezanov's superiors in St. Petersburg. Thus, in May 1807, with the *Juno* newly resupplied, Rezanov took leave of his young fiancée and again traveled across the Pacific via Sitka, landing at Kamchatka in September. Alas, while traveling through Siberia he became ill, fell off his horse, was kicked in the head, and died, and with him died many of the dreams of Russian America.

Unfortunately for Japan, before embarking on his journey across Siberia Rezanov had issued some muddled instructions to two subordinate naval officers—Nikolai Khvostov and Gavril Davydov. Those instructions would affect Japanese relations with foreigners in the north for decades to come.

Russian and Japanese Clashes

In 1806, from his headquarters at Unalaska in the Aleutian Island chain, Rezanov had written Czar Alexander the following message:

By strengthening our American establishments, and by building more vessels, we shall be able to force the Japanese to open trade with us. . . . I do not suppose that Your Highness would charge me with a crime when with worthy coworkers. . . . I should next year go down to the shores of Japan to destroy their settlement at Matsama [*sic*], to drive them out from Sakhalin, and to spread terror on the shores . . . the sooner to compel them to open up trade with us.[19]

Revenge against distant Japan was the last thing on the czar's mind then, since Russia was in the midst of war with France, but Rezanov did not wait for an answer. Acting without state authority, he gave Khvostov and Davydov orders to attack Japan. In the ships *Juno* and *Avoss*, retrofitted for war, Rezanov wanted his officers to attack Japanese posts on Sakhalin and the southern Kurile Islands and burn Japanese vessels and stores. According to some biographers, any Japanese taken prisoner were to be transported to an island in Alaska's Sitka Sound, named "Japonovski" for the occasion, and then used to help colonize Russian territories in America.[20] Quite mysteriously, however, before he died Rezanov also issued another, contradictory, directive, asking Khvostov and Davydov to inspect the Aleutians instead.

Khvostov and Davydov found it easier to carry out the first set of instructions. In mid-October 1806, Khvostov reached Sakhalin and sacked and looted a Japanese outpost, taking several Japanese guards prisoner. His men nailed a copper plate to the entrance of a local temple, warning that if the Japanese did not agree to trade with Russians on Sakhalin the Russians would lay waste to northern Japan.[21] Any Ainu met were treated kindly, given medals, and declared to be under the patronage and protection of Mother Russia.

Khvostov then retreated to Kamchatka to wait out the winter. But when news of his attack reached Edo, it created a panic and resulted in the Shogunate sending reinforcements north as fast as it could. Among the frontier outposts strengthened were Sōya and a garrison at Shana, on Etorofu, one of the southern islands in the Kurile chain. Then, in the spring, Khvostov and Davydov, in the *Juno* and *Avoss*, respectively, sallied south to raid Etorofu. They sacked the first settlement they found, giving the Ainu what they took from the Japanese, and taking several more Japanese guards captive.[22]

On June 3, the Russians landed at the Shana fort, which now had over two hundred soldiers, and a battle erupted. The Japanese were armed with

Russians attacking Ainu in northern Japan.
From the woodblock print series "Publication on the Ainu People of Japan," n.d.

bows and arrows and swords and lances, and some guns and cannon, but Edo's 150-year-old policies of isolation had not encouraged technological innovation. Japanese guns were antiquated matchlocks, the cannons could only fire in one direction, and the warriors had had no experience with war for generations. Using a nighttime attack, a few dozen Russians routed the Japanese, most of whom fled into the hills and eventually made their way back to Hakodate, in Hokkaidō. The man in charge of the fort, Matadayū Toda, took responsibility and committed suicide.[23] The Russians burned all the buildings to the ground, and then left in their ships. Two members of their party, however, who had become drunk and passed out in a shed after a victory celebration, were left behind. Discovered by the Ainu and a few remaining Japanese, they were speared in their sleep, their heads salted and later sent with their effects to Hakodate.

Khvostov and Davydov next sailed further south past Hakodate, setting fire to a Japanese junk on the way. Then they returned to Sakhalin and found more Japanese buildings to burn. Then they headed south across the Straits of La Perouse, burning two more ships near Rebun Island, eventually arriving at Rishiri. In Motodomari Harbor, where MacDonald would eventually be confined, they looted and destroyed a merchant vessel as well as a Shogunate ship, the crews of which promptly fled. They also landed and burned the Japanese outpost and storage sheds and searched for any Japanese in the vicinity but could not find them.

Then the Russians left, but before doing so they released eight prisoners they had brought with them, giving them a boat on which to sail to Sōya and a letter for the Japanese authorities written in Russian on one side and phonetic Japanese on the other. The letter announced, in essence, that the Russians had taken their actions because Japan had refused to trade with Russia and the czar was angry; that if the Japanese authorities changed their minds, the two nations could be friends; if not the Russians would come back with many more ships and wreak more of the same havoc.[24]

❖ ❖ ❖

The Russians' effect on Japan was electric and lasting, resulting in the militarized environment that MacDonald later encountered. The Japanese had no way of knowing that Khvostov and Davydov had acted without the sanction of the Russian state. In the capital of Edo, word of the debacle spread like wildfire, the Russians sometimes said to have been not sixty but five hundred in number, and even twelve feet tall. In the north, samurai on the coast braced for all-out war. To control the situation, the Shogunate prohibited talk about the incidents and temporarily took control of the northern frontier away from the Matsumae Clan.[25]

Most seriously, the raids exposed the technological weaknesses of Japan's antiquated defense system and the lack of a strong military presence in the north. Little could be done immediately about technology, but defenses could be beefed up. New surveys of the poorly understood north were commissioned, and reinforcements were sent to existing garrisons. In 1808, in addition to 250 troops from the Tsugaru and Nanbu domains, 2,000 troops from Sendai and 1,600 from Aizu were quickly dispatched north. The Aizu troops, in particular, manned areas such as Sōya, Rishiri Island, and Sakhalin, but to stay there year-round was a tough assignment, even for men used to chilly climes. The graves of many Aizu samurai on Rishiri Island today are evidence of the toll that malnutrition and disease took. At the Sōya Garrison, in 1807 alone, over 70 Tsugaru men died of dropsy.[26]

On December 25, 1808, the Shogunate ordered troops in the north to fire on any approaching Russian ships and to capture them.[27] Three years later, this order had a direct effect on the next Russian official to enter the area.

❖ ❖ ❖

In 1811, Captain Vasilii Mikhailovic Golovnin was conducting a survey of the Kurile Islands for the Russian government on the sloop *Diana* after returning from Sitka in Russian America. Golovnin knew full well about the Khvostov and Davydov debacle and had no intention of meeting Japanese, but on Etorofu Island he accidentally ran into some. Naively thinking he could handle the situation, but depending on Kurile Island Ainu to do the interpreting (since none of the Japanese knew Russian and none of the Russians knew Japanese), Golovnin and six of his men were taken captive. He was taken to Hokkaidō and imprisoned at Matsumae, all-in-all spending over two years in captivity.

Only when the Japanese were convinced that Khvostov and Davydov had acted unilaterally (and not as representatives of the Russian state), and only after some more Japanese castaways had been returned, were Golovnin and his party finally released. They were sent home with a letter from the local authorities reiterating both Japan's prohibitions against Christianity and the standard Seclusion policy:

> Our countrymen wish to carry on no commerce with foreign lands; for we know no want of necessary things. Though foreigners are permitted to trade at Nangasaky, even to that harbour only those are admitted with whom we have for a long period maintained relations, and we do not trade with them for the sake of gain, but for other important objects. From the repeated solicitations which you have hitherto made to us, you evidently imagine that the customs of our country resemble those of your own; but you are very wrong in thinking so. In future, therefore, it will be better to say no more about commercial connexion.[28]

After Golovnin, the attacks that the Shogunate had once feared from Russia never came, and the Russian threat slowly receded. But like a rock thrown into a still pond, these early nineteenth century clashes would send shock waves far into the future, all the way to MacDonald's time.

MacDonald at Sōya

By 1848, when MacDonald arrived, the military presence at Rishiri Island had ended and the Sōya Garrison had been substantially reduced, yet the system established to deal with foreign threats from the north remained intact.[29] The real concern of authorities was the huge increase in mainly American whaling ships cruising in the Sea of Japan, and passing through the Straits of Sōya.

There were no professional English-speaking interpreters stationed at Rishiri or Sōya, for in fact no one in all of Japan could truly speak the language. But many of the people MacDonald met were receptive to English and fascinated by foreigners. In his writings, he notes that on the way to Sōya from Rishiri, whenever a ship was spotted the "officers would direct my attention towards them and say 'America Ship!' but on looking I could easily distinguish them from such and would answer 'no! no!' with a shake of the head."[30] One of the samurai repeatedly inquired after MacDonald's health by using the word "sick," which he had already learned from his captive.

In prison at Sōya, MacDonald had considerable communication with his captors. He says he was repeatedly visited by "a great many officers [who] came into my prison no doubt from curiosity." One of the officers kept a key to his sea chest because, he was told, "the common people should not see what I had," but whenever he wanted to get a book from the chest they would open it, and "4 or 5 others would be present, I suppose to see what I took out and what I returned."[31]

During initial interrogations, Tangaro, his guard-companion from Rishiri, served as his "interpreter," which presumably meant that he and MacDonald communicated in sign language and whatever limited English and Japanese words they had taught each other on Rishiri. Although simple interchanges would have needed few language skills, when samurai officers collected in his prison "to hear the wonders of the world from me" or when he was informed of the number of cannon and troops at Sōya, a considerably more sophisticated communication would have been required. He was examined by a doctor dressed in silks, whose "head was shaved and was a fit subject for a phrenologist" and who was introduced with the European word

"Doctor." The doctor took his pulse and peppered him with questions, wishing, among other things, to know "whether America, England, and France were larger than [Hokkaidō]." He "could not believe it but that Japan was larger."[32]

After Tangaro left to return to Rishiri, MacDonald writes that "his place as interpreter was taken by the person who had been keeper of Inoes over George Howe and his party. He was so appointed on account of his slight knowledge of English."[33] Howe was the second mate on the *Lawrence*, a U.S. whaling ship wrecked on Japan's coasts two years earlier, who had been forwarded to Nagasaki with six other men and then deported on a Dutch ship. It was because of Howe's group that, when MacDonald first arrived wet and cold on Rishiri, he had been offered Japanese sake with the English words "grog-yes." "The name . . . puzzled me," MacDonald writes, "but on inquiry afterwards I learned that it arose from the fact of the crew of the 'Lawrence,' who had been in that quarter, answering 'Grog? Yes! Fetch it on.' when it was offered to them."[34]

❖ ❖ ❖

The defense system in the north had been established out of fear of the Russians, but it is thanks to this system that MacDonald was meticulously recorded from the moment he entered Japanese custody. On his second day in Sōya, as he writes, "an inventory of my goods and chattels was taken . . . in the guard room. . . . Everything was closely inspected. My quadrant, some India rubber, and my slate appeared to excite their curiosity."[35]

In what is a gold mine for historians, the Japanese inventory of MacDonald's effects survives. When his *Narrative* was posthumously published in 1923, Naojirō Murakami—a noted historian at Tōkyō's Imperial University—was one of its editors, and he did a yeoman's job of locating and translating old records so they could be attached to the book as appendixes. Thus we know that MacDonald's revolver (the one that did not fall overboard) was approximately .33 caliber and about $5\frac{1}{3}$ inches long, that he had a map of the world, a leather hat, a couple of knives, a flint, some tobacco, and "a kind of spectacles."

His India rubber is presumably what puzzled Japanese officials described as "two balls of pine resin, large and small" or "a ball of pitch." His slate may be "one varnished board." The quadrant, which most Japanese had never seen, is certainly "one box containing an article like a telescope."

Most intriguing in the inventory of items in Mac-Donald's possession is his "twenty-three large and small books with covers," "fifteen books without covers," and "one bundle of different kinds of books."[36] For anyone doing research into the complex saga of Ranald MacDonald, the next burning question is: What were the titles of these

Advertisement for Georg Langsdorff's book, in *Whalemen's Shipping List*, September 19, 1848.

books? The normally detail-minded Japanese could not record the titles because they could not read English. And in his *Narrative* MacDonald merely says that he limited his books to a "simple English Bible, prayer book (Church of England), a dictionary, grammar, history (English) and geography &c—all in compact form."[37] Yet this hardly amounts to the thirty-eight to fifty books the Japanese records imply he had with him when he landed—after having already lost an untold, additional number on first capsizing his boat.

Might MacDonald have had any books on Japan that would have helped him prepare for his adventure? In the English world, Japan was almost a terra incognita, and books on it were few and far between. Engelbert Kaempfer, a former resident at the Dutch factory in Nagasaki, wrote one of the first histories of Japan, published in 1727 and widely read, but by 1848 it was antiquated. Carl Peter Thunberg, who also worked at the Dutch factory, wrote about Japan in the late 1700s, but his focus was on botany. In 1848, the most contemporary and useful books on Japan had all been written by Russians, who did include considerable detail on the places that MacDonald would visit, including Rishiri Island, Cape Sōya, Matsumae, and Nagasaki.

MacDonald had certainly heard the broad outlines of the Russian adventures as a sailor, or even as a child. In the early 1800s, Sitka, Alaska, became a hub for explorers and travelers in the North Pacific and a clearinghouse for information on Japan. Sitka had one of the largest libraries on the Pacific

Coast, with books in many languages. As the headquarters of Russian America, Sitka was visited by most Russians who had been to Japan, and it was also a rendezvous spot for American ships in the sea-otter trade. Golovnin passed his time in Sitka by, among other things, meeting American sea captains, many of whom were hired by John Jacob Astor and plied the route between New York, Canton, and the place of Ranald MacDonald's birth—Astoria, Oregon.[38] In fact, for a brief period between 1810 and 1812 Sitka was furnished supplies by the Americans at Fort Astoria. And starting in 1840, Sitka was supplied by the Hudson's Bay Company from Fort Nisqually (in today's Washington State), which had been founded by Ranald MacDonald's father. Although Archibald McDonald never visited Sitka, many of his contemporaries did, including George Simpson and Duncan Finlayson, both of whom knew Ranald well.

The most intriguing possibility is that MacDonald's chest might have contained books by Kruzenshtern, Langsdorff, or Golovnin. Kruzenshtern's *Voyage Round the World* had been translated and published in English in 1813. The original edition of Langsdorff's *Voyages and Travels in Various Parts of the World* had subscribers that included prominent royal families of Europe as well as John Quincy Adams, then minister to Russia from the "United American Free States" and later president. The book appeared in print in several editions in English starting in 1813, and there were even editions for young readers issued in 1816 and 1819. Langsdorff's book was also sold at New England whaling ports in the 1840s.[39]

Yet, of all the books authored by the Russians, Golovnin's *Narrative of My Captivity in Japan* was most specific to Japan, and the most popular. It was widely published in English translation in 1818, 1824, and 1852, and until Perry arrived in Edo Bay in 1853, it remained the most informative book in English on Japanese society and geography. In fact, if MacDonald had read Golovnin's work before landing in Japan, he would have had an excellent idea of what he was about to encounter during his sojourn there, for many of Golovnin's experiences and observations had an uncanny parallel to his. In particular, MacDonald would have learned a great deal about Matsumae, where he was next headed.

CHAPTER 10

Under Control of the Matsumae Domain

R anald MacDonald's two-week confinement at the Sōya military post
ended on August 23, 1848, but he gained neither his freedom nor the
ability to observe more of his surroundings. Favorable winds had finally come
up, allowing one of the larger junks to take him to Matsumae—a castle town
on the spur-like Oshima Peninsula in the far southwest corner of Hokkaidō,
from where the Matsumae Clan administered the entire northern frontier.
Matsumae would be his first stop on a longer journey all the way south to
Nagasaki, on Kyūshū, where regulations required all shipwrecked foreign
sailors be sent before being deported.

On the way to the pier, the streets were again cordoned off, with ceremonial curtains blocking the view, and the junk thus made a bigger impression
on MacDonald than the town. The junk had a number of military officers, a
physician, and a crew of around twenty-four, and it seemed quite large to
him. But he was disappointed rather than reassured by the ship's size, since
he knew a larger vessel would stop at fewer places and he would see less of
the Hokkaidō coastline. Again, all his effects, including his whaleboat, were
carefully put on board.

As when he had traveled from Rishiri to Sōya, MacDonald keenly
observed the level of technology in use, and Japan's 250 years of isolation

must have made him feel like the time-traveling protagonist of Mark Twain's *A Connecticut Yankee in King Arthur's Court*. The junk was lined with a forest of upright spears on the quarter deck and covered with white banners displaying heraldic patterns—patterns that to him looked like fake cannon ports. The designs were, he decided, "the false teeth of a people who have long and happily chewed the cud of a fancied and traditional invincibility, who cannot yet be said—so far as I know—to have felt the touch of any naval power, ancient or modern." Most puzzling to him was what is called the *sagari*, or "hanger," a huge decorative swatch of black rope that hangs over the prow of these coastal junks like a figurehead. An "enormous ugly dangling 'what you may call it,' swinging and dipping with the motion of the waves, into the limpid sea, was beyond my comprehension."[1]

After being put into a small cabin toward the stern, MacDonald was told he could be bound and beaten if he tried to escape, but at times he was given the run of the deck. The junk had a high bow and poop deck and, in conformance with regulations, only one mast. He noted the way the sails were reefed, the shape of the anchor, the hawser, and the general rigging. The large and heavy rudder had a huge tiller, but there were "no rudder chains or wheel for steering." Inside the main cabin, he was fascinated by the sight of the captain and his men praying before a Buddhist altar. "With such a rig, in such a vessel, freighted with fish salted and dried, and with kelp, did I enjoy a lubberly voyage from one prison to another."[2]

The junk was a variant of the single-masted cargo ships so often disabled in storms on Japan's eastern coast, and like them its open-sea capabilities had been crippled by regulations. It sailed in a point-to-point fashion, out of sight of land for ten or twelve hours at the most, and dropped anchor at a small village along the way. MacDonald was not allowed to land or told the village's name, but a kind local representative did come on board and gave him some fruit. On the ship, MacDonald was not alone; as in Rishiri and Sōya, he was often accompanied by a young servant, whom he refers to in his journal as *musuko*, the Japanese word for "son," or "boy."

✵ ✵ ✵

On September 7, the ship finally arrived in the bay of Matsumae, and MacDonald was told to remain below. All in all it had taken fifteen days to sail only around 350 miles. A large number of samurai officers of the Matsumae

Domain came out to meet the junk, and this time he greeted them on one knee. Their leader, he noted, was around five foot six "with remarkable eyes and plump health" and dressed in Japanese formal wear that MacDonald struggled to describe as a pair of "silk trousers with garters below the knees, the bottoms inserted in the tops of his white linen mokasins and a mantle of black silk with the coat of arms or "mondogro" [*mondokoro*] of the Government of Matsumai."[3]

The same man's first words were "*Nipponjin!*" [a Japanese!], which MacDonald assumed to be an expression of surprise over his own Asiatic appearance. Another junior officer then appeared, sliding across the mats on his knees to take a position next to him. This man, by "odd words of English and signs, made himself understood and interpreted" for MacDonald and his superior. The superior officer said, "You by and by Nagasaki go away. Carpenter." Imitating the act of "hitting with a hammer with the right hand and bringing the left thumb and forefinger together as if holding a nail, [he] said 'ship,' by which I inferred that they would repair a ship for my conveyance."[4]

And then MacDonald astounded his captors. As he later noted in his journal, he turned to the leader and

> I then asked . . . why take all that trouble, why not allow me to remain among them, to hear what would be his answer to such a request, he being a great man. The interpreter appeared to understand me and interpreted accordingly. The only result was a loud laugh and an answer of "no, no, you Nagasaki go away."[5]

After his elite visitors left, MacDonald remained on the junk while preparations were made for his landing. He whiled away the time smoking Japanese tobacco in a pipe he had been given and talking with his boy servant. His cabin was closed, the weather was sultry, and he began pacing. Finally, around six thirty in the evening he was transferred to a smaller boat with several officers and transported across a bay, covered with welcoming vessels of all sizes, decorated with flags and lanterns. On shore, he was met by a line of soldiers and men with a palanquin to transport him, but a large crowd had also gathered, nearly all holding lanterns. Like many early foreign visitors to Japan, he found the intensity of their curiosity disturbing: "I could not stand their gaze (as if I was a wild beast). I made good my retreat into the palanquin which I made to answer a double purpose—for what the Japanese had provided that I should not see the country, I made use of that I should not be stared at."[6]

Shut in a tiny box, rolling and swaying, MacDonald was carried out of the castle town of Matsumae, over hills, valleys, and streams, his bearers stopping only occasionally to rest. His escorts included fifteen officers and troops. Finally, sometime after midnight, they arrived at a small village and he was led through a line of guards to a wooden building, surrounded by a high wall with "sharpened spikes of iron and bamboo." It made him suspect he was being "taken into a dark dungeon," but he was actually put into a room, where he would be confined for nearly three more weeks. MacDonald understood the name of the place to be "Erametz" or "Eremetz," actually Eramachi, a fishing village only a few miles north of the town of Matsumae.[7]

MacDonald did not know it, but he was in the hands of Matsumae officials, who had already read several reports on him. Three weeks after his landing on Rishiri Island, they had received and forwarded a report to the Edo Shogunate, requesting instructions. They had been told to handle him in the same way as other recent foreigners, and they were thus acting in accordance with an already established procedure. Save for officials in the southern city of Nagasaki itself, the Matsumae officials had more experience dealing with foreigners than anyone else in Japan.

A Visit to Modern Matsumae

In those days, the Matsumae castle town was the business, administrative, and population center of all of Ezochi (Japan's northern frontier, including Hokkaidō, Sakhalin, and the Kuriles). It was so powerful that early European explorers often mistakenly called all of Hokkaidō "Matsumae." Today, however, among Japanese, the town has the reputation of being a rather inconvenient and remote place.

In 1998, I visited Matsumae with the little delegation from the U.S. Friends of MacDonald society, in conjunction with the 150th anniversary of MacDonald's landing in Japan. To follow MacDonald's route, after touring Rishiri Island and the Wakkanai–Sōya area, we theoretically should have sailed straight down to Matsumae, yet this is nigh impossible today as there are no regular ferries. Nor is it easy to drive from Sōya down the western coast of Hokkaidō, for it would take days. From Wakkanai, therefore, most people take a train to Sapporo, the modern capital of Hokkaidō, and then another to the eastern coast of the island, to the port of Hakodate. From there, it is a two-and-a-half-hour journey by train and finally bus to Matsumae. In train-laced Japan, Matsumae has been very much left out; even the ultramodern train line that zips through the thirty-four-mile-long undersea Seikan Tunnel, linking the islands of Honshū and Hokkaidō, goes close to Matsumae but does not stop anywhere near it.

Going by land has some advantages, however, as it allows one to reflect on how the castle town's isolation came to be, on the larger context in which MacDonald's visit to Matsumae occurred, and on the indirect contribution he made to Hokkaidō's development. Hokkaidō is the most "un-Japanese" of all the main Japanese islands, physically similar to the more lush regions of the American Pacific Northwest. It is characterized by beautiful forests, large-scale farms, and modern-looking towns. The island has a "Western" look partly because it was the last area of Japan to be settled, and because much of its agricultural and urban infrastructure was created in the late nineteenth century, after the fall of the Shogunate, with the help of contract American and European advisors.

✳ ✳ ✳

Although Matsumae was traditionally the power center of Hokkaidō, and Hakodate relatively insignificant, when Commodore Perry forced Japan to interact with the outside world in 1853–54, he demanded use of Hakodate as a provisioning port for American ships because of its superior harbor. This inadvertently set in motion a sequence of events that caused Hakodate to prosper, at Matsumae's expense, both as an international port and (until recently) as the main gateway to Hokkaidō. As a result, Hakodate today has a population of nearly three hundred thousand, a large airport, and good connections to the outside world by ferries and trains. It is also a romantic tourist spot for Japanese tourists, who enjoy its foreign atmosphere and dramatic history.

In 1867, some eighteen years after MacDonald's departure, a limited civil war erupted in Japan between forces faithful to the feudal Tokugawa Shogunate and reformers who wanted to restore the emperor's power and modernize Japan. The old regime lost, but holdouts sailed north from Edo to Hakodate, hoping to create an independent state on the northern frontier. They holed up in Goryōkaku—a French pentagonal-style fortress originally built by the Shogunate to defend against threats from the north, especially the Russians—and their bloody defeat in 1869 marked the final end of Japan's feudal era. As part of this so-called Hakodate War, the nearby castle town of Matsumae was also attacked; two-thirds of it was destroyed, and it never recovered.

When Hakodate was first opened to the outside world the panicked government magistrate found he did not have enough qualified English-speaking interpreters to deal with all the ships that visited. He notified officials in Nagasaki, where most of the professional interpreters resided, and urgently asked for help. At least one of the men sent in response—Yashirō Iwase— had been one of MacDonald's pupils during his confinement in Nagasaki in 1849. Iwase subsequently worked in Hakodate as an official interpreter for foreign visitors and a translator of important documents, thus aiding in the modernization of the area.[8]

❖ ❖ ❖

From Hakodate to Matsumae, our little group was escorted by Yumiko Kawamoto, a member of Japan's FOM society, who flew up from Tōkyō to join us. A linguist, Kawamoto specializes in teaching Japanese to foreigners at Waseda University, and—unlike most researchers delving into MacDonald's story in Japan, who tend to focus on his teaching of English to Japanese—much of her research has been focused on MacDonald's acquisition of the Japanese language.

As noted previously, MacDonald began compiling a glossary of Japanese words almost as soon as he landed in Rishiri, but some of his Japanese guards were from feudal domains in northern Honshū Island, where different dialects are spoken even today. One of Kawamoto's goals was therefore to ascertain which of MacDonald's vocabulary entries might be in northern Honshū dialects. To this end, she was trying to compare his vocabulary list with a Russian-Japanese list compiled by a Japanese castaway who had wound up in Russia in the same general era. Since this castaway was from the northern Tōhoku region of Honshū Island, Kawamoto reasoned, his list would help identify which of MacDonald's entries might have been influenced by the Tōhoku dialect of the time. It would not only shed interesting light on MacDonald's language-learning skills but also illuminate how the dialect itself has changed over the years.

At Matsumae, we were met by local representatives and historians at the town's local cultural and history center. They gave us a lecture about the region and its connection to MacDonald, and afterward showed us a multi-volume set of hardback books on the township's history, designed for academics, and then presented us with a smaller, single-volume paperback version, designed for public consumption. Remarkably, all of the books are published by the township itself, despite the fact that Matsumae is a tiny, isolated dot on the map of Hokkaidō today, with a declining population of around 12,000 people—many of whom are senior citizens. Yet, perhaps because Matsumae was once the island's power center and because many of its residents were born and raised in the area, there is a palpable sense of pride in local history. As Tomisato Nagata, our senior host and regional authority pointed out, the land was created by *senjin no ase*, or "the sweat of our forebears."

A Colorful Past

The first residents of the Matsumac area were probably Ainu, but official Japanese settlement itself dates back over eight hundred years, making it the oldest Japanese site in Hokkaidō. The big northern island has historically been Japan's "frontier," and as is often true of frontiers everywhere, many of the first Japanese settlers were refugees—clans or families or individuals fleeing military defeats or tax collectors or difficult circumstances on Honshū to the south. The Japanese established forts in southern Hokkaidō and prospered by trading with the Ainu and selling goods along the western coast of Honshū. But in A.D. 1456 the Hokkaidō Ainu staged a large-scale revolt against the Japanese, and fighting continued off and on for nearly a hundred years. Out of this conflict emerged a Japanese clan that took the place name of "Matsumae" as their name. The Matsumae Clan built a castle in the area and established their rule, which lasted, with only a brief interruption, until the very end of Japan's feudal period.

If the Hokkaidō in which MacDonald first arrived physically resembled the land of his youth, the Matsumae Clan's rule over Hokkaidō also bore several parallels to the Hudson Bay Company's Charter over "Rupert's Land" in North America. During Japan's feudal period, the Tokugawa Shogunate presided over domains, which were in turn controlled by *daimyō*, or local lords. In 1605 the Matsumae *daimyō* was granted official control over his domain with three provisos: (1) no one was allowed to enter or exit the domain without his permission and directly trade with the Ainu; (2) any Japanese crossing the sea to trade had to be reported, but the Ainu were to be free to move anywhere they wanted; and finally, (3) all Japanese were to be strictly prohibited from mistreating the Ainu. The Shogunate, in essence, gave the Matsumae Clan monopoly trading rights over all of Hokkaidō in return for its help in securing the northern frontier. Concerns for treatment of the Ainu were not simply humanitarian, but to ensure the safety of the then vastly outnumbered Japanese population.[9]

Within the feudal structure of Japan, the Matsumae Domain was quite an exception. The Shogunate normally required *daimyō* to annually alternate their residences, switching between the domains and the capital (accompanied by their main retainers). But Matsumae was too far removed, so the pilgrimage requirement was reduced to once every five years. Taxes were normally levied on domains in the form of rice, but, again, Hokkaidō was too far north to grow rice. The Matsumae Domain was thus given monopoly rights to trade with the Ainu, and these rights were in turn parceled out to retainers, who set up trading posts throughout the area. Japanese manufactures were traded for such things as herring, seaweed, eagle's wings and tails (for arrow feathers), and bear and other wild animal furs. These were then traded throughout the other Japanese islands, making the castle town of Matsumae extremely prosperous for the time, in some respects analogous to the Fort Vancouver of MacDonald's childhood.

Despite this envious arrangement and the fact that the prosperity of Matsumae depended on trade with the Ainu, abuse of the native people by subcontracting merchants led to frequent revolts. In the far north, particularly, the Kunashir-Menashi Uprising of 1789 stunned the Shogunate. It resulted not just from mistreatment, but from the fact that the northernmost Ainu (especially in the Kurile Islands) were being sandwiched between Russians expanding south and Japanese expanding north. The uprising required the central government to send reinforcements from other clans on northern Honshū to beef up the Matsumae forces, and demonstrated that in order to secure its northernmost borders Japan needed at least the passive allegiance of the Ainu.

When the Russian empire expanded east and began making forays into Japan's northern frontier, the Matsumae Domain was initially responsible for handling the situation. When Adam Laxman—the first Russian emissary to Japan—visited Hokkaidō, it was the Matsumae castle town to which he was brought in 1793, and Matsumae where negotiations took place and Japanese castaways were returned. After the abortive mission of Rezanov to Nagasaki in 1804, and the depredations committed upon Japan's northern frontier by his lieutenants in 1806, the Shogunate decided that security of the north could not be entrusted to the Matsumae Clan alone. Between 1807 and 1822, the Shogunate therefore took control away from the clan and controlled the northern territories from offices established in the town, using soldiers from other domains. But whether the central government or the Matsumae Clan was in control, whenever foreign intruders and shipwrecked sailors appeared in the north, they were almost always brought to the castle town of Matsumae. And the experiences of these foreigners both foreshadowed and contrasted Ranald MacDonald's.

Golovnin

The Russian, Golovnin, as noted earlier, had had the ill luck to be captured in 1811 while surveying the Kurile Islands, shortly after the attacks by Rezanov's men. With seven other men, including a Christianized Kurile Ainu named "Alexei" serving as interpreter, Golovnin was taken to Hakodate and then to Matsumae, all in all remaining captive for two years and two months. Like MacDonald, Golovnin was a man of great objectivity about the world and its peoples. Also like MacDonald, he had the rare ability to turn adversity into a positive experience.

In the beginning, Golovnin and his men were treated quite harshly, as the Japanese were still smarting over the 1805 attacks by the Russians and fearing more. From Kunashiri, the Japanese transported the prisoners to southern Hokkaidō, binding their hands and arms so tightly that they bled and festered. But at the same time, the Japanese also showed traces of kindness, some of the guards devoting themselves to brushing gnats and flies off the faces of the Russian men.

Along the way, Golovnin noted that in southernmost Hokkaidō the Japanese did not allow Ainu villages, that the Japanese population seemed exceedingly industrious, and that there was a great deal of settlement (at least compared to Russia). In Hakodate, the Shogunate's local magistrate interrogated the captives, and huge crowds of curious citizens flocked around them. When they finally reached the Matsumae castle town, the welcoming population of soldiers and citizens seemed vast to Golovnin. But the Russians were shut up nearby in what he described as "cages" inside a prison, Golovnin himself sharing with two other officers a dark space, "six paces square and ten feet high." The building was surrounded by two walls, one with sharp wooden stakes, and the entire place was heavily guarded day and night.

On October 1, the Russians were led, bound by ropes, to the magistrate's office on the castle grounds. Here, their interrogations began, but a problem immediately developed with the Japanese interpreter who, Golovnin realized to his terror, really knew no Russian and was distorting their responses. Luckily, a Japanese interpreter named Kamajirō Uehara knew the Kurile language, and, with the Russian-speaking Kurile Ainu named Alexei, who knew a little Japanese, the two sides were somehow able to communicate.[10] The Russians were asked at great length about their identities and sent back to their prison cells, and then a few days later, they were recalled for more interrogations. This pattern continued with increasing frequency.

To the Matsumae and Shogunate officials, desperately in need of information about the outside world and deeply concerned about what the Russians were doing in the north, Golovnin could not have fallen into their hands at a better time. They bombarded him and his men with questions about the world at large and about Russia's military strength. As Golovnin later wrote, the questioning started to seem like torture:

> The number of questions the [magistrate] asked was incalculable. If he put one interrogatory concerning any circumstance connected with our case, he asked fifty which were unimportant, and many which were ludicrous. This so puzzled and tormented us, that we sometimes made very irritable replies. On one occasion, we stated plainly, that we had rather they would put an end to our existence at once than torture us in the way that they did.[11]

The Japanese asked even more specific questions after going through boxes of French and English books that had been found with Golovnin. Books with diagrams of instruments and machines, especially "filled them with amazement."[12] But when they realized Golovnin was not the advance guard of an impending Russian invasion, they began treating him better. They gave the Russians tobacco, warm clothing, and bearskins to ward off the growing cold, and they arranged to have physicians regularly visit the prisoners to make sure they stayed in good health.

It soon became apparent to the Russians that in exchange for better treatment, the Japanese planned to make maximum use of them. A young Matsumae man named Teisuke Murakami was brought in so that the prisoners could teach him their language and Murakami could then check all the Russian documents, as the Japanese required all official translations to be double-checked by two translators. As Golovnin wrote, "[Murakami] had an excellent memory, and pronounced the Russian words with such facility, that we suspected he had previously learned the language, and was purposely concealing his knowledge of it, or, at least, that he was acquainted with some other European tongues."[13]

The Japanese also had the Russians assist in translating a variety of documents they had, particularly those related to relations with Russia. Unbeknown to Golovnin, the Shogunate had made intelligence on Russia and the acquisition of at least some Russian-language skills by Japan's linguists a top priority. For the past two hundred years, almost all Japanese contact with the Western world had been filtered through the Dutch in Nagasaki; the only European language that official government interpreters really knew was Dutch, yet there were important questions requiring knowledge of Russian that needed to be answered. For example, had Khvostov and Davydov been acting as renegades when they had raided the north in 1806–7, as Golovnin claimed, or had their actions been state-sanctioned? Due to language problems, the Japanese government was still not certain of the true meaning of the various written messages and demands the Russians had then left, including some on Rishiri Island specifically addressed to the lord of Matsumae. To further their understanding, the Japanese asked Golovnin, in a painstaking process, for any French, English, and especially Dutch equivalents of Russian words in documents.[14]

Fearing they were going to spend the rest of their lives in Japan as captive teachers, the Russians in desperation plotted to escape. Early one April morning, in 1812, six of the men escaped from a hole they had secretly dug under a fence, and fled into the hills around Matsumae, hoping to make their way to the coast, find a large boat, and then make their way to the Asian mainland or the Russian Kuriles in the north. It was a hopeless cause, not only because of the extraordinary distance but because the Russians were so conspicuous. After wandering fourteen days (during which time Golovnin hurt his leg), the men were finally caught on the coast at the village of Kinoko, about thirty-six miles north on the Oshima Peninsula. They were returned to a prison for common criminals in the castle town, but Golovnin in his objectivity was nonetheless able to write later, "We naturally thought this treatment severe; but it must be borne in mind, that the Japanese laws respecting criminals are far more humane than those of most European nations."[15]

Attitude and deportment play a major role in the way people are evaluated and treated in Japan, and this was especially true in the feudal era. To the surprise of the Russians, their desperate escape effort and the way Golovnin took responsibility for it impressed the Japanese officials. Combined with a change in local magistrates and the gradual realization that Golovnin and his party meant Japan no harm, their treatment improved and they were soon transferred back to their original quarters.

While the Russians waited and waited to learn what would become of them, they kept vocabulary lists and tried to learn Japanese, but when they asked to be taught to read and write they were told that "Japanese laws prohibited the teaching [of] Christians to read and write their language."[16] Their role as teachers for the Japanese, on the other hand, did not stop. In March of the following year, an academician from Edo and an official "Dutch interpreter" from Nagasaki came all the way to study with them. The academician began translating a Russian work on arithmetic and physics. The interpreter would later translate a book on vaccinations, brought back to Japan years earlier by a castaway who had spent time in Russia. As Golovnin noted, "He used to refer to a French and Dutch Lexicon, for the purpose of acquiring through the French such Russian words as he did not know; he then searched for these words in a Russian Lexicon, which he had in his possession . . . and as he possessed an excellent memory, and considerable knowledge of grammar, he made rapid progress in Russian."[17]

This "academician" was Sannai Adachi, who had already translated a Russian book on arithmetic, brought back by the castaway Kōdayū, who had lived in Russia many years and made it back alive. The interpreter was Sajurō Baba, one of the best in his field. Because the Russians who raided northern Japan in 1807 had left a letter in French, in 1808 the Shogunate had ordered its "Dutch interpreters" in Nagasaki to begin studying French from the Dutch factor, or trading-post superintendent, in Nagasaki and, shortly after that, to also study Russian. Baba had already translated a Dutch book on Russia and spent two years in Edo learning Russian from Kōdayū.[18]

Golovnin and his companions were eventually sent back to Hakodate. In

October 1813, they were finally released to a Russian ship that had come to rescue them in exchange for delivering some Japanese castaways. All their effects from the time of their capture were returned to them, meticulously inventoried and cared for. Like Ranald MacDonald, Golovnin came away with a very positive impression of his captors. Of the average level of knowledge among the population, he wrote that the Japanese "are the most enlightened nation in the world." Of his treatment, he stated, "[W]e had also experienced the generosity of a pacific people, whom some Europeans, perhaps less civilized, regard as barbarians."[19] All of Golovnin's men made it home alive except for one officer. He had identified with the Japanese so much that, when forced to return to Russia with Golovnin, he committed suicide.

More Foreigners

After Golovnin's departure, concerns about Russia faded, and control over Hokkaidō reverted to the Matsumae Clan. By 1830 the clan's main headache was that American whalers were swarming into the newly discovered "Japan Grounds." After 1842, Matsumae forces were no longer required to automatically fire upon ships that came too close, and they were now allowed to supply them with wood and water if in trouble, but they still had to warn and chase them away. And more and more shipwrecked men started turning up on Japanese soil, asking for help.

In the sparsely populated vastness of the northern frontier, monitoring these ships and their crews created a severe headache for Matsumae officials, for it meant that warriors had to constantly scramble up and down the long coasts. In cases like MacDonald, if the sailors could not be made to leave, they had to be caught, transported over 1,800 miles south to Nagasaki, and then deported on Dutch ships. And, as always, no one in all of Japan could yet really speak English.

The obligation to handle these foreigners nearly ruined the Matsumae Domain. Usually, the foreigners did not come alone, but even if, like MacDonald, they did, regulations required that an entire ship had to be used, requiring a crew of fifteen, a *metsuke* or supervising officer, and fifteen samurai, for a total of over thirty people, just to get them south to Nagasaki. This was an extremely expensive operation. And as at least one Japanese historian has pointed out, under the feudal system this meant that authorities ultimately recouped their costs by forcing poor Ainu and Japanese laborers to work in ever more wretched conditions.[20]

The Lawrence Crewmen

Two groups of American sailors arrived in Matsumae-controlled territory shortly before MacDonald, and both proved extremely problematic. The first group consisted of seven men who claimed they were survivors of a whaling ship named the *Lawrence*, which, they said, had sunk in a gale on either May 27 or 28, 1846, in the Pacific, about three hundred miles off the coast of Japan. The men said they had sailed from Poughkeepsie, N.Y., under the command of a Captain Baker in the summer of the previous year, but the *Lawrence* is a ship of mysterious origins. It was not mentioned either in the authoritative *Whalemen's Shipping List* or in Poughkeepsie newspapers, and none of the ship's log books or records appear to have survived. It is entirely possible that the men really were deserters who had concocted a story calculated to win sympathy, for such tactics were not unheard of then. Nonetheless, the basic parameters of the men's experience once in Japan are easily confirmed in Japanese records of the time; it is in the details where the Japanese and American versions vary dramatically.[21]

The English version of the story comes from accounts by George Howe, the second mate, and Murphy Wells, the ship's carpenter. Howe afterward wrote the most detailed report, which was later published in the December 29, 1847, edition of the *Batavia Courant* (in today's Indonesia) and widely reprinted in English-language newspapers throughout the Pacific and the United States. The story convinced many Americans that the Japanese had been extraordinarily cruel to the shipwrecked sailors; after being forwarded to the U.S. secretary of state in 1848, the report was one factor in the government's later decision to send Commodore Perry to Japan with an armed fleet. MacDonald was well aware of Howe's story when he embarked upon his adventure.

According to Howe, he and six crewmates made it into a whaling boat when the *Lawrence* went down, and after eight days reached land (at Iturup, in the southern Kuriles), nearly starving. There, the Americans encountered some Japanese and were told to leave, but they pleaded for food and aid as their boat was too small for the open sea. The men were imprisoned in a "town" for eleven months, during which time, through sign language and by drawing on paper, they were daily questioned "regarding our country, religion and every other particular that could be thought of." Despite being fed rice, fish, and water, they all fell sick, and, according to Howe, "what with this, the miserable situation we were in, and the bad treatment we met with from our guards, who frequently struck us, and insulted us in every possible way they could, we gave up all hopes of ever getting out of our prisons alive."[22]

The men were put on board a junk and stowed in the hold. According to Howe it was "a dark filthy place and during the time we were in here, some three or four months, not a sin-

Sketch of imprisoned *Lawrence* crewman, identified only as "George," but presumably George Howe.

gle moment were we allowed to step on deck to breath the fresh air or see the light." Finally, they arrived "at a city called Matsumai, where the emperor's son lived." They were examined again, this time by a Japanese interpreter who spoke Dutch, which one of the crewmen could understand. Then they left again, "to another city," where they were transported in "a box, the lid of which was fastened down upon us." Here they were again interrogated but also forced to tread and spit upon a print of the crucifixion. After nearly seventeen months of what Howe called "close and strict confinement, privation, and ill-treatment" (which the Japanese denied), the men were deported from Nagasaki on a Dutch ship to Batavia.[23]

There is no evidence that the *Lawrence* crewmen were ever in the castle town of Matsumae—indeed, surviving Japanese documents show that the crew was only taken to nearby Hakodate before being sent on to Nagasaki. But while in Hokkaidō and Iturup, the sailors had been under the control of Matsumae forces. The Americans' poor sense of where they were is understandable, given that, like MacDonald, in the beginning they did not comprehend Japanese and were kept from seeing much of anything. But one thing is certain: while in the north, the *Lawrence* crew had a miserable time in the custody of Matsumae forces.

The Lagoda Crewmen

Two years after the *Lawrence* sank, yet another group of American men landed in territories under Matsumae control. From a New Bedford whaling ship called the *Lagoda*, their stay in Japan overlapped with Ranald MacDonald's, yet they never met him until the day they were all deported. Their experience, rather than resembling MacDonald's, was far closer to that of the *Lawrence* crewmen.

Japanese records show that around June 7, 1848, a party of fifteen sailors in three boats landed near the village of Kosago on the western coast of the Oshima Peninsula, slightly north of the Matsumae castle town. Guards were sent north, only to find that the men had gone to Ishizaki, another nearby village. When troops were then sent there, arriving the following morning, it proved impossible for them to communicate with the Americans except through sign language, but they did learn that the men were whalers. Each boat was given a bundle of firewood and rice, and the men were ordered to leave. The next day, however, the same men landed at the village of Eramachi (where MacDonald would later be confined). Here, the *Lagoda* men were ordered to leave again, but the men pleaded that their boats were too small for ocean travel. They also told the Japanese their mother ship had sunk and the captain and many fellow crewmen had drowned. The Japanese guards subsequently housed the crewmen under strict guard and reported the matter to the authorities. As with Golovnin and the *Lawrence* crewmen, the *Lagoda* men's effects were itemized and inventoried in minute detail. The Shogunate ordered that the men be handled according to the same procedure used for the *Lawrence* crewmen and be sent on to Nagasaki.[24]

Later, in the spring of 1849, the U.S. Navy would take the depositions of six of these crewmen, which survive in U.S. Senate documents, along with that of Ranald MacDonald's. In their basic outlines, the men's accounts of their experience at the hands of the Matsumae officials square quite well with the Japanese records, but again, it is in significant details that the accounts diverge dramatically.

The *Lagoda* whalers consisted of nine Hawaiians and six white men of whom Robert McCoy was something of a leader. McCoy was twenty-three and intelligent, and his account describes the numerous Japanese soldiers they encountered, "armed with swords and match-locks," with officers "cased in armor" and wearing "japanned hats." At Eramachi, he claims, the crewmen wanted to leave but the locals told them their boats were too fragile and small, and, that since they would surely perish in it, the Japanese would give them a bigger boat. The men eventually concurred and were taken to a house in Eramachi, where their things were "tallied," and they were told to wait twenty days for the boat.

In the interim, according to McCoy, the men were also told that they would be housed in a better place, but upon arriving they discovered it was a prison, and that they were under guard. After twenty days passed they were told to wait another twenty days, and after that they were told to wait until January. In desperation, one night in July of 1848, McCoy and another American, John Bull, cut through the roof of the privy of their quarters and fled, hoping to find a Japanese boat and use it to locate an American whaling ship in the area. The pair became lost in the woods, however, and were caught the next day and returned to prison. According to McCoy, the men quarreled among themselves, and Bull was then separated from them. On July 25, McCoy again attempted to escape, this time with a different crewman named John Martin, by again cutting through the roof of their quarters. The two were quickly discovered and Martin was caught, but McCoy ran to the sea, stripped, and swam out to a nearby rock. When the Japanese came to get him in a boat, he swam back through the surf to the beach and in the process nearly drowned. He was treated, but he and Martin and Bull were thereafter put into a small barred "cage," with a tiny hole in it, through which they were fed. The *Lagoda* men were told that they would be sent to Nagasaki and that from there they could make their way to Korea.

Ten days later, all of the men were taken to a junk off shore, but the three men who had attempted to escape found they were to be housed in separate cages between decks, and that one of the cages was only five feet high, six feet long, and four feet wide. According to McCoy, before being transferred, "we had some wrangling in the cage between ourselves, when the soldiers wished to take out Martin." According to Martin's deposition, the wrangling was "a sham quarrel, with a view of effecting an escape." Either way, according to the Americans Martin was then taken out and whipped with ropes about the size of a middle finger. Shortly thereafter, in August, the junk sailed with them to Nagasaki, where they went through the usual interrogations and procedures. As we shall see later, two of the *Lagoda* crew would die before the men were deported (along with MacDonald) in the spring of 1849.[25]

❖ ❖ ❖

A century and a half later, the introductory history book published by the Matsumae township briefly describes the visit of the *Lagoda* crewmen. It does not mention the ship's name but it repeats both the official Japanese account of the sailors' stay in Matsumae and their story of having survived a shipwreck. Oddly, neither this book nor the township's huge multivolume history series mentions a fact that caused many in the West to later dismiss the sailors' story. Unlike the mysterious *Lawrence*, which has never been identified, the *Lagoda* is a well-documented ship: its men were bona fide deserters who told the Japanese a whale of a story. The Japanese had no way of knowing this then, but after a flurry of reports in America that one New England paper noted caused "much painful anxiety at home," the *Lagoda* was confirmed as still very much afloat and its captain alive and well. Of the men, the paper wrote, "Their falsehood . . . will not, therefore, be productive of much benefit to themselves."[26]

Revisiting History

After our introductory lecture at the Matsumae Cultural Center in 1998, our hosts took us on a tour of sites related to MacDonald's time. As with most modern Japanese towns, almost all of Matsumae's mid-nineteenth-century buildings are gone, the victims of earthquakes, fires, wars, and relentless modernization. Yet the township's biggest tourist attraction today remains its history, and the centerpiece of that is a rebuilt castle—the only one in all of Hokkaidō featuring a feudal-era design. The castle is perched on a hill with a grand view of the bay, and from it today one can see a pachinko gambling parlor on a road below and, on occasion, during the town's "Old Day's Festival," formations of motorcyclists parading in samurai outfits. During MacDonald's time, the castle offered a good vantage point from which to observe any foreign ships passing in the area. Rather small by Japanese standards, it has been rebuilt at least twice since he left, but its thick walls and centerpiece *donjon*, or center tower, as well as exhibits of local history inside, make it easy to imagine what it might have been like when Golovnin was in the area, or when MacDonald passed by, hidden in his palanquin, on his way to Eramachi.

To further capitalize on its unique history, Matsumae has replicated part of the old castle town itself nearby. A highly ambitious venture and part of a local revitalization effort, the attraction has re-creations of feudal-era shops, as well as the quarters of citizens and craftsmen. In the streets there is even a palanquin of the sort that conveyed MacDonald, but—as any large foreigner who tries to squeeze into its

Friends of MacDonald in front of Matsumae Castle, 1998.

confines soon discovers—a ride in such a litter for very long would be torturous. A rebuilt magistrate's office shows the rigid control Matsumae officials maintained, not only over foreigners but also Japanese citizens. As a pamphlet notes, the office was in charge of inspecting and taxing any Japanese people, ships, and cargo entering the northern frontier; on a ritualized white sand space in the courtyard, suspicious intruders were stripped and checked for signs of prior sword wounds and tattoos—anything that might indicate an unsavory past.

Twelve miles north up the western coast of the Oshima Peninsula is Eramachi, where both the *Lagoda* crew and MacDonald were incarcerated. Today Eramachi is a gray-looking fishing village made up of low, stuccowalled houses and a few shops, with a harbor for fishing boats. Little is left from MacDonald's days, but next to the harbor stands a simple wooden memorial post, with Japanese text inscribed on it that reads: "Site of Detention Center for Foreign Castaways."

The facility's purpose was confinement, but it was far better than a jail for common criminals. In fact, it had just been specially built or adapted to house the *Lagoda* crew shortly before MacDonald's arrival. According to Japanese records, the ship carrying MacDonald from Sōya was supposed to have landed at Esashi, which is even further north, but unfavorable winds caused Matsumae officials to take him to Eramachi. Local historians today also claim that Matsumae officials chose Eramachi because they were afraid that housing Americans in the castle town would reveal the weakness of its military defenses.[27]

Confinement at Eramachi

In his posthumously published *Narrative*, MacDonald's description of his prison at Eramachi is completely at odds with that of the *Lagoda* crew. Although in his journal he mentions being led into what he feared was a "dark dungeon," in his *Narrative* he says he was led by a man whom he called the "governor" (in reality, the local official in charge) to "what seemed to be an apartment for dwelling, without anything to give it a prison look." With paper sliding screens, a fireplace and tea kettle ready, it "offered a cheerful welcome." But he quickly perceived two English letters—a "J" and a "C"— written on the wall in charcoal, and in the roof he noticed a patch of new boarding about eighteen inches square. Furthermore, on a pillar in the middle of the room, he found the names of "Robert McCoy," "John Brady," and others written in English in pencil. Using sign language and the word "America," his hosts let him know that fifteen Americans had been incarcerated in the same place, had tried to escape through the hole in the roof, and—as he understood it—on being apprehended had been executed. The last point, according to MacDonald's *Narrative*, was emphasized by one of the samurai, who unsheathed his long sword and symbolically drew it across his throat, pointing to an iron bludgeon hanging nearby and making the "sign of striking" when he mentioned "McCoy." MacDonald had no reason to doubt his captors, writing later that "the reported murder, or at least death of the Captain of the 'Lawrence' recurred to me, and I believed that my 'fifteen' predecessors had shared the same fate."[28]

Nonetheless, in both his official 1849 deposition and *Narrative* Mac-Donald describes his treatment at Eramachi as very good, in the latter writing: "Throughout, in all matters, they treated me with very great kindness

and gentle delicate consideration." He was well fed, and
had "four or five" waiters,
including a man whose job it
was to taste his food to make
certain it was all right. By the
"governor," he claims he was
also given Japanese clothing,
bedding, "a box of confec-
tionery," a formal greeting
card, and—most remarkably,
in light of the experience the
Japanese had just had with the
Lagoda sailors—"two knives, a
large and a small one." He was
also given a "rude wooden
spoon" that had been made by
the *Lagoda* sailors. [29]

The day after his arrival,
MacDonald asked for his
books, but he was at first
refused. The books were in his

Tomisato Nagata, in front of post marking the
Eramachi Detention Center for Foreigners,
September 1998.

sea chest that had been brought down with him from Sōya. The chest was
sealed with strips of paper so that it could not be opened without someone
knowing, and whenever anything was taken out or returned, it had to be
done in the presence of others. In one of the more surprising passages in his
posthumously published *Narrative*, MacDonald describes pleading for his
Bible, using the Japanese word *kami*, or "god," which he had already picked
up. Not only did his captors give it to him, he says, but at his request they
built him a ritual shelf for it. "They seemed to respect it; in taking it up pay-
ing it their usual compliment to books of a good character by putting it up to
the forehead."[30]

This might not seem unusual today, but Christianity was then strictly
prohibited in Japan, and the officials with whom MacDonald interacted had
a grave responsibility to make sure it did not spread. For a brief period in the
early seventeenth century—right after the establishment of the Seclusion
Edicts and the banishment and execution of foreign priests—Matsumae and

southern Hokkaidō had become a refuge for Christians fleeing persecution on Honshū. This happened because the area was a frontier and regarded as semi-autonomous, and there was work in the local gold mines, but when Christianity itself was banned in Japan, the lords of Matsumae, perhaps fearful of the central government, became particularly zealous in carrying out their duty. As a nearby monument to 106 martyrs today testifies, more Christians were executed in the Matsumae area than in any other place in northern Japan. By the beginning of the eighteenth century, officials were still occasionally uncovering Christians who had gone underground, but by MacDonald's time if there were any practicing, it was a family secret kept hidden for generations.[31] In a stroke of luck, MacDonald had not only arrived in Japan when Matsumae officials were no longer required to automatically fire upon foreign intruders, but also at a time when officials were apparently somewhat more relaxed about religious matters as well.

Many years later, in a letter to his editor friend, McLeod, MacDonald would allude to the sympathetic attitude that his captors displayed toward his religion, especially at mealtimes:

> In saying grace I bring my hands together locking my fingers, my thumbs naturally would form a cross. It was observed by my attendants & directed my attention to it. I would often hear the word Padre. Since, I have often thought that at the time of the persecution the Christian faith was not wholly extinguished but that some of my attendants were Christians at heart following the faith planted by St. Francis Xavier.[32]

Leaving for Nagasaki

On October 1, MacDonald finally departed Eramachi. He was marched in procession down to a beach and seen off by a multitude of officers and samurai, dressed up and armed for the occasion. Exactly where this beach was is a matter of speculation today, but local historians have found an entry in a diary written by a samurai named Shigenao Kimura indicating that on October 1 an "American" named "Makidon" was shipped to Nagasaki from Satsumae—another village just south of Eramachi. Today, the spot is a simple harbor, consisting mainly of a breakwater and a few fishing boats.[33]

MacDonald was transported by boat out to a large junk off shore called the *Tenjinmaru*, which was decorated much like the junk from Sōya. It was a single-masted ship of around 150 tons, and it normally carried fish and other maritime products down the Japan Sea side of the Japanese islands, all the way around to Osaka, on the Pacific side. Surrounded by smaller boats, with their decorative curtains, swab, glittering lances, and flags, the ship appeared to him "more a phantasmorgia than an actual scene of human life."[34] Unlike his trip from Sōya to Matsumae, MacDonald was put in a small grated cabin, "in fact, caged," and remained there for the rest of the voyage, "unable to see anything outside except on two or three occasions." The boat creaked and pitched far more than American ships, but the voyage to the bay of Nagasaki was made in the unusually fast time of under two weeks. Japanese records show it stopped once on the eighth day during a heavy rain and fog on the island of Hikoshima, near the entrance to the Shimonoseki Straits between Honshū and Kyūshū Islands, and once again the next day at Yobuko on northwestern Kyūshū Island. As with his trip from Sōya to Matsumae, Mac-Donald had a sizable escort. Records show that in addition to the regular crew he was accompanied by fourteen men, including samurai, regular soldiers, and a physician.[35]

MacDonald's posthumously published *Narrative* states that he traveled down the eastern coast of Japan on his way to Nagasaki, but this was the result of an editorial mistake. In reality, nearly all ships from the north then sailed down the western side of the Japanese islands, through the Sea of Japan rather than the Pacific, on the eastern side.[36] The cooped-up Mac-Donald caught only furtive glimpses of land, but as he traveled south the temperature felt warmer and the coastline seemed lush, so he decided that it was "altogether of a better and more habitable Country."[37]

CHAPTER 11

Arrival in Nagasaki

The Tenjinmaru arrived in the Bay of Nagasaki, on the southern island of Kyūshū, on October 11, 1848.[1] It had been a fast yet rough voyage from Matsumae, with many members seasick on the last portion, but MacDonald was fine, despite having been confined the whole time. A number of officials boarded the junk to question the exotic captive and, as usual, a language problem immediately arose. Two of Nagasaki's professional "Dutch interpreters"—seventy-four-year-old Sakushichirō Uemura and twenty-nine-year-old Einosuke Moriyama—were on hand to help. The older man proved unable to understand much English, so Moriyama, the talented junior, did most of the questioning, but even he had trouble. Although MacDonald did not know it at the time, his arrival was like a gift from heaven for the Nagasaki interpreters, for they desperately needed to learn English.

✳ ✳ ✳

The officials who came on board included Tatsunoshin Shirai, a high-ranking assistant to the central government magistrate, responsible for foreigners. He and the other officials did have some English books and an atlas in their possession, and through the interpreters they asked MacDonald the standard set of questions posed to foreigners who had entered Japan illegally. Mac-Donald had already been asked these same questions many, many times before at Rishiri, Sōya, and Matsumae.

When asked where he was born, MacDonald answered "Oregon," adding that he lived in Canada and had last sailed from New York. Later, MacDonald would write that he told them he was by birth a British subject but that he "belonged to the Commercial marine and [was] a citizen of the United States. I was desirous that they should regard me as belonging to both nations (British and American) in order [that] in the event of a vessel of either of them visiting Japan my case might attract their special attention."[2] Having heard of the American sailors who had preceded him in Matsumae, MacDonald now also felt he had a duty to get out of Japan and somehow tell "the people of the United States that some of their countrymen were imprisoned in Japan and in all probability would remain in prison for life."[3] He presumably knew that in 1846 Britain and the United States had finally settled the "Oregon Question" but he apparently believed the treaty would soon unravel, for he writes that he thought "a war might arise therefrom, and that some of the vessels of either side might approach the Japanese coast."[4]

The officials were most eager to know why MacDonald had entered Japan, and why he had left his ship on the open sea in such a small boat. Afraid of being punished (or worse) if he said he had done so out of adventure and curiosity, he replied that he had had some "difficulty with the captain." Moriyama, the younger interpreter, struggled to understand the word "difficulty" in this context and was forced to hand MacDonald a Dutch-English dictionary, asking him to look it up. He somehow got the gist of MacDonald's reply across, for Japanese records state that MacDonald had "quarreled with his captain and taken his leave on the open sea."[5] MacDonald, for his part, understood through Moriyama that the officials had said he "had a great heart."[6] Given the context, in reality they probably told him he was a *kimottama no futoi yatsu* (a "gutsy" man), written with the characters for "liver." Indeed, in a vocabulary list MacDonald compiled (that survives), he gives the English definition of *kimo* (liver, with a secondary meaning of "spirit") as "heart."[7]

Moriyama informed MacDonald that he would be taken to the central government office in Nagasaki the following day, to appear before the *bugyō*, or magistrate. The rains were heavy, however, and he was not landed in the inner harbor until two days later. Then, for the first time, he could clearly see

Kyūshū Island.

Nagasaki, which was one of Japan's larger cities. In the harbor there were Japanese junks, and at least three large, armed Chinese ones, as well as a Dutch ship anchored off a tiny island on which there was a Dutch trading post. As in Matsumae, MacDonald was placed in a palanquin on shore, but this time it was left open, affording him a good view as he was borne through the town, escorted by rows of soldiers and officers and interpreters. The streets were paved with stone in the middle. The thousands of houses were single-storied, unpainted wooden structures with windows of "oiled paper," and wooden shingles or tiles. The larger, wealthier homes had walls around them, topped off by what he thought was broken glass (more likely ceramic shards) to prevent intruders—a design still used in some areas today. Compared to northern Japan, the local people seemed more accustomed to strangers, and not so intensely curious about him.[8]

Before long, the party arrived at the Nagasaki magistrate's office, or what MacDonald thought was the "governor's residence." There were huge crowds of spectators in front, but he was ushered into a filthy, shed-like space with dirty matting, and his soldier escorts were replaced by men "looking grim, with inferior swords and daggers—like jailers."[9] After a simple meal, he was visited by Moriyama, who told him the magistrate would be asking questions that he, Moriyama, would formally interpret. Magistrates were regularly rotated by the Edo Shogunate, and that year the man in charge was Ido Tsushima-no-kami Sadahiro, a name which—in the Japanese order of family name, given name—likely registered on MacDonald as little more than a long-winded jumble of vowels and consonants.

Moriyama warned MacDonald that before entering the hall where he was to be interrogated, he would be required to tread on a bronze metal plate with an image of the "Devil of Japan." MacDonald replied that he would have no problem doing so because he "did not believe in images," and Moriyama was obviously pleased, replying, "Very Good! Very Good!"[10] As

MacDonald passed into the room, he put his foot on the plate. He was unable to see it clearly, he would later claim, "in consequence of the Crowd, who pressed me forward. It appeared to be a metallic plate of about a foot in diameter on which I thought I could see the representation of the Virgin and Infant Savior."[11] Here, MacDonald's extraordinarily pragmatic response must again have greatly reassured his captors, for as he writes in his *Narrative*, "Told to put my foot on it, being a Protestant, I unhesitatingly did so."[12]

Like most North Americans, MacDonald was reluctant to act in too submissive a fashion. In his deposition given to the U.S. Navy in 1849, he notes that he was asked to kneel in Japanese fashion. When he got down on only one knee, "they insisted upon my getting down on both knees, which I finally assented to. Soon after this I heard a hissing noise and was told by the Interpreter that the Governor was coming, and that I must make 'compliments to him,' which was to bend low and not look up. I made a low bow to the Governor, though not before I had taken a look at him."[13] The magistrate was, he later observed, "rather short—'chunky.' " In MacDonald's Narrative, this interchange is described even more dramatically, and somewhat amplified, perhaps by his editor. In that version, when the magistrate entered with great pomp—preceded by soldiers holding a ceremonial naked sword, hilt up—MacDonald claims he refused to bow, despite being ordered to do so. Nearly everyone else in the room, including the soldiers, prostrated themselves, but MacDonald declined: "I . . . kowtow . . . to no man! I just would not do it." Instead, he says, he stared respectfully but fearlessly at the magistrate, "curious to read my fate at the hands of His Excellency." The magistrate eventually spoke a few words, and although MacDonald did not understand them, he was later told that they again meant, "You must have a big heart."[14]

When this formal, First Interrogation began, MacDonald was asked many of the same questions he had endured on the boat, but in greater detail. The officials wanted to know where he had come from, the position of his family, why he had left the ship, and so forth. But this time he was also asked if he believed in God. On replying in the affirmative, Moriyama queried him about the nature of this God, and MacDonald says he then started to recite the "Apostle's Creed," which he had been taught as an Episcopalian. As soon as he mentioned the words "Jesus Christ" and "born of Virgin Mary," Moriyama interrupted him, hurriedly whispering, "that will do! that will do!" to stop him.[15]

In his interpreting, Moriyama apparently left out all of MacDonald's ref-

Scene in a typical magistrate's office, in this case in Matsumae's reconstructed castle town (Matsumaehan yashiki). Suspicious people were questioned in front of a magistrate, scribes, guards, and, in the case of foreigners, interpreters. MacDonald would have been treated to a similar but more elaborate scene in Nagasaki.

erences to "Jesus" and "Virgin Mary." For a professional interpreter—normally required to translate everything with precision and neutrality—such an omission was a radical act that could have cost him his job, if not his head, but it may have helped ensure better treatment for MacDonald. A surviving Japanese document called *Nagasaki kakidome* [Nagasaki notes] hints at how Moriyama probably translated MacDonald's words. He is listed as being a fisherman from Canada, who said he believed in neither Buddhist nor Shintō gods but tried to cultivate his spirit and achieve happiness and clarity of mind by worshiping Heaven.[16]

The First Interrogation complete, MacDonald was taken to a former Buddhist retreat nearby, called Daihian, and led into a barred room about seven feet by nine feet, with *tatami* mat floors. This would be his home for the next six months, but he would return to the magistrate's office at least twice for repeat interrogations and undergo questioning in his prison. Other foreigners who wound up in Japanese custody in the nineteenth century were nearly driven batty by the constant quizzing they had to endure, but MacDonald never complained.

The MacDonald Depositions

Modern knowledge of what transpired in MacDonald's interrogations in Nagasaki has until recently depended on his own accounts, which are reliable but limited by his own perspective. Discoveries in Japan of records from two separate interrogations at the magistrate's office have broadened the view. Some sections of these records are nearly undecipherable, and the dates are not entirely clear, but the first record of an interrogation appears to be marked November 13; Dutch sources confirm the second one as dated November 30, 1848. Through these records, we can read MacDonald's replies to the Japanese questions, filtered through Japanese interpretations of what he said.[17]

In the record of the First Interrogation, MacDonald states his name, age (24), country (Canada, in North America), and occupation (pilot, or navigator). He says he was born in a place in North America called *Oregon,* and that his father was from a land called *Skotto* (Scotland) in Europe. He describes separating from his father at an early age; being educated or raised at a trading post in Oregon; and then, at ten, traveling with a friend to *Roburutsuran-do* (Rupert's Land, which a note at the end of the interrogation identifies as *Egeresu* ["English"] territory), where he attended school for four years. From there he says he moved to *Kanada,* where he was, among other things, in the "dry goods business," but lost money, found his future limited, and thus moved to *Sagu Haruhoru* (Sag Harbor), where he began living in November 1845. On December 4, 1845, he left to go whaling on a ship called the *Puri-mouto* (*Plymouth*), captained by a man named *Etowaru* (Edwards).[18]

The Japanese were particularly interested in MacDonald's movements between Sag Harbor and Japan, and he describes that period in considerable detail. He mentions the outbreak of disease on the *Plymouth* near *Rayode-jinerou* (Rio De Janeiro) in the land of *Burajiri* (Brazil), the death of several men, and the hiring of replacements. From the eight *Santo uisu* (Sandwich) Islands, he mentions whaling in the Northwest, near *Kamushikatto* (Kamchatka), and in the Sea of Okhotsk, occasionally returning to Oahu for reprovisioning. He mentions the loss of several men at sea, hiring replacements in the Hawaiian Islands, and his promotion to an *anjinyaku* (pilot, or navigator) in August 1847. He describes visits to the Ladrone Islands, Bataan, and eventually Hong Kong, where another crewman died and five new men were hired, then going back to Bataan and hiring another man, and

then finally heading for the Sea of Japan via the Ryūkyū Islands and eventually whaling off the shores of Hokkaidō. He even proudly lists the number of
barrels of whale oil the *Plymouth* took in as "around 4,800,"which is very
close to its recorded final tally of 4,870.[19]

The main goal of the interrogators was to find out what MacDonald was
doing in Japan. He told them that he had had many arguments with his captain, and that in the Sea of Japan the two had argued over the way the crews'
shares of the whaling proceeds (what was called the "lay") were being calculated. According to MacDonald, his original contract stipulated that he was
supposed to have been given one barrel of profit for 180 barrels taken, but
Edwards violated this arrangement, and MacDonald distrusted him greatly
for it. On June 29, the crew argued with Edwards, and MacDonald says he
"was unable to restrain his anger" and asked to leave the ship on a boat with
provisions. His goal, he claims in the records, had not been to go to Japan but
China. He had only landed on Rishiri Island because high winds and waves
had overturned his boat, and he had lost his compass, most of his food, and
other effects in the sea.[20]

The Second Interrogation (for which records also survive) covers essentially the same ground as the first, except that it is considerably more
detailed. Intriguingly, in this interrogation MacDonald mentions that his
mother had died shortly after his birth, and that when he went to school in
Rupert's Land (Red River) at the age of ten, he had met his *stepmother* and
siblings, "for the first time." Allowing for errors in translation and nuance,
the statement clearly shows that MacDonald was fully aware of his background, if not his royal roots, at age twenty-four.[21]

The Second Interrogation goes into considerably more detail about the
voyage of the *Plymouth* in the Pacific. MacDonald says the ship spent over
three months in Oahu, was in the Sea of Okhotsk and Kamchatka in June
1847, and by the time they returned to Oahu, many of the crew were sick
from disease (presumably scurvy). In Hong Kong they took on one "East
Indian" and four men from Luzon, which brought the crew number up to
thirty-six as they entered the Sea of Japan. On leaving the *Plymouth* in his little whaleboat in the Japan Sea, MacDonald says he took food for four or five
days with him, as well as some money with which he intended to buy more,
if necessary, at some of the smaller islands he had spotted in the area. When
his boat capsized, he lost most of the money, along with most of his cooking
implements and uneaten food, as well as other equipment. As for his pistol

(an obvious concern to the worried Japanese), he says it was something he had received from a fellow American sailor on board; it was of little use, he had no powder for it, and he regarded it as more of "a plaything." Of his quadrant (which the Japanese refer to as an "octant"), MacDonald explains that he had received it upon becoming a navigator and that it was used to take measurements of the sun and determine directions.[22]

In response to questions about being in the Sea of Japan, he gives his captors a short history of whaling, explaining that in previous years countries such as France and England had caught whales near Greenland but then moved on to "New Holland" (Australia) and gradually expanded to places such as Kamchatka and the seas around Japan. He tells of nearly two hundred whaling ships from France, England, America, Holland, and even Denmark in the area, many of which he has personally seen or passed. The crews, he tells his interrogators, occasionally visit each other when they have time. Whale oil, he explains, was among other things used in "steamships," which must have surprised his interviewers, since they had never seen steamships before.[23]

Finally, MacDonald reaffirms that he had originally had no intention of coming to Japan, and that he had never heard of Rishiri Island before. Having been in distress, he says he is relieved to have been brought to Nagasaki. As in his preliminary interrogation on board the ship in Nagasaki Harbor, he tells his captors that he believes in neither Buddhist nor Shintō gods, tries to cultivate his spirit and achieve happiness and clarity of mind by worshiping heaven, and does not pray out loud.[24]

❊ ❊ ❊

As MacDonald later wrote, "[O]n each answer to a question, reference was made to my answer as taken down on a previous occasion."[25] Asking the same questions over and over in multiple interrogations was (and still is) a way to check answers for continuity, and the Japanese had good reason to do so, for they did not trust MacDonald. But above and beyond this, they also needed to ask him the same questions over and over because none of the official interpreters could really understand his responses with any confidence, as no one in all of Japan then had a real working knowledge of English. In fact, without the help of a Dutchman named Joseph H. Levyssohn, the two Mac-Donald interrogations at the magistrate's office in Nagasaki for which records survive would never have been possible. Levyssohn's memoirs note that the Japanese asked him to help because they feared MacDonald's arrival on their territory had not been "accidental" and "must have served some specific purpose such as proselytizing or spying."[26]

In 1848 Levyssohn was the "factor" or superintendent of trade at the tiny Dutch trading post on an island in Nagasaki Bay. He was fluent in English, and his name is affixed to both surviving interrogation records with a statement that he wrote down MacDonald's answers in Dutch, which was then translated into Japanese by two professional "Dutch interpreters"—one senior and one junior. It was a tedious and awkward process. The interpreters turned the examiners' questions into Dutch, Levyssohn turned them into English for MacDonald, who then replied in English, which was written down in Dutch by Levyssohn, and translated into written Japanese by the "Dutch interpreters." But it worked. For obvious reasons, MacDonald was not disclosing his true motives in leaving the *Plymouth*, but the rest of his replies are rendered quite accurately, even after being filtered through two languages.

That such a linguistic crisis should exist in Japan—where none of the professional interpreters had a working knowledge of one of the world's most important languages—was humiliating to Nagasaki officials. Understanding how this crisis came about, and why MacDonald's appearance was so fortuitous for the Japanese, requires some additional background information.

Nagasaki and the World

In 1848 Nagasaki was the only port where the Shogunate sanctioned true trade with the outside world, and that only with the Chinese and the Dutch. The Dutch sent one ship per year then, and to manage this trade they were allowed to maintain a staff of less than a dozen men, who were required to live on a 15,000-square-meter, fan-shaped artificial island called Deshima. The island was surrounded by a high wooden fence with a double row of iron spikes and connected to Nagasaki via a narrow stone bridge, guarded on both ends. Every five years, the Dutch had to make a pilgrimage to the capital of Edo and pay respects to the Shogun, but other than that they were virtual prisoners. They were not allowed to bring wives or women, and they were kept strictly isolated from the local population. When occasionally given permission to enter Nagasaki on short excursions, they were accompanied by interpreters and officials that included professional spies. To prevent contacts with ordinary Japanese women, they were provided with professional prostitutes. As one resident put it, "A European condemned to spend the rest of his life in this solitude would truly be buried alive. . . . One can vegetate here in the most absolute moral nullity, foreign to all that is taking place on the world scene."[27]

Japan's problems with Europeans had begun over three hundred years before MacDonald arrived, in 1543, when a few shipwrecked Portuguese on the southern island of Tanegashima taught the local people how to make guns. Six years later, after a visit by the famous Jesuit Francis Xavier, Portuguese and Spanish missionaries began proselytizing in Japan, converting large swaths of the population in southern Kyūshū Island, including several local *daimyō*, from Buddhism and the native Shintō faith to Christianity. Trade with Europe also had begun, centering around Nagasaki and nearby Hirado. The Dutch and the English also arrived, and for a brief period multinational trade flourished.

But Japan was not yet a unified nation. A trio of warlords still vied for supremacy, and their attitudes toward foreigners fluctuated wildly. In general, they favored trade but feared Christianity. They viewed the Portuguese and Spanish with particular suspicion, partly because of their missionaries' success in converting people, and partly because of their history of subverting local rule in other nations. As early as 1587, the warlord Toyotomi Hideyoshi, who had gained the ascendancy, ordered Catholic priests to leave the country. He put Nagasaki under central government control and ten years later set the tone for a horrific period of persecutions, rounding up twenty-six missionaries and their followers and sending them to Nagasaki, where they were executed on Nishizaka Hill. Yet Hideyoshi remained in favor of trade.

Around 1600 Japan was finally unified under the Tokugawa Clan, its members thereafter serving as hereditary Shogun for the next two and a half centuries. In the beginning, the Shoguns cracked down on Christianity while tolerating trade, but they came to see any contact with the outside world as inherently threatening to Japanese society and their rule over it. They thus enacted an elaborate system of controls on religion and foreigners, as well as on the social behavior of ordinary Japanese.

In 1612, the Shogunate prohibited Christianity in areas it directly controlled, including Nagasaki (where local churches were destroyed); shortly thereafter the ban was extended nationwide. Two years later, a large group of notable Japanese Christians was banished to the Philippines, and in 1622 fifty-five Christians were martyred in Nagasaki. Still, partly to offset Portuguese power during this time, the Dutch and British were allowed to establish trading posts in nearby Hirado. The British soon closed theirs because of poor profits, but the Dutch did not.

In 1626 the Shogunate's magistrate in Nagasaki instituted the annual *fumi-e* (trampling picture) system for all citizens, requiring them to step on an image of the Virgin Mary and renounce Christianity. The next year, he presided over the execution of 350 more Christians. Then, over a period of six years starting in 1633, the Shogunate began issuing a series of edicts that formed the backbone of Japan's Seclusion Laws: foreign ships were only allowed to visit Nagasaki Harbor; construction of large ocean-going ships was prohibited; traveling overseas was banned; and those already abroad were prohibited from returning home. Most foreigners had already been expelled, but their Japanese wives and mixed-race offspring were also banished. To consolidate power domestically, the Shogunate forced feudal lords to regularly travel to Edo, regulated the possession of swords, banned guns, and established strict controls over religion and domestic travel.

In an ultimately futile attempt to maintain a type of social and political stasis, society was divided into four hereditary castes: samurai-warriors, farmers, craftsmen, and merchants, with the samurai at the top and the merchants on the bottom. The activity and even clothing of each caste was strictly regulated. An awesomely effective system of local social controls—the *goningumi* system, requiring families to monitor each other's activities—was also put in place.

When MacDonald arrived in Nagasaki Harbor in 1848, one of the first things he spotted was Deshima, the tiny island on which the Dutch had their trading post. First built in 1636 to hold Portuguese, the site had been given to the Dutch five years later, partly as a reward. In 1638 a heavily Christianized domain on nearby Shimabara Peninsula had revolted. After much struggle, the Shogunate forces finally defeated the rebels and sent the heads of four leaders to Nagasaki for display, while those of ten thousand followers were placed on bamboo spikes around the local castle as a warning. Christians throughout Japan were thereafter systematically exterminated, forced to convert, or driven underground. All Portuguese were banished from Japan, but since the Dutch had always been more interested in trading than proselytizing and since their ships had helped the Shogunate by bombarding the Shimabara rebels, the Hollanders were allowed to take over Deshima and maintain a trading post there.

For over two hundred years, a handful of Dutchmen in Nagasaki Harbor thus monopolized all of Japan's official trade with Europe. Under control of the Batavia-based Dutch East India Company (which functioned in Southeast Asia much like the Hudson's Bay Company in North America), they first mainly exported gold, silver, and copper; later

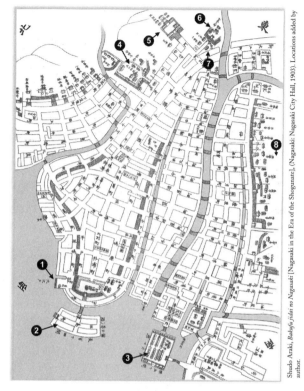

Old Nagasaki. (1) Landing site. (2) Dutch trading post at Deshima. (3) Chinese trading post. (4) Magistrate's office. (5) Suwa Shrine. (6) Matsu-no-mori shrine. (7) Daihian. (8) Approximate location of Shifukuan, where *Lagoda* crew was incarcerated.

Shudo Araki, *Bakufu jidai no Nagasaki* [Nagasaki in the Era of the Shogunate], (Nagasaki: Nagasaki City Hall, 1903). Locations added by author.

they exported handicrafts such as lacquerware and pottery (which became sensationally popular among well-off Europeans). They imported silk, sugar, wool, and some European manufactures. As gifts to the Japanese rulers whom they needed to appease, the Dutch traders occasionally brought exotic animals such as ostriches, camels, and even an elephant, greatly astounding the populace of Nagasaki.

Because of the Dutch presence, Nagasaki thus became the gateway for almost all knowledge the Japanese had of the outside world. Conversely, almost all of the official knowledge that Europeans and Americans had of Japan was filtered through Nagasaki and the Dutch. And at the center of this flow of goods and information, making it all possible, were the professional "Dutch interpreters" of Nagasaki.

Japanese "Dutch Interpreters"

Prior to the Seclusion Laws, many Japanese had learned to speak Portuguese fluently and many missionaries had learned to speak Japanese. But with the expulsion of the Portuguese, all that changed. The Hollanders on Deshima were forbidden to learn Japanese. Nagasaki officials used Dutch to communicate with the Hollanders, but the only Japanese who spoke it were the so-called "Hollands Tolk," or "Dutch interpreters." These men were part of a hereditary cadre of professional interpreters from notable families; they worked for the central government and performed all the interpreting tasks required. They were divided into grades such as "senior," "junior," and "apprentice," and they could only rise in the ranks after years of study and observation. For menial tasks—such as helping the Dutch men sell privately imported goods—there was also a group of men of lower-class birth called *uchi-tsūji*.

When MacDonald arrived, there were around 140 "Dutch interpreters." Their duties included far more than just helping the Dutch perform odds and ends at Deshima. They had to meet the annual ships sent from Holland, verify their nationality, and compile lists of the crews and ladings. They had to accompany the Dutch on periodically required gift-giving trips to the capital of Edo and help them answer questions. They had to serve in the Edo Observatory (an astronomy and research institute), and they occasionally had to work at Uraga Bay near Edo, or even travel to Matsumae in the far north to help interrogate shipwrecked foreigners.

The "Dutch interpreters" also had to translate written documents from Dutch into Japanese. Most foreign books were banned, but after 1720 some that did not deal with Christianity were permitted, fostering the development in Japan of a movement known as *Rangaku*, or amateur "Dutch learning." Using translations, often done with the help of the Nagasaki interpreters, Japanese scholars were able to learn of Western advances in anatomy, cartography, astronomy, and medicine. But one of the most important documents that the Nagasaki interpreters had to translate was an annual report, submitted by the Dutch, on the affairs of the world. After two centuries of isolation, these reports became one of the few sources of information for officials to learn about events happening in Europe, America, and Asia; it was through them that officials to their horror learned how, during the 1839–42 Opium War, the British had humiliated once powerful

China, forcing it to end its policy of isolation and open several new ports to trade.[28]

Through the Hollanders, the Japanese "Dutch interpreters" occasionally met other European nationalities. The men on Deshima sometimes brought Javanese men with them as servant slaves and hired foreign doctors to work for them whom they passed off as "Dutch." Three of these doctors became famous in Japan for teaching Western medicine to Nagasaki interpreters and "Dutch" scholars. In Europe and America, they became famous for the books they wrote, which provided a rare glimpse of the mysterious Empire of the East. Philipp Franz Siebold, a German physician who arrived in 1823, is a household name in Japan today. He fell in love with Japan and a courtesan named Taki, by whom he had a daughter, but in 1829, after he attempted to ship a map of Japan home to Europe, he was banished forever. Despite a desperate (and unheard of) attempt to demonstrate his loyalty to Japan by applying for Japanese citizenship, he was forced to leave alone.[29] Yet, like all the others in Dutch employ on Deshima, even Siebold communicated with the Japanese in Dutch, going through the professional interpreters.

New Languages

Political upheavals in the landscape of Europe at the beginning of the nineteenth century brought Nagasaki interpreters into direct contact with languages other than Dutch. As linguist-historian Tsutomu Sugimoto notes in his book *Nagasaki tsūji* (Nagasaki interpreters), "For Japan, the dawn of the nineteenth century meant that the nation's Seclusion policies, at least in terms of language, were beginning to collapse."[30] The Shogunate could try to keep Japan isolated from the outside world and frozen in time, but it could not stop the outside world from changing.

Holland's global power peaked at the dawn of the nineteenth century, and for a brief period during the Napoleonic Wars (1796–1807), the country was taken over by the French. Because Britain was at war with France, the British regarded Dutch ships and possessions as fair game, so to avoid being attacked by British warships, the Dutch chartered several American vessels (even a Danish ship) and used them to sail from Batavia to Deshima as part of their regular trade with Japan.

Eventually, British ships captured and briefly held Java and Batavia, and for a while in 1813, the lonely Dutch trading factory on Deshima became the

Nagasaki official, as seen by a British artist in 1845.

From Edward Belcher's *Narrative of the Voyage of the H. M. S. Samarang.*

only place in the entire world where the Dutch flag flew.[31]

Other European nations, jealous of the Dutch monopoly, also tried to initiate their own contacts with Japan around this time. As already noted, the Russians sent their emissary Rezanov straight to Nagasaki in 1804. In order to communicate with the Japanese, Rezanov brought Japanese castaways as interpreters, but castaways often created more problems than they were worth. If they knew the languages of their benefactors, the Japanese did not trust them. And the castaway's own Japanese-language skills often left much to be desired, for many were poor, uneducated fishermen who spoke radically different dialects. Furthermore, these humble men were often filled with terror at the thought of interpreting for powerful Japanese samurai officials, as it was, after all, technically illegal for them to return to Japan. In the worst cases, these amateur interpreters became bargaining chips, pawns in high-stakes international gambling, with sometimes tragic results. One of the castaways brought by Rezanov, named Tajurō, "thrust a razor through his mouth into his throat" in an attempt to commit suicide.[32]

In hopes of alleviating potential language problems, Rezanov brought a letter from the czar to the emperor that was in Russian, Japanese, and Manchurian, the Japanese part translated by Japanese castaway-translators at Irkutsk. The Nagasaki officials first appeared overjoyed to receive the translated letter, but two days later they returned—begging for "a true, literal translation of it into Dutch. They said that the letters and words were indeed Japanese, but the letter itself was 'unintelligible,' and no sense could be made of it." Of what was readable, they complained that "the handwriting [was] very bad and the language only that in vulgar use."[33]

Like other arrivals in Nagasaki, the Russians found the Japanese with whom they interacted fascinated by information on the outside world—information they were normally denied. "That Russia had possessions in America," Rezanov's physician wrote, "appeared to them very extraordinary."[34] The Japanese "Dutch interpreters," the Russians found, were also desperate to learn whatever they could of the new language they had encountered. "The first thing they inquired was how they were to ask in Russian, *What do you call this?* On being informed, they inquired the names of various objects, desired to know the numerals . . . and immediately began to make use of the information they had obtained. The inquisitiveness, the readiness at learning, and the memory of these people, surprised us exceedingly."[35]

Because of problems communicating with the Russians, the Shogunate ordered the Japanese "Dutch interpreters" in Nagasaki to begin studying Russian. Yet Rezanov had arrived with his letter from the czar not just in Russian and fractured Japanese but Manchurian. And, when his subordinates Khvostov and Davydov had attacked northern Japan, they had left at least one threatening communication to the authorities in French, which was then one of the "international languages" of Europe. In February 1808, the Shogunate therefore commanded that the Nagasaki Dutch interpreters begin studying French, and in October it ordered the "Chinese interpreters" to learn Manchurian. Broken Russian could be learned from some castaways repatriated from Russia, but French was much more problematic, as there were no Frenchmen or castaways to learn from. The interpreters, therefore, were forced to study under the imperfect tutelage of the Dutch factor posted at Nagasaki.[36]

Then, on October 14, 1808, the Japanese government was forcefully made aware of the importance of English. A British man-o'-war, the *Phaeton*, brazenly sailed into Nagasaki Bay looking for Dutch ships to capture. In a clever act of deception, it flew a Dutch flag, in accordance with an established procedure in Nagasaki, and thus fooled the local Nagasaki officials, interpreters, and two Dutchmen who sailed out to meet it. The British grabbed the Dutchmen and, when they realized no Dutch ships were in Nagasaki at the time, demanded provisions from the Nagasaki officials, threatening to burn any Japanese or Chinese ships in the harbor. The poor magistrate of Nagasaki, who ruled over the city on behalf of the Edo Shogunate, had no troops under his own command and was forced to mobilize them from surrounding domains. To stall, he provided the British with food and water, but the reinforcements were slow in arriving, and the *Phaeton* sailed away, after releasing the two Dutchmen. With Nagasaki's weak defenses exposed, the magistrate wrote out an apology that night and committed *seppuku*, or ritual suicide. In neighboring Nabeshima Domain—which had been unable to supply troops in time and was later determined to have been derelict in its duty—several senior councilors also killed themselves.[37] For years thereafter, the British, along with the Russians, were put on a Japanese blacklist of foreign powers.

The Problem with English

The Shogunate thus next commanded several of its interpreters in Nagasaki to study English, but they had the same problem as they had had with French. English was extraordinarily difficult for them, and because all Europeans except the Dutch were banned, there were no native English speakers available as tutors. The Japanese were therefore forced to try to learn written English from dictionaries compiled with the help of the Dutch on Deshima, or from the Dutch nationals themselves—and the Dutchmen's command of English was far from native.

Study of English thus proceeded in this unsatisfactory fashion for several years, the interpreters rarely given the chance to try out their command of the new language. After 1808 no ships openly flying the British flag came to Nagasaki. Then, in 1825 the Shogunate issued its most drastic interpretation of the Seclusion Laws, ordering all domains to automatically drive off any foreign ships sighted; the demand for English skills thus withered to almost nothing. Not until after 1842, when the law was relaxed and more foreign ships began appearing off Japan's coast, did the need for English again become critical. But even then, the dilemma was the same: how to learn English when no English speakers were allowed in Japan?

In August 1845—a mere three years before MacDonald landed in Japan—another British warship dared to come to Nagasaki, this time on a peaceful mission. A frigate named the H.M.S. *Samarang* was conducting a survey expedition in the Pacific and it sailed into Nagasaki Bay, hoping to obtain provisions. Amazingly, the Japanese warily allowed the captain, Sir

Edward Belcher, to land on a small island and take measurements. They provisioned his ship but refused to accept anything from him, out of fear that he would construe it as an invitation to trade. At first the Japanese tried to talk with Belcher in Dutch, but he refused. Belcher, for his part, tried to speak with Japanese officials in English but found any meaningful discussion impossible. As a result, both sides communicated in Chinese, using a Chinese interpreter Belcher had brought along and the professional "Chinese interpreters" of Nagasaki. Belcher later noted the curiosity and desire for information about the outside world among the Japanese officials he met. Many of them, he observed, "spoke Dutch, and some a little French."[38]

Belcher had the impression that there must be a school in Nagasaki where young men were being taught English, in addition to other languages, but he met no one capable of working as a professional interpreter. Einosuke Moriyama, one of the young Nagasaki interpreters ordered to study English, was not around, for that summer he was working in the Edo area, where he interpreted during the July visit of the U.S. whaler *Manhattan*. Then he had been described by the Americans as someone "who had been taught Dutch, and who could speak a few words of English, but who could talk still more intelligibly by signs."[39]

Nonetheless, Belcher observed a keen interest in English among some younger Japanese who boarded his ship. As he wrote,

One of the young students understood English slightly, could pronounce a few English words, and readily caught at every expression, recording it in his note book. He had proceeded so far as to write several of the names of the Officers in English, when it was probably noticed by some of the authorities; and as my readers have, doubtless, frequently noticed a dead silence amongst a collection of noisy sparrows, followed by a sudden chirrup and flight, without any visible cause, so it happened with these young students; who, without any apparent authority, hurried off very suddenly to the boats."

Another, older official to whom Belcher had offered a penknife as a gift replied very distinctly in English, "I must not."[40]

✦ ✦ ✦

By the summer of 1848, the need for English-speaking interpreters had reached a crisis level. In the space of three years, an American whaler, the *Manhattan*, as well as two U.S. naval warships commanded by Commodore Biddle, had sailed into the entrance of Edo Bay, only miles from the capital. The British warship, the H.M.S. *Samarang*, had brazenly entered Nagasaki Bay. And on the northern frontier, there were reports of hundreds of American whaling ships, some of whose crews had landed on Japanese soil without permission, or been taken into custody after a shipwreck. In this context, MacDonald could not have fallen into Japanese hands at a better moment. He was educated, cooperative, and he even had language books with him. He claimed to have been stranded in Japan, but he also seemed in no particular hurry to leave.

CHAPTER 12

Nagasaki Days: Teaching English and Learning Japanese

Most non-Japanese today know Nagasaki for its victim status—for the fact that it was nearly destroyed by an American atomic bomb on August 9, 1945. Japanese people, however, also think of Nagasaki as a cosmopolitan port city with an exotic, almost foreign history. Over the centuries, the Portuguese, Spanish, English, Dutch, and Chinese have all left their mark on the area's architecture, food, language, and religion. For historians interested in Japan's relationship with the outside world, Nagasaki is a gold mine. For those researching the story of Ranald MacDonald, it is a modern Mecca, and the place most central to his Japan adventure.

Over seventy thousand residents (including many Christians) were killed in the 1945 bomb blast, but Nagasaki's hilly terrain shielded large pockets and swaths of the city from its effects, leaving a surprisingly large number of historical sites intact. The home of Masatoshi Kakikoshi, a local Friends of MacDonald society member, illustrates this. In 1998, Kakikoshi was living in the century-old house of his wife Akiko's family, on the side of a hill not far from where MacDonald was imprisoned long ago. On the day of the A-bomb blast, Akiko, then a teenager, had felt poorly and stayed home, instead of going to work at a local factory with her compulsory labor group. An enormous wind roared, the ceiling collapsed, and "black rain" later fell on the house, but the main force of the explosion was blocked by the hills between her house and the blast's epicenter. A heavy metal door on a backyard storage shed—at a slightly higher elevation than the house—was scorched and permanently twisted from the blast and heat. Her friends working on the other side of the hills, as well as her younger brother, were never found.

Many sites related to Ranald MacDonald were gone long before the war. Deshima—the tiny, fan-shaped island he noted in Nagasaki Bay, where the Dutch traded—was an early victim of rapid population expansion and landfill measures. By the mid-twentieth century, it was already prime real estate in Nagasaki's downtown area. But at the beginning of the twenty-first century the city was painstakingly excavating and re-creating the old trading post as part of a costly, decades-long project.

The magistrate's office, where MacDonald was first interrogated, was destroyed after the Shogunate later collapsed. The office was only around a mile west of where MacDonald first landed, but his palanquin bearers must have huffed and puffed, as the area is very hilly. Today, as then, the area is something of a "power center," with a branch of the Bank of Japan, houses of presidents of big corporations and local justices, and, until recently, the residence of the governor of Nagasaki Prefecture. Monuments and markers among the modern buildings indicate former historical sites.

The Nagasaki Prefectural Library now sits atop the site of the magistrate's office, and its archives contain important surviving documents related to MacDonald. To commemorate the 150th anniversary of MacDonald's arrival in Japan, in the summer of 1998 the library held an exhibit of some of the materials, including a ground plan of the building in which he was imprisoned and samples of dictionaries that his interpreter-pupils later compiled. Of these, the *Egeresugo jisho wage* ("Japanese translation of a dictionary of English words"), compiled in 1851–54, is particularly famous in the context of the history of English studies in Japan. It shows how the Nagasaki interpreters were still dependent on the Dutch language, even at that late date, as the cover page is titled not in English, but in the Dutch words *Engelsch en Japansch Woordenbook*. Also exhibited was the original *Hankachō*, or "Record of criminal acts," a summary of decisions rendered by the Nagasaki magistrate during MacDonald's stay. It lists all the American sailors who were deported in the spring of 1849 after having illegally entered Japan. MacDonald is simply described as a steersman from Canada who had landed in distress on Rishiri Island in a small boat and sought help.

From the magistrate's office, MacDonald was conveyed another half mile west to his prison, following a road along the foothills of Mt. Tateyama, just north of the Nakashima River. He never mentions it in his *Narrative*, but he passed the Suwa Shrine on his left and could not have missed it. Founded in 1625, it is one of the largest shrines in Shintō, Japan's native animistic religion, and to this day its rituals and ceremonies are tightly woven into the lives of the local populace. During MacDonald's time, the interpreters regularly prayed at Suwa for the safe arrival of Dutch ships; a popular annual Noh drama staged on the shrine grounds was also one of the few festivities the Deshima Dutchmen were allowed to attend. A modern pamphlet issued for foreign tourists highlights the shrine's complex history, noting that it now has an "automobile blessing space"; a memorial to the much-beloved physician Siebold; and a tree planted by American president Ulysses Grant during a visit on June 27, 1879, after Japan was opened to the outside world. The structures on the site have been rebuilt several times. Many were destroyed at the beginning of the seventeenth century by Christian zealots when, as the pamphlet notes, "Nagasaki became a Christian enclave, and both Shintō and Buddhist religious facilities fell under a period of persecution." Other buildings were destroyed by fire in 1857, but shortly thereafter rebuilt, surviving until today, even through World War II."[1]

After passing Suwa Shrine, MacDonald's entourage roughly followed a street today known as the "approach to Matsu-no-mori Shrine." This second shrine is small, set among huge trees only a few hundred yards further west, but it has wooden buildings that have survived intact since 1713. MacDonald may not have been allowed to enter the grounds, but he certainly saw the huge camphor trees there or smelled their fragrance; already hundreds of years old when he was in the area, some are today over seventy-five feet tall and nearly twenty-four feet in circumference.

Daihian

Until recently, the precise location of MacDonald's prison was unknown, having long since disappeared from city maps. From Japanese records it was known to have been somewhere between Suwa and Matsu-no-mori shrines, in a place called Daihian, a retreat originally built in 1704 as an adjunct of a large, once-Chinese temple on the other side of the Nakashima River. Daihian altogether was about 1,200 square yards in size, the main building con-

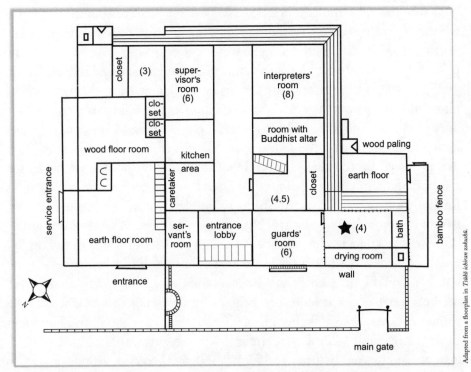

closet (3) super-visor's room (6) interpreters' room (8)

closet
closet

wood floor room

kitchen area

room with Buddhist altar

wood paling

caretaker

earth floor

closet

(4.5)

service entrance

earth floor room

ser-vant's room

entrance lobby

guards' room (6)

★ (4)

bath

drying room

bamboo fence

entrance

wall

N

main gate

Adapted from a floorplan in *Tsūkō ichiran zokushū*.

Daihian floor plan. Star indicates room in which MacDonald was presumably incarcerated.

taining a variety of rooms of different sizes that could be used for guards and servants, and for meetings. In the late nineteenth century, the retreat was replaced by a restaurant and then covered over by a residential community.

MacDonald describes Daihian as a cluster of buildings surrounded by a stone wall about six feet high, "topped with broken glass." He was put into an older building that appeared newly refurbished, entering via a "lobby." His room was partitioned off with high bars "about four inches thick and the same distance apart." It seemed to him that the walls of the building in which he was placed had been removed and replaced with the bars, and that about twelve or fifteen feet off in front of them there was a "wooden screen about twenty-five feet high." His room in the building was only seven by nine feet in size, but he also had access to another room off to the side, with toilet and bath facilities.[2] MacDonald had no way of knowing that by Japanese standards his "prison" was quite deluxe. Daihian was being used as a *zashiki rō*, or a prison cell with *tatami* mats, ordinarily used to confine political offenders or the insane. The accommodations were substantially better than a *rōgoku* (written with the characters for "prison" and "hell"), where common criminals were thrown.

During his over half a year of confinement, MacDonald was only let out of his room for repeat interrogations at the nearby magistrate's office. He was allowed to use a Japanese futon and to wear clothes given him by the magistrate of Matsumae, and, because it was still typhoon season when he first arrived, he was provided with mosquito netting to sleep under. Food was brought on a tray that he noted was "japanned," or lacquered, and he ate off a low tea table in the room. He asked for his books but was denied them, and when he requested his Bible, he was told by Moriyama, "Don't mention name of Bible in Japan, it is a bad book." But he was also told that if he were well behaved, the magistrate would give him nearly everything he wanted.[3]

After several interrogations, and after he had begun teaching English to the interpreters, MacDonald's treatment did improve markedly. Indeed, he was given nearly everything he wanted, except his freedom. As he writes, "I was served with almost lordly state, with all personal comforts, including baths, hot and cold, and with five or six waiters, all neat, clean, and with appropriate livery, to wait upon me at my four meals a day; with extras on my Sundays."[4] This is the reason, only a few years after his "liberation" from Japan by the U.S. Navy, that one prominent American writer would describe him as having been "living in clover."[5]

At the time, Japanese faced prohibitions against eating the meat of four-legged animals and they did not use dairy products, but Nagasaki officials were already used to the habits of the Dutch. MacDonald was thus fed the normal Japanese staples of fish, rice, and plenty of vegetables and fruit, as well as tea, but when he requested meat they provided him with pork once a week. And they gave him bread, obtained from the Dutch.

All these rarities they seemed to take a pleasure in procuring for me, and were effusively demonstrative in the way of polite ceremonial in most regularly laying before me, on my table, with appropriate table service of knife, fork, spoon. . . . [T]hey [also] very kindly made me a comfortable arm chair, according to order and directions from myself. . . . For bed, I found the national mat and bed clothes and pillow quite comfortable, and very convenient in my 7 X 9. These were out of sight during the day. Literally as the Governor promised, I "lived better and better."[6]

Even MacDonald's Bible was soon returned to him, and, as had been the case at Matsumae, his jailers built him a shelf in the corner of the room to display it. And on the European New Year's Day, he found presents sent over from Joseph H. Levyssohn, the Dutch factor on Deshima. Levyssohn had obtained special permission from the magistrate, and his own journal entry describes delivering coffee, sugar, butter, cigars, and four loaves of bread. A grateful MacDonald, in his writings, describes receiving a "bottle of exquisite coffee" and "more precious still to me—sixty-eight numbers of the *London Atlas* newspaper, and *Weekly Dispatch*, the whole with his polite card of compliments."[7] Levyssohn also tried to deliver some alcohol, with permission, and he may have been worried about MacDonald's staying warm, as it was very cold (and would snow heavily a week later, despite the fact that Nagasaki is about the same latitude as San Diego, California). But MacDonald was a teetotaler, and Levyssohn notes that he declined "to take wine or liquors."[8]

At Daihian, as had been true on the voyage from Matsumae, the authorities went to extravagant lengths for a solitary foreigner. Yet MacDonald was worth it to them. As Levyssohn later wrote, it "was only thanks to [MacDonald's] good behavior, his decent manners and the fact that he was teaching English to some of the Dutch interpreters that he, in return, was treated politely and well."[9] In fact, after the annual Dutch ship in Nagasaki Harbor left without him on it, one of MacDonald's main fears came to be that he would never get out of his room. As he later wrote of his interrogators, "[T]he object of their questions appeared to be to ascertain if I had any influential friends at home who would seek for me. If I had, they would send me away; if I had none, then they would imprison me for life in Japan."[10]

Modern Nagasaki's MacDonald Memorial

In the late 1980s, Nagasaki researchers finally pinpointed the site of MacDonald's former prison. This, in turn, led to the erection of a modest stone memorial to him on November 1994. It stands on the narrow road leading to Matsu-no-mori Shrine, and given the turbulence of Nagasaki's overall history—in which MacDonald is but a tiny, usually forgotten footnote—it is perhaps understandable if relatively few people see or are even aware of it.

The Nagasaki Memorial is similar to that on Rishiri, far to the north. Erected by the local Rotary Club, it features a small bas-relief image, based on the sole surviving daguerreotype portrait of MacDonald as a young man,

Ranald MacDonald monument in Nagasaki.

showing him in a high collar and cravat with then-fashionable sideburns. As with the Rishiri Memorial, his face has a definite Asian cast to it. The inscription (translated) simply says: "Fascinated by Japan, Ranald MacDonald landed on Rishiri Island in 1848 and was sent under escort to Nagasaki. On this site he became the first person to teach English conversation to Japanese, and thus laid the foundation for the dramatic progress in English studies later made in Japan." As in Rishiri, the text is by Akira Yoshimura, who helped popularize MacDonald's story in Japan with his historical novel, *Umi no sairei*.

Perhaps out of concern that the memorial does not impart enough information, a plaque has also been erected next to it as a sort of afterthought, with more detailed information in both Japanese and English. In addition to the basic facts, it notes that

[a]lthough for a brief period of about six months, MacDonald taught English conversation to 14 Japanese students including Einosuke

Moriyama and thereby exerted an important effect on Japanese subsequent diplomatic relations. After his return to the United States, MacDonald submitted a report to the American government referring to Japan as a civilized country and to its people as polite and cultivated.

In truth, after his visit to Japan, MacDonald nearly disappeared into the mists of unrecorded Japanese history. A series of articles on him appeared in the Osaka edition of the *Asahi* newspaper in 1888 and brought him to the attention of a few scholars. After that, his name was only mentioned occasionally, mainly in the context of obscure and scholarly articles on the history of English teaching in Japan, specifically on the acquisition of English by the Nagasaki "Dutch interpreters." Only in the past two decades of the twentieth century did research in Japan begin to expand much beyond the basic outlines of the story, much of that effort the result of work by members of the Japan-based Friends of MacDonald society.

The society's first meeting was held in Tōkyō in October 1988, only a few months after the American organization was formed. A study group had existed before, but this was the first formal association of MacDonald fans and researchers from throughout the country, and it subsequently helped bring his name into greater prominence. The thirteen participants represented a wide variety of interests, and included a member of the newly formed American society. There was a strong contingent of English-language teachers, as well as prominent academics and independent scholars from throughout the country, all of whom have helped to popularize MacDonald. Nagasaki itself was represented both indirectly and directly. All serious researchers into MacDonald's story have visited Nagasaki numerous times—Akira Yoshimura (author of the popular novel on MacDonald) perhaps holding the record at over one hundred visits. From Nagasaki itself, where there has been great interest in MacDonald (especially among the local medical community), two physicians attended. One, Dr. Masami Obama, was a community leader active in the Nagasaki Rotary Club; he would not only head the Nagasaki branch of the organization in the 1990s but also be instrumental in creating MacDonald's monument.[11] Today, there are more members of the Friends of MacDonald society in Nagasaki than anywhere else.

A Teacher of English

When MacDonald is mentioned in Japan today, he is almost always described as "the first English teacher," and his name is far more likely to appear in books about English studies than in those about history. This description of him is easy to remember, and it makes good advertising copy—especially in a nation where English learning has become an obsession and a multibillion dollar industry—but it is not entirely correct. Since, prior to MacDonald's arrival, the Nagasaki interpreters studied English from the Dutch factor on Deshima, more conscientious descriptions refer to him as the "first native teacher of English conversation in Japan." Yet even this title is inadequate. While not documented, it is safe to assume that some Japanese did try to learn English from Englishmen even earlier, at the English trading factory at Hirado at the beginning of the seventeenth century.

It is through MacDonald's teaching of English to the Nagasaki *interpreters*, who were desperate to learn the language, that he made his true contribution. To merely call him a "teacher of English" is to ignore the significance of what teaching English at that particular junction in history meant, and what the interpreters went on to do. Several, such as Einosuke Moriyama, later played a major role in negotiations with the English-speaking foreigners who came to force Japan open. And although it is rarely mentioned in history books, without the skills of these interpreters it would have been difficult for Japan to preserve her independence in the mid-nineteenth century. Instead of experiencing a successful political, social, and technological revolution and eventually becoming a ranking world power, Japan might have been colonized or carved up by Europeans or Americans, as happened to the rest of Asia.[12]

Exactly how MacDonald came to teach Moriyama and other interpreters is itself something of a mystery, but one of the men presumably petitioned authorities for permission to study under him. The officials had received information from Matsumae that MacDonald was different from other foreigner castaways, and they knew he was intelligent and educated. Given that he had arrived in Japan with a large number of books and that it was his secret intention to become an interpreter, and given that they had a desperate need to learn from a native speaker, the decision to use him as a teacher could not have been very difficult. Nonetheless, it must have been politically awkward; because of his illegal entry into Japan, MacDonald was, after all, a "criminal."

There is, surprisingly, no official record at *all* on the Japan side of Mac-Donald having taught English in Nagasaki. All research on this most important part of his contribution to Japanese history is thus based on his own writings and comments, and on the ability to confirm them using Japanese sources. Why should this be so? The simplest answer is that interpreters, sworn to confidentiality, are notoriously tight-lipped. But even long after the main interpreters had retired, long after the feudal government that employed them had collapsed and the men theoretically no longer had any obligation to remain silent, they consistently left no diaries or personal records. As Kazuo Katagiri, one of Japan's main experts on the Nagasaki interpreters, laments,

> [T]here were a large number of interpreters throughout the Edo period, and they played an important historical role, either orally or with their ink brush pens. In retrospect, it seems extremely unusual for a professional group such as the Dutch interpreters to come to an end with its members not even expressing their individual opinions, or even leaving a record of themselves.[13]

MacDonald had fourteen pupils, whom he called the "tsooze-gada," from the now-archaic Japanese word for interpreters, *tsūji-gata*, and using a quill pen he kept a record of their names on a scrap of Japanese paper. This paper survives in the archives of British Columbia in Canada and it was reprinted in MacDonald's posthumously published 1923 *Narrative*. Unfortunately, MacDonald struggled to render the names phonetically, and in places his handwriting is difficult to decipher. This, combined with the propensity of editors ignorant of Japanese to introduce errors, has led to a severe corruption of his list in subsequently published articles and books, with disastrous results for researchers who did not refer back to the original material.

The left column below indicates the pupils' names, as MacDonald remembered or understood their names, and is from his original list. The right column shows the actual names of the interpreters (rendered with modern romanization), as they have been confirmed by researchers, particularly Chisato Ishihara (a Tōkyō-based expert on the history of English studies and a founding member of Japan's FOM society).

1. Nish Youitchero	Nishi, Yoichirō
2. Wirriamra Saxturo	Uemura, Sakushichirō
3. Moreama Yeanoske	Moriyama, Einosuke
4. Nish Kataro	Nishi, Keitarō
5. Akawa Ki Ejuro	Ogawa, Keijirō
6. Shoya Tamasabero	Shioya, Tanesaburō
7. Nakiama Shoma	Nakayama, Hyōma
8. Enomade Dinoske	Inomata, Dennosuke
9. Suzuke Tatsuetsero	Shizuki, Tatsuichirō
10. Hewashe Yasaro	Iwase, Yashirō
11. Judgero Hory	Hori, Jujirō
12. Shigie Taganotske	Shige, Takanosuke
13. Namra Tsenenoske	Namura, Tsunenosuke
14. Motoke Sozemon	Motoki, Shōzaemon

As Ishihara discovered, the interpreters who studied under MacDonald had an average age of thirty-two years, but within that average the range was remarkable. Shizuki, a junior interpreter, was a mere lad of seventeen. Uemura, who along with Moriyama had first met MacDonald in the port, was a senior interpreter, already seventy-four-years old in an era when most men expired in their mid-forties. He had even studied English under the local Dutch factor long ago in 1809, when the Shogunate first ordered the Nagasaki interpreters to learn both English and Russian.[14]

As MacDonald describes it, "their habit was to read English to me: one at a time. My duty was to correct their pronunciation, and as best I could in Japanese explain meaning, construction, etc."

He had a hard time teaching them pronunciation, and some of the English consonants, particularly anything with a letter "l," he observed, "were impracticable to them." Discussions "as to signification and different applications of words were, at times, a little laborious, but, on the whole, satisfactory." And he was aided by the fact that his pupils "were all well up in grammar, etc., especially Murayama; that is to say, they learned it readily from me."[15]

MacDonald found he had a natural aptitude for teaching; one he never before realized he possessed. He greatly enjoyed the teaching experience but attributed much of his success to the quality of his students. "They were all very quick and receptive," he writes. "They improved in english wonderfully, for their heart was . . . in the work, and their receptiveness . . . was, to me, extraordinary; in some of them phenomenal."[16]

In this, MacDonald was greatly aided by the fact that his pupils were highly motivated professional interpreters who already knew Dutch, but even so the Japanese men faced enormous obstacles. While today Japanese and North American cultures share much, materially, intellectually, and even linguistically (modern Japanese is replete with English and pseudo-English terms),[17] back then a vast chasm separated peoples' values, modes of thought, and ways of expressing things. And although the interpreters used dictionaries, unlike today there were no bookstores selling English-Japanese dictionaries tailored to different levels of skill and interest. In fact, there were only two or three Japanese-English dictionaries or grammars in the entire world then, and all were extremely problematic.

English–Language Challenges for Japanese

Six years after the Shogunate first ordered the "Dutch interpreters" to learn English in 1811, several of them compiled a textbook, introducing English letters and their pronunciation, and giving examples of English words and conversational phrases. Then, in 1814 they compiled a true dictionary with over 6,300 terms, listed in English alphabetical order. Both of these books were impressive undertakings, but they were compiled with the help of the Dutch on Deshima, who were not native English speakers, and they were primarily based on existing Dutch-English grammars or dictionaries. In 1841, a book on English grammar also appeared in Japan, but it was a Japanese translation of a Dutch translation of Lindley Murray's *Murray's English Grammar*, a best-seller in the English-speaking world at the beginning of the nineteenth century. As a third-generation translation, it contained many errors.

The 1814 dictionary, titled *Angeria gorin taisei* (A compilation of English words) reveals some of the problems the interpreters faced. Its Dutch roots are revealed in the title, where "English" is represented by the Japanese-Dutch word, *Angeria-go*. Inside, English terms are neatly handwritten in brush and ink, with Japanese translations of their meaning given in *kanji*, or Chinese ideograms. But translations of meaning are useless in learning how to pronounce English, so each word has beside it a pronunciation key written in *katakana*, an angular phonetic script of around forty-eight different symbols.

Japanese pronunciation resembles Spanish or Italian, with nearly all words ending in vowels and the language overall having a fairly limited set of phonemes. But this simplicity of pronunciation makes it extremely difficult for Japanese to learn foreign languages that have more complex pronunciations or inflections, or languages that rely heavily on consonants, such as "r" or "l" or "th" sounds for which no exact equivalents exist in Japanese. When *katakana* is used to try to represent English pronunciation, the result can be a severe mangling of the original sound. It is a problem that plagues many Japanese-English dictionaries even today, and a reason it is infernally hard for Japanese who rely on such dictionaries to pronounce English correctly.

In *Angeria gorin taisei* it is easy to see how the Japanese interpreters struggled to represent English sounds using *katakana*. If the *katakana* characters are back-rendered into *rōmaji*, or the modern roman-alphabet representation of Japanese, "comet" comes out quite well, appearing as "kometto"; "amber" become "emuburu"; and "kettle" becomes "kettoru." But "Liberal Art" becomes "re-ruaru aruto" and "pair of spectacles" comes out as "pe-ru ofu spekite kerusu." This does not even include the problems of translating concepts that did not then exist in Japan, such as "parliament," the meaning of which is given as "a building for officials."[18] Prior to MacDonald's teaching, it is easy to understand why the few English-speaking visitors to Japan had such a terrible time understanding what the interpreters were trying to say to them.

MacDonald's Favorite Pupil

Of all MacDonald's pupils, his favorite was Einosuke Moriyama, who was close to him in age. Moriyama was, MacDonald later wrote,

> [B]y far, the most intelligent person I met in Japan. . . . When with me he always had books in Dutch, and a Dutch and English dictionary . . . the books were on different subjects, but principally on the commerce and customs of European nations. . . . [He] told me that he had a large library; and also, that he was studying Latin and French.[19]
>
> His countenance when in repose was a mild dignity observable in our clergymen, when in deep thought he had that peculiar habit of nibbling his finger nails. . . . [He] appeared to derive inspiration after

Courtesy Shinkichi Nohtomi

Einosuke Moriyama (undated, but after 1853).

mature reflection. Suddenly his countenance would beam with animation. . . . He showed a great desire to learn English, and much aptitude in doing so. His greatest difficulty was in pronouncing words with "th" as in "thought," "thunder," "the," etc., etc. It was always amusing after many attempts and knowing his failure he would again and again renew it, until he thought he had mastered it.[20]

It is Moriyama, more than any other of MacDonald's pupils, who has fascinated historians in Japan. One reason is that interpreters usually are shadowy figures in history, but Moriyama is remarkably well documented. He participated in many of the most important meetings with American, Russian, and British military missions to Japan in the mid-1850s and accompanied the first Japanese mission to Europe in 1862. His name (also rendered as Takichirō Moriyama) thus appears not only in official Japanese documents but in the published journals and articles of Americans and others who met him and recorded their impressions. In fact, of all of MacDonald's pupils, Moriyama is the only one whose birth and death dates (1820–70) are known. He was first buried in Nagasaki's Honrenji Temple, where a tombstone still remains. His official grave is now in Tōkyō's Honmyōji Temple grounds, where it is maintained by his descendants and erroneously marked as "Japan's first interpreter." Even Moriyama's appearance is well documented; a lithograph portrait of him was created in 1854 by Perry's men, and—apparently alone among MacDonald's students—a photograph later taken of him also survives.

Moriyama has also attracted great interest among linguists because there is enough historical information to track the progress of his English skills. He was, after all, the same man described by Americans three years before MacDonald's arrival, in 1845, as someone "who had been taught Dutch, and who could speak a few words of all English, but who could talk still more intelligibly by signs."[21] But by 1853, when Commodore Perry led a fleet of American warships into Edo Bay and forced Japan to change its Seclusion Policy, Moriyama made a far different impression.

Most of the actual negotiations in 1853–54 were done by using Dutch as an intermediary language, as the English ability of most of the Japanese "Dutch interpreters" was simply not good enough for official business. Edward Yorke McCauley, who served with Commodore Perry on the U.S. squadron, wrote that there were

[O]ne or two of the Interpreters who read English very fluently, without understanding it to any extent, but one of them astonished us very much, the first time he took up an Illustrated News and read a piece about the Japanese Expedition, their speaking English is of course very limited from want of practice: A chief Interpreter . . . came on board one day, and made Capt. A. a long speech in English . . . but on asking him a question [the Captain] soon found that his new friend had to prepare, the day before, any English he might want to use.

Of Moriyama, McCauley had nothing but praise, describing him as "a well read, and intelligent man, as far as I could guess, listening to his Dutch. I heard him one day, when unable to recollect the word calomel, ask what was the general name for the Protochloride of mercury." Elsewhere in his memoirs, he describes talking in off-hours with Moriyama in English about Japanese customs of suicide (which fascinated Americans no end and which Moriyama once threatened to perform in front of the Americans to stop them) and marriage. A very loquacious Moriyama told him that he was married to a beautiful woman and had a mistress, and (in a grand exaggeration) that he had been married five times.[22]

S. Wells Williams, a missionary and publisher based in China, was also along on the same Perry mission. Williams spoke Mandarin and had learned a smattering of Japanese from accompanying the *Morrison* on its abortive attempt to repatriate Otokichi and other Japanese castaways in 1837. In his journal, he wrote that "[a] new and superior interpreter came . . . named Moriyama Yenoske, who had recently returned from Nagasaki. . . . He speaks English well enough to render any other interpreter unnecessary, and thus will assist our intercourse greatly."[23]

MacDonald and Japanese

When Moriyama and the other interpreters first met MacDonald, they were greatly aided by the fact that he, too, was something of a linguist. In addition to English and French, MacDonald knew a smattering of Dutch, or was at least willing to learn it, for, while incarcerated, he kept a list of Dutch phrases too, with their English counterparts. He recorded only twenty-three phrases, mostly relating to the weather or simple questions and answers such as "Is it possible? Yes, it is possible." Yet he clearly used them to help his pupils understand the meaning of English phrases or to better communicate with them.

Kenji Sonoda is one of the few people to analyze MacDonald's Dutch phrases. A former member of the local FOM branch and an assistant professor of English Studies at the School of Allied Medical Sciences in Nagasaki University, in the 1980s and 1990s Sonoda chose to do what few writers about MacDonald have done. He went beyond the basic parameters of the story outlined in MacDonald's error-ridden, 1923 autobiography and carefully compared the 1923 work with earlier drafts and other original materials in the British Columbia Archives in Canada. Then he wrote various scholarly papers, dissecting many of the more interesting and contradictory facets of the MacDonald saga, which were subsequently published in history and "English studies" journals in Japan.

In particular, Sonoda has focused on MacDonald's acquisition of Japanese in Nagasaki. Of teaching the interpreters, MacDonald himself wrote that "[m]y duty was to correct their pronunciation, and as best I could, in Japanese, (Lingua Franca—pigeon Japanese), to explain meaning and construction, etc."[24] Yet in a report submitted to the U.S. Senate after being removed from Japan by the U.S. Navy, MacDonald is described as having said that "Moreama was his best scholar, though he [MacDonald] thought he himself knew more of the Japanese language than his pupil did of English."[25]

In fact, MacDonald's own mastery of Japanese, even if limited, was an even more extraordinary feat than his teaching of English to the interpreters. As noted earlier, although it was against the law for foreigners to learn Japanese, shortly after his capture he created a quill pen from a crow feather and surreptitiously began compiling a vocabulary and phrase list, which he maintained to the end of his stay in Nagasaki. On thick, durable Japanese paper, in tiny handwriting, this list survives (along with his list of Dutch phrases and part of his journal) in the British Columbia Archives in Canada. For linguists, it is a priceless resource. But without an understanding of the problems MacDonald faced, it is easy to underestimate the accomplishment it represents.

Photo No. BA-99999, Courtesy British Columbia Archives, Province of B.C.

Part of a page of MacDonald's vocabulary list, showing how he struggled to render Japanese words in the roman alphabet. "*Fta toru*," or "uncover," is usually written today as "*futa wo toru*," but it is a logical rendition of the sounds he would have heard. The penciled numbers on the list were added by later editors.

In trying to learn Japanese, MacDonald had one advantage over the "Dutch interpreters" who were trying to learn English—he could hear the language he wanted to learn being spoken all around him. On the other hand, he lacked access to any dictionaries or grammar books that would have helped him to understand the stream of sounds he was hearing and to break them down into recognizable words and patterns. The dictionaries and grammar books the interpreters possessed would have been useless to him, even if they had let him use them. The 1814 *Angeria gorin taisei*, for example, had English words written in English, but the Japanese definitions and pronunciations were written in Japanese *kanji* (Chinese ideograms) and phonetic scripts, both of which MacDonald was utterly unable to read.

Japanese is not an intrinsically "difficult" language. Pronunciation is quite simple and easy to master. The basic grammar is also simple: nouns have no gender, nor (usually) do they take any singular or plural form; there are no definite or indefinite particles, and verb tenses are extremely limited. The true difficulties most Westerners face can instead be summarized as follows: (1) Japanese bears little resemblance to Indo-European languages and thus provides little frame of reference; (2) the simplicity of the language means there is far more vagueness and implied meaning in conversations than in European languages, and there are a huge number of homonyms, or words that sound alike but have different meanings; (3) the hierarchical nature of Japanese society means that language employed by different genders and classes of people can differ radically, with maddening degrees of formality and politeness; (4) there are many dialects; and (5) the writing system is unusually complex, even for Japanese themselves.

There are four separate writing systems in use in Japan today. *Kanji* consists of thousands of ideograms imported from China, awkwardly crammed on top of native Japanese grammar and used to represent both concepts and sounds. *Hiragana* is a cursive phonetic script of over forty-eight symbols. *Katakana* is an angular phonetic script of the same number of symbols, today used primarily for emphasis and to represent foreign words. *Rōmaji* ("Roman-letters") is the alphabetization of Japanese, and today it is used seemingly everywhere in advertising, but there are three different competing systems of alphabetization in use.

In 1848, the Nagasaki interpreters and the "Dutch" scholars were the only people in all Japan who knew the roman alphabet. In fact, in the entire world then, there was only one romanized Japanese-English and English-Japanese dictionary that MacDonald could possibly have read, had he had any access to it. MacDonald may have even seen it, as the Nagasaki interpreters likely had obtained a copy from the Dutch. Titled *An English and Japanese and Japanese and English Vocabulary*, it was published in Batavia by William H. Medhurst in 1830. But the interpreters probably howled in laughter on first reading it, for Medhurst had never been to Japan or met Japanese people and he could not speak Japanese. Medhurst had had some knowledge of Chinese and, working with Chinese scholars, he had managed to compile his dictionary from words identified in Japanese books he had been given. But as Medhurst himself cautioned in his introduction, "the whole has been written by a Chinese, who understands neither English nor Japanese."[26]

For MacDonald, one of his greatest challenges in trying to learn Japanese was thus not only to listen to the sounds around him and identify individual words, but in his glossary to try to render them in the English alphabet in a way that made sense—in other words, to invent his own system of romanization. He managed to incorporate around five hundred Japanese words and phrases into his glossary. To those used to a more standard system of romanization, his lists may appear error ridden, but the inconsistencies reflect a mighty struggle, for when transliterating sounds MacDonald had to decide how to best represent them. How, for example, to best represent the "e" sound, as in English words such as "been" and "seen"? The Japanese word for snow, usually romanized today as *yuki*, he decided to write as *youkee*, which for native English speakers in many ways is a more logical representation of the actual Japanese pronunciation.[27] And figuring out a written pronunciation guide for terms was only one of the problems. Without some sort of semantic context, for example, it is very hard to tell if a guard bringing food in the morning and saying *hai, gohan desu,* means "good morning" or "here's your food" (the latter in this case).

To present-day speakers of Japanese, many words in MacDonald's vocabulary list also appear confusing because they are now archaic. *Konata*, which he defines as "he," is an upperclass (samurai) word no longer in use, now superseded by *kare*. In addition, Japan is a land of radically different dialects, and many of the guards and others with whom he came in contact were from Nagasaki. The Japanese word MacDonald lists for "good," therefore, is not today's standard Japanese, or *ii*, but the *yōka* of Nagasaki. Similarly, in his glossary MacDonald renders the Japanese word for "maid" as *sara*, which to most modern Japanese sounds like "plate." Since "plates" were brought to him by a maid or servant, it might be thought that he had confused the two, but according to linguist Yumiko Kawamoto, who has also extensively analyzed the vocabulary list, *sara* was then indeed a Nagasaki dialect word for an unmarried young woman, or a young "maid."[28]

Over the years, MacDonald's ability in Japanese has also been underestimated because of the way in which his vocabulary list has been reproduced. Malcolm McLeod, the first editor of MacDonald's manuscript, rewrote the list in the late nineteenth century, while compiling the words into alphabetical order. And in 1923 McLeod's list was copied one more time by W. S. Lewis and Naojirō Murakami when they included it in their edition of MacDonald's posthumously published *Narrative*. By carefully comparing the various iterations of the list, scholar Sonoda discovered that over 135 errors were introduced at various stages in the editing process. In other words, nearly one-quarter of the words that most readers see in the back of MacDonald's posthumously published 1923 autobiography—the primary source of information on him today—are not as MacDonald originally wrote them.[29]

How did MacDonald acquire his Japanese? His captors were not allowed to teach him and he had no dictionaries or grammar books to help him. Of his own ability, he would years later write conflicting opinions: that he had only acquired "a smattering" or that he could eventually speak a sort of "pidgin" Japanese; that he had acquired "a good deal" of the language, and elsewhere that "I picked up their language easily, many of their words sounding familiar to me—possibly though my maternal ancestry."[30]

Ultimately, his remarkable ability to get along with people in the most trying circumstances probably helped the most, for in learning an alien language it is constant, repetitive communication that is most critical. MacDonald was popular among almost all the Japanese he met. He was, he writes, "naturally sociable," and he always made friends. He found the Japanese themselves "naturally chatty; always in a vein of good humor," and he felt "in rapport" with them. He even detected an odd sense of kinship, writing: "In looks, facial features, and complexion (and bronzed somewhat, by sealife), I was not unlike them. Apart from that, there seemed to be some subtle undefinable sort of racial sympathy between us."[31]

Without eliciting suspicion, MacDonald constantly questioned people, using what he called a "pumping" process. He had plenty of visitors, from all walks of life. "Men of all sorts—students, officers, priests, and people in general of the respectable classes," he notes, came to stare at him "as a natural curiosity." The visitors were all men, except that on one occasion the captain of his guards brought his wife and daughter and three other females to see him in his jail. MacDonald found himself fascinated by the women's dress and hairstyles, and particularly—according to the custom of the time for married women—the blackened teeth of the guard's wife. The women giggled a great deal, and as they were invariably trained to act around men in those days, exhibited a "smiling good nature and artlessness calculated to make a favorable impression."[32]

The visit by the women, or memory of it, may have held a special significance for MacDonald. In the British Columbia Archives today, along with his vocabulary list, there is a clearly treasured, brush-painted image of a woman and child. Unfortunately, however, someone apparently informed on his friend, the captain of the guards, for to MacDonald's great dismay, he was later told that the man had been punished for bringing women, and—as he understood it—that "his head had been chopped off."[33] The real fate of his friend was certainly not so severe, as the Japanese expression for "fired" is *kubi ni natta*, or "lost his head."

✣ ✣ ✣

In his posthumously published *Narrative,* MacDonald says he picked up much colloquial speech from his interpreter-pupils, and that he drew most of his comfort and companionship from them. But researcher Sonoda disputes this notion, noting that by virtue of their position the interpreter-pupils had to be extremely circumspect in what they told MacDonald. He suggests instead that MacDonald's main tutors were his ever-present guards or attendants who, like the captain above, sometimes became close friends. He notes that on the back of the surviving vocabulary list, MacDonald carefully listed the names of twenty-eight of his guards, as well as the names of the captain whose head was "chopped off" and his wife. Indeed, on doing further research into the archives—comparing different versions of the drafts that would become the 1923 *Narrative,* Sonoda discovered that the paragraph in which MacDonald claims that he picked up the language from his interpreters originally said "guards," and not "interpreters."[34]

CHAPTER 13

Leaving Nagasaki

For over six months Ranald MacDonald lived in his tiny room in Nagasaki, cut off from information about the world around him. The interpreters, the officials, and the guards he befriended were hardly forthcoming.

They were, he noted, "studiedly reticent on all subjects pertaining to the country" and ever "on their guard against saying too much in exposition of their affairs and general public or even private life." He found ordinary people friendly but realized there was an elaborate spy system in effect in Japan and that from "the habit of intrigue in the *governing classes*, watch and ward have become the 'order of the day.'" Of the people around him, he observed, "each one seemed afraid of another informing on him." But among some of the more intelligent men he met, he detected an unvocalized frustration with Japan's feudal system. Their minds, he later wrote, were "acute enough to pierce the veil of their old traditional life, which, to them, was as the rotting shroud of a dead past."[1]

❖ ❖ ❖

MacDonald was not the first foreigner to make such an observation. On the

Rezanov mission to Nagasaki in 1805, Langsdorff had noticed that someone was always checking the interpreters, "the government's mistrust . . . mainly at fault." But one interpreter did manage to confess to him that "he considered all the strict regulations of the Japanese government as extremely ridiculous . . . and wished very much to travel and see foreign countries." Even more shockingly, in an act which could have cost him dearly if overheard, the man criticized the short-sightedness of Japan's rulers, including the emperor.[2]

Japan's feudal government could not afford to tolerate much questioning of the ancestral laws, especially those regulating overseas contacts, as the entire social system was predicated on a type of social stasis. Yet thinking-people wanted to know about the outside world. On Rezanov's visit, officials had been so fascinated by scientific instruments, especially a static electricity-generating Leiden bottle, that many had come back, wanting "to feel the effect of the electricity, or to see some experiments." When the Russians made a "montgolfier" hot air balloon out of Japanese paper and sent it soaring (nearly burning down part of Nagasaki in the process), the citizens were amazed.[3] Similarly, when MacDonald was incarcerated, a mini-parade of people came to see him, merely out of curiosity.

No one could have been more frustrated by the Shogunate's policy than the Nagasaki interpreters, for they had more access to unfiltered international information than anyone else in Japan. By the mid-nineteenth century, they knew Japanese technology was increasingly backward and the Seclusion Laws futile—but they were required to be transmitters of information and to keep their opinions to themselves. When Siebold, the famous Deshima physician, was banished in 1829 for smuggling a map out of Japan, the local repercussions had been widespread. They included death sentences, suicides, and banishment to remote islands for those suspected of directly helping him. Many interpreters who had contacts with Siebold—interpreters whom MacDonald's pupils knew well—had been imprisoned.[4]

Even subtle criticism of government policy could have dire consequences. While not a government interpreter, Chōei Takano, a *rangakusha*, or scholar of Dutch learning, had studied medicine and other subjects under Siebold in Nagasaki and was a noted translator of texts. Around the time of the *Morrison* affair of 1837 (when Shogunate forces had fired on an American ship trying to return Otokichi and other Japanese castaways), Takano wrote a critique of the Seclusion policy, couching it in the form of a dream.

He was thrown in jail, later became a fugitive, and ultimately was forced to commit suicide.[5]

In this context, while MacDonald is known for teaching English to the interpreters in Nagasaki, he actually did far more than that. He imparted information about the outside world, all of which was filtered through the interpreters. Officials asked him over and over again about the whaling industry and world geography. In his private conversations with Moriyama and Uemura, he notes, "They would not consciously give me any information, but were very inquisitive on several subjects; on which I told them all I knew." Moriyama, in particular, repeatedly grilled him about the governments, armies, and navies of European nations. Getting the Japanese to reconsider their ancestral laws was out of the question, but MacDonald tried. Later in life, he would write, "I endeavored to impress upon them among other things that the advancement made by Western nations in improving and having a better knowledge would soon be extended to Asia and the possibility of their deriving advantages &c &c. For as of that early date I had heard of the possibility of having a Rail-Road across the continent [of North America]."[6]

External Pressures on Japan

In the mid-nineteenth century, many Westerners regarded the Dutch trade with Japan with a mixture of jealousy and scorn. The jealousy sprang from the fact that Holland was the only European nation allowed to trade with the mysterious but presumably rich Japan. The scorn came from the fact that by the mid-nineteenth century Holland was a relatively insignificant power. Critics also complained that the Dutch humiliated themselves and dishonored all Christians by kowtowing to Japanese authorities simply to maintain their monopoly—which they had obtained by helping suppress the Shimabara Christians in 1638.

By the mid-nineteenth century, the United States government had interests in Japan beyond direct trade. It wanted better treatment for its shipwrecked sailors. As a new Pacific power, it saw relations with Japan as a way to further trade with China and counter British influence in the area. And as the age of steamships dawned in the Pacific, American officials hoped someday to open up coaling stations in Japan.

Viewed from the outside, the pressures mounting on Japan were so obvious that in 1844, four years before MacDonald's arrival King William II of Holland took the unprecedented step of writing the Shogunate directly. The Dutch East India Company normally handled all contact with Japan, but Siebold—back in Holland and worried about Japan's future—had strongly recommended that the king send a personal letter, and even drafted one for him.[7] Writing in a most respectful and solicitous tone, William commended the Japanese government for having ordered that foreign ships in trouble no longer be fired upon and instead be treated kindly. He acknowledged the Seclusion Edicts and ancestral laws but did not mince words. He explained the changes occurring in the outside world, the rise of British power, and the recent British victory over giant China in the Opium Wars. Stressing that no nation could remain in isolation forever, he wrote,

> This, All powerful Emperor, is our friendly advice: ameliorate the laws against the foreigners, lest happy Japan be destroyed by war . . . peace can only be maintained through friendly relations, and . . . these are only created by commercial relations.[8]

But when the Shogunate's final response came, it was the equivalent of a polite form letter, reasserting the immutability of the ancestral laws.

Other American Prisoners in Nagasaki

Of all the Nagasaki interpreters, Einosuke Moriyama had a particularly clear view of the problems Japan faced, but to MacDonald he never revealed the depth of his knowledge, or his previous experience with English-speaking people. He had interpreted during the visit of the *Manhattan* to Japan in 1845, and in 1846 he had participated in the interrogations of the *Lawrence* crewmen. Furthermore, in 1848—while interacting with MacDonald— he was participating in the interrogations of the *Lagoda* crew. If Moriyama was MacDonald's best pupil, it was partly because he had had the most practice.

The *Lawrence*, it will be recalled, had been wrecked off northern Ezo on May 27, 1846. Seven survivors had been taken into custody by the Matsumae Clan and, after a year in the north, transported to Nagasaki. Arriving in August 1847, they were interrogated and incarcerated at a local temple. Unlike MacDonald, they later complained of unwarranted cruelty by their captors.

The interrogations were conducted in English, but because the Japanese "Dutch interpreters" were not yet fluent, Dutch factor Joseph Levyssohn did the actual questioning. George Howe, the *Lawrence*'s first mate, claims that the Japanese wanted to ascertain the sailors were not British, as Britain had been placed on the Shogunate's blacklist, and that Levyssohn told them, "If there are any John Bulls amongst you, you had better not say anything about it." Levyssohn denies this, but in a later report, Murphy Wells, the ship's carpenter, roughly corroborates Howe's account, writing that the Japanese "threatened to cut off our heads, because they thought we were English, whom they hate; but when we told them we were Americans, they said nothing more, except to ask us of what religion we were." When told to tread on a Christian icon, the men hesitated, and, according to Howe, "the guards drew out their swords and threatened to kill us, and so compelled every one of us to trample on the print, and spit upon it." The men had already spent a year as prisoners in the far north under harsh conditions. Even if exaggerated, their accounts clearly reveal their despair of ever getting home. Howe later referred to their stay in Japan as one of "close and strict confinement, privation, and ill-treatment."[9]

After two months of incarceration in Nagasaki, the men were finally deported on a Dutch ship to Batavia, with the help of Levyssohn. But according to Howe, just before obtaining freedom one man gave up hope, and, saying "he would rather die than suffer so much any longer," tried to escape from prison, whereupon he was "inhumanely murdered by the Japanese." Wells's account is more detailed and says, "While we were in Japan, in prison, one of our comrades, Thos. Williams, endeavored to make his escape, but was caught and taken back to prison in a dying state, owing to wounds inflicted on him with some deadly weapon; there was a gash over his forehead which bled profusely. The poor fellow lived about six hours. The natives brought a coffin, into which they compelled us to place the corpse, when they took it away."[10]

Levyssohn's account of the *Lawrence* crew, published in 1852, is entirely different. His version was essentially the official Japanese one—that the man later died of disease after the Japanese did everything possible to help him. "Upon entering the compound," Levyssohn writes, "one of the men, who came from Canada and who had long been suffering from a disease that would later cause his death, tried, in a state of lightheadedness, to escape. This attempt was soon foiled, and the Japanese commander, in order to prevent any repetition of such incidents, had the poor souls tied up."[11] Japanese records show officials acknowledging the death, but ascribing it to an illness that they tried hard to cure, and not to maltreatment or murder.[12]

Moriyama's name appears on the interrogation records of the *Lawrence* crewmen, but what he felt about this incident is a mystery. He spoke Dutch with Murphy Wells, who understood some of that language, yet one thing is clear: for at least two months in 1846 he and other interpreters had had an opportunity to listen to native English on a daily basis.

❖ ❖ ❖

The year MacDonald arrived in Nagasaki, Moriyama helped interrogate the notorious crew of the whaling ship *Lagoda*. Like the *Lawrence* crewmen, these unfortunate fifteen souls had a terrible time in Nagasaki; so much so that, even though their stay overlapped with MacDonald's, they almost seem to have been in a different country.

From the beginning, the *Lagoda* men were nothing but trouble for the Japanese. Deserters, who had already made escape attempts at Matsumae, they arrived in Nagasaki shortly before MacDonald, at the beginning of September 1848. Their voyage took place during the hottest time of the year, and the cooped-up men feared they would die of suffocation.

Twenty-three-year-old Robert McCoy, from Philadelphia, was the most intelligent and articulate man in the group and something of a leader. Physically huge (one account says 300 lbs.), he was also extremely strong willed. In the mid-nineteenth century, when Japan still maintained a fossilized system of feudalism—with an extreme emphasis on hierarchy, McCoy had the "live-free-or-die"–type of American personality that—unlike the friendly and eager-to-please MacDonald—could only create problems.

When the *Lagoda* crew arrived in Nagasaki, officials including Moriyama met them and asked the regular set of questions. The men demanded their whaleboats and freedom, but the officials refused and told them permission had to come from the Shogunate at Edo, which would require a month and a half. The men nonetheless believed they would then be able to leave on the annual Dutch ship for Batavia. Like the *Lawrence* crew before them and MacDonald after them, the *Lagoda* men were taken to the magistrate's office, forced to trample on the cross, made to bow before the magistrate, interrogated, and then incarcerated in a local Buddhist temple. They were subsequently subjected to repeat interrogations, and, with Moriyama present, they reasserted that they had been shipwrecked. McCoy found Moriyama's interpretations "very incorrect."[13]

On September 6, the men were interrogated without Levyssohn present. According to McCoy, the Japanese interpreter (presumably Moriyama) said "he doubted our story, and believed that we were mere spies, and came to examine the country, and nothing else." Still, the Americans believed they would be allowed to leave as soon as permission was obtained from the "emperor." On September 20, Levyssohn sent over presents, in this case "coffee, sugar, Holland gin, and some flasks of wine," as well as clothing and newspapers. He tried to get permission for the Dutch physician on Deshima to look at the men, but the Japanese authorities denied it.[14]

After a month and a half, the men were told that permission to leave on the Dutch ship had not yet been received. They had been told how long it took to get answers from the capital, but not of the delays common in a molasses-like bureaucracy. Increasingly frustrated, they began quarreling among themselves, despite admonitions against doing so by Levyssohn. Finally, two of them wrote a letter to Levyssohn, begging him to get word to an American government consul somewhere, in hopes that they might be rescued.

Around November 1, in a desperate attempt to try to reach the Dutch ship in Nagasaki Harbor before it left, McCoy broke out of prison. After a night of travel and no success, he hid in the mountains but was captured the next day. Returned to prison, he was re-interrogated, confined in stocks, tied up, and then separated from his companions and thrown into a common jail. When he learned the annual Dutch ship had left, he went on a hunger strike. Only after Levyssohn intervened on his behalf was he reunited with his crewmates.

As de facto guardian of the Dutch monopoly with Japan, Levyssohn was placed in a difficult position. He knew scores of American whaling ships regularly passed near Nagasaki, but none would dare visit because of Japan's Seclusion Laws. Furthermore, he knew that by law, foreign sailors could only be deported on the annual Dutch or Chinese ship, so if the Dutch ship left without the men, they would remain incarcerated another year. As a precaution, he therefore took the exceedingly risky step of writing a letter to the U.S. consul in Batavia, notifying him of the men's plight. He placed it, along with the note from the *Lagoda* men, on board the *Josephine and Catherine*, which finally left for Batavia on November 8.

On the night of December 14, the still undaunted McCoy and two other *Lagoda* men—John Bull and Jacob Boyd—burned a hole in their prison floor and dug under a fence to escape. Reaching the shore of Nagasaki Bay at two o'clock in the morning, they tried to get to a boat but failed when a barking dog alerted local residents. After hiding and moving about the area for twenty-four hours, the escapees were finally caught by soldiers. This time they were bound in the painful style used for common prisoners, their hands hauled up high behind their backs. Later, they were put in stocks.

Thereafter things went downhill rapidly. On or about December 16, all the *Lagoda* men were thrown into a common prison for criminals, with miserable conditions, but the three escapees were kept separate from the others. The next night, one of the Hawaiian crewmen, known as "Maury," was found dead, the Americans claiming he had hung himself.

As the weather grew colder and it snowed in Nagasaki, some of the *Lagoda* men fell ill. On January 24, 1849 (New Year's Day in the old Japanese calendar) one man—Ezra Goldthwait—died. The Americans became convinced the Japanese were trying to poison them with strange medicines, and their suspicions were reinforced when John Water—who came down with symptoms similar to those of Goldthwait—recovered after he *stopped* using the medicinals.

In the interim, McCoy befriended one of the guards, who gave him much valuable information. When some of the Americans told their captors that the U.S. government would come to help them and punish the Japanese for their cruelty, this guard reportedly told them that "the year before, at the City of Yedo, a common soldier had knocked down an American commodore, and that the Americans had taken no notice of it." Why then, the guard asked, would the Americans take any notice of a few poor sailors?[15] When eventually relayed to American officials, this statement about Commodore Biddle's 1846 visit had lasting reverberations and profoundly affected the way in which the Americans believed they should deal with the Japanese.

Unlike MacDonald, McCoy did not have daily contact with the interpreters, but through his guards he learned enough colloquial Japanese to communicate. Always dogmatic and overconfident, he later boasted that "I can understand nearly everything said to me in Japanese without difficulty. I am better acquainted with the Japanese language than Morreama, the interpreter, is with the English."[16]

Sometime in March 1849, McCoy learned from his guard friend that there was another American sailor imprisoned in Nagasaki—MacDonald—but he "was cautioned not to mention it, as it would cause the guard to lose his head." On another occasion, McCoy was told a story that corroborates (and gives further credence to) the claims of the *Lawrence* survivors—that "one of a party of Americans, who had been in the same prison, in 1846, broke out and escaped into the country; and whilst the soldiers were recapturing him, in defending himself he struck one of the chiefs on the head with a stone, when he was cut down and overpowered. He died from his wounds a few days afterwards, being left alone in his prison."[17]

❖ ❖ ❖

No one ever told MacDonald that other Americans were imprisoned in Nagasaki, but he began to suspect so, in an amusing context. He was occasionally asked to translate "certain sailor terms," such as "Shiver my timbers!" (and presumably other, more profane expressions). He found it impossible, not only because of his limited Japanese but because Japanese people do not swear in the manner of Westerners. Nonetheless, from this he deduced that his captors must have picked up the terms "from British or American sailors about the place."[18]

MacDonald later indicated that he felt an obligation to get word to the outside world so that other American sailors in Japan could be freed. Instead, it was the other way around, for it was the plight of the *Lagoda* crew that resulted in MacDonald's release. And it was the plight of all shipwrecked sailors in Japan that gave a humanitarian pretext to the United States' decision to force Japan to end her policy of isolation.

American Sailors Become a Political Issue

In the North American press, reports about Japanese mistreatment of shipwrecked Americans inflamed public opinion. The accounts were amplified in the retelling, and since Japan had no relations with the outside world they were relentlessly one-sided. The stories had, after all, originated with embittered seamen, who had little love in their hearts for Japan. Murphy Wells, of the *Lawrence*, later wrote, "It is anxiously hoped the American Government will not suffer this treatment, but more particularly so sanguinary an act towards hapless shipwrecked American seamen to pass without ample retribution."[19]

In the fall of 1849, the *New York Courier and Enquirer* described the *Lagoda* men as having been "treated with the utmost inhumanity and cruelty . . . beaten upon the slightest pretext, shut up in cages like wild beasts, excluded from light, air and exercise, and fed just enough to prevent starvation. . . . Nothing could be more inhuman than the treatment they received during the long period of their captivity." Another editorial concluded that, "The Japanese, by not only refusing such assistance, but by treating all such unfortunate foreigners as enemies, forfeit all claim to respect as a civilized people, and may justly be regarded as hostile to the human race." The writer went on to reiterate former president John Quincy Adams's position that no nation has the right to isolate itself from others, and to advocate that unless the Japanese changed their policy a U.S. naval force should be maintained off the coast of Japan "to inflict summary chastisement upon them for any renewal of such barbarities upon American citizens, as they have heretofore inflicted with entire impunity."[20]

American readers were unaware of Japan's Seclusion Laws and they could not understand how shipwrecked or destitute sailors could be put in any sort of prison. In the West, helping ships or sailors in trouble was a duty. Levyssohn—the Dutchman who went out of his way to assist the *Lawrence* and *Lagoda* crews as well as MacDonald (and was profusely thanked by all of them)—referred to it as "a sacred obligation."[21] But further inflaming American sentiment was the Japanese attitude toward Christianity. Reports of seamen being forced to trample on sacred icons seemed to confirm impressions that Japanese were barbaric. And it is easy to forget today how insulting it was to Americans at the time—even to MacDonald, who was raised under the British flag—to be forced to bow. In feudal Japan of the 1840s, bowing often meant dramatic prostration before a superior, and it was carried to great extremes. To U.S. citizens, recently liberated from European monarchism and colonialism, such kowtowing was absolute anathema.

On the other hand, readers of the first accounts of shipwrecked sailors in Japan did not know that some of the men were deserters. Furthermore, they tended to forget how obstinate and unruly American sailors—especially whalers—could be. In fact, the *Lagoda* crew nearly drove the Japanese to distraction.

When Nagasaki officials later released the *Lagoda* men and MacDonald to the U.S. Navy, they provided an extensive report. It correlates closely with later depositions given by the *Lagoda* men and documents their various escape attempts. The report carefully notes that each time the men were captured they begged for forgiveness, which was granted with warnings and the imposition of increased restrictions on their freedom. It details the men's various illnesses and the medical treatments they were given; of MacDonald, it states that "he . . . has never complained of being ill." It notes the deaths of the two *Lagoda* crewmen in some detail, but here the accounts of the Japanese differ dramatically from those of the American crewmen. Robert McCoy and John Bull had claimed that they were not allowed to bury the men on their own, Bull writing, "They refused us, laughing and scoffing at our request." The Japanese report stresses that the men "begged and obtained permission to bury" their comrades, and says that Nagasaki officials initiated an investigation into the death of the Hawaiian islander—the implication being that he could not have hung himself undetected in a crowded cell and may have been murdered by his crewmates. Most tellingly, the report notes: "The [*Lagoda* men] gave so much trouble that the Japanese authorities scarcely knew what course to pursue towards them."[22] Other Japanese surviving records are even more explicit, saying that MacDonald "was extremely well-behaved and polite towards the officials, but the [men of the *Lagoda* crew] seemed truly of low birth, and were so rude and insulting that the officials were at a loss what to do with them."[23]

Public Opinion

In North America, people at first believed the sailors' reports and routinely denounced the Japanese. But American attitudes soon underwent a 180-degree shift as the official Japanese perspective was factored into the interpretation of events. First of all, some of the men were learned to be deserters. Second, after Japan was finally opened to the Western world in 1853, the American public "discovered" and fell in love with its new Pacific neighbor. Even Honolulu-based newspapers *The Polynesian* and *The Friend*—previously so sympathetic to sailors and so critical of Japan's policies—turned against the men. In 1854, immediately after Commodore Perry negotiated a treaty of Amity and Friendship with Japan and came to agreements on the treatment of sailors, *The Friend* ran an article stating,

This disposition of the Japanese to treat with care and attention shipwrecked men, is quite contrary to the generally received opinion of the world in this respect, and in justice to the Japanese, it is but fair to state, that the restraints hitherto imposed upon American seamen, about which so much has been said and written, were rendered necessary by their over-bearing lawlessness, and vicious conduct.[24]

In truth, mid-nineteenth century whaling crews could be a rough and unruly lot, for they were often abused and treated more like slaves than freemen by ship's officers. Partly because of this, modern Japanese and American historians have been inclined to discount the men's tales of suffering in Japan, or at least interpret them in a more relativistic fashion (sometimes not even mentioning the crewmen's assertion that their friends were murdered).[25] In this view, the sailors' bad experiences were caused by cultural misunderstandings. Used to a calorie-rich diet, on normal Japanese fare the Americans would have felt they were being deliberately starved. Not used to palanquins (which might be a luxury for ordinary Japanese) or to cramped quarters (which might be perfectly adequate for smaller Japanese), the sailors would have seen these conditions as cruel treatment.

When writers do describe the *Lawrence* and the *Lagoda* sailors, they invariably use MacDonald as a benchmark. The Dutch factor on Deshima, Joseph Levyssohn, was one of the first to do so. In his 1852 book he denigrated the *Lagoda* crewmen for their "bad behavior" and supported the position of the Nagasaki authorities, quoting an article based on information he had supplied, saying that "insofar as the shipwrecked had any cause for complaint concerning their harsh treatment, it was wholly due to their misbehavior and their repeated attempts to escape. This appears to be in complete agreement with the truth since *Ranold Macdonald . . .* had traveled to *Japan* on his own accord, presumably in the pursuit of adventure, and whose manners the Japanese found in no way objectionable, *had no complaints about his treatment there.*"[26]

When posthumously published in 1923, even MacDonald's own *Narrative* disparaged the *Lagoda* crew. In it he, too, sides with the Japanese viewpoint, describing the sailors as men who were "young, violent, habitually quarreled amongst themselves, and gave much trouble." Similarly, he says that "throughout their whole detention . . . they were according to their own account, well and certainly not cruelly treated; as prisoners ever, however."

He claims that "no punishment was inflicted" and that one American died a natural death, "not withstanding all medical care and humane treatment." Of the Hawaiian man who may have hung himself, he cruelly notes that he had done so "in the manner of his people, without compunction."[27]

Yet this passage was authored decades after MacDonald had left Nagasaki—after later, negative accounts about the *Lagoda* crew had appeared in the press. Stylistically, it also smacks of a section reworked by his editor friend, Malcolm McLeod. At the time of his release from Nagasaki, MacDonald held an entirely different opinion. After disembarking in Hong Kong from a U.S. Navy ship on which he had just spent several weeks with the *Lagoda* crewmen, he wrote Samuel C. Damon on May 24th, 1849, in Honolulu, saying,

> [I]t is a shame how they have abused 15 American sailors belonging to the *Lagoda* . . . of this party the Japanese killed one man & a poor Sandwich Islander hung himself in despair.[28]

The truth of what happened to the *Lawrence* and *Lagoda* crews probably lies somewhere between the official Japanese accounts and the stories of the embittered sailors. The language barrier amplified misunderstandings, but the men may indeed have had the misfortune to meet with cruelty or guards who could not deal properly with a situation that escalated out of their control. The guards had little impetus to advertise to their superiors what had really happened, and Japanese officials had little interest in letting overseas governments know if maltreatment had occurred—especially if doing so might encourage foreign governments to send warships to attack them. And Levyssohn had little incentive to complain too loudly of mistreatment of the sailors, as it might jeopardize the Dutch trading monopoly.

To judge the *Lagoda* and *Lawrence* men based on MacDonald's experience is thus overly cruel. MacDonald was alone, and far easier to control than a large group of men of varying temperaments, ages, and cultures. Unlike them, he was also in Japan voluntarily. Although he yearned to be released from his jail, he had gone to extraordinary lengths to get to Japan and initially, at least, had no desire to leave.

U.S.S. *Preble* (1839–63). Lithograph by A. Hoen & Co.

U.S.S. Preble Arrives in Nagasaki

An hour or so before sundown on April 17, 1849, MacDonald heard six cannon shots, the first two in quick succession and the others spaced out. He knew this was the local custom in signaling the arrival of the annual Dutch ship, but it was too early for that. The other possibility was that the cannons were summoning troops to Nagasaki from surrounding areas in case of a non-Dutch foreign ship. Sure enough, in the next few days, soldiers swarmed into Nagasaki. A United States man-o'-war had been spotted in the offing, and it had specific orders to retrieve any stranded American sailors. Joseph Levyssohn had succeeded in doing what the *Lagoda* crewmen had begged him to do—to get word of their plight to the outside world.

Levyssohn's letter, along with the note from the *Lagoda* crewmen, had been sent to Batavia in November 1848. From there it had been forwarded to the Netherlands consul in Canton, China, who on January 25, 1849, forwarded it to his U.S. counterpart. The note from the *Lagoda* men, originally addressed to Levyssohn, was short and to the point. Having just learned they could not leave Japan on the *Josephine and Catherine*, the two writers said it had "sunk our spirits greatly." They promised to try to keep the other men under control, but complained that the Japanese "had deceived us so often, we can put no dependence in them. We do not ask them to help us, if only they let us go. . . . If not, our American navy cruising on this side will hear of it, and claim us as American citizens. If they are ignorant of this, please to inform them of it, and the consequences. . . ."[29]

The day after receiving Levyssohn's communication, the U.S. consul in Canton forwarded it with a cover letter to Commodore D. Geisinger, commander of the U.S. East India Squadron, then in Whampoa, near Canton. The consul asked Geisinger to send a portion of his squadron to secure the release of "fifteen seamen" in "Nangasacki." In a truly speedy turnaround for the time, Geisinger replied on the very same day that he would order the U.S.S. *Preble*—under Commander James Glynn and then in Hong Kong— to Japan.

Glynn's sailing instructions, issued on January 31, were specific, and they evidenced a sophistication about the problems of negotiating with authorities in Nagasaki. He was to sail to Nagasaki and obtain the immediate release of the fifteen survivors of the "shipwrecked crew of the American whaler 'Lagoda'." If the men were handed over, or if they were not in Nagasaki, he was to return to Shanghai. At this time, Americans generally did not understand that the Japanese emperor was kept powerless in Kyōto and that real power resided in the Shogun in Edo, but they knew Edo was the center of power. If the Nagasaki authorities claimed to need permission from Edo (which would require waiting a month and a half), Glynn was told to sail to Edo and try to communicate directly with the "imperial court." Glynn was advised to be "conciliatory, but firm" in all his negotiations, and he was to "be careful not to violate the laws or customs of the country, or by any means prejudice the success of any pacific policy our government may be inclined to pursue." He was reminded that protection of the American whaling fleet was of deep concern to the U.S. government, and also ordered, during his cruise, to give "American commerce and interests the fullest protection in your power." Most significantly for the fate of Ranald MacDonald, Glynn was told that if he learned of any *other* American seamen besides the *Lagoda* men confined in Japan, he should also "demand their release and surrender."[30]

Before leaving Hong Kong, Glynn had three letters for Japanese officials translated (into Japanese) with the help of Charles Gutzlaff, then the "Chinese Secretary" for the local British government office. Gutzlaff, it may be

recalled, was a missionary linguist who had studied Japanese and in 1849 had employed
Kyūkichi (one of the three
castaways who had attended
school at Fort Vancouver
shortly after Ranald MacDonald's departure to Red River).
The first of these little-known
letters represented Glynn's
polite but simple request for
the return of any shipwrecked
sailors in Japan. The second,
apparently never presented,
proposed that an American

Commander James Glynn.

From *Harper's New Monthly Magazine,* October 1898.

agent be stationed in Japan to help solve any future problems with shipwrecked seamen. Regarding their mistreatment, it noted, "[O]n this very
point we are perhaps more ready to war than on any other" and (referring to
the War of 1812 with Great Britain) "on this point we have warred with the
most powerful nation on the Globe." The final letter, also apparently never
used, was the most ambitious of all, proposing that the United States be
allowed a coaling depot in Japan in the future for use of its steamships.[31]

The *Preble* left Hong Kong on February 12, 1849, but an outbreak of
smallpox soon caused her to turn back to port and be quarantined. It was a
harbinger of things to come, as during her long assignment in the Pacific in
the 1840s, the *Preble* would suffer one of the highest crew mortality rates
from disease in the entire U.S. Navy. Nonetheless, the forced return had an
auspicious result for MacDonald, because in Hong Kong Glynn saw a newspaper article from the December 1848 edition of the Honolulu seamen's
paper, *The Friend*, authored by Samuel C. Damon. The article summarized
what was then known about MacDonald's attempt to enter Japan through its
northern frontier, and—while somewhat skeptical of his chances for survival
after leaving his whaling ship—did let Glynn know that another North
American sailor might be somewhere in Japan.[32]

On March 22, the *Preble* at last set sail again, and on April 18, after a
three-day stop at the Ryūkyū Islands, finally reached the entrance to Nagasaki Bay. The weather was mild and clear, with light breezes. At 11:30 A.M.,

with all hands at general quarters save for eighteen who were sick, the ship anchored in twenty-seven fathoms of water.

Officials in Nagasaki had elaborate procedures to confirm the identity of ships approaching their harbor and to control them. One of these involved having a small boat sail alongside the foreign ship and, with a long pole, foist onto its deck a bamboo container with a written message (usually in Dutch, sometimes French). The message conveyed questions about place of origin and purpose of coming, and—if the ship were to be allowed into the harbor—prohibitions on disembarking or discharging of firearms, as well as instructions where to anchor. Glynn was not the commander of a merchant ship, however, but the U.S.S. *Preble*, a 127-foot, 560-ton sloop, with a crew of 141 men and fourteen cannon. For a man-o'-war it was small, but Glynn was determined to show he could not be trifled with. In an act that horrified the Nagasaki bureaucrats, he promptly ordered the communication thrown overboard.

U.S.-Japan Negotiations Begin

The first Japanese to board the *Preble* was none other than Einosuke Moriyama, accompanied by seven officials. Although the Americans later reported that he "spoke tolerably good English, but understood only as much as he wanted to," Moriyama interpreted almost all negotiations until they departed and he greatly impressed them with his ability.[33] These conversations with the Japanese were all transcribed and survive, both as handwritten copies in the National Archives of the United States as well as published U.S. House and Senate documents. Although they do not reveal what sort of accent Moriyama had (presumably peculiar, with heavy overtones of Dutch and Japanese), they do show he had already made remarkable progress during his six months under MacDonald's tutelage. They should be required reading for modern American and Japanese negotiators.

Despite the extreme tension, initial conversations went well. A new spot to anchor was negotiated, but Glynn refused to let any of the Japanese men sail with him when repositioning his ship in the harbor. Through Moriyama, Glynn was first questioned by Tatsunoshin Shirai, the same military officer who had met MacDonald on his arrival in Nagasaki. Shirai wanted to know why Glynn was in Japan, what country and port he came from, details about the ship, what his official title was, and whether he had written or oral orders to come to Japan and retrieve Americans. Important for MacDonald, Glynn responded that he had written orders to retrieve not just shipwrecked sailors in Nagasaki, but *any* Americans confined in Japan, and to take them back to Hong Kong. Shirai, for his part, was eager to learn from whom Glynn had received his orders, how he knew there were any Americans in Japan, and whether he had full power to negotiate their release. But he also asked Glynn whether he was in need of water, firewood, and provisions. Glynn knew the Japanese would not ask for payment and that in the Japanese system there was a danger in incurring obligations, so he tried to insist on being allowed to pay. Shirai asked if the Americans had brought any shipwrecked Japanese sailors, to which Glynn replied, "If I had found any, I would have brought them with pleasure."[34]

As soon as Glynn had the chance, he got right to the point, again directly asking Shirai if there were any American seamen in Japan, and if so whether they were in Nagasaki. Shirai answered that there were fourteen men, out of an original number of sixteen, and that two had died. "We are very sorry that they died," he explained, "but [we] could not do anything to prevent it."[35] It is unclear whether Glynn did the math and realized there was an additional sailor beyond the fifteen *Lagoda* men for whom he had come. Nonetheless, he was a smart negotiator and deliberately did not reveal how many sailors he *thought* were in Japan. Among the Americans a real fear existed that the Japanese might not tell them who they had. They knew, for example, that during the failed visit of the U.S.S. *Columbus* to Edo Bay in July 1846, the Japanese had not mentioned the *Lawrence* crew, shipwrecked in the far north that May.[36]

Luckily for MacDonald, Shirai had included him in his count of "American seamen," and he explained that one of the men (MacDonald) had arrived in Nagasaki shortly after the *Lagoda* men. Glynn then asked the most critical question: "Will it be necessary that my demand for the release of the seamen be referred to the Emperor?" And here the first hint of conflict occurred, as Shirai responded, "This is a question which I cannot satisfactorily answer to *officially*."[37]

The next day, on April 19, Glynn met Sehei Matsumura, another "high military official" of Nagasaki, who came on board with much pomp and circumstance. After Matsumura congratulated the American commander on his safe arrival, Glynn protested against the scores of small boats surrounding his ship—which were clearly making him nervous—and asked that they be removed. Matsumura explained that he did not have jurisdiction over the boats and asked why America had sent a warship to Japan in the first place. He also wanted to know the dimensions of the ship, and how many men-of-war the United States possessed. Glynn replied that it was common practice for the United States to send ships to protect its citizens from "injustice or oppression" and that he was in Nagasaki to relieve his "distressed countrymen." He presented Matsumura with an official written communication for "His Excellency the Governor of Nangasacki"—formally asking for the release of the detained sailors. "My superior officer," Glynn had written, "has heard that fifteen persons have been cast upon your coast, on one occasion, and one alone on a second occasion—making sixteen in all—from American vessels."[38] From this statement it would appear that Glynn's superior Geisinger knew in advance of MacDonald's confinement in Nagasaki, but more likely it was a ploy by Glynn—who had just learned of another sailor's presence the previous day—to give his demand more weight.

The interrogations on board the *Preble* were recorded by hand, in a simple question and answer format. The language in the reports has clearly been edited, as both Japanese and Americans speak in grammatically precise, clear English. Yet everything had to be filtered through the interpreter, Moriyama, in a slow, consecutive fashion, with him looking up many words in his dictionary and bowing to Matsumura each time he addressed him. Responses to questions on both sides were obviously measured, given after what must have been fascinating internal discussion.

Because Glynn spoke in the same language as the transcripts (English), as one would expect, his speech sounds native and sophisticated in the reports, whereas the Japanese questions and answers are straightforward (having been filtered through a struggling interpreter). Had the dialogs been recorded in Japanese, the situation would have been reversed. How well the Japanese actually understood Glynn at times is debatable, especially when he used long sentences such as: "A free intercourse and reciprocal understanding between myself and the people, as well as the authorities, will tend not only to a better acquaintance, but lead to a more correct understanding between us." Yet despite language problems and the extreme tension of the situation, communications were successfully established. Records for that day show (in parentheses) that when Glynn was asked his age, the answer was "given after some humor."[39]

On April 22, with Moriyama interpreting, another conference was held between Glynn and Matsumura on board the *Preble*. This time, tensions started rising as soon as Glynn asked Matsumura if he had brought an answer to his letter to the magistrate. Matsumura's replies and Glynn's reactions to them form an uncanny pattern that to this day is repeated over and over again in negotiations between Americans and Japanese. Then as now, Japanese answers usually drive the Americans to distraction:

> *Matsumura:* To-day he could not send an answer. He will send a reply "another time—not now."
> *Glynn:* When will the governor send me an answer?
> *Matsumura:* I cannot say when. In a "short time" I think the governor will send an answer.
> *Glynn:* What do you mean by a "short time?"
> *Matsumura:* I cannot say, for I don't know when an answer will come.
> *Glynn:* Tell the governor that if I can get the shipwrecked sailors, I wish to depart immediately; but if I am unsuccessful in getting them, then I am ordered by my superior officer "to do something else."
> *Matsumura:* Whether the men will be given up or not, I cannot say, but will report your remarks to the governor.[40]

Exasperated, Glynn demanded a written response to his written request, and a clear explanation of what the Japanese meant by "a short time." After much vacillating by Matsumura, Glynn demanded a response the next day. Then he wanted to know if the sailors were in a "prison," but Matsumura, speaking through Moriyama, claimed not to understand what a prison was, and replied in a brilliant obfuscation that, "the men do not walk about, but are *'in a place by themselves.'* "[41]

Most pressing to Glynn, who constantly feared being attacked and could not afford to dawdle in Nagasaki, was to learn whether the magistrate of Nagasaki would have to get permission from the "emperor" of Japan, whom he thought lived in Edo. But he could not get Matsumura to tell him if the magistrate had written the emperor, and when he demanded to know how long it took to get a message to and from Edo, the following dialog ensued:

> *Matsumura:* I really do not know.
> *Glynn:* What? Born in this country, and living here all your life, and being in an official position, cannot you tell me the time it would

take to go from here to Yedo and back?

Matsumura: I think thirty days.[42]

Glynn was ready to tear his hair out in frustration, but as often happens in such situations, he put considerable blame on the interpreter—in this case Moriyama. As his men later reported, "[T]he evasions made by the interpreter to the queries put to him were characteristic of this suspicious people—a people among whom the system of espionage and mutual responsibility has well-nigh destroyed everything like frankness, truth, and confidence."[43] In fact, Glynn had no idea of the problems Americans and Japanese could then have communicating. He wanted to salute his visitors, but they had no such custom. He wanted to (and did) shake their hands, without realizing it was a slightly repulsive act for them. And he could not understand why they did not look him in the eye when talking—at one point even demanding that they do so.

Glynn wanted precise and immediate responses, but he did not know that vagueness is an art form among Japanese and that direct answers are often considered impolite, if not dangerous. Nor was he aware how hard it is to interpret Japanese statements (which often do not require specifying subject or gender or singular or plural or complex tenses) into logical-sounding English. And he did not know that negative questions, such as "can't you come back tomorrow?" could result in answers with "yes" that really meant "no," as in "yes, we cannot come back tomorrow."

Finally, although Glynn realized responsibility was diffused among the Japanese officials, he did not appreciate the tremendous pressures they were under. They would have *loved* for him to collect the American sailors and leave *immediately*. With knowledge of the disastrous visit of the British warship, *Phaeton*, the officials lived in dread of what the commander might do if his demands were not met. But they also had ancestral laws to consider and a Byzantine hierarchy to report to, and any misstep might have dire consequences. As Levyssohn wrote later, "[O]ne must bear in mind the exaggerated fear some Japanese officials have of falling out of favor with their superiors, as a result of which they would then feel obligated to take their own life."[44]

As luck would have it, a new magistrate had just arrived from Edo. He did not bring permission, but his arrival presented an opportunity. The magistrate sent Levyssohn a "very secret and urgent oral request . . . by mouth of the junior interpreter Einoske," requesting ideas for a solution.[45] Levyssohn was not feeling well—he was coming down with a fever that would incapacitate him—but he obliged.

At the end of a meeting with Moriyama on April 22, Glynn received his first break. Levyssohn had translated Glynn's letter of April 19 to the magistrate into Dutch (for the Japanese interpreters), and Levyssohn, better than anyone else, knew the insurmountable nature of the problems both sides were having. He knew Glynn was under orders to retrieve the seamen and what could happen if they were not delivered. He knew the Nagasaki magistrate did not have the authority to release the men and that it would take longer to obtain permission than Glynn could afford to wait, cooped up on his ship in the harbor. He also knew that Japanese law required shipwrecked sailors to be given only to the Dutch or Chinese for deportation, and that no provision existed for handing them over directly over to a foreign military ship, especially one that had suddenly appeared in Nagasaki Harbor. The Dutch factor's solution was thus brilliant.

As Levyssohn explained in a letter to Glynn, he had proposed to the magistrate that the Japanese meet with the Americans to explain their treatment of the sailors. At this meeting, Levyssohn reasoned, the Japanese could also explain their laws and regulations with Glynn. The Japanese could then release the seamen—not to the Americans but to the Dutch on Deshima—whereupon they could be transferred to the Americans in a way that would satisfy Japanese law.

On April 23, Glynn again met with Tatsunoshin Shirai in the *Preble*'s cabin, desperate for more definite answers. Shirai explained that Levyssohn's proposal had been submitted to the magistrate with a plea that normal procedures be waived. In two days, he added, Levyssohn would visit the *Preble*. But Glynn, still unhappy with the vagueness of the situation, demanded to see the magistrate and not a local Dutchman. When Shirai qualified all his remarks about dates with "I think," Glynn lost his temper and threatened to leave and report to his government that Japan had *refused* to release the sailors. He demanded to see Levyssohn on Deshima instead of on board ship (which would have been against Japanese law), and he began talking in the tone of a teacher scolding a schoolboy:

> Stop!. . . Now, I do not want to know what you "think"; you have had ample time, certainly, to think. I can think also. I have thought a great deal. It is time that matters should come to a crisis—that some-

thing definite was arrived at. . . . I want a "positive promise" as to whether I am to get the men or not. . . . I want no prevarication. I want a straight up and down answer.[46]

Shirai and Moriyama tried desperately to keep the situation under control. When Glynn turned exasperated to Moriyama, gesturing, and threatening to call off all further discussions, the interpreter is quoted as saying, "But stop; pray hear me. What do you do so for? . . . it is not good, it is not Japanese custom."[47] Finally, at the end of the meeting the commander obtained a firm promise that he could have the men in three days.

On April 25, Glynn had another meeting with Matsumura. Levyssohn was too ill to attend, and sent his assistant, Bassle, in his stead. But before Bassle could board the *Preble*, Moriyama insisted on boarding first, so he could officially "invite" the Dutchman on board. Bassle brought an offer of provisions from Levyssohn, but Glynn, in a snit, refused it, saying he could not accept them from a Dutch "potentate" and would only accept them from the magistrate of Nagasaki, and that he was going to tell his superior that the Japanese had refused. All was not in vain, however, as Bassle had brought with him the previously described document from Nagasaki officials, explaining the treatment they had given the *Lagoda* men and Ranald MacDonald. The original was in Japanese, which the Japanese had rendered into Dutch. Bassle orally translated the document into English for the sake of the Americans, who wrote it down.

Escape from Nagasaki

On April 24, six days after the *Preble*'s arrival, both Shirai and Moriyama came to MacDonald's cell in Nagasaki. They told him a new magistrate had arrived from Edo and that it had been decided to move him to Deshima. They asked if he knew why, and when he answered in the negative, they told him a ship had arrived from his "country." In his interrogations, MacDonald had said that he was from three places—Oregon, Canada, and New York—so he asked the two men if the ship was from Oregon. When they said no, that it was from "New York," he answered that yes, indeed, New York was the place he had sailed from.

Early in the morning on April 26, dressed in clean Japanese clothes, MacDonald was carried to the magistrate's office in a palanquin and led into a shed. There, he saw the *Lagoda* crewmen for the first time, all appearing "very pale and thin." Led from the shed to the courtyard, he was made to kneel apart from them in front of the old magistrate and his replacement, who were seated together. The sailors were officially notified of the decision to release them, and informed they would first have to go to Deshima, to the Dutch factory. They were also read the decision of the magistrate's office—the same content as the official *Hankachō*, or "Criminal Record." Surviving in written form, it lists the thirteen surviving sailors of the *Lagoda* and Ranald MacDonald, and briefly describes how they arrived in Japan and broke Japanese law. At the end, it warns them to "never engage in fishing off the coast of Japan again."[48]

After thanking the magistrates, the North Americans were again borne through crowded streets to Deshima in palanquins, the *Lagoda* crewmen singing sea shanties along the way. On crossing the tiny bridge from Nagasaki to Deshima, they were searched, and then greeted by Levyssohn, who told them not to kneel before him because, as he said: "This is a Christian house!" They were fed a hearty, Western-style meal with tables and chairs and cutlery and Dutch Java coffee, and then taken out to the *Preble* in a boat bearing the Dutch flag, accompanied by Levyssohn's assistant, Bassle.[49]

Glynn had been told Japanese laws were usually not recorded in book form, but on the *Preble* his Japanese visitors now handed him a variety of documents (translated into Dutch), explaining that it was their policy to treat foreign shipwrecked sailors well and deport them on Dutch ships to Batavia or Chinese ships to China. The Japanese also requested that American ships not cruise so close to Japan. And with that they left.

Glynn had promised to leave as soon as the sailors were delivered to him, but when the sun set on April 26, he was still at anchor in Nagasaki Harbor, waiting for a better wind. Now, he had a new problem. The Japanese had not only returned the American sailors and MacDonald, but—with typical thoroughness—given Glynn all four of the whaleboats with which the men had come to Japan, along with all their "tackling, Harpoons, &c., &c." MacDonald's boat probably never made it out of Nagasaki Harbor, though, for the *Preble*'s deck log notes how two of the total were found unserviceable, "and having no means of carrying them, they were cast adrift."[50] Finally, to the enormous relief of the Nagasaki officials—who had just drafted another letter demanding that Glynn leave—on April 27 the wind came up and the *Preble* departed.

Aftermath of an Adventure

What did MacDonald really think of his sojourn in Japan? In his 1923, posthumously published "autobiography," he has nary a complaint about his treatment, lavishing praise on everyone, including Moriyama, Shirai, Levyssohn, and even the magistrate. In an oft-quoted passage that makes him sound like something of an intercultural-relations saint, he says,

> I have never ceased to feel most kindly and ever grateful to my fellow men of Japan for their generous treatment of me . . . throughout my whole sojourn of ten months in the strange land, never did I receive a harsh word, or even an unfriendly look . . . [of all the peoples I have met, both] civilized and uncivilized, there are none to whom I feel more kindly—more grateful—than my old hosts of Japan; none whom I esteem more highly.[51]

In reality, MacDonald wrote this passage on May 24, 1889, as part of a letter sent to his editor friend, Malcolm McLeod. McLeod had wanted MacDonald to expand on how he felt about his treatment in Japan, and MacDonald was more than willing to oblige, even thanking the samurai in Matsumae who had once threatened him—"the gentleman who made the sign of passing his sword across his throat."[52]

Yet immediately after leaving Japan, MacDonald had not felt as generous to his hosts as he did in 1889. In his deposition taken on board the *Preble* on April 30, 1849, only three days out of Nagasaki, he had stated, "The common people appeared to be amiable and friendly, but the government agents were the reverse."[53] Later he would tell friends that "he thought every moment they would chop off his head."[54] Furthermore, on May 24, right after disembarking from the *Preble* in Hong Kong, he wrote to Damon, the missionary editor of the Honolulu *Friend*, complaining bitterly that the Japanese had forced him to tread on an image of the Virgin and Savior, kept his books from him, and told him the Bible was a "bad book." "I wish," he wrote, "that those civilized savages may be taught to understand the right due to Christians, for what they had done to me they would do to others, and have done it, it is a shame how they have abused 15 American sailors belonging to the *Lagoda*."[55]

How does one reconcile these two conflicting views of MacDonald's treatment in Japan? While on board the *Preble,* the *Lagoda* crewmen, brimming with resentment over their treatment, may have influenced his statements. But MacDonald had an innately forgiving and generous character, and decades later when he put together his autobiography, a mini love affair was going on between North America and Japan. The context in which he wrote his opinion, therefore, had changed. Furthermore, by 1889 he had a burning desire to achieve recognition for his adventure to Japan, and he was able to view it as the true highlight of his life. He could afford to be generous to everyone.

Initial resentments aside, there is no question that MacDonald ingratiated himself to his hosts and made many deep friendships. And in this sense, his experience was profoundly different from that of the *Lagoda* and *Lawrence* crewmen. In Japan today, his affection for Moriyama, in particular, has been a focal point of much of the material written about him. Akira Yoshimura's 1989 historical novel, *Umi no sairei,* contains a scene that may not differ too much from reality, depicting the two men when they part. MacDonald, tears welling in his eyes, says to Moriyama: "I had hoped to stay in your country to teach English and become an interpreter . . . but that is not permitted. It saddens me greatly, as does parting with you, but I shall never forget the friendship you showed me." Moriyama then takes MacDonald's hand and, with his voice breaking, thanks him for his teachings and wishes him luck.[56]

✳ ✳ ✳

Reports of the *Preble*'s voyage to Japan quickly appeared in English-language newspapers and magazines throughout the world, giving the stories of the *Lagoda* crewmen and MacDonald wide exposure. On August 28, 1850, the men's full depositions, as well as documents relating to Commodore Biddle's visit, the *Lawrence* crew, and negotiations between Glynn and the Japanese were compiled into U.S. House *Executive Document* (vol. 10, no. 84), entitled "Imprisoned American Seamen." And on April 12, 1852, the same documents were included in the U.S. Senate *Executive Document*, no. 59.

The Senate documents took the form of a message from President Millard Fillmore transmitting to the Senate, as requested by Secretary of State Daniel Webster, "certain official documents relative to the empire of Japan, and serving to illustrate the existing relations between the United States and

Japan." One section of MacDonald's deposition stands out like a jewel, illustrating his grasp of history and drama, and it is often quoted. When the *Preble* first arrived in Nagasaki Bay, one of the interpreters had asked MacDonald what the rank of its captain was, relative to the leader of the United States. In attempting to illustrate the political hierarchy of a democracy, he replied: "First, I gave the people, which they could not comprehend, then the President of the United States, the Secretary of the Navy, commodore, post captain, and commander."[57]

The Senate documents also contain two prophetic letters from Commander Glynn. One, dated February 24, 1851, is addressed to owners of a prominent New York shipping firm, advocating the opening of Japan, saying that "we could convert their selfish government into a liberal republic in a short time; such an unnatural system would at the present day fall to pieces upon the slightest concussion. But it is better to go to work peacefully with them if we can." The other letter, dated June 10, is addressed to President Fillmore, and in it Glynn further clarifies his views, essentially outlining the very strategy the government would adopt for the Perry expedition. He advocates sending a naval officer on a U.S. warship, with a plainly written (and thus easy to translate) letter from the president, asking for trading and associated rights. The officer, he stresses, should "be a man of matured judgment, and of ready tact" and should deal with the Japanese with firmness and respect, treating them as equals, assuring them that the United States had no intention of interfering with their internal affairs or religion. He would require great patience, Glynn warns, "to sustain himself under trying circumstances not designed to annoy him, and spirit to repel every attempt to exact from him any humiliating act of ceremonial deference to the native authorities."[58]

In his letter to the president, the only sailor Glynn directly mentions having rescued in Japan is the *Lagoda* deserter, Robert McCoy, who had told him of Japanese guards belittling Commodore Biddle's failed mission in 1846. But there is evidence that Glynn did solicit opinions from MacDonald about Japan that were never recorded. Much later in life, MacDonald would write that "in my interview with Capt. Glynn of the U.S. ship Preble I suggested that in the event of another visit to Japan for the purposes of opening trade that *models of Western Ingenuity* should be *taken* & exhibited &c."[59]

❖ ❖ ❖

"Conference Room at Yokohama, Kanagawa, Japan, March 1854." Portman sketch from William Speiden's journal. Moriyama (C) is in the middle, interpreting; Tatsunosuke Horii (D), another famous interpreter, is bowing in front of him. Commodore Matthew C. Perry (A) is at the far end of the table on the left, and he has with him a Dutch interpreter (Anton Portman) and a Chinese interpreter (S. W. Williams). Japanese officials on the right include the portly Ido Tsushima-no-kami (second from rear), who had interrogated MacDonald in Nagasaki.

In November 1852, under orders from President Fillmore, Commodore Matthew C. Perry set sail on his famous expedition to Japan. He arrived in Edo Bay in July 1853, met Shogunate officials, and presented, along with a letter from Fillmore, U.S. requests for "friendship, commerce, a supply of coal, and provisions and protection for our shipwrecked people."[60] Then he left for Hong Kong, giving the Japanese time to think matters over, and returned in March 1854 to negotiate an agreement. The Perry expedition eventually resulted in treaties between Japan and the United States, and became the catalyst for the collapse of the Shogunate in 1868 and the eventual transformation of Japan from a feudal to a modern state. Perry can be seen as an early American imperialist, yet in his dealings with Japanese officials he was firm but respectful, and patient. His intentions were peaceful, and by arriving with a naval squadron that included heavily armed steamships and by bringing samples of new technologies, such as a miniature steam train, photographic equipment, and a telegraph—the keys to modern industrial society, which few Japanese had ever seen—he was able to psychologically overwhelm his hosts. While his arrival in Japan could have resulted in disaster, he achieved his goals without firing a shot.

As for MacDonald's pupils, at a time when Japan risked losing its independence to Western powers, they were able to perform their jobs in a highly sophisticated fashion. Official negotiations with Perry were conducted in Dutch and Chinese, but often—as in the case of Moriyama—the interpreters were able to use their English to impress the visitors and establish friendships and to further their own understanding of the nuances of foreign demands. From MacDonald, the pupils had learned not only grammar and vocabulary, but what is equally essential for an interpreter—a knowledge of body language, expressions, nuance, customs, and history. And they had been exposed to a North American, instead of a Dutch or European, world perspective.[61]

As researcher Chisato Ishihara notes,

In the wake of visits by Perry and [the Russian] Putiatin, many of MacDonald's direct pupils—as well as the interpreters who probably learned from those pupils . . . were sent to Edo, Uraga, Shimoda, and Hakodate. Others worked in Nagasaki, where they helped Japan in her foreign relations after the nation was opened, teaching English, propagating Western culture, and serving as an unseen force in the nation's modernization. At the risk of death, placing his faith in his fellow man, a single twenty-four-year old young man had infiltrated Japan when it was still firmly closed to the outside world. His pupils took the seeds he sowed and made them flower throughout Japan.[62]

CHAPTER 14

Creation of the Narrative

On March 3, 1854, Einosuke Moriyama boarded Commodore Perry's flagship in Edo Bay. He had just arrived from Nagasaki to serve as chief interpreter in the negotiations, and according to one of the Americans, "He inquired for the captain and officers of the 'Preble,' and asked if Ronald McDonald was well, or if we knew him." What the Americans answered is unknown, but it is safe to say that no one knew where MacDonald was.[1]

After leaving Nagasaki, the U.S.S. *Preble* had let MacDonald off in Hong Kong on May 22, 1849. The ship's deck log shows he was handed over to the U.S. consul at 3:30 P.M. that day, along with the *Lagoda* men. The consul's report to Washington records receiving him (as an "American"). A letter MacDonald wrote on May 24 survives, saying he was leaving on a different ship the next day. The letter gives neither the name of the ship nor his destination, yet in it he says, "I have been busy ever since I came ashore in writing a detailed account of what befell me in Japan to be sent to Washington for the information of the Government."[2]

Had MacDonald chosen to return directly to North America with his account, he might have secured his place in history. He had a certain notoriety, as news of his entry into Japan and retrieval by the *Preble* was widely publicized. And leading up to the Perry expedition, interest in Japan was reaching a fever pitch. In a March 1853 article entitled "Japan," the popular *Putnam's Monthly* declared that Americans needed to know more about the mysterious Asian nation:

> Whatever method be chosen to diffuse information—whether by press, in books; or by reviews in quarterly and monthly periodicals, and by leaders in daily newspapers; or by oral teaching in lectures before lyceums and scientific societies—we hail the contributor with a cordial welcome, and we will do our part to spread the knowledge.

The problem, the editors noted, was that

> books on Japan are scarce. . . . Locked in the archives of the Jesuit mission rooms; hidden under the unfamiliar language of Holland or Russia; buried beneath the dust of the East India Company. . . . Our booksellers ought to thank President Fillmore for opening a new channel of trade in books, as well as for the attempt to open Japan.[3]

But in Hong Kong, MacDonald found himself "a penniless waif on the ocean of life," and he decided to "ship again before the mast." On a ship somewhere in the Indian Ocean near Madras, he was wrecked and had to swim to shore, for dear life, through shark-infested waters, a knife at his belt. In the process he lost all of his possessions, except "the clothes I had on and a little bundle, in a handkerchief, containing, with other little precious things, only a few of my notes in Japan."[4] Other than a dozen or so pages that survived, the bulk of MacDonald's written account of his adventure in Japan thus sank to the bottom of the sea.

Thereafter, for four years, the record of MacDonald's movements becomes exceedingly murky. Ever the adventurer, he visited Calcutta, Madras, Bombay, Java, and Singapore, and he took part in the 1851 Australian Gold Rush, mining for a time at Ballarat.[5] Before going to Australia, he was apparently in London, and afterward, on his way home to North America via the Cape of Good Hope, he visited most of the capitals of Europe, including Paris, London, and Edinburgh. Toward the end of his life, he boasted that there was "not a city of any note on the face of the globe he [had] not visited." One friend of his later claimed that in Australia, "He acquired a good stake and went to England with some £16,000 where he went it high for luck, no doubt posing for some native Prince." Somehow, he made the acquaintance of the Duchesses of Manchester and Gordon. Then, in the spring of 1853, he showed up in St. Andrews (see map p. 113), near Montreal, in today's Quebec, Canada, where his father had relocated after retiring from the Hudson's Bay Company.[6]

Homecoming

St. Andrews today is a largely French-speaking, Catholic community, but in 1853 it was

Christ Church, St. Andrews East, built in 1821.

Photo © 2000 Frederik L. Schodt.

mainly English-speaking and Protestant, with many inhabitants of Scottish highlander descent. Christ Church, St. Andrews East, built in 1821, still stands, with two beautiful stained-glass windows donated by Jane Klyne McDonald, who died in 1879; beneath the windows are inscribed the names and death dates of herself, her husband, and the ten children who died before her. Her step-son Ranald, still alive at the time, is not listed. In the nearby cemetery, the nearly illegible epitaph on Archibald's worn gravestone notes that he died on January 15, 1853, at the age of sixty-two, and that "[a]mongst others of his works, it may be said that he was the pioneer, or one of the pioneers, of civilization in Oregon. In short, his life was one of much usefulness." Sadly, Archibald just missed his long-estranged son's return home.

❖ ❖ ❖

In 1844, suffering from aches and pains, and nostalgic for civilization, Archibald McDonald had finally decided to retire from the fur trade. He left

Fort Colvile in September on the long and arduous journey over the Rockies, his large family in tow. One son had already died after a long illness. Another was in school in England, and two were still at school in the east. But there were six other children—a daughter born in February 1834 and five younger boys born after Ranald had left for Red River that spring—with one on the way. The baby was born on the trip, but while wintering in Edmonton, three of the older boys died of scarlet fever. The family thus finally arrived, heartbroken, in Montreal in the fall of 1845, after stopping to visit Edward Ermatinger in St. Thomas.

Instead of retiring in St. Thomas as originally planned, Archibald McDonald purchased a beautiful estate near St. Andrews. As a retired chief factor in the Hudson's Bay Company, he was well provided for, and some of his investments—such as those in fledgling railroads—paid off handsomely. Both Archibald and Jane became influential members of the local community, Jane succeeding to a degree rare among "country-born" women. As the United States and Britain negotiated over final control of the "Oregon Country," Archibald found himself being interviewed by some of the highest officials in Canada about the West. He wrote to an old friend that—"[s]o engrossing is that subject now become that my very lap dog from Oregon was hailed here as a perfect wonder."[7]

But Archibald's time was limited. In his first will, written in 1834, he had bequeathed £300 to his son, Ranald. In an 1835 revision he had reduced the amount to £100. And then, shortly before he died, on May 19, 1852, he revised his will one last time, leaving out any mention of Ranald altogether.[8]

Some writers have assumed that Archibald never heard from Ranald after he went to sea and presumed him dead, but this was always unlikely. Between 1849 and 1853, Ranald's name appeared in English-language magazines and newspapers in China, Hawaii, San Francisco, Sag Harbor, New Bedford, and New York, among other places. Even if Archibald had never seen these mentions of his son, someone would have told him about them, for with his long tenure in the HBC he was still indirectly connected to one of the world's best commercial intelligence networks. In fact, recently uncovered letters indicate father and son were indeed in at least sporadic communication. On April 3, 1852, the month before he removed Ranald from his will, Archibald wrote to a relative in Fort Colvile: "From Ranald, the Hero of Japan, I had several letters since his withdrawal from Jedo—He sticks to the sea, and last sailed from London for Sidney. But I trust he will now prefer digging for Gold in Australia to the precarious & uncertain life of a sailor."[9]

Why did Archibald write Ranald out of his will if he knew he was still alive? It is too simplistic to view this as a slighting of his "half-breed" son over his other progeny. Archibald had made considerable sacrifices to educate Ranald, and he clearly had felt betrayed by his youthful rebelliousness. As time passed, his other children (all mixed-blood) had their own pressing needs. With no sign of Ranald returning, Archibald may simply have erased his name in frustration, especially if he thought the young man had made his own fortune. Given his character, Archibald likely would have reinstated his son if he had lived long enough to meet him again. As it was, his wife in effect did just that, in her will bequeathing her stepson $400. Still, years later in 1892, in a desperate attempt to get his Japan story published, MacDonald would try to borrow money from his half-brother Allan, who had been left the care of the family property, reminding him that "out of my Father's Estate I got nothing. Altho our mother had left me $400.00 I never got a cent but of that I did not mind."[10]

A greater puzzle is why Ranald MacDonald's stay in St. Andrews is so poorly documented. It is not clear exactly when he arrived or left. Surviving letters place him in the summer of 1853 at the house of his lawyer friend, Malcolm McLeod, who helped him join Local Branch 516 of the Masons, and they also indicate that he visited nearby Lachine. A half-century later, his half-brother Benjamin recalled that he had returned from Australia with rock specimens in which gold had been discovered, and "demonstrated and explained to the family how they washed the gold from this chalk formation by crushing it." Yet Benjamin recalls this as happening not in 1853, but 1858, and says that MacDonald "was on his way from Australia to British Columbia" to join the Gold Rush there. The dates conflict, but MacDonald may have arrived in St. Andrews in 1853, returned to Australia, and then come back to St. Andrews again in 1858, before heading to British Columbia. Indeed, one of the first drafts of his *Narrative*, edited by McLeod between 1853 and 1857, has a cryptic note saying, "He is now an adventurer in Australia."[11]

MacDonald's visit to the Montreal area should have been newsworthy for two reasons. First, he had returned from Japan, which was a subject of great curiosity, even in Montreal. Second, he had been in Australia, a far away place with which Canadians were then obsessed. As a family friend wrote in July 1, 1853, "Emigration to Australia is at present become a mania, the rich Gold mines attract immense numbers to that distant Country, in the hope of making large fortunes in a few years."[12] Yet the local newspapers appear to have ignored MacDonald, and his father's friends (including Edward Ermatinger)—who left such gossipy correspondence detailing their lives—either never mentioned him or those letters have never been found.

Malcolm McLeod

The one local man who did write about MacDonald was the lawyer Malcolm McLeod. It is thanks to him, in fact, that we know much at all about Mac-Donald today, for he ultimately compiled MacDonald's story and saved many of his later letters. Yet McLeod is also a reason MacDonald never achieved the recognition he deserved.

The two men became fast friends in the summer of 1853. They had a great deal in common; they were three years apart in age, bachelors, part-Indian, with shared roots in the Hudson's Bay Company culture. Yet in other respects, they were mirror images of each other. MacDonald was stocky, highly physical, with enough adventures to fill several books but little experience in the "civilized world," and he had lived mainly around men. McLeod was wiry, bald, highly educated, and intellectual, and, at the time of MacDonald's visit, in poor health, living at home with his mother, five sisters, and a brother. He had experienced few adventures compared to Mac-Donald, but what experience of the wilderness he had was a central part of his adult identity.

Many years later, in a letter to McLeod, MacDonald would reminisce eloquently on the reasons former HBC personnel—whether Scottish, French Canadian, or Iroquois—had such strong bonds:

> You have, I have seen it, have seen with nature face to face, moun-tains, prairies, forests, lakes and rivers, in its primitive state even the human, the savage, the Child of Nature we have seen in that condi-tion as Adam at the creation. . . . [W]e two are about the only who have witnessed those conditions on the Pacific slope. We have wit-nessed the grandeur & solemnity of the temple of the great archi-tect—no mark or sign of civilization within thousands of miles of us, but what we ourselves represented. A spot, a dot, & a blot. Yes, that is

the Answer and a strong bond it is, I say.[13]

Malcolm McLeod, ca.1890s.

Photo No. I-61532. Courtesy British Columbia Archives, Province of B.C.

McLeod's father, John, was a Scotsman who, like Archibald McDonald, had joined the Hudson's Bay Company. He had helped Highland colonists in Lord Selkirk's Red River settlement, early on crossed to the Pacific, and subsequently risen in the ranks of the organization, serving at various HBC posts. In 1819 he had married a mixed-blood woman named Charlotte Pruden "in the custom of the country" and sired his first son in 1821. In 1826, in what would always be a source of enormous pride to Malcolm, John McLeod took him over the Rockies in the winter, although how much of this trip the five year old really remembered is subject to debate. Like Ranald MacDonald, Malcolm McLeod was baptized at Red River, in 1826. His father's marriage was also solemnized there, in 1829, by the Reverends David T. Jones and William Cochran.[14]

But instead of Red River, Malcolm McLeod was sent to Edinburgh, Scotland, for his education. He proved to be an accomplished student, excelling in English, French, Greek, Latin, mathematics, and (importantly for his later interests) ancient geography. His high school teacher described him as "not more distinguished by superior endowments and proficiency in learning, than by excellence of disposition and the most blameless propriety of conduct."[15] The superior education helped him later to study law in Montreal and be admitted to the bar there in 1845, making him a real success among the "country born." Yet McLeod always felt that the achievements of his father—who had died prematurely of cholera in 1849 and never made the coveted post of chief factor—had not been fully recognized. He thus spent much of his life trying to right an imagined wrong. In the process, he failed to realize that his father suffered from real character flaws that had kept him from advancing and that he—Malcolm—might have inherited some of them.

Governor George Simpson, in his famous 1832 "Character Book," described John McLeod:

> A correct well behaved well Meaning Man, who is always most anxious to discharge the duties with which he is entrusted in a satisfactory manner and would on no consideration do an improper thing. Very firm when he finds it necessary to make a stand; but not bright, on the contrary so confused that it is next to impossible to understand what he means to be at either verbally or on paper. Deficient in point of Education and quite a clown in address and should consider himself fortunate in his present situation which is more valuable than a man of his abilities could reasonably aspire to in any other part of the World.[16]

Malcolm McLeod was far more educated and intellectual than his father, but he was dogmatic and had a habit of representing his own accomplishments in a grandiose way. His intelligence, moreover, was betrayed by a talent for disorganization. Much later, after his death, a colleague recalled him as follows:

> He was a tall spare stern looking man, but in conversation, he was one of the liveliest and most interesting men I ever met. His knowledge of the Northwest dated, as he was fond of telling, from the time when he moved along the Banks of the McKenzie River on his mother's back. . . . He had an extensive knowledge of the Law and had read even into the Laws of Scotland which he was fond of quoting, but he seemed to lack the power to classify his knowledge and to make it applicable to the case at issue. He never did an unkindness to anyone. As far as this world's goods were concerned he could not keep them with him and when a wave of prosperity would come to him he was as reckless as any Indian in squandering his money.[17]

Assembling the Narrative

As a lawyer and the initial executor of Archibald McDonald's will, McLeod was deeply involved in the affairs of the McDonald family. In 1853, one of the matters presumably discussed with Ranald MacDonald would have been the fact that he had been left out of his father's final will, in effect disinherited. After so many years, MacDonald could not have been expecting much, but the cutoff surely came as a disappointment. There was also the complicated matter of his true relationship to the woman he thought of as his mother, and his royal Chinook origins. If we are to believe MacDonald's published *Narrative* and surviving letters, he did not know all the facts at this time, nor was he told them.[18]

McLeod, nonetheless, began to assemble the *Narrative* while MacDonald stayed with him in 1853. MacDonald had fragments of his journal from Japan, plus his vocabulary list, and a few other items, all of which he shared and eventually left with McLeod. Around the kitchen table, he told McLeod the story of his Japan adventure, and McLeod, fascinated, wrote it down in pencil, asking questions as needed. From the beginning, McLeod planned to edit and publish the story as a book.

✦ ✦ ✦

McLeod continued corresponding with MacDonald after he left St. Andrews in 1853. A few years later, in 1857, McLeod had a manuscript to sell. In a letter drafted March 18, he talks of sending it to the Canadian publishers Dix, Edwards & Co., and explains the following "facts" in a somewhat confusing fashion. Given the date, the letter further reinforces the idea that MacDonald knew of his true ancestry long before he claims in his *Narrative*, and also that he had left the Montreal area in 1853–54:

> Mr. McDonald (the son of a Chief Factor of the Hudsons Bay Company, by an Indian Chieftain(ess), and by his Mother, now the Chief of the once dominant Oregon tribe of Chinooks) was, my guest about three years ago.
>
> For the express purposes of publication I took notes of his most interesting conversation about Japan and his adventures there. In preparing the narrative for publication I have adhered most strictly to his text. Mr. McDonald was perfectly competent to write his own story, having received a good education, but his 'Nature,' bold but modest, would not allow him. In ought that seems to contradict this in the course of the narrative, blame me.[19]

Nearly twenty years later, in 1875, McLeod described this first version of the *Narrative* as being a

small work on Japan, with a glossary of over five hundred Japanese words and phrases in ordinary use, there. . . . In writing up the work I had to look into all available works on Japan, and the trade—and general foreign policy of that country, and also of its neighbour China. I was drawn to the little (a leisure) task, by the story, with a few notes, and a well told narration from an old native born British Columbian.

In the same passage, McLeod reveals his opinion as to why no publisher was interested:

[It] was not published . . . because the magnificent and very full United States Government report, on Japan, of the day, on the conclusion of the Commodore Preble expedition to that country for the release of certain American shipwrecked mariners, held in confinement, there, took the ground from me.[20]

MacDonald's story had already appeared in abbreviated form in reports on the *Preble* mission to Japan led by Commander Glynn (not Commodore Preble), but this would hardly have affected sales of a new book. Of much greater impact were Commodore Perry's expeditions to Japan 1853–54, for they had already produced a brief flood of books on Japan, with nearly every subsequent visitor seeming to write a memoir of some sort. In this sense, McLeod's timing was truly unfortunate, as even if published in 1857, Mac-Donald's book might still have been overlooked. And in the United States (by far the largest potential market), the initial fascination with Japan was soon superseded by the bloody Civil War between North and South.

Still, the problems were not just timing. They were in part due to the style McLeod introduced. Had MacDonald written the work in his regular style, the text would have seemed remarkably modern, especially if copyedited. Yet for some reason he was reluctant, perhaps because he believed he should defer to his better-educated friend. And since McLeod in effect thus became MacDonald's editor and cowriter, the result was far less readable than it would have been otherwise.

McLeod was not always a bad writer. But he was a lawyer and later a political propagandist, used to writing in a jerky, legalistic style with a great deal of nested logic. When he put MacDonald's story together in 1857, he tried to express himself in a flowery literary mode that was already archaic. The combination of the legal and inflated literary styles, plus an inherent tendency toward disorganization—produced a text that can be insufferably difficult to read, with frequent use of "anon" and "viz" and Latin phrases, and digressions from the subject, followed by "to proceed with my narrative." The following section, mercifully edited out of an earlier draft, is an extreme example:

> Events since, in hurrying sequence, there; thence; and thither, from all quarters, have been as echoes of these whisperings, set flying as by trumpet blast . . . growing over every Sea and Land. Anon shall come the acclaim—*T's done!* East to West uttering speech, in all amity, in pure Anglo-Saxon—Angezoram lingua. Wonderful truly![21]

Several pages of MacDonald's original journal, as well as many of his later letters to McLeod, survive in the British Columbia Archives, and they can be compared with the text of the final *Narrative*. Although it takes time, in doing so careful researchers can discern which parts of the *Narrative* are MacDonald's and which are McLeod's. In places McLeod has embellished or added to the text, and in others he has used MacDonald's prose almost verbatim. Contextual and expository information about world or Japanese history is authored by McLeod, as are most of the sections about Canadian politics, the Canadian Pacific Railroad, and MacDonald's youth. The most straightforward sections—describing what happened between leaving Lahaina and being deported from Nagasaki—are essentially the work of MacDonald.

A Project Shelved—For a Quarter of a Century

The first version of the manuscript may have been rejected, but McLeod was not one to give up easily. He brought a messianic zeal to his projects, and spared no time and expense on them.

As for MacDonald, he was never one to stay still. The Caribou region of British Columbia was the site of a Gold Rush around 1858, and for Mac-

Donald—who had grown up in the Pacific Northwest and learned much from his Australian experience—participating in it was a logical choice. With his half-brother Allan, he set up a packing business between Port Douglas and the Fraser River gold mines, and ran a ferry across the Fraser at Lillooet; later, he was joined by Benjamin. In 1861 or 1862 he teamed up with John Barnston (another part-Chinook son of an HBC officer and a former lawyer) to form a company to create a road to the new mines. Known as the Bentinck Arm and Fraser River Road Company, it was a considerable undertaking. MacDonald had to write a prospectus, satisfy the British Columbia government (then not part of the Dominion of Canada) on the merits of the road, and within a specified period complete a pack trail for mules and later a wagon road. In exchange, the men were granted a charter, allowing them to levy a toll. But the project required some $60,000 dollars in start-up capital, a fortune in those days.[22]

McLeod and MacDonald continued to correspond. As McLeod writes, in purple prose,

> [For eight or nine years after our meeting], I was in constant correspondence with him, in associate service as old fellow British Columbians, with considerable proprietary interests in the Country, invested many years before by our respective fathers—the first true and effective pioneers of whites and civilization in that intensely (then) barbarian land—when, there, to white men—life was—night and day—ever a struggle, with its watch and ward, and combat oft, against its treacherous truculent hordes.[23]

Elsewhere, McLeod indicates that the correspondence was not quite as constant. Now and then, he says, he would hear of MacDonald "in connection with some bold and successful feat in exploration." And now and then, up to 1862, he says that MacDonald wrote "for aid in raising a collateral of $60,000, for opening a waggon road from Bellacoola (Pacific Shore) to the Carriboo gold region, under charter."[24]

Then, around 1862, the correspondence stopped, for a quarter of a century. McLeod had his career as a barrister and, after not hearing from MacDonald in British Columbia, shelved his attempts to publish the *Narrative*. He moved closer to what would become the political center of Canada, living near Ottawa (see map p. 113), where he became more and more politically active. This led to his re-using some of the information on Mac-Donald and on Japan, and it ultimately brought him back into touch with MacDonald.

* * *

Perhaps because of his education, McLeod was a thorough British imperialist. He regarded the expansionist United States to the south as a threat to the national "nexus" of British Canada. Even within Canada, he perceived two camps, one British and one "American," and he was firmly in the former.[25] Canada was then far smaller than today, and at "Confederation" in 1867, when the colony became a self-governing dominion, it consisted only of the provinces of Ontario, Quebec, New Brunswick, and Nova Scotia. For McLeod, it was imperative that Canada quickly expand westward and solidify itself against the United States.

Toward that end, he took up the cause of Red River, where the Métis and half-breed populations chafed under the rule of the Hudson's Bay Company. He had relatives there, and unlike Edward Ermatinger—who published letters defending the Company and disparaging the independence movement—in 1862 McLeod published a "memorial" or petition to the government, advocating British takeover of the settlement from the Company; later, he would take credit for in it warning the government of coming problems. "I did this," he wrote, "as a North Wester, personally and intimately connected with many of the chief families in the settlement and, moreover having, by inheritance, proprietary rights in it."[26]

McLeod also began to advocate the construction of a transcontinental railroad and propose routes. He was not the first to do so, for it was then a popular theme in Canada and the United States. Yet because of his love of geography, his upbringing, and his work on the Japan-related *Narrative*, he had a unique perspective. For McLeod, a Canada that spread from the Atlantic to the Pacific, linked by a railroad, would do more than help complete the global reach of the British Empire and defend against the U.S.; as MacDonald had also foreseen, it would make trade with Japan and China far easier.

On May 27, 1869, McLeod began writing a series of letters to the editor of the *Ottawa Times*, advocating "A British Railway to the Pacific—An Imperial Necessity." These letters ran in other newspapers as well, and were signed with his nom de plume "Britannicus," thus becoming known as the "Britannicus Letters." With information from his father's journals and those of Archibald McDonald, as well as other HBC records, McLeod proposed specific routes from Montreal to—*not* coincidentally—"Bellacoola, Pacific tide water at the head of the North Bentinck Arm."[27] His letters were long and meandering essays, filled with descriptions of advantageous and disadvantageous terrains, statistics on distances and heights of passes, and so forth. He provided excruciating detail, and pretended to have great personal knowledge of the continent, despite the fact that he had only seen its western portion as an infant. Taking the position that he "knew the country," he would write later that he saw himself as "a 'leather-stocking' guide (as it were) through the pathless forest to be traversed, to meet the lurking foe, and—as my brave old father and grandfather did—forward, westward, the path of empire in emprise boldly dare to cleave."[28]

The seventh letter in the series ran in the June 24, 1869, edition of the *Ottawa Times*, and in it McLeod outlined the final leg of his proposed route, from the Fraser River area to the Pacific in British Columbia. He noted there had been no scientific survey of the area yet, but that routes for pack trails and wagon trains had been explored and formally reported. Among the best routes, he claimed, was one explored by two personal friends, Ranald Mac-Donald and John Barnston. McLeod then described MacDonald's charter and quoted liberally from his company's prospectus.

To show, as McLeod wrote—"that my humble authority is not quite a nonentity"—he digressed to give a lengthy outline of MacDonald's Japan adventure and quoted from one of the first English-language books to mention him—Richard Hildreth's 1855 *Japan: As It Was and Is*. McLeod also mentioned having seen the name of MacDonald's main pupil, "Mooryama," in the British and U.S. treaties subsequently signed with Japan. MacDonald, McLeod pointed out to his readers, "[I]n his own humble way contributed to obviate the difficulty and inconvenience of Dutch interpretation in the communication of British thought and sentiment to a people, who, of all others I know of, have the closest affinity of spirit to the British race. They, in fact, in heart and mind, are the British of the East. They require but the *iron link* to bend them in cognate bonds."[29]

In 1873 McLeod became district magistrate for the counties of Ottawa and Pontiac, and in 1887 he was appointed Queen's Counsel, keeping offices right across the street from Parliament. But he always kept writing. In 1869, the newly constituted Dominion of Canada had finally purchased Rupert's Land from the HBC, and in 1871 British Columbia had joined Canada on the condition that a railway be constructed. To further promote a railway and help populate the new Canadian vastness with immigration, in 1872 McLeod published *Peace River.* This was Archibald McDonald's journal of an 1828 trip from the Hudson Bay to the Pacific, to which McLeod added copious statistics and geographical notes, relying on information from his father and other HBC records. The notes took up twice as many pages as the original journal.[30]

Between 1872 and 1880, McLeod also published five pamphlets containing his "Britannicus Letters," and in 1889 he wrote *The Problem of Canada*, which again discussed the Canadian Pacific Railroad and potential trade with Asia. Most of McLeod's writing and publishing was done at his own considerable expense, but he contended that the railway-related pamphlets had really been commissioned by Sandford Fleming, the ultimate architect of Canada's transcontinental railroad and a major figure in Canadian history today. Since McLeod believed his work had greatly helped in building the railroad, in 1889 he appealed to the government for remuneration, with another "memorial" pamphlet. But the fact that his contribution was hard to quantify in monetary terms (or any terms) proved to be a sore point. In 1892 he issued another pamphlet in conjunction with the Oregon Indemnity, attempting to obtain remuneration for the services of his father, whom he felt had always been ignored. But this, too, was unsuccessful.[31]

MacDonald and McLeod Reconnect

It was the railway pamphlets that reconnected McLeod to MacDonald, in an extraordinarily roundabout fashion. On November 22, 1887, McLeod saw a mention in the local press of a "Murayama," described as the editor and proprietor of the Osaka edition of Japan's famous *Asahi* newspaper. Not knowing that "Murayama" was nearly as common a name as "McDonald," McLeod assumed the man must have been MacDonald's favorite pupil in Nagasaki, Einosuke Moriyama. It was a real stretch, but he sent a letter to Japan (via the new Canadian Pacific Railway), enclosing a copy of his "Britannicus" pamphlet that mentioned MacDonald, a sample of MacDonald's writing, as well as the list of his interpreter pupils. By the time the letter arrived, Murayama had passed away and his son had taken over the paper.

Unable to speak English, the son gave the letter to Junichirō Oda, an editor who had studied in England and worked as a translator.

This had two important results. First, McLeod's letter about MacDonald was translated and printed in the Osaka *Asahi* over a six-day period between January 24 and 29, 1888, under the title of *Kaikyū no Shokan* (A letter from the past). This was the first time MacDonald's long-forgotten story had been confirmed in the Japanese media. Second, when Oda was sent to England as a foreign correspondent that year, he decided to visit McLeod along the way. This was no easy feat, as it required sailing from Yokohama to San Francisco, traveling by train to Chicago, Washington D.C., New York, then Ottawa, and leaving for Liverpool by ship via Montreal. Nonetheless, Oda spent August 24–27 visiting McLeod in Ottawa and gave him valuable information on the Japan of MacDonald's time, as well as the Japanese language—much of which McLeod incorporated into the working draft of the *Narrative*. Oda's visit also resulted in a short article in the September 1 edition of the *Ottawa Daily Citizen*. Titled "An Interesting Visitor," and mentioning MacDonald, it was reprinted across Canada.[32]

After losing touch with MacDonald around 1862, McLeod considered that his friend "had died possibly alone, in some of his adventures in the wild,"[33] but this was hardly the case. MacDonald simply was not in McLeod's orbit.

❖ ❖ ❖

In fact, MacDonald had remained very much in the news for some time, although in no way connected to Japan. In 1864 he played a leading role in Robert Brown's widely publicized Vancouver Island Exploring Expedition for the British Columbia government. This time he did not lose his journal, and it survives in very readable form, a note by Brown declaring it could be "generally relied upon—His opinions on some points were however rather accounted singular and possibly dogmatic."[34] Brown's own journal frequently mentions MacDonald and his sense of humor, which was much prized. A Sunday, August 28 entry, for example, describes a man named "Cave," giving a sermon to half-a-dozen men in a local settlement:

Our general jester . . . (MacDonald) probably overpowered by the unaccustomed homily of Mr. Cave, quietly fell asleep on the sack of flour which he used [as] a pew much to the scandal of the parson but delectation of all the Congregation & snored most audibly until he was aroused by a vigorous kick from the nearest Colonist when he had the impudence to look around most unconcernedly and proceed apparently to make notes of the heads of Mr. Cave's discourse; but in reality to post up his diary for the last 24 hours.[35]

The Expedition's artist, Frederick Whymper, published a book in 1868 with an amusing engraving of MacDonald and a description of him that, while containing some errors, sheds light on his life. Whymper depicts MacDonald as one of the great yarn-tellers around the campfires, with a "story often begun and never ended—the narrative of his eventful life." He describes him as having run away to sea when young and having spent time in prison in Japan after being shipwrecked there, only to be rescued by "Commodore Perry." In Australia, Whymper says, MacDonald "mined, made money, and spent it; had once kept a gambling-house and dancing booth at the 'diggings.' " In British Columbia he had " 'run' a ferry on the Fraser River, kept a grog-shop at Lillooet, and played the 'honest miner' in Cariboo." Whymper, who became good friends with MacDonald, describes him "as usual, thoroughly good-tempered."[36]

MacDonald remained active in the Pacific Northwest after the Vancouver Island expedition. In her 1997 book, *Ranald MacDonald: Pacific Rim Adventurer*, writer Jo Ann Roe unearthed much new information, showing his further ventures in ranching, mining, exploration, and business. Descriptions also survive from people who knew him during this period. A half-brother describes him in 1863 as having been "very active," with curly hair and side whiskers. He remembers him as weighing "over 225 lb" (Whymper says "300"). A distant cousin, Christina Williams, depicts him in 1874 as having made and lost (through "bad luck and trickery of sharpers") $60,000 in the Caribou mines, and while in Bonaparte Station as often "dancing all night with the ladies and showing them the little courtesious, polished attentions noticeable for their absence among the rougher elements of the West." Later he stayed with this cousin's family and helped with her fur-trading books, and is described as "a jolly, likeable fellow and an entertaining talker, telling of early times in the Northwest." Still, there is an almost mythological aspect to accounts of this period, one man later writing that, "I was sitting in my tent one stormy winter day in the year 1882, on the line of the Canadian

Illustration by Frederick Whymper in *Travel and Adventure in the Territory of Alaska.*

"The Rampant Raft." The raft was made of wood from an Indian lodge, lashed together with ropes; holes were made with "pistol bullets." "The current acting on the stern of our craft with 300 lbs.—Macdonald's weight, as steersman—took it underwater several feet, while the bows were elevated in the air."

Pacific Railway in the midst of the Cascade range, when an old man entered; wet and cold. He said he was looking for work and then related the story [of his life and adventure in Japan]."[37]

Even on the frontier, MacDonald remained in touch with the world. In a January 14, 1874, letter, he wrote his half-brother Benjamin from Hat Creek, Bonaparte, pooh-poohing rumors of a local Indian uprising and exhibiting sympathy for their plight but also commenting intelligently on Canadian national politics and concluding his letter with, "Give my love to Mother & tell her that I will shortly write her, should you write to Alex or Allen or to MacLeod [sic], say that I often think of them."[38]

By 1885 MacDonald had finally exhausted his wandering spirit. He settled down near old Fort Colvile and would remain there until his death. But around May 1889, he read a reprint of the Canadian article describing how McLeod had been visited the previous November by Junichirō Oda. With this information, he quickly wrote his old friend again:[39]

My dear Malchom
After so many years you must consider me as if risen from the dead; it is over a quarter of a century since I wrote you from Victoria British Columbia. . . . From our local paper the "Colville Miner," I learn that a certain Mr. Oda a partner of Mr. Muryama had been on

a visit to you. Then followed a short paragraph of my adventures in
Japan, etc. etc.

I am well but as poor as the proverbial church mouse . . . .

With my very best regards to your sisters,
I am
dear Sir
Your Old Friend
Ranald MacDonald[40]

The Project Restarted

The two men quickly resumed their long-lapsed friendship and marveled at
the ease of corresponding, now made possible by the new transcontinental
railway.[41] McLeod was surprised that MacDonald's "fine and elevated character seems to have been unscathed by the hardships and temptations of the
rude pioneer life on our Pacific slope." He was also amazed by MacDonald's
clear recollection of everything that had happened to him in Japan such a
long time ago.[42]

Around this time, McLeod was about to prepare his petitions to the
Canadian government, hoping for remuneration for his father's service in the
HBC, under the Oregon Indemnity provided for by the United States. He
told MacDonald that he, too, might be able to make a claim on the U.S. government, as the legal descendant of Comcomly. McLeod also determined to
repackage the *Narrative* for another try at publication.

But then McLeod took steps that would make the *Narrative* nearly
unreadable. In rejecting the first manuscript, one of the Canadian publishers
had said it was too short but might make a "good magazine article." Stung by
this criticism, McLeod nonetheless wrote on May 4, 1889, "I had to
acknowledge the force of the objection, & in response said that I could easily
'pad' it with a brief history of the Japanese & a statement of European communications with them—a subject but little known to the general public."[43]

Never having been to Asia, let alone Japan, and living in eastern Canada,
McLeod was forced to rely on a few books on Japan in his possession and on
a flawed collection in the Ottawa Parliament library. To make matters worse,
since he was ever-enamored of new technologies that might bridge North
America and Asia, he decided to incorporate information not just on Japan

Photo © 2000 Frederik L. Schodt.

Parliament Building, Ottawa, Canada. As viewed from McLeod's offices
across the street, at 172 and 138 Wellington Street.

and on railroads, but also on a Pacific telegraph cable, to make the *Narrative* more "interesting."

McLeod did add some new information from MacDonald, incorporating nearly verbatim, for example, most of the contents of a long letter his friend wrote him on May 24, 1889, with reminiscences of all the people who had helped him in Japan. Yet McLeod took the word "pad" to an extreme. A June 2 letter from MacDonald reveals his (MacDonald's) understanding that his own story was to comprise one-quarter of the entire book (the rest to be "statistics in connection of the cable telegraph"), that he was "to get half after the expenses are paid," and that the dedication was to be authored by Sandford Fleming.[44] Excited by the prospect of publication, even under these conditions, MacDonald two weeks later went out and had his photograph taken in the town of Colville and sent it to McLeod.

McLeod meanwhile submitted the new manuscript to a Montreal publisher, William Drysdale and Co., but the submission did not go well. Drysdale was diplomatic. He was "deeply interested," he said in a July 23 letter, but added that "unless the Govt or CPR would undertake to subscribe for a certain number of copies I feel certain the work would not pay expense of printer . . . unless you are in a position to guarantee the publishers against loss I fear it will be very difficult to place the work."[45]

Remarkably, Drysdale had located a native Japanese to write a critique of the padded manuscript, and it reveals much about the evolution of the *Narrative* and the problems plaguing this version. It was authored by K. J. Takahashi, a Presbyterian minister, one of the few Japanese nationals then living in eastern Canada, and a man with an astounding grasp of English for the time. Takahashi started out by praising MacDonald's story (McLeod later incorporating much of this praise verbatim into his final draft). He realized MacDonald had done something greater than simply teach English to the Nagasaki interpreters and had indirectly aided Japan's later transition from a feudal to a modern state. He lamented that MacDonald and his pupils were unknown in Japan and blamed it partly on the former feudal government's policies of secrecy. "We of today," he wrote, "would gladly acknowledge his immense service so long cast into cruel oblivion: and if he happens to revisit the country now, our people will never be slow to show him their sincerity in this respect."[46]

Most Japanese are polite, and Takahashi at first found it difficult to make direct criticisms. Gradually he warmed to the task. McLeod had included a reworked version of MacDonald's vocabulary list and introduced many errors in the process. Not realizing this, Takahashi thought the list contained far too many inaccuracies and needed "to be recast." But knowing it had been illegal for foreigners to learn Japanese, he was impressed with MacDonald's ability to have compiled *any* vocabulary list at all, especially while in prison.

Takahashi's real problem was with the other material, which formed the bulk of the huge manuscript. In a twisted attempt to broaden the appeal of the book, McLeod had let his pen wander far beyond the main theme, adding several chapters on Japanese language and literature, religion, racial origins, and history. These chapters were a spectacular intellectual goulash, a mixture of recycled and often flawed information and his own wild theories. (This was, after all, a man who had once tried to demonstrate that Queen Victoria's lineage could be traced back to Adam and Eve.) He had even added a voluminous section trying to prove that the Japanese were directly descended from the Phoenicians and the land of Canaan, a theory with no basis in fact, but resembling crackpot theories that occasionally surface in

Japan even today, claiming the Japanese are descendants of the lost tribes of Israel. Like most late-nineteenth-century Japanese, Takahashi loosely subscribed to his own nation's mythology, in which the Yamato, or modern Japanese people, were believed derived from a sixth-century B.C. emperor of divine origin. Still, McLeod's notion of Japanese coming from Canaan was too much. "As it stands," Takahashi wrote, "the theory does not seem to claim so much of soundness as of novelty."[47]

Of the voluminous information on the Canadian Pacific Railroad and McLeod's other pet projects, Takahashi wrote that all of it "had nothing in direct to do with Japan." Of McLeod's additions in general, there was not enough to make the book popular, as "the author lacks of one essential element, that of personal observation, which is everything in this practical age; while on the other hand he has almost too much to say of his own theory and his past views now confirmed." While readers might be interested in MacDonald's story, Takahashi observed, "they will not care to pay for all the rest of the work, which, in fact, covers more than half of the whole. It would have been infinitely better if the author confined himself to the McDonald narrative only."[48]

❖ ❖ ❖

McLeod was nonetheless reluctant to remove his own material. An August 11, 1889 letter from MacDonald reveals that the manuscript then still contained accounts of the earliest navigation of the Pacific and the discovery of Japan, and that McLeod was still determined to include his pet projects, with statistics. Ever-deferential, MacDonald thought this was a good idea, but of Takahashi's criticisms he gently said, "[F]rom his standpoint as a Japanese gentleman and patriot he may not approve of your treating of Pacific Railroad and steam communication and telegraph matters in the same book."[49]

To further flesh out MacDonald's own skeleton narrative, McLeod began sending him more questions about his stay in Japan, especially about the northern islands and the Ainu. He left spaces beneath numbered questions and had MacDonald return the letters, with answers filled in. In one written reply, MacDonald complained that "[t]o answer some of your questions one would think that I was perfectly free with all the material of a scientific explorer instead of a close prisoner and every precaution taken to exclude my observation. I fear that I have added little or nothing to what you have and it is so long since & then not being allowed a pen, and every obstacle put in my way to acquire information, many things are forgotten." In a response to McLeod's requests for maps and drawings, MacDonald noted that he was a horrible artist but did supply a sketch of Rishiri Island, remarking that, "who would think that I would be called upon at this time of day to make a sketch of what I saw near 50 years ago?" When McLeod later wanted to flesh out the story of his birth, he wrote back, "I have not the remotest idea of the ceremonial dress of the Chinooks of that time." If MacDonald was uneasy about what McLeod was doing to his story, he was also helpless, and diplomatic, writing, "Not having read the manuscript I don't know what you have inserted and what you had left out. I now regret that I was not by you so as to take up the thread and explain where anything was obscure and might recall such incidents that might have a bearing on the subject."[50]

Yet Another Attempt at Publication

In 1891 McLeod made another major push to get the *Narrative* published. It was a tumultuous year for MacDonald, as his house burned down in February, and in the summer his interview with Mrs. Custer would upset him greatly. McLeod had also written, regarding the book, that he was at his "wits end," saying that "publishers will not understand it or rather not undertake the risk for the reason that it is too high a class for the general reader but that the book is well worth publication & if we wish to see it in print we are to pay for it ourselves." For MacDonald, who had never been able to keep money about him, this began a sad process that lasted until his death, of desperately trying to raise the funds to publish the book.[51]

McLeod tried a variety of Canadian and U.S. publishers, including Harper's and Putnam in New York, but he was always rejected or asked for a guarantee of sales. One of the best candidates turned out to be W. Foster Brown & Co. of Montreal, and to stimulate interest and gain advance orders a promotional flyer was created, with ordering information. Beneath the headline *"New Book! A Canadian in Japan. Over Forty Years Ago!"* Malcolm McLeod is listed, in large type, as the "author." The forthcoming book is described as "A Narrative adventure of Ranald MacDonald in Japan, the first teacher of English in that country, employed by the Japanese government during 1848–1849: with a compendium of the Origin, History, Resources, Characteristics, etc., of that interesting Country." It was to be a massive work, of "500 pages, with maps and illustrations. Price $2.50." The first part contained the history of discovery, trade, and settlement of countries on the North Pacific and then the story of Ranald MacDonald, "in his own graphic words as noted by the author." MacDonald's story is described as equal in interest to "that of Defoe's Robinson Crusoe" but with "the hero . . . still alive, and in vigorous intellect." The second part contained McLeod's information on Japan, including "several chapters" on the origin of the Japanese and the Ainus, "the New constitution of Japan, treaties with Great Britain, and Commercial regulations with all powers." To bolster sales, the flyer included an endorsement (dated November 11, 1891) from railroad architect Sandford Fleming. In it Fleming reveals that he has read large portions of the manuscript. He summarizes MacDonald's story, mentioning that Mac-Donald is the grandson of "King Kum Kumly"; he praises McLeod for his help promoting the Canadian Pacific Railway; and he puts himself down for ten copies.[52]

By the end of 1891, MacDonald had distributed as many flyers and secured as many advance orders as he could locally. He desperately wanted to help McLeod, and needed $400 to help reach a total of $900, but both men were on hard times. When MacDonald applied for a loan at the bank, he was turned down because he was too old. "Very hard pressed for money," at the beginning of January 1892 he tried to sell his ranch to his cousin Donald, but this did not work. Donald tried to sell some cattle to help him, but the cattle were rejected for being of poor quality. MacDonald began pestering friends and relatives for money, but to no avail. He even wrote McLeod, begging him to write Donald to urge him to do everything possible to help. Mac-Donald sent $55 in March, and another $255 in June, but he never made the entire $400, despite traveling all the way to Ravalli, Montana, to plead for more money from relatives living on the Flathead Reservation there. As McLeod would later lament, "We were both too poor to meet the cost—viz $900—for the work was large."[53] Then, on May 30, 1892, Foster Brown & Co. returned McLeod's manuscript—for lack of orders.

McLeod was still not ready to give up. "The World's Columbian Exposition" was planned in Chicago for September 1893, and he thought he could interest Chicago publishers. North America was in the throes of a severe economic depression, but this giant fair was designed to feature the dramatic progress made since the continent's "discovery," four hundred years earlier. Immigration from Europe was soaring, and new technologies such as telephones, bicycles, phonographs, and electric lights were all the rage; the era of the frontier and the heroic individual had ended, and the economic landscape was increasingly dominated by consumers and corporations and nation states, all more closely linked than ever before. Washington, where MacDonald lived, had become the forty-second state three years earlier, and it was represented at the fair with its own section, as were Canada and Japan. In their letters MacDonald and McLeod talked of making the book available in all three sections. McLeod thought it would be a good opportunity to "catch the popular breeze."[54]

❖ ❖ ❖

Throughout, McLeod kept making changes to the book, couching parts of it in third person, then first person, and experimenting with various titles for different markets, eventually settling on *Japan: Story of Adventure of Ranald MacDonald, First Teacher of English in Japan, A.D. 1848–1849.* Then, at the end of 1892, McLeod finally took Takahashi's advice and cut the book drastically, confining himself to MacDonald's story. He became even more upbeat about its prospects. In a letter sent in early 1893, he reported that the manuscript was something to "rival all intelligences; and at the same time, in its singular heroism—foolish though it may seem—to touch the sympathy of mankind in general." He saw it as something that beat "all romance—all Robinson Crusoes & such like tales" and thought it would "take like hot cakes."

He also laid out the terms to MacDonald. The book, he wrote,

> will long survive you: and in the meantime will I have every hope— will be a source of revenue to you . . . for the evening of your days. My intention is myself to publish it—paying the printer as the work piece is done. The work tho done entirely in your own name, & as coming from your own mouth.
>
> As the real author, I shall be entitled to take the copyright & deal with it as mine: but as I have no desire to make money out of it, I shall when I am prepaid my outlay—probably abt $400—for a first issue say of 500, shall transfer what of it commands—for the printer, presumably will require some continuum, interest, to yourself entirely."[55]

MacDonald wrote back, saying "may all you predict about it come to pass. I am not unmindful of the many weary hours you have devoted to the work of love, what I regret very much, is your cutting off so much of original matter of interesting reading, but of that you are the best judge."[56]

By October 24, 1893, however, things were not going so well. "I may say," MacDonald wrote, "it was certainly disheartening and somewhat disappointing to us after reading your letter to learn that the long expected book is not yet published, in fact is as far off as it was a year ago with the exception that you propose to have it published in England, Canada, and the United States simultaneously in the copy right fields after having three or four type written copies taken."[57]

MacDonald finally did receive a completed copy of the manuscript. He wrote a long letter to McLeod covering various matters, with one line saying, "I can assure you that I am pleased with it," and McLeod would later use this sentence to "prove" that MacDonald officially approved of everything he had done. As for MacDonald, despite the many errors of fact in the manuscript (which he must have noticed), he wanted to make only one correction, and that was of McLeod's description of his Chinook mother. "I scratched one word Terra Cotta leaving Egyptian Brown," he wrote. "Why I cannot tell but it grated in my ear."[58]

With a copy of the *Narrative*, MacDonald finally began to take matters into his own hands. He arranged to get part of his story published in the local paper, the *Kettle Falls Pioneer*, and on November 16 the serialization was announced, MacDonald being described as "a fine hale old gentleman whose manners are of the old time school of punctilious courtesy." Excerpts thereafter appeared in print for the first time, in three segments during November and December of 1893. He was aided in this by a Mrs. L. G. P. Hawkins, a local resident of Kettle Falls, who was also an editor, a member of the state press association, and a history buff. She tried and failed to find him a publisher in Spokane and was hoping to get him an offer from San Francisco, or even Denver, Colorado.[59] But time was running out, and on August 5, 1894, MacDonald died.

*   *   *

With MacDonald's death, McLeod abandoned hope of ever publishing the *Narrative*, in September 1895 depositing all his files in Montreal's McGill

University. A penciled note gives only a brief history of his involvement in the project (and MacDonald's significance) and laments his failure to get the book published:

> That the story has not been published to the world is assignable to causes that derogate not to the merit of the wondrous deed. In the conception and execution, with utmost success, of his idea in this way MacDonald has well earned historical record: and it is sad to think that in his old age (three score and ten)—faultless for he was ever of deep religious life, a noble character—he was left to die in poverty and distress in the land he had so honored by his life service.[60]

Of the typewritten copies of the manuscript, McLeod explained that one had been sent to MacDonald before his death and another had been sent (with photographs) to a "J. R. Quain" of London, but never returned. Of MacDonald and himself, McLeod wrote: "The views he and I—as primal British Columbians—held as to the connection with Japan, and via Japan, China, were, under the circumstances, far in advance of our time, and were so vague and seemingly impractical, and out of the run of events of the world then in international communications as to make it 'folly.' "[61]

In 1897, three years after MacDonald's death, McLeod followed him. But on May 3, shortly before his own death, he had deposited his own manuscripts and papers in the Parliament Library in Ottawa. They would continue to collect dust there for several years until discovered by the American woman, Eva Emery Dye, who would write the first biography of MacDonald.

Biography of Ranald MacDonald Finally Published

As noted previously, Dye was the author of the romantic 1900 biography *McLoughlin and Old Oregon*, about HBC Chief Factor John McLoughlin. She had planned to title it *The King of the Columbia*, only to find that all the old Hudson's Bay Company men referred her instead to MacDonald. She never met him, but the two did correspond.[62] Dye would later claim that, "in his last years Ranald McDonald desired me to write the story of his life," but there is no evidence of this. On the contrary, he wanted her help in publishing *his* already-written autobiography, concluding one letter with, "Now be sure to write soon and tell me what prospects there are for the sale for such as work as I describe. . . . Don't be so hard on me as Mrs. General Custer."[63]

After MacDonald's death, Dye wrote McLeod several times about the whereabouts of the manuscript but obtained no response and was on the verge of giving up. Then, on a trolley one day in Portland, she happened to sit next to a Baptist pastor from Walla Walla, Washington, who had known MacDonald in his last years. According to the pastor, MacDonald had claimed that "he had a manuscript stolen by some one in Canada, some account of his travels and doings in Japan."[64]

Dye then enlisted the assistance of a friend—a private secretary of the premier of British Columbia and a former newspaper editor—who happened to be traveling to Ottawa. The friend learned that McLeod had died but managed to arrange to bring the collection of his papers back to Victoria, where they were deposited in the British Columbia Legislature (and later moved to the British Columbia Archives next door). Dye immediately traveled to Victoria, obtained a typed copy of the *Narrative,* and was allowed to borrow much of the correspondence between McLeod and MacDonald. This material—along with her own correspondence with MacDonald, his published deposition, and correspondence with people who had personally known him—she used to write her own book, published in 1906 as *McDonald of Oregon: A Tale of Two Shores.*[65]

Dye has been accused of "publishing a considerable portion of [MacDonald's manuscript] verbatim . . . without mention of [his] actual authorship of the material"[66] This is a somewhat harsh criticism, as Dye clearly acknowledges her sources in her foreword. All in all, given the limits of information flow in her day, she did a fairly good job, and achieved quite a coup simply in locating the manuscript. But she was not a professional historian. Her trademark was romanticized history for the masses, glorifying European-American conquest of the wilderness. Despite its title, in her book MacDonald's story comprised but a small part of the whole. There was a section on the Japanese castaways who arrived in Fort Vancouver in 1834, and much information on Dye's frontier heroes, such as Daniel Boone and John McLoughlin. The last section in *McDonald of Oregon* detailed the destruction of Indian resistance to U.S. settler-based culture during the bloody Yakima (Puget Sound) War of 1856.

This sweeping treatment of history created an exciting mix, but it diminished and clouded MacDonald's own story. In the back of the first edition, even the Chicago-based publisher, A. C. McClurg, garbled the message with a blurb that confused MacDonald with his interpreter pupils in Japan, describing the book as a "[c]hronicle of the earliest Japanese refugees to land in America, and of the first Americans who visited Japan later to act as interpreters to Perry."

MacDonald's Narrative Finally Published

Nearly thirty years after MacDonald's death, in 1923, the *Narrative* was finally published in its entirety. Yet even then it appeared not as a stand-alone book, but as a "book within a book." The full title required a deep breath, being *Ranald MacDonald: The Narrative of his early life on the Columbia under the Hudson's Bay Company's regime; of his experiences in the Pacific Whale Fishery; and of his great Adventure to Japan; with a sketch of his later life on the Western Frontier, 1824–1894.* The book contained the full text of *Japan: Story of Adventure of Ranald MacDonald, First Teacher of English in Japan*—the original and final MacDonald/McLeod *Narrative* tailored for a U.S. market—heavily supplemented with commentary by editors William S. Lewis and Naojirō Murakami.

This book remains the bible for all those interested in MacDonald's saga. It is based on MacDonald's manuscript copy, which after his death made its way into the hands of a Spokane newspaperman and eventually the holdings of the Eastern Washington State Historical Society. William S. Lewis, the Society's corresponding secretary and an expert on the history of the Northwest, edited the book with Naojirō Murakami, who was a professor at the prestigious University of Tōkyō, a "Commissioner of Historical Compilation for Japan," and fluent in English. It is hard to imagine a more qualified pair.

Lewis and Murakami knew the MacDonald/McLeod manuscript had problems, but for historical purposes they chose to reprint it as is. Since their main task was to authenticate MacDonald's story (which to many seemed hard to believe), they added copious supporting materials, appendixes, and footnotes (on top of McLeod's footnotes). The result was 333 pages, including recollections of those who knew MacDonald, photographs, illustrations, and translations of original Japanese government documents. Even MacDonald's vocabulary list is included. The MacDonald-related bibliography alone represented a herculean task in pre-Internet and Interlibrary Loan days, and required the cooperation of people from around the world.

When published in a limited edition of one thousand copies, in the United States the reaction was highly favorable. *The New York Times* ran a review on September 16, praising MacDonald for possessing "heroic traits which call to mind the type of Ulysses and Marco Polo." But in Canada, Frederic W. Howay, a noted expert on the history of the Pacific Northwest, was scathing. "The book contains," he wrote in his review, "the reminiscences of an old man, written, it would seem, entirely from memory, after a lapse of forty or fifty years . . . the few pages in which he speaks of fur-trading days are filled with inaccuracies and exaggerations, and exhibit a manifest effort to magnify his deeds and his and his family's importance."[67]

The Lewis and Murakami book thus had contradictory effects. By verifying MacDonald's adventure, it gave him a better foothold in history. But because it was based on the McLeod-edited *Narrative*, it inherited many of the problems he had introduced. And although Lewis and Murakami had little choice, loading their book with so much supplementary material made an already confusing narrative even harder for ordinary readers to navigate. To understand MacDonald's story properly, and to distinguish it from that of McLeod's, required a great deal of outside knowledge, as well as an ability to read between the lines. For many readers, MacDonald and his adventure would thus remain confusing, and hard to define.

CHAPTER 15

The MacDonald Legacy

On the afternoon of August 12, 1994, I attended a small ceremony at the gravesite of Ranald MacDonald. I was struck by the fact that for a man with such a dramatic life, in death he rests in such a peaceful place. He is buried in an old Indian cemetery a few miles from the Canadian border, in a remote area of northeastern Washington State, near Toroda, in Ferry County. It is a stunningly beautiful spot, surrounded by meadows, steep hills, and the pines of the Colville National Forest; the Kettle River, a tiny tributary of the mighty Columbia, runs nearby. The view from the gravesite is probably the same as it was in 1894.

The ceremony was held to commemorate the one hundredth anniversary of MacDonald's death and to mark his contribution to U.S.-Japan relations. I had come from Portland on the trip mentioned at the beginning of this book, organized by the Friends of MacDonald committee and the Oregon Historical Society, and our own members included Japanese, Japanese-Americans, Canadians, and Hawaiians. At the gravesite, we were joined by local residents, including some of MacDonald's descendants, tribal members from the Colville Indian Reservation, and representatives from the Japanese American Citizen's League and the Japanese Consulate in Seattle. A kilted bagpiper from Canada performed a Scottish lament, and its notes reverberated mournfully through the valley. Speeches were made, a prayer was read, and a few rocks from Rishiri Island were placed on MacDonald's tombstone, joining flowers and Japanese and American flags. The tombstone, erected in 1951, states the following:

RANALD MACDONALD

1824–1894

SON OF PRINCESS RAVEN

AND

ARCHIBALD MACDONALD

HIS WAS A LIFE OF ADVENTURE

SAILING THE SEVEN SEAS

WANDERING IN FAR COUNTRIES

BUT RETURNING AT LAST

TO REST IN HIS HOMELAND

"SAYONARA"—FAREWELL

ASTORIA	EUROPE
JAPAN	THE CARIBOO
AUSTRALIA	FT. COLVILLE

Over the years, MacDonald has slowly started to receive more recognition, and his grave reflects this. At first it was unmarked and almost forgotten. By 1917, a wooden cross was in place. In 1938 a simple cast concrete cross was erected. Finally, in 1951 the present granite tombstone was added, its inscription penned by a local lawyer.

Ceremonies were also held at the gravesite in 1938 and in 1951, but the 1994 centennial commemoration was larger in scale and pomp than anything previous; the governor of Washington declared a "Ranald MacDonald Day," and politicians from faraway Japan sent commemorative letters to be read. MacDonald might have wished for less emphasis on the "United States" in the 1994 ceremony, since during his life he was referred to as British, Canadian, and American (not to mention "Columbian," "Oregonian," "Chinook," and "half-breed"); but the multicultural makeup of the audience at least reflected the diversity of his own being.

One of those in attendance at the 1994 ceremony was Richard Slagel. A representative of the local Ferry County Historical Society and a member of

Toroda gravesite ceremony, 1994.

the Friends of MacDonald, Slagel served as a bridge to the past, for as a young man he had also attended the 1938 ceremony. He had then helped pour concrete for the cross, erect it, and etch MacDonald's name on it by hand. He had even photographed the 1938 event with a box camera and carefully preserved the prints. One shows the cross with the flags of the United States, Japan, and Canada. Another shows one of the main speakers, Jennie Lynch, then quite up in years but known as a very "active Indian lady."[1] Jennie was MacDonald's niece, a daughter of his half-brother Benjamin.

❖ ❖ ❖

On February 5, 1894, already seventy years old and complaining of various aches and pains, MacDonald wrote his old friend McLeod. In typically neat penmanship, he stated, "Ben's daughter Jenee by an Indian woman who had married a Mr. Nelson and living on the Colville Reservation up Kettle River about 60 or 70 miles, had lost her husband over a month ago, leaving her a widow with small children, had written to me and even sent her team for me. I was unable to go or risk my health, but will do so as soon as the weather is milder."[2] At the beginning of August, MacDonald finally made good on his promise. For a man who had already circled the globe and traversed the North American continent, the seventy-mile journey should have been easy, but Jennie had to send a team of horses for him. He was not feeling well, and in the last few years he had injured a hand, lost much of his hearing, and had trouble recovering from the flu.

On August 5, while visiting Jennie in her property's guest-house cabin, MacDonald suddenly took ill, collapsed, and died in her arms. His last, gasped words—reportedly "Sayonara, my dear, Sayonara"—were surely some of the most incongruous ever uttered in northeastern Washington in 1894 and initially must have mystified his niece. But if this seems an almost too-perfect way for MacDonald to have expired, it was very much in keeping with the intrinsically romantic, poetic nature of his life.[3]

✳ ✳ ✳

According to Slagel, at the 1938 gravesite ceremony Jennie Lynch recounted her memories of MacDonald's final visit and confirmed his final words. She was old enough to have performed a native dance for General William Tecumseh Sherman on his visit to the area in 1877, but in 1938 she still lived on the property where MacDonald had died, only a half mile from his gravesite. Her land was originally part of the huge Colville Indian Reservation, but when gold was discovered nearby and whites surged into the area, the Indians had been pressured to sell much of the northern half of their reservation. Before that happened though, allotments of land had been given to those with Indian blood in the area.

By the time of the 1994 ceremony Jennie Lynch had long since passed away, but one of her granddaughters, Rosalie Dunn, was in attendance. Two great-grandchildren from a different branch of the family, Janine and Mike Stanton, were also present, and they still lived across Kettle Creek on Jennie Lynch's old land, in a large extended family spanning three generations. On their property, the cabin in which Ranald MacDonald died still stood, weathered, surrounded by tall grass, and gradually falling apart from age, its presence making it easy to imagine his last moments.

Photo © 1994 Frederik L. Schodt.

The Stanton cabin in which MacDonald died, as seen in 1994.

❖ ❖ ❖

Since 1994, the cabin on the Stanton land has collapsed, but MacDonald's local stature has only increased. His gravesite is marked on Washington State maps as an officially designated Washington State Park Heritage Site. In August 2000, plaques in both Japanese and English were placed in front of the cemetery, illustrating how MacDonald risked his life to enter Japan. In October of the same year a mural was also erected on West Kettle Road, near the cabin in which he died. Commissioned by the Ferry County Historical Society, it stresses his Native American heritage and contribution to international diplomacy. As so often happens with MacDonald, when memorials rely on his published *Narrative* they are not always error free; a map of Japan on the plaques by the cemetery shows him sailing from Hokkaidō to Nagasaki along the wrong side of Japan—a result of Malcolm McLeod's misinterpretation of a letter MacDonald sent him.[4]

The 1990s saw a resurrection of sorts for MacDonald in both North

America and Japan, resulting in monuments, events, and writings about him. In North America alone, there have now been over seven books on Mac-Donald published, including this one and two editions of his autobiography. Not all are non-fiction, for 1999 also saw publication of Peter Oliva's novel, *The City of Yes*, which incorporated MacDonald's saga into a unique semi-autobiographical account of a modern Canadian teaching English in Japan. The number of mentions of Ranald MacDonald in magazines and books in both North America and Japan is now too large to easily catalog.[5]

Interest in MacDonald nonetheless still comes in cycles, spanning decades, driven by a few individuals with a particular passion for his story, who eventually move on to other things. In North America, a surprising number of academics—even experts on Japan and its foreign relations—have yet to hear of MacDonald, and almost no research on him has been done by professional historians. One of the few articles in English to appear in a scholarly journal is appropriately titled "'A Home Which Is Still Not a Home:' Finding a Place for Ranald MacDonald." Authored in 2001 by Gretchen Murphy from the English Department at the University of Minnesota, it deals with the difficulty of placing MacDonald in an appropriate context.[6]

The nature of MacDonald's *Narrative*—the fact that its publication was so delayed and that it contained so many editorial problems—partially explains his marginal position in history, but it is only one factor. Others also bear looking at, as they directly relate to the way all histories are created.

Finding a Place in History

Throughout his life—whether whaling, mining, or exploring—MacDonald lived on a type of frontier. As such, while he achieved some notoriety, he lacked the connections needed to interest publishers and to exploit his notoriety in the logical market for his book, which was the cities on the eastern seaboard of the United States.

In the final five years of his life, MacDonald was, in a sense, a publisher's dream, but his basic disposition both helped and hurt him. He spent enormous energy trying to promote the *Narrative* and help its publication, and he was willing to sell his land, travel great distances, and even jeopardize his relationships with relatives to raise money. Yet had he been less deferential to Malcolm McLeod, he could have sought out a more qualified editor or made the corrections himself, for he was a better writer than his friend. In fact, during his forties and fifties, if MacDonald had put as much energy into getting his *Narrative* published as he did in his late sixties, he would have succeeded. At the very minimum, he could have raised the money required for self-publication, or for the then-popular form of subscription-based publication, which required getting advance orders. But when MacDonald was younger, there were always new adventures to be pursued. And given the wealth of adventures he had in his long life, it is even possible that he did not realize that entering Japan had been the defining act of his existence, until he was an old man, living in out-of-the-way Fort Colvile.

In his quest for broader recognition during his lifetime, MacDonald's heritage unquestionably put him at a huge disadvantage, but some writers have been cruel in the way they assert this. John C. Jackson, author of the 1996 book *Children of the Fur Trade: Forgotten Métis of the Pacific Northwest*, writes that

> Marginality was as disfiguring as a blatant birthmark, a sensitivity that had to be lived with because amputation of part of one's being meant the perpetual burden of buried consciousness and pretense. Métis men like Ranald McDonald or David McLoughlin who ran away from themselves often became wanderers, lonely recluses, and sterile bachelors. As self-outcasts they put themselves off from the weed of their being and all too often wasted their genetic brilliance in alcoholic rivers of no return.[7]

Given that David McLoughlin (the son of Chief Factor John Mc-Loughlin and MacDonald's childhood friend) was trained as a physician, married a Kootenai woman, and had nine children, and given that there is no evidence either he or MacDonald was an alcoholic or a lonely recluse, this description seems almost libelous. One might also think that being single was some sort of social crime, a harsh accusation even in the context of nineteenth-century morals. Yet William S. Lewis, the man responsible for publishing MacDonald's autobiography in 1923 and a presumed admirer, echoes Jackson. Of MacDonald he writes: "He never married and the social prejudices against his mixed-blood, together with his secret resentment thereof, probably prevented him from taking his proper position in the world."[8]

In the long run, it is probably the *blurred* nature of MacDonald's ethnic makeup and nationality that has most hindered his recognition. As University of Winnipeg's Jennifer Brown, an expert on Métis history, explains, in the late nineteenth century the word "half-breed" was itself an "objectifying" term to be used for people who didn't make it into the dominant elite. Most mixed-bloods who wished to move in a higher circle, and who could, put the Indian part of themselves behind in order to become part of the dominant society.[9] MacDonald, on the other hand, considered himself a full citizen of the civilized world, but at the end of his life he also had an overt identification with his native ancestors. Born under the British flag, and later given U.S. citizenship, he may have compromised some of his rights as a U.S. citizen in the 1890s by registering as a member of a Native American tribe, for American Indians were generally not given full citizenship until 1925. As he writes in his *Narrative*, in a way that could just as well have referred to ethnic characterization, "I am and have ever felt myself to be a man of two flags; proper, in a way, to both. Yet, let me say, scarcely quite content with either."[10]

Unfortunately for MacDonald, most written history is "national," and it attempts to explain a shared history or illuminate a national or ethnic perspective. One need not look far to see how this affects MacDonald's story even today. MacDonald himself once cautioned an American writer, "There were no such boundaries as Montana, Idaho, Washington or Oregon or British Columbia in those days."[11] But U.S. writers still invariably do downplay British contributions to the Northwest and stress the U.S. aspect of his identity. And many Canadians take offense at those who suggest that MacDonald was anything but a Canadian, even though Canada was a British colony in MacDonald's time. Historian Frederic W. Howay, who wrote the particularly spiteful critique of MacDonald's *Narrative* in 1923, was writing from the context of modern Canada (where the history of the fur trade is an important part of its national identity) when he complained: "The many years that he spent in British Columbia are passed over almost unnoticed. The consequence is that the text is of little interest and of less value to the student of Canadian history."[12]

In fact, the problem of national context plagued MacDonald's *Narrative* from the beginning, as there were in effect two authors—MacDonald and McLeod—with two different agendas. McLeod, the editor and ghost writer, worked on the *Narrative* as part of his own dreams for Canada and the British Empire. MacDonald, the subject and ostensible author, merely wanted to see his story published. As McLeod reluctantly tailored the books for different markets, the title changed accordingly. At first it was the horrifically awkward, *JAPAN: The Canadian There!* When publishers in Chicago were targeted, it became *A Columbian in Japan 40 Years Ago.* Finally, it resolved to the more neutral *Japan: Story of Adventure of Ranald MacDonald . . .* , which was then sandwiched into *Ranald MacDonald: The Narrative of his Life, 1824–1894,* the 1923 book ultimately edited by Lewis and Murakami, an American and a Japanese.

In 1892 MacDonald lived only a few miles from the Canadian border. But on July 18, he wrote to McLeod,

> A Columbian is more preferable to Canadian on this side of the line . . . many have asked me about the book, when it would be out, what was its title, &c. I observed when I told them (A Canadian in Japan &c) there appeared to be some dissatisfaction, in fact some told me that I was no Canadian & [it] ought to have another name. . . . By all means call it A Columbian not that I object to Canadian as Canadian but for the success of the work, [the Canadian publishers] have had their opportunity & would not take it, to me it looks like casting pearls before swine, as you justly remarked they are Hog-headed.[13]

For North American researchers pursuing MacDonald's story today, it is not just the U.S.-Canada border that gets in the way. The most important research on him has been done in Japan but remains untranslated, so most English-speaking researchers face a considerable language barrier. For academics, MacDonald's story is also peculiarly interdisciplinary. There are scholars, for example, who specialize in the history of Japan's early contacts with the West or in the North American fur trade (including the Hudson's Bay Company and the Red River Métis). But the interests of these two communities rarely intersect.

Finally, with MacDonald there is always the problem of succinctly defining exactly what he did. To say that he was "the first teacher of English in Japan" makes it sound as though he flew to Japan and taught English at a local high school. Yet to say—"Ranald MacDonald risked his life to enter Japan when it was closed to the outside world, taught English to interpreters desperate to learn it and thus indirectly helped Japan preserve her independence and contributed to global understanding"—is too complicated. Ultimately, the extraordinary-ness of his adventure is related to the fact that as a young man he conceived of doing something no one else would have considered doing alone, and against all odds carried it off. He was not a passive victim of fate. Nor was he backed by an armed fleet. His plan was all his own, and so was its execution, his only weapons the force of his personality and his goodwill. In a sense, for MacDonald's era and station in life, going to Japan in 1848 was like an individual in our time deciding to go to the moon, alone, and somehow doing it.

A Brighter Future

Many of the same factors that have kept MacDonald from assuming his rightful place in history may yet bring him greater prominence in the future. Each generation must interpret the past according to its needs, and there is now a real need for heroes who can transcend national and ethnic boundaries. MacDonald, by doing so, offers us a new view of nineteenth-century North America and the North Pacific. And as a true cultural and racial hybrid—in the best sense of the word—he assumes heroic proportions because of his success in carving his own path in life, in an often unfriendly world.

In fact, MacDonald also teaches us that ordinary individuals can indeed do extraordinary things, but that it is sometimes necessary to revisit, even rewrite, history to recognize them. MacDonald may have undertaken his trip to Japan solely in the spirit of adventure. He may figure in history almost like Mathias Rust, the now largely forgotten German youth who in 1987 flew a Cessna into the Soviet Union and brazenly landed in Red Square. But in the long run of history, who is to say that Ranald MacDonald—by entering Japan when it was closed to the outside world and teaching the professional interpreters—did not change the course of history as much as other, far better known figures? It often takes time to appreciate the larger context of what an individual has achieved, and in MacDonald's case he was far, far ahead of his time. His life should be exciting enough to keep historians, novelists, and screenplay writers busy for decades to come.

❈ ❈ ❈

On August 4, 2001, the first "Ranald MacDonald Day Celebration" was held in the tiny town of Curlew, a few miles from his gravesite. Given the relative

Ranald MacDonald Day Celebration. Curlew, Washington, August 4, 2001.

isolation of the area, and the fact that the town itself has only a few buildings, it was a truly remarkable event. The local county newspaper described it as representing a "new plateau" for a "story that was untold for almost 100 years."[14]

The event was conceived by Mary Warring, the president of the local Ferry County Historical Society and a member of the Friends of MacDonald society. She lived a short distance from MacDonald's grave, and had become fascinated by his story ever since moving to the area as a retired school administrator. Warring saw MacDonald's ability to bridge cultural barriers as particularly relevant to our times and also as a potential unifying force in the local community. For her, MacDonald was a vehicle to help reduce tensions in an area where the lives of many residents—not only newcomers and old timers, but also whites, Métis, and Native Americans on the Colville Indian Reservation—rarely intersect.

Warring conceived of the Celebration as a full day of events commemorating MacDonald's life. She was able to attract broad-based support for her idea, enlisting sponsorship from the Ferry Country Historical Society, the Curlew Chamber of Commerce, and even the Japanese FOM. The day

RANALD MACDONALD
1824 — 1894
SON OF
PRINCESS RAVEN
AND
ARCHIBALD MACDONALD

HIS WAS A LIFE OF ADVENTURE
SAILING THE SEVEN SEAS
WANDERING IN FAR COUNTRIES
BUT RETURNING AT LAST
TO REST IN HIS HOMELAND
"SAYONARA" FAREWELL

ASTORIA   EUROPE
JAPAN   THE CARIBOO
AUSTRALIA   FT. COLVILE

Photo © 1994 Frederik L. Schodt.

Gravestone of Ranald MacDonald, Toroda, Washington, with rocks from Rishiri Island placed in front.

began with a seminar in the local civic hall exploring the "The Social and Economic Forces That Influenced the Personality and Career of Ranald MacDonald" and ended in a country-western dance, but the highlight was a parade down the town's very short main street in the afternoon. Local people, as well as visitors from Tōkyō and Rishiri Island, and MacDonald's distant relatives from Montana and Canada, all participated. Many were in costumes representing different stages of his life story, some riding in a stagecoach and others walking. There were people dressed up as fur traders; explorers; Captain Edwards of the *Plymouth*; MacDonald's father, Archibald; Einosuke Moriyama and other samurai; and even Elizabeth Custer. The Colville Confederated Tribes sent costumed dancers, singers, and drummers. The role of Jennie Lynch, the niece in whose arms MacDonald died in a nearby cabin, was enacted by her great-granddaughter, Janine Stanton, wearing moccasins and riding a striking brown horse. Jennie Lynch's granddaughter, Rosalie Dunn, served as parade marshal.

Even the press came. A reporter from Seattle's National Public Radio station walked around with a tape recorder and mike, marveling that such an unknown figure could draw participants from Japan, Canada, and other areas of America to such an isolated spot. Like all those who report on MacDonald, he struggled to place MacDonald's story in context and then to succinctly describe his accomplishments. When the story aired, it represented some of the broadest publicity MacDonald has ever received, and led off with the following:

This is a story about Ranald MacDonald, not Ronald, the hamburger chain clown. It's Ranald, spelled with an 'A.' Ranald was a 19th century adventure-seeker and humanitarian whose incredible life is only now getting the recognition it is due. Among people who know his story, MacDonald inspires amazing devotion.[15]

❖ ❖ ❖

Were MacDonald himself alive today, he would certainly marvel at how, over a century after his death, Rishiri Islanders could travel all the way to his remote gravesite to pay homage to him. He would observe how the economies of Japan and North America have become so tightly integrated, and how the peoples of both regions have so much friendly interaction. And to any reporter willing to listen, he would probably reply (with a twinkle in his eye), exactly as he did in a letter at the end of his life:

In all this I flatter myself that I have broken the seal that made Japan a Sealed Empire to the West—at all events cracked it so bad that it made it easy for Commodore Perry to do the rest of the business and secure a commercial treaty. . . . I in the meantime to wait for my reward from Govt.[16]

Artwork on previous page based on Photo No. 562 [13-28]; used courtesy of Museum of N. W. History Collection, K. Ross Toole Archives, University of Montana, Missoula. Background text from MacDonald's Nagasaki deposition, used with permission of the Matsuki Collection, Kyūshū University.

Deposition of Ranald MacDonald on the U.S.S. Preble

The following deposition, taken on board the U.S.S. *Preble* shortly after leaving Nagasaki, is transcribed from a handwritten copy in the National Archives and Records Association, Washington, D.C. (See Microfilm Publication M89, Letters Received by the Secretary of the Navy from Commanding Officers of Squadrons [Squadron Letters], 1841–1886, Roll 4, East India Squadron, vol. 4, 12 February 1848–19 June 1850.) Except for punctuation, correction of old-fashioned spellings, and the sentence, "They gave me a suit of Japanese clothing," the U.S. Senate and House documents listed in the Bibliography are an almost exact copy of this original.

Deposition of Ranald MacDonald

Before me, James Glynn, commanding the United States Ship Preble, personally appeared this thirtieth day of April, Eighteen hundred & forty nine, Ranald MacDonald, who being duly sworn, deposes as follows:

I was born in Astoria, Oregon. I am now twenty four years of age. I shipped at Sag Harbor, in the whaleship Plymouth, Captain Edwards, on a whaling voyage, on the second day of December, Eighteen hundred and forty five.

Being off the islands of Japan, I left the Ship at my own desire, agreeably to a previous understanding with the Captain; he was to furnish me with a boat, etc. and drop me off the Coast of Japan, under favorable Circumstances for reaching the shore.

Ranald MacDonald further deposes,—That on the twenty-eighth day of June, Eighteen hundred and forty eight, after losing sight of the Plymouth, I hauled on the wind, standing to the Northward and Eastward for the land. In entering a bay, I observed some rocks ahead. I endeavored to tack but failed. I then wore to the Southward & Westward, just clearing the rocks. I kept on the wind until I cleared them. I then ran free to the Northward and Westward, standing for the opposite side of the bay. I passed through a channel in the reef, and anchored under a shelter, where I tried my pistols by shooting a sea lion. I then got under way, & stood for the bottom of the bay, where I landed, having understood from the Captain that it was inhabited. But finding no inhabitants, I made an experiment of a premeditated design, which was, to see if I could capsize my boat, and right her again. In this I succeeded to my satisfaction. I then ascended the heights to take another look at the Ship. With a view to lengthening my absence from the ship, I remained two nights in this bay. In the meantime I made an excursion into the interior, but saw nothing of interest.

That, knowing there were inhabitants on the Island of Timoshee, (Or Dessey of the Japanese) about ten miles distant, I put to sea, on the third day, to go there with a view of representing myself as destitute.

That, between the two islands, about ten o'clock in the morning, I turned out the reef in my sail, capsizing my boat intentionally, making no effort to save anything but my chest, which I wanted for ballast and for trimming my boat. My rudder was let go also. Unstepped my mast, righted my boat, restepped my mast, set my sail & stood towards the land. I saw a vessel that day about six P.M. to the Northward. That night I spent in the boat, lying off and on. Next morning early I approached the land and was becalmed. I first discovered smoke, and when day broke, saw some natives launching a boat. They came towards me, within a hundred yards: on my beckoning they approached me timidly, and I jumped into their boat, fastening the painter of my boat to theirs, and made signs to go ashore.

On landing they took hold of my wrists, one on each side, in a gentle manner, put sandals on my feet and led me to a house. Here a breakfast was provided for me in their best manner, and they also gave me dry clothes. I remained in this house eight days, when four Matsumai officers arrived from *Soya*. These officers took me to the Capital of the Island, situated on the sea shore to the Northward and Westward. There I was imprisoned. At first my apartment was quite small, but on my remonstrating they enlarged it by moving the partitions.

After remaining here thirty days, an officer arrived and took me to a town, called Soya, on the island of Yesso, distant about twenty-five miles. I was placed in prison in Soya, and remained there about fifteen days, waiting for a junk, which I was secretly told they expected from Matsmai. This vessel not arriving, I was placed in a small boat, and after a day's journey met a junk, and was taken back to Soya, where I was delayed four or five days longer, after which I was put on board this junk and sent to Matsmai. On the passage stopped to get wood and water. On board this vessel I was permitted to go about abaft the mast. I arrived at Matsumai after a passage of fifteen days, on the sixth day of September. Here they put me in confinement, where I remained until the first of October. Whilst here, I learned that I had been preceded by fifteen other Americans, who had made attempts to escape. Here they gave me a suit of Japanese clothing and gave me sweet-meats, and in all other respects treated me kindly. I was given a rude spoon which had been manufactured and left by one of the party of fifteen Americans who had been imprisoned here before me. On the First of October, I left in another junk for Nagasaki; arrived at Nagasaki on the fifteenth; remained on board two days and landed on the seventeenth.

I was taken in the first place to a small enclosure, adjoining the Town Hall. Here I was met by an Interpreter (Morreama Einaska) who told me that in front of the first door of the Town House, I would see an image, and to put my foot on it, telling me that this image was the "devil of Japan." In passing the door I put my foot on it, but was not able to see it clearly in consequence of the Crowd, who pressed me forward. It appeared to be a metallic plate of about a foot in diameter, on which I thought I could see the representation of the Virgin and Infant Savior. In the Town House I was requested to kneel after the Japanese fashion, upon a mat. I attempted one knee, but they insisted upon my getting down on both knees, which I finally assented to. Soon after this I heard a *hissing* noise and was told by the Interpreter that the Governor was coming, and that I must make "Compliments to him," which was to bend low and not look up. I made a low bow to the Governor, though not before I had taken a look at him.

The Japanese inquired my name, my place of birth and port from whence I sailed and my place of residence. I answered them, Oregon, New York & Canada, with the hope that in the event of an American or English Vessel arriving here, either of them would take an interest in me and that I might be restored to my own liberty, and for the opportunity of giving information to the people of the United States, that some of their countrymen were imprisoned in Japan, and in all probability would remain in prison for life. They then inquired the name of the ship I had left, the name of her Captain, and my reasons or motives for leaving the Ship. I told them that I had some difficulty with the Captain. They finally asked me, "If I believed there was a God in Heaven." I answered, Yes; that I believed in the Father, Son & Holy Ghost, and in our Lord and Savior, Jesus Christ.

I was then told I had permission to leave the Hall and I was then taken in a *Cago*, attended by a number of soldiers, to my prison, which I was told was a sort of temple or priest's house. I remained in this prison up to the present time. During this time I was taken to the Town Hall twice, and also questioned on several occasions, at my prison. The day after being put in this prison, I asked for my books, particularly my bible. The Interpreter told me, with a good deal of fervor or interest, "not to speak of the Bible in Japan; it was not a good book." During these interviews, the object of their questions appeared to be to ascertain if I had any influential friends at home who would seek for me; if I had, they would send me away; if I had none then they would imprison me for life in Japan.

About the Seventeenth of April, I heard signal guns. (About three months before I had been told that when the Dutch Ship, or any ship, appeared approaching the Coast, that guns would be fired.) I was told by my guard, secretly, that these guns announced the approach of a yearly Dutch ship, and they were also fired to call in the troops from the neighboring towns & districts. On this occasion there were fired six guns; two were in close succession, being repeated at longer intervals. In the hands of the same soldiers the next morning, I saw sheets of paper with writing on, which did not appear to be a letter. On inquiry he told me it was a list of soldiers who had arrived at Nagasaki from some neighboring cities. The number he gave me thirty five hundred and four. I asked how many soldiers there were in Nagasaki on ordinary occasions. He said that the ordinary number was "six hundred and fifty, but on this occasion he thought there were about six thousand, besides an unknown number of attendants or followers, an extraordinary force.

On the afternoon of the twenty fourth, the Chief Serai Tatsunosen, accompanied by the Interpreter Morreama Einaska, came to me in my prison and told me that as a new Governor and a number of gentlemen had arrived from Yedo, they had decided to send me to the Dutch factory. After a while they asked me if I knew the reason of this. I replied "No," then they told me that a vessel had arrived from my country. As I had hailed from three different countries, I asked if the ship was from "Oregon," that having been assigned as the place of my birth. They said, "No, from New York." I told them that was the place I sailed from. From thence I was taken to the Dutch factory at Decima & delivered over to the Dutch Superintendent of Trade, where I was kindly treated. The superintendent sent me to the ship. I have heard other cannon fire before the arrival of the Preble, which I suppose was a salute on the arrival of the winter fleet of Chinese junks. I was told there was five cannon in Soya but I never saw any except those I saw on coming from Nagasaki. The troops that I have seen in Japan were clothed in a coat of mail, with hats of paper, Japanned, broad rimmed, low crowned, & fitting close to the head. These hats did not appear to be worn for defense. They were armed with two swords and in addition to these, with bows and arrows, and also with matchlocks, (the ignited match being carried at the waist.) I never saw any mounted cavalry, but heard of such being in the country. The matchlocks were with very short breeches to the stock, which was brought against the cheek in firing, as shown to me by one of the soldiers. In firing, they kneel upon the right knee, throwing the left foot forward, keeping both eyes wide open.

The common people appeared to be amiable and friendly, but the Government agents were the reverse.

During my imprisonment I had a number of scholars among the Japanese interpreters, which probably procured me more kindness than I would have otherwise met with—"Morreama" speaks better English than any of the Japanese I heard attempt it. Two or three of the other interpreters speak a little English. I was told that there was an abundance of mineral coal in Japan, and some not far from Nagasaki.

That I was fully under the impression that the fifteen men, whoever they might be, who had preceded me from Matsmai, were still in Japan, &

doomed to perpetual imprisonment; & that I believed that their liberation depended entirely upon the success of my efforts to return to Civilization, & send them relief.

Upon the arrival of the ship there appeared to be a general excitement among the Government agents. On the morning of the twenty sixth of April, the Interpreter came to my prison, & exhibited a letter, translated into English, purporting to be a communication to the Commanding Officer of the Preble, requiring him to leave the harbor of Nagasaki, on the reception of the fifteen men.

The Interpreter wished me to give him the relative rank of the Captain of the ship, by counting in the order of Succession from the highest Chief in the United States. First I gave the People, which they could not comprehend, then the President of the United States, the Secretary of the Navy, Commodore, Post Captain and Commander. This rank appeared to be sufficiently elevated to excite their surprise.

(Signed) Ranald McDonald.
Sworn & subscribed before me this thirtieth day of April, Eighteen hundred & forty nine.
(Signed) James Glynn
Commanding U.S. Ship Preble
In presence of—
Silas Bent, Act. Lieut. U.S.N.
Henry Wilson, Purser, U.S. Navy

Ranald MacDonald and the Chinooks

R anald MacDonald was descended from the famous Chinook chief
Comcomly. Beyond this, there are many contradictions in the story
of his background, made more puzzling by the complicated racial environment of late-nineteenth-century North America.

As noted, in his *Narrative* MacDonald claims not to have known of his
royal birth while growing up. He believed, he says, that his step-mother, Jane
Klyne, was his real mother and that she was "German Swiss," born in
Switzerland. He says that he learned of his own background in the Astoria
area, after returning from Japan, presumably around 1858. But much of
MacDonald's *Narrative* was ghostwritten by his friend, the lawyer Malcolm
McLeod. McLeod was close to the McDonald family, himself a mixed-
blood trying to live in mainstream white society, and along with MacDonald
he may have been trying to protect Jane Klyne.

If MacDonald believed himself to be Jane Klyne's son while growing up,
he had to have known that she was part Indian and (by extension) that he
was, too, since all women and children west of the Rockies were then at least
part Indian, and he himself had a distinctly dark complexion. The only plau-
sible interpretation of his assertion in the *Narrative* and elsewhere is that as
a child, although he knew he was part Indian, he still believed that part-

Indian Jane Klyne was his true mother. When he became a young man, he had to confront the negative attitudes of white society toward "half-breeds" and thus tended to emphasize her "whiteness." When he later learned Jane Klyne was not his true mother, the shock was assuaged by learning that his real mother had in fact been Chinook royalty. This encouraged him to identify with his Chinook roots, while still being the educated son of a European man of social standing. Still, MacDonald must have realized Jane Klyne was not his true mother far earlier than he claims in his *Narrative*, for when interrogated in Japan in 1848, at age 24, he clearly referred to her as his "step-mother."

MacDonald must also have suspected that he was Chinook far earlier than he claims. His father often referred to him in letters as a "Chinook," and called him "Tool," or "Toll Toll," from a Chinook word apparently meaning "the boy." In an April 1, 1836, letter to Edward Ermatinger, Archibald also refers to his son as "a kinsman of King Comcomly." And in his own *Narrative*, Ranald MacDonald refers to having been nursed by members of Comcomly's family for his first year or so, after his true mother's death, and to having been a favorite of Comcomly (after the chief's death he was even referred to by elders as "Comcomly," or "Comly MacDonald"). In a June 4, 1891, letter to McLeod, MacDonald wrote,

> I recollect the old King, who took me in his arms when on our way to Fort Langly. I must have been about four years old. Before that at Fort Vancouver I recollect an old woman who used to call me Quaame, qua-ame meaning my grandchild. I also remember the one they called the Princess. . . . I believed she was my Aunt, she hardly ever noticed me. Why my family ever kept it dark was always a puzzel to me. Edward Ermatinger of St. Thomas called me Kum Kumly & so did Peter W. Dease.[1]

Before MacDonald died, he registered himself as "Kumkumly" with the Lake Tribe in northeastern Washington. He was not particularly knowledgeable of Chinook traditions, but probably could speak *Chinook wa-wa*, or the trade pidgin of the Northwest. According to an 1891 article in the *Astorian*, a newspaper in the place of his birth, he was regarded as "the only lineal descendant of King Kumkumly, and is still described by all the Indian tribes, particularly down this way, as their only chief, although he cannot speak any of the Indian dialects with great fluency. Were he to visit Astoria, there is not an aborigine within 500 miles of here who would not flock to pay his respects to the man whom all the Northwest Indians recognize as their head."[2]

McDonald's private awareness of his roots aside, his *public assertion* of his rights as a descendant of Comcomly came late in life. In 1889 McLeod was trying to gain remuneration for his own father's services, and he told MacDonald that in the mid-1840s his (MacDonald's) father, Archibald, had considered making a claim against the U.S. government, based on his son's lineage. When McLeod suggested to MacDonald that he might be entitled to some compensation, this coincided with both men's efforts to get the *Narrative* published and to gain more publicity for it.

MacDonald was not Comcomly's only potential heir, as Comcomly had many wives and many children. Early whites in the Astoria area were acutely aware of Chinook lineage issues, and in 1825, only a year after MacDonald's birth, Governor George Simpson wrote in a letter,

> Two boys of the Cheenook Tribe accompany me across the Mountain this season for the purpose of being put under the charge of the Rev.d Mr. Jones; one of them belongs to a family of the first rank in the River, he is the Grandson of Comcomly King of Chief of the Cheenooks say the eldest son of his only son Cassacas Prince of Wales so that our young protegee is the heir apparent to the Throne; I feel a good deal of interest in this lad on account of the respectability and uniform good Friendly conduct of old Comcomly towards the whites and shall request the favor of Mr Jones to pay him particular attention.[3]

By the time MacDonald began asserting his claim in the 1890s, most of Comcomly's direct descendants were dead, but MacDonald still had competitors, although none contested his claim. His childhood playmate at Fort Vancouver, William McKay, who became a doctor and outlived him, was the son of Comcomly's oldest daughter, who had married Thomas McKay, the step-son of John McLoughlin. William McKay would theoretically therefore have been ahead of MacDonald in line of succession, but there is no record of his disputing MacDonald's assertions.

Before he died, MacDonald wrote that he had long ago learned of his royal roots from "Celiast," the daughter of a famous Clatsop chief in the Astoria area, who had also married a white man. Celiast's son from this marriage, Silas B. Smith, became a successful lawyer and local historian, and at the beginning of the twentieth century, he represented surviving Chinook tribe members in a suit against the U.S. government. In 1891 Smith wrote to author Eva Emery Dye, saying of MacDonald that "[h]is mother was not a daughter of Kumkumly but simply a relative."[4] In a 1902 deposition about the Chinook tribe and its lineage, Smith mentions McKay and his descendants but omits all mention of MacDonald.[5] But that could partly be because MacDonald was by then dead and had no heirs. It should also be kept in mind that Smith was the descendant of a Clatsop chief who was not part of Comcomly's far-flung confederacy of tribes but something of a rival.

Just before his death, MacDonald realized the need to document his claims. He was convinced that he could rely on the mother of a friend of his, the widow of George Barnston, a former chief factor in the Hudson's Bay Company, for corroboration. Like MacDonald's own true mother, she was a Chinook of royal descent, from Astoria, but in the 1890s she lived in Ottawa. On MacDonald's urging, McLeod drafted an affidavit for her to sign, testifying to the facts as MacDonald understood them. For reasons which will never be known but could include old age and a desire to shield herself and family, she refused. As MacDonald wrote back to McLeod in 1891,

> You certainly surprised me when you state that Mrs. Barnston refused to say that my Mother was a daughter of King Kum Kumly. I depended so much on her memory and knowledge of that part of the country that she could give a truthful assurance of the fact.[6]

Five years after MacDonald's death, in 1899, the Portland *Oregonian* newspaper ran an article about Comcomly's descendants, featuring a granddaughter of his, known as "Princess Mary," who at 73 would have been two years younger than MacDonald. Her eldest son, a "Prince Louis Duchesne," is described as the hereditary ruler of the Chinooks, following the death of Dr. W. C. McKay, who "had succeeded to hereditary rule (vox et pretereo nihil) on the death of [Comcomly's son] Che-nam-us in 1845." MacDonald, alas, is not mentioned.[7]

Endnotes

Abbreviations Used in Endnotes

For purposes of brevity, publications also cited in the Select Bibliography are abbreviated in the Endnotes. References to the William S. Lewis and Nao-jirō Murakami 1923 edition of *Ranald MacDonald: The Narrative of his Life 1824-1894* are indicated with the acronym LMRM.

Archives and libraries with primary source material are indicated as follows:

BANC	Bancroft Library, University of California (Berkeley, CA)
BCA	British Columbia Archives (Victoria, B.C., Canada)
BFO	British Foreign Office, China Correspondence (London, U.K.)
CMS	Church Mission Society (London, U.K.)
EWSHS	Eastern Washington State Historical Society (Spokane, WA)
HBCA	Hudson's Bay Company Archives (Winnipeg, Manitoba, Canada)
HCMSL	Hawaiian Children's Mission Society Library (Honolulu, HA)
HPL	Hakodate Public Library (Hakodate, Hokkaidō, Japan)
JJT	J. J. Talman Regional Collection, D. B. Weldon Library, University of Western Ontario (London, Ontario, Canada)

MAT   Matsuki Collection, Center for The Study of Kyūshū Cultural History, Department of Literature, Kyūshū University (Fukuoka, Kyūshū, Japan)

MHS   Minnesota Historical Society (St. Paul, MN)

NAN   National Archives of the Netherlands, Vereenigde Oostindische Compagnie (VOC) Collection (The Hague, Netherlands)

NARA National Archives and Records Administration (Washington, D.C.)

NBWM New Bedford Whaling Museum/Dartmouth Historical Society (New Bedford, MA)

NPL   Nagasaki Public Library (Nagasaki, Japan)

OHS   Oregon Historical Society (Portland, OR)

PAC   Public Archives of Canada (Ottawa, Canada)

PAM   Public Archives of Manitoba (Winnipeg, Manitoba, Canada)

Chapter 1—Fort Colvile and the Custer Interview

1 Elizabeth B. Custer, "An Out-of-the-Way 'Outing,'" *Harper's Weekly* (18 July 1891), pp. 534–35.

2 Ibid., p. 534.

3 Ibid.

4 Ibid.

5 Ibid.

6 "Ranald MacDonald's Monument, Toroda Creek, State of Washington," *British Columbia Historical Society*, vol. 11 (July–October 1951), pp. 223–27. Quote is attributed to an unidentified letter from Ranald MacDonald to Malcolm McLeod.

7 LMRM, pp. 60–61, an account of Eleanor Haskins Holly.

8 Custer, "An Out-of-the-Way 'Outing,'" p. 534.

9 The Hudson's Bay Company's Fort Colvile was often spelled with one "*l*," whereas a nearby U.S. military fort later erected was spelled with two. In his letters, MacDonald uses two "*l*"s, but for clarity here I have used one.

10 Pamphlet on Fort Colvile, issued by National Park Service, U.S. Department of Interior.

11 F. W. Howay, William S. Lewis, Jacob A. Meyers, eds., "Documents—Angus McDonald: A Few Items of the West," *Washington Historical Quarterly*, vol. 8, no. 3 (July 1917), pp. 197–99.

12 Peter C. Newman, *Caesars of the Wilderness: Company of Adventurers, Vol. 2*, p. 500.

13 Robert Ignatius Burns, *The Jesuits and the Indian Wars of the Northwest*, p. 140.

14 NARA, *Census of the Lake Indians of the Colville Agency, Washington, 30 June 1892 & 1893*. In the 1892 *Census*, MacDonald's Indian name was given as "Cum Cum li-ti no," and he was described as a "66"-year-old male "widower." In the 1893 *Census*, he merely appeared as "Ronald McDonald," "single" and aged "64." Quite commonly, ages and marital status were recorded incorrectly.

15 Custer, "An Out-of-the-Way 'Outing,'" p. 534.

16 Ibid., pp. 534–35.

17 Ibid., p. 535.

18 Ibid.

19 "The New Eden, First Glimpse of a Glorious Land; Like a Paradise, Seen by a Revered Hero's Widow, Mrs. General Custer; Her Charming Sketch of the Upper Columbia Region and a Quaint Pioneer," *Kettle Falls Pioneer*, 6 August 1891.

20 BCA, MS-1249, "Malcolm McLeod Papers," box 9, folder 13, Ranald MacDonald to Malcolm

McLeod, 29 August 1891.

21 Ibid.; BCA Microfilm, F919-3, "Ranald MacDonald, Lands and Works Department, B.C.," Letter from Lt. Colonel Moody to Sir James Douglas, Governor of B.C., 4 January 1860. In the letter, Moody mentioned that the duchess, "one of the most worthy ladies in the realm," had recommended MacDonald for an appointment.

22 BCA, MS-1249, box 9, folder 13, MacDonald to McLeod, 27 August 1891.

23 Ibid., folder 11, typescript copy of letter from Ranald MacDonald to *Kettle Falls Pioneer*, 31 August 1891.

24 Ibid., 3 September 1891.

25 BCA, MS-1249, box 9, folder 13, MacDonald to McLeod, 28 (25?) May 1889.

26 Ibid., 29 December 1890.

27 "The Oldest Native Astorian: A Brief Sketch of the Life of the Grandson of King Kumkumly, the Old Indian Chief," *Morning Oregonian*, 12 February 1891.

28 Harvey W. Scott, *History of the Oregon Country*, vol. 2, pp. 139–40; "Long Live Com-Comly," *Spokane Falls Review*, 27 November 1893, p. 2.

29 BCA, MS-1249, box 9, folder 11, "MacDonald, Ranald 1824–1894, 'Correspondence Outward—Letters to Mrs. C. H. Dye, Ranald MacDonald to Eva Emery Dye,'" 24 July 1892.

30 LMRM, p. 84.

31 EWSHS, MS 25, William S. Lewis, box 2, p. 16.

32 "Mrs. Custer's Letter," *Worcester Sunday Telegram*, 20 December 1885; Shirley A. Leckie, *Elizabeth Bacon Custer and the Making of a Myth*, pp. 242, 275. Mrs. Custer was to visit Japan in 1903, viewing the people as rather "small" with "primitive" industry, and writing that "[t]he Japanese takes himself very seriously and we do not dare smile when there is something doing that someone's great grandfather did and that is not now quite up to the 20th Century."

33 Blaine Harden, *A River Lost: The Life and Death of the Columbia*, pp. 153–55.

34 *Steven's County Miner*, 14 June 1888; "The Chinese Evil," *Spokane Falls Review*, 27 November 1890.

35 *Kettle Falls Pioneer*, 23 November 1893.

Chapter 2—The Mouth of the Columbia River

1 A. G. Harvey, "Chief Concomly's Skull," *Oregon Historical Quarterly*, vol. 40, no. 2 (June 1939), pp. 161–67.

2 George Vancouver, *The exploration of the Columbia River by Lieutenant W. R. Broughton, October, 1792: an extract from the Journal of Captain George Vancouver*, pp. 21–24.

3 Ibid., pp. 24–27.

4 Paul W. Dale, ed., *Seventy North to Fifty South: The Story of Captain Cook's Last Voyage*, pp. 195–237, 347.

5 Alexander Walker, *An Account of a Voyage to the North West Coast of America in 1785 and 1786, by Alexander Walker*, ed. Robin Fisher and J. M. Bumsted, pp. 139, 196.

6 Frederic W. Howay, ed., *Voyages of the "Columbia" to the Northwest Coast, 1787–1790 and 1790–1793*, pp. vi; for a description of Kendrick's mission to Japan, see Jim Mockford, "The Lady Washington at Kushimoto, Japan, in 1791," in William S. Dudley and Michael J. Crawford, eds., *The Early Republic and the Sea: Essays on the Naval and Maritime History of the Early United States*, pp. 82–99.

7 Howay, *Voyages of the "Columbia,"* pp. 398–99.

8 Ibid., p. 399.

9 Ross Cox, *The Columbia River, or scenes and adventures during a residence of six years on the western side of the Rocky Mountains among various tribes of Indians hitherto unknown; together with "A Journey across the American Continent,"* ed. Edgar I. and Jane R. Stewart, pp. 70–71.

10 Charles Bishop, *The Journal and Letters of Captain Charles Bishop on the North-West Coast of America, in the Pacific and in New South Wales, 1794–1799*, ed. Michael Roe, p. xxvi.

11 Ibid., p. 10.

12 Ibid., pp. 11–12.

13 Ibid., p. 56.

14 Ibid., p. 116.

[15] Ibid., pp. 118, 124.

[16] Howay, *Voyages of the "Columbia,"* p. 395.

[17] Robert Stuart, *The Discovery of the Oregon Trail; Robert Stuart's Narratives of His Overland Trip Eastward from Astoria in 1812–1813*, ed. Philip Ashton Rollins, p. 271.

[18] Bishop, *The Journal and Letters of Captain Charles Bishop*, p. 118.

[19] William Clark and Meriwether Lewis, *The Original Journals of the Lewis and Clark Expedition, 1804–1806*, ed. Reuben Gold Thwaites, vol. 3, pp. 197, 346.

[20] Ibid., p. 217.

[21] Ibid., pp. 230, 238.

[22] Hubert Howe Bancroft, *The Works: The Native Races, Vol. 1., Wild Tribes*, pp. 225–26.

[23] Clark and Lewis, *The Original Journals of the Lewis and Clark Expedition*, pp. 241, 301, 306, 327.

[24] In 1998 the 112-foot ship *Lady Washington* even re-enacted MacDonald's landing in Japan. See *The Columbian*, 26 June 1998.

[25] Interview with Bruce Berney, eastern Washington, 13 August 1994.

[26] Washington Irving, *Astoria, or, Anecdotes of an Enterprise Beyond the Rocky Mountains* (1836 ed.; 1961 reprint), vol. 1, p. 9.

[27] Ibid. vol. 1, p. 66. Gabriel Franchère, *Adventure at Astoria, 1810–1814*, ed. and trans. Hoyt C. Franchère, p. 57.

[28] Irving, *Astoria*, vol. 1, pp. 67–68.

[29] Ibid., vol. 2, pp. 404–5.

[30] Ibid., vol. 1, pp. 11, 192; see also *The Complete Works of Washington Irving: Astoria*, ed. Herbert L. Kleinfield, p. 28.

[31] J. B. Tyrell, ed., *David Thompson's Narrative of His Explorations in Western America, 1784–1812*, p. 500.

[32] Irving, *Astoria*, vol. 2, pp. 429–31.

[33] Elliot Coues, ed., *New light on the early history of the greater Northwest. The manuscript journals of Alexander Henry, Fur Trader of the Northwest Company and of David Thompson, Official Geographer and Explorer of the Same Company, 1799–1814*, vol. 2, p. 850.

[34] Jean Murray Cole, *Exile in the Wilderness: The Biography of Chief Factor Archibald MacDonald, 1790–1853*, p. 93.

[35] *Montreal Gazette*, 21 January 1853, p. 3.

[36] Benjamin MacDonald, "Narrative of Benjamin MacDonald," *Washington Historical Quarterly*, vol. 16, no. 3 (July 1925), pp. 196–97.

[37] Newman, *Caesars of the Wilderness*, p. 345.

[38] John S. Galbraith, *The Little Emperor: Governor Simpson of the Hudson's Bay Company*, p. 63 (quoting from E. E. Rich, *Journal of Occurrences in the Athabasca Department*, p. 392).

[39] Frederick Merk, ed., *Fur Trade and Empire: George Simpson's Journal*, p. 105.

[40] Cox, *The Columbia River*, p. 172.

[41] LMRM, pp. 89–90.

[42] BCA, MS-1249, box 9, folder 13, MacDonald to McLeod, 10 August 1891; MacDonald claimed he heard this story from a Captain Thomas Butler of Salem, Massachusetts.

[43] LMRM, p. 93.

[44] M. Nichols, "Jane Klyne McDonald, 1810–1879," *British Columbia Historical News*, vol. 21, no. 4 (Fall 1988), p. 2; Clifford Merrill Drury, *Elkanah and Mary Walker; Pioneers Among the Spokanes*, pp. 104, 256.

[45] LMRM, p. 98.

[46] EWSHS, "Donald MacDonald Letters," Donald MacDonald to N. B. Wheeler, 30 March 1916.

[47] OHS, MSS 1089, "Eva Emery Dye Papers, Letters from MacDonald, Ben, and Donald, and Duncan; and McCarthy," Benjamin McDonald to Eva Emery Dye, 29 November 1904.

[48] Rev. Samuel Parker, *Journal of an Exploring Tour Beyond the Rocky Mountains, under the direction of A.B.C.F.M.*, pp. 191–92.

[49] "Diary of Reverend George Gary—II," *Oregon Historical Quarterly*, vol. 24, no. 3 (September 1923), p. 267.

[50] Sir Edward Belcher, *Narrative of the Voyage of H.M.S. Samarang, During the Years 1843–1846*, vol. 1, p. 308.

51 Jean Murray Cole, ed., *This Blessed Wilderness: Archibald McDonald's Letters from the Columbia, 1822–1844*, p. 222; Archibald McDonald to John McLeod, 8 August 1842.

52 LMRM, p. 120.

Chapter 3—A Fateful Non-Meeting at Fort Vancouver

1 LMRM, pp. 121, 127.

2 Ayako Miura, *Kairei*, vol. 2, pp. 141–42.

3 Interview with Kōichi Saitō, Neah Bay, 19 September 1997.

4 Miura, *Kairei*, vol. 3, p. 342.

5 Hitoshi Tomita, ed., *Umi wo koeta Nihon jinmei jiten.*

6 Ibid., p. 170; Katherine Plummer, *Saisho ni amerika o mita nihonjin*, pp. 88–109; for information on the *Forester*, also see Jones, ed., *Astorian Adventure*, pp. 157–68.

7 Joseph Heco, *The Narrative of a Japanese: What he has seen and the people he has met in the course of the last forty years*, vols. 1 and 2. Heco is buried in the foreigners' section of the Aoyama Cemetery of Tōkyō. Like Manjirō, he has his own society that helps to preserve his memory and promote his name.

8 Hisakazu Kaneko, *Manjiro, the Man Who Discovered America*, pp. 95–97; Foster Rhea Dulles, *Yankees and Samurai: America's Role in the Emergence of Modern Japan*, p. 49.

9 Official English translation of Prime Minister Ryūtarō Hashimoto's words, read by Mayor Kōichi Saitō, musical program, Bellevue, Washington, October 1, 1997.

10 Robert H. Ruby and John A. Brown, *Indian Slavery in the Pacific Northwest*, pp. 76–77, 88–91.

11 Ibid., p. 92.

12 LMRM, p. 98; OHS, MSS 1089, Eva Emery Dye, "Letters from Ranald MacDonald, Box 1 of 20," Ranald MacDonald to Eva Emery Dye, 31 October 1892.

13 Glyndwr Williams, "Governor George Simpson's Character Book," *Beaver* (Summer 1975), pp. 4–18.

14 Cole, ed., *This Blessed Wilderness*, pp. 92, 97–98; idem, "Ranald MacDonald—His Ancestry and Early Years," paper delivered at the Annual Meeting of the Friends of Ranald MacDonald Society, May 1989.

15 John Ball, *Born to Wander, Autobiography of John Ball, 1794–1884*, p. 62.

16 OHS, MSS 1089, "Eva Emery Dye, Letters from Ranald MacDonald, Box 1 of 20," Ranald MacDonald to C. H. Dye, 31 October 1892.

17 HBCA, B.223/b/10, fol. 15d, Chief Factor John McLoughlin to the Governor, Deputy Governor & Committee of the Hudson's Bay Company, 28 May 1834.

18 Cole, *Exile in the Wilderness*, pp. 172–73.

19 Glyndwr Williams, ed., *Hudson's Bay Miscellany 1670–1870*, p. 221.

20 HBCA, B.223/6/10, fol. 9d, John McLoughlin to William H. McNeil, 16 May 1834.

21 Ibid., b/10, fol. 10b, McLoughlin to McNeil, 20 May 1834.

22 Ibid., fol. 19, McLoughlin to McNeil, July 1834.

23 Frederick Holman, *Dr. John McLoughlin, the Father of Oregon*, pp. 182–83.

24 Rev. Z. A. Mudge, *A Memoir of Cyrus Shepard, Embracing a Brief Sketch of the Early History of the Oregon Mission*, p. 137, Shepard to Mudge, 23 December 1834

25 E. E. Rich, ed., *The Letters of John McLoughlin, from Fort Vancouver to the Governor and Committee, First Series, 1825–1838*, pp. 128–29, John McLoughlin to Governor, Deputy Governor & Committee of the Honble. Hudson's Bay Company, 18 November 1834.

26 Ibid.

27 HBCA, A 6/23, p. 265, Hudson's Bay Company to John McLoughlin, 28 August 1835.

28 Eva Emery Dye, *McLoughlin and Old Oregon: A Chronicle*, pp. 12–13.

29 Photocopy of letter from Eva Emery Dye to Rev. Otis Cary, Kyōto, Japan, 31 May 1913 (courtesy Beth Cary); Eva Emery Dye, "A Hero of Old Astoria," *Oregon Historical Quarterly*, vol. 12, no. 3 (September 1911), pp. 220–23.

30 "Reviews," *Washington Historical Quarterly*, vol. 7, no. 4 (December 1906), pp. 435–37.

31 Eva Emery Dye, *McDonald of Oregon: A Tale of Two Shores*, p. 9.

32 Ibid., p. 69.

33 Ibid., pp. 69–70. Among the details Dye provided—probably true—are that most of the original crew of

the junk had perished of starvation and disease and their bodies had been preserved on ship. On the basis of no contemporary historical record, however, she also claimed that in addition to enslaving the three sailors, the Makah had "killed some at the Ozette village."

34 Ibid., pp. 69–70.

35 Letter from Bruce Berney to author, 20 January 1999.

36 LMRM, p. 106; BCA, MS-1249, box 8, folder 2, p. 24.

37 Dorothy O. Johansen, "Book Reviews: *Ranald MacDonald, Adventurer,*" *Pacific Northwest Quarterly*, vol. 32, no. 4 (October 1941), p. 449.

38 Marie Leona Nichols, *Ranald MacDonald, Adventurer*, p. 55.

39 Ibid., p. 54.

40 Interview with Jean Murray Cole, Ottawa, Canada, 19 November 1999.

41 Evelyn Iritani, *An Ocean Between Us*, p. 35.

42 Jo Ann Roe, *Ranald MacDonald: Pacific Rim Adventurer*, p. 16.

43 BFO, "General Correspondence: China, 1815–1905," F.O. 17–153, Charles Gutzlaff's Communication Relative to the "Preble's Visit to Japan," 23 May 1849; ibid., Charles Gutzlaff to J. G. Bonham, 11 January 1849. In this letter, Gutzlaff recommended Keoukitch (Kyūkichi) for continued employment in his office. He described Kyūkichi's extraordinary odyssey, including capture in North America, and said he was "the most intelligent" of the three men, praising his English and Chinese ability and adding, "He is a man that can be implicitly depended upon in the performance of any duty requiring secrecy and caution."

44 PAC, Hargrave Collection Microfilm, series 1, C73, p. 967, John Rae to James Hargrave, 12 February 1835.

45 LMRM, p. 39. According to this version, told to Eleanor Haskins Holly of Kettle Falls, Washington, MacDonald determined to go to Japan when he learned of his Indian blood, while a young man at St. Thomas, Canada.

46 Howay, Lewis, and Meyers, "Documents—Angus McDonald," pp. 188–229.

47 Rev. Parker, *Journal of an Exploring Tour Beyond the Rocky Mountains*, p. 162.

48 "The Historical Conference," *Oregon Historical Quarterly*, vol. 6, no. 3 (September 1905), pp. 311–15.

49 Dye, *McDonald of Oregon*, pp. 70, 76.

Chapter 4—Education at Red River

1 Cole, ed., *This Blessed Wilderness*, pp. 99–101, Archibald McDonald to John McLeod, 20 February 1833, and pp. 97–98, Archibald McDonald to Edward Ermatinger, 20 February 1833.

2 HBCA, E/12/3, Duncan Finlayson (1795–1862), "No. 3 Containing Journey from Vancouver to York Factory thence to Lachine & England, 1833–1835."

3 John Perry Pritchett, *The Red River Valley, 1811–1849: A Regional Study*, pp. 16–17. Selkirk is quoted as saying, "... when I was but a youth I developed an antipathy for the United States due almost solely to the buccaneering of John Paul." During the Revolutionary War Jones was ordered to harass British shipping and take hostages. He chose to raid the Selkirk estate because he believed himself to be one of their illegitimate and unacknowledged offspring.

4 Ibid., p. 45; Newman, *Caesars of the Wilderness*, pp. 196–97. Quote is from an anonymous person addressing Selkirk, in Beckles Willson, *The Great Company*.

5 Cole, *Exile in the Wilderness*, p. 51.

6 The battle is memorialized in Winnipeg with a plaque at Main St. and Rupertsland Avenue.

7 *Rupert's Land to Riel, vol. 1, Manitoba 125: A History*, pp. 102–3, 126–27.

8 HBCA, E.12/5, Isobel G. Finlayson, "My Notebook," 1840, p. 99 (printed no.).

9 John S. C. Abbot, "The People of the Red River," *Harper's Magazine* (January 1859), pp. 169–76.

10 HBCA, E.12/5, Finlayson "My Notebook," p. 89.

11 "A Visit to Red River," *Harper's New Monthly Magazine*, vol. 13, issue 77 (October 1856), p. 665.

12 Ibid., p. 670.

13 Alexander Ross, *The Red River Settlement: its rise, progress, and present state*, pp. 243–44.

14 Pritchett, *The Red River Valley*, pp. 233–34, George Simpson to Andrew Colville, 31 May 1824.

15 "A Visit to Red River," p. 665.

16 Alexander Gregor and Keith Wilson, *The Development of Education in Manitoba*, p. 20.

17 John West, *The Substance of a Journal During a Residence at The Red River Colony, British North America*, pp. 30, 92.

18 Merk, *Fur Trade and Empire*, p. 181, George Simpson to Andrew Colvile, 20 May 1822.

19 Jennifer S. H. Brown, "Ultimate Respectability: Fur Trade Children in the 'Civilized World,'" *Beaver* (Winter 1977), p. 4.

20 PAM/ HBCA, film no. 4M101, E4/1A, "Red River Settlement Register of Baptisms, 1820–1841," p. 115d.

21 CMS, Class "C," C.1, North West America Mission (Rupertsland) (John West), C.1/M Mission Books (Incoming Letters) 1822–1862, p. 90, 2 November 1834.

22 Raymond M. Beaumont, "The Rev. William Cockran: The Man and the Image," *Manitoba History*, no. 33 (Spring 1997), pp. 2–15.

23 PAC, C73, "Hargrave Collection," p. 1002, Donald Ross to James Hargrave, 13 March 1835.

24 HBCA, E4/1A, p. 115d.

25 Ibid., film no. 4M101, E3/16, p. 244.

26 CMS Class "C," C.1 North West America Mission (Rupertsland) (John West), C.1/M Mission Books (Incoming Letters) 1822–1862, Rev. W. Cockran to the Secretaries, 8 June 1835. Cockran's journal is presumably off by one day, as he listed officiating at a marriage on the 8th, and not the 9th, which is the date given in other records for the McDonalds' marriage.

27 Ibid., p. 142, Reverend D. T. Jones's Journal, 19 June 1835.

28 Ibid., 14 July 1835.

29 BCA, MS-1249, box 9, folder 13, "Letters to Malcolm McLeod, 1889–1894," Ranald MacDonald to Malcolm McLeod, 24 October 1893.

30 OHS, MSS 1012, file no. 4, "Archibald McDonald, Letters to Edward Ermatinger, 1830–1837" (photostats), McDonald to E. Ermatinger, 1 April 1836.

31 *Dictionary of Canadian Biography*, vol. 8, pp. 714–15; also, Pritchard, *Glimpses of the Past*.

32 *Dictionary of Canadian Biography*, vol. 8, pp. 713–14; Rich, *The Hudson's Bay Company, 1821–1870*, vol. 3, p. 427.

33 Pritchard, *Glimpses of the Past, in The Red River Settlement, From Letters of Mr. John Pritchard, 1805–1836*, p. 24.

34 CMS, Class "C," C.1, North West America Mission (Rupertsland) (John West), C.1/M, Mission Books (Incoming Letters) 1822–1862, reel A-77, "Report of the State of Religion and Morality and Education of the Red River Settlement and Grand Rapids, by the Rev. Messrs. Jones and Cockran (5 June 1835), pp. 62–71.

35 HBCA, E10/1, vol. 1, fol. 24d; letter of Colin Robertson is referred to in HBCA search file under "John Pritchard," in communication from Judith Beattie to Paulette M. Chiasson, 28 May 1984.

36 HBCA, E 5/8, Red River Settlement Census.

37 W. L. Morton, "The Canadian Métis; An appreciation of Marcel Giraud's magnificent study of the western half-breeds, 'Le Métis Canadien,' published by the Institute d'Ethnologie in Paris," *Beaver* (September 1950), pp. 3–7.

38 CMS, Class "C," C.1, reel A-77, "Report of the State of Religion and Morality" (5 June 1835), pp. 62–71.

39 CMS, Class "C," C.1, North West America (Rupertsland) (John West), C.1/M Mission Books (Incoming Letters), 1822–1862, Cockran to the Secretaries, 18 October 1835, p. 135.

40 Ibid., Rev. W. Cockran to the Secretaries, 5 August 1835, pp. 75–79.

41 Ross, *The Red River Settlement*, pp. 237–39.

42 Ibid., p. 132.

43 William J. Fraser, *St. John's College Winnipeg, 1866–1966; A History of the First Hundred Years of the College*, p. 12; Thomas F. Bredin, "The Red River Academy," *Beaver* (Winter 1974), pp. 10–17.

44 HBCA, Search File Extract from Report from George Simpson to Governor and Committee, dated York Factory, 21 July 1834, p. 11, in L029162 to T. Bredin, 21 October 1970.

45 CMS, Class "C," C.1, Jones and Cockran Report to Secretaries, 5 June 1835, p. 69; Bredin, "The Red River Academy," pp. 10–17.

46 CMS, Class "C," C.1., North West America Mission (Rupertsland) (John West), C.1/M Mission Books (Incoming Letters), 1822–1862, Reverend D. T. Jones's Journal, 9 June to 14 October 1835, pp. 142–49.

47 CMS, Class "C," C.1, Jones and Cockran Report to Secretaries, 5 June 1835, p. 68.

48 Elizabeth Custer Interview, *Harper's Weekly*, 18 July 1891.

48 CMS, Class "C," C.1, North America Mission (Rupertsland) (John West), C.1/M Mission Books (Incoming letters), Rev. David T. Jones's Journal, 27 August 1836 to 18 July 1837, p. 230, 10 February 1837.

50 LMRM, pp. 132–33.

51 HBCA, D 4/22, fol. 47–47d, George Simpson to the Reverend D. T. Jones, 24 June 1836.

52 BCA, MS-1249, box 9, folder 13, MacDonald to McLeod, 25 December 1891.

53 PAC, Hargrave Collection, series 1, C73, p. 833, John Macallum to James Hargrave, 12 August 1834.

54 Ibid., series 1, C-74, pp. 1520–22, Macallum to Hargrave, 14 December 1838.

55 Bredin, "The Red River Academy," pp. 12, 14.

56 McLeod, *The Letters of Letitia Hargrave*, p. 177.

57 OHS, MSS 1012, file 5, Archibald McDonald to E. Ermatinger, 25 January 1837.

58 Ibid., file 7, McDonald to E. Ermatinger, 1 February 1839.

59 Ibid., file 8, McDonald to E. Ermatinger, 10 March 1839.

60 CMS, Class "C," C.1, North West America Mission (Rupertsland) (John West), C.1/M, Mission Books (Incoming Letters), 1822–1862, p. 135, Rev. David Jones to Clerical Secretary, 20 October 1836.

61 Ibid., D. T. Jones's Journal, p. 226, 14 November 1836.

62 Ross, *The Red River Settlement*, p. 239.

63 CMS, Class "C," C.1, p. 230, D. T. Jones's Journal, 10 February 1837.

64 Jane Lewis Chapin, ed., "McLoughlin Letters, 1827–1849," *Oregon Historical Quarterly*, vol. 37, no. 1 (March 1936), p. 46, Simon Fraser to John McLoughlin, 20 April 1827.

65 Ibid., p. 60, John McLoughlin to John Fraser, 14 February 1836.

66 Grace Lee Nute, ed., "Notes and Documents: Documents Relating to James Dickson's Expedition," *Mississippi Valley Historical Review*, vol. 10, no. 2 (September 1923), pp. 173–81, George Simpson to J. H. Pelly, 31 October 1836.

67 Nute, ed., "James Dickson: A Filibuster in Minnesota in 1836," *Mississippi Valley Historical Review*, vol. 10, no. 2 (September 1923), pp. 127–40, William Nourse to John Siveright, 15 September 1836.

68 Nute, "Notes and Documents," pp. 173–81, George Simpson to J. H. Pelly, London, 31 October 1836.

69 M. Elizabeth Arthur, "General Dickson and the Indian Liberating Army in the North," *Ontario Historical Society*, vol. 62, no. 3 (September 1970), pp. 151–62.

70 Martin McLeod's journal survives in the MHS archives.

71 Chapin, "McLoughlin Letters, 1827–1849," pp. 58–59, John McLoughlin, Jr., to John Fraser, 11 October 1836.

72 The sword can be seen today at the Manitoba Museum of Man and Nature in downtown Winnipeg.

73 OHS, MSS 1012, file 6, Archibald McDonald to E. Ermatinger, 2 February 1838.

Chapter 5—A "Trial in Business" at St. Thomas

1 OHS, MSS 1012, Archibald McDonald, "Letters to Edward Ermatinger, 1830–1837" (typescript copies of photostats), file 4, Archibald McDonald to Edward Ermatinger, 1 April 1836.

2 Ibid.

3 Ibid. Comcomly was famous for his prohibitions on liquor among his tribesmen, but his son Cassacas ("Prince of Wales") was an exception. The "princess" is presumably not Ranald's mother, but Cassacas's wife.

4 Ibid., file 5, A. McDonald to E. Ermatinger, 25 January 1837.

5 Ibid., file 6, A. McDonald to E. Ermatinger, 2 February 1838.

6 Ibid., file 8, A. McDonald to E. Ermatinger, 10 March 1839.

7 Ibid.

8 OHS, MSS 1012, file 11, A. McDonald to E. Ermatinger, 30 March 1842.

9 C. O. Ermatinger, *The Talbot Regime, or the First Half Century of the Talbot Settlement*, pp. 179–80.

10 JJT, "The Edward Ermatinger Papers," Memoirs of Edward Ermatinger, part A, pp. 19, 39.
11 Ermatinger, *The Talbot Regime*, p. 223.
12 Ibid., p. 227.
13 JJT, "Ermatinger Family Collection," series 1, file 62, printed letter from William Stayner, General Post Office, to E. Ermatinger, St. Thomas, 1 November 1838.
14 Ermatinger, *The Talbot Regime*, p. 225.
15 "Prospectus," *St. Thomas Standard*, 7 May 1844.
16 LMRM, pp. 115–17; also BCA, MS-1249, box 8, folder 1, p. 62.
17 HBCA, reel 3M60, series 1, D5/6, pp. 125–26, Archibald McDonald to Governor Simpson, 15 April 1841.
18 PAC, "Hargrave Collection," microfilm series 1 C76, p. 3699, Francis Ermatinger to J. Hargrave, 1 January 1848.
19 Ibid., C73, p. 700, John Macallum to James Hargrave, 18 December 1833.
20 JJT, "The Edward Ermatinger Papers," Memoirs of Edward Ermatinger, p. 22.
21 T. C. Elliott, ed., "Letters of Dr. John McLoughlin," *Oregon Historical Quarterly*, vol. 23, no. 4 (December 1922), pp. 367–68, John McLoughlin to Edward Ermatinger, 1 February 1836.
22 Lois Halliday McDonald, ed., *Fur Trade Letters of Francis Ermatinger, written to his brother Edward during his service with the Hudson's Bay Company, 1818–1853*, p. 216.
23 OHS, MSS 1012, file 6, A. McDonald to E. Ermatinger, 2 February 1838.
24 McDonald, *Fur Trade Letters*, p. 223, letter 28, Francis Ermatinger to Edward Ermatinger, 6 February 1840.
25 Ibid., p. 229, letter 29, F. Ermatinger to E. Ermatinger, 15 March 1840.
26 Ibid., p. 232, letter 30, F. Ermatinger to E. Ermatinger, 10 March 1841.
27 Ibid., p. 12, letter 26, F. Ermatinger to E. Ermatinger, 12 July 1838.
28 Ibid., p. 213, letter 27, F. Ermatinger to E. Ermatinger, 26 February 1839.
29 Ibid., pp. 250–56, letter 33, F. Ermatinger to E. Ermatinger, 4 March 1843.
30 Ibid., p. 260, letter 35, F. Ermatinger to E. Ermatinger, 4 April 1844.
31 Ibid., p. 265, letter 36, F. Ermatinger to E. Ermatinger, 23 March 1845.
32 BANC, MSS P-W 4 (film), "Selected Items Relating to the Fur Trade from Material in the Huntington Library," Francis Ermatinger to Edward Ermatinger, 24 December 1847.
33 OHS, MSS 1012, file 14, A. McDonald to E. Ermatinger, 12 December 1846.
34 HBCA, Microfilm series 1, reel 428, HBCA Ref. No. A 36/9, "Officers' and Servants' Wills," 27 June 1834, with Codicil of 26 June 1835.
35 OHS, MSS 1012, file 4, A. McDonald to E. Ermatinger, 1 April 1836.
36 McDonald, *Fur Trade Letters*, p. 186, letter 21, Frank Ermatiger to Edward Ermatinger, 11 March 1836.
36 Ibid., p. 251, letter 33, F. Ermatinger to E. Ermatinger, 4 March 1843.
38 Ibid., p. 200, letter 23, F. Ermatinger to E. Ermatinger, 1 June 1837.
39 JJT, "The Edward Ermatinger Papers," Memoirs of Edward Ermatinger, part B, pp. 27, 33.
40 PAC, Hargrave Collection, series 1, C-77, p. 4912, Frank Ermatinger to James Hargrave, 21 December 1851.
41 BCA, MS-1249, box 9, folder 11, "MacDonald, Ranald 1824–1894, 'Correspondence Outward—Letters to Mrs. C. H. Dye, [typescript copies], Ranald MacDonald to C. H. Dye,'" 24 July 1892.
42 OHS, MSS 1012, file 7, A. McDonald to E. Ermatinger, 1 February 1839.
43 Ibid., file 9, A. McDonald to E. Ermatinger, 2 April 1840.
44 HBCA, E94/1, "Ermatinger Papers," "John Tod Correspondence 1826–1862," John Tod to Edward Ermatinger, 1 March 1841; also microfilm at PAC, C-375, "Ermatinger Papers," vol. 2, p. 77.
45 OHS, MSS 1012, file 10, A. McDonald to E. Ermatinger, 5 March 1841.
46 Ibid.
47 Ibid.
48 LMRM, pp. 117–18
49 BCA, MS-1249, box 8, folder 2, "Story of Adventure of Ranald McDonald, First Teacher of English in Japan, A.D. 1848–49," p. 44.
50 LMRM, pp. 38–39.

51 Brown, "Ultimate Respectability: Fur-Trade Children in the 'Civilized World,'" p. 9.
52 Robert E. Bieder, "Scientific Attitudes Toward Indian Mixed-Bloods in Early Nineteenth Century America," *Journal of Ethnic Studies*, vol. 8, no. 2 (Summer 1980), pp. 17–30.
53 Ibid., pp. 26, 30.
54 Hubert Howe Bancroft, *History of the Pacific States of North America, Vol. 23, The North West Coast* and *Vol. 2, 1800–1846*, p. 651.
55 Merk, *Fur Trade and Empire*, p. 181.
56 PAC, "Hargrave Collection," series 1, C-79, p. 7443, Edward Ermatinger to James Hargrave, 11 January 1861. Ermatinger was apparently referring to a son of George Barnston, a close friend of Ranald Mac-Donald and also part Chinook.
57 Edward Ermatinger, "Notes of the Liverpool Financial Reform Association's Tract entitled 'The Hudson's Bay Company versus Magna Carta and the British People,'" 1857.
58 HBCA, E94/3, Miscellaneous Correspondence 1829–1872, p. 263, Peter C. Pambun to Edward Ermatinger, 22 June 1858.
59 OHS, MSS 1012, file 10, A. McDonald to E. Ermatinger, 5 March, appended on, 21 April 1841.
60 HBCA, PAM, reel 3M60 Series 1, D5/6, pp. 125–26, Archibald McDonald to George Simpson, 15 April 1841.
61 Thomas E. Jessett, ed., *Reports and Letters of Herbert Beaver, 1836–1839*, p. 77.
62 OHS, MSS 1012, file 9, A. McDonald to E. Ermatinger, 2 April 1840.
63 Ibid., file 11, A. McDonald to E. Ermatinger, 30 March 1842. Being hired as an "apprentice clerk," would have given Ranald more opportunity for promotion. It was the same position in which the Ermatinger brothers entered the Company.
64 HBCA, reel 41, HBC Letter Book, A 6/26, "London Correspondence Book Outwards—H.B.C. Officials 1842–45," p. 22, William Smith to Archibald McDonald, 31 August 1842.
65 OHS, MSS 1012, file 11, A. McDonald to E. Ermatinger, 30 March 1842.
66 McDonald, *Fur Trade Letters*, p. 254, letter 33, F. Ermatinger to E. Ermatinger, 4 March 1843.
67 OHS, MSS 1012, file 12, A. Mcdonald to E. Ermatinger, 15 March 1843.
68 Ibid.
69 PAC, reel 3M62 series 1, D 5/8, Archibald McDonald to George Simpson, 27 April 1843.
70 OHS, MSS 1012, file 12, A. Mcdonald to E. Ermatinger, 15 March 1843.
71 HBCA, E94/1, "John Tod Correspondence 1826–1862," "Ermatinger Papers," John Tod to Edward Ermatinger, 20 March 1843.
72 LMRM, p. 133.
73 PAC, reel 3M66, D5/11, p. 135, Archibald McDonald to Sir George Simpson, 20 April 1844.
74 OHS, MSS 1012, file 13, A. McDonald to E. Ermatinger, 22 March 1844.

Chapter 6—Sag Harbor's Japan Connection

1 PAC, Hargrave Collection, microfilm series 1, reel 75, p. 2524; Archibald McDonald to James Hargrave, 21 March 1843.
2 LMRM, pp. 133–34.
3 BCA, MS-1249, box 7, vol. 1, "Ranald MacDonald's Adventure in Japan, as First Teacher of English There, A.D. 1848–1849," p. 4.
4 Ibid.
5 LMRM, pp. 37, 41–42.
6 *The Whalemen's Shipping List*, 17 March 1843, 14 April 1843, 29 August 1843, 17 October 1843, 24 October 1843, 8 November 1843, 2 January 1844, 23 April 1844, 4 February 1845.
7 BCA, MS-1249, box 9, folder 11, "MacDonald, Ranald 1824–1894, 'Correspondence Outward—Letters to Mrs. C. H. Dye,' MacDonald to C. H. Dye," 24 July 1892. In this letter, MacDonald mentioned meeting William Glenn Rae, son-in-law of John McLoughlin and head of the HBC post on Montgomery Street, San Francisco. Rae arrived in 1841 and committed suicide in 1845; BCA, MS-1249, box 9, folder 13, MacDonald to McLeod, 11 August 1889.
8 "A Sailor's Attempt to Penetrate Japan," *Friend*, December 1848, p. 91.

9 PAC, film 3M70, series 1, D5/15, p. 223, Archibald McDonald to George Simpson, 7 October 1845.

10 BCA, MS-1249, box 9, folder 13, MacDonald to McLeod, 20 May 1889.

11 Herman Melville, *Moby-Dick, or, The Whale*, p. 121.

12 Harry D. Sleight, *The Whale Fishery on Long Island*, p. 17; "American Whale Fishery," *Living Age*, vol. 9, no. 100, 11 April 1846, p. 102.

13 Melville, *Moby-Dick*, pp. 122, 172.

14 Ibid., p. 37.

15 LMRM, p. 40.

16 Howard C. Gardiner, *In Pursuit of the Golden Dream: Reminiscences of San Francisco and the Northern and Southern Mines, 1849–1857*, Dale L. Morgan, ed., p. 11.

17 Ibid, p. 11.

18 Melville, *Moby-Dick*, p. 37.

19 Gardiner, *In Pursuit of the Golden Dream*, p. 12.

20 Ibid., p. 13.

21 Sleight, *The Whale Fishery on Long Island*, p. 25.

22 George A. Finkenor, *Whales and Whaling: Port of Sag Harbor, New York*, p. 66.

23 *Sailor's Magazine*, vol. 15, no.12, August 1843, p. 367, letter of Capt. Edward Richardson, Sag Harbor, L.I., 3 April 1843.

24 Erastus Bill, *Citizen: An American Boy's Early Manhood Aboard a Sag Harbor Whale-Ship Chasing Delirium and Death Around the World, 1843, being the Story of Erastus Bill Who Lived to Tell About It*, pp. 52–53.

25 Donald R. Bernard, *The Life and Times of John Manjirō*, p. 45.

26 "Japan," *Friend*, 2 February 1846.

27 NBWM, Old Dartmouth Historical Society, Whaling Museum Library, microfilm roll: 1009, catalog no. 1073, "Log of the *Manhattan*," 16 March 1845.

28 Ibid., 18 April 1845.

29 "Japan," *Friend*, 2 February 1846.

30 NBWM, "Log of the *Manhattan*," 20 April 1845.

31 *Friend*, 1 February 1846.

Chapter 7—A "Staging Ground" in the Hawaiian Islands

1 *Friend*, 1 June 1846; *The Polynesian*, 1 January 1847.

2 LMRM, pp. 135–36.

3 Ibid., pp. 137–38.

4 "A Sailor's Attempt to Penetrate Japan," *Friend*, 1 December 1848.

5 BCA, MS-1249, box 9, folder 13, MacDonald to McLeod, 4 December 1893.

6 "A Sailor's Attempt to Penetrate Japan."

7 Mary Charlotte Alexander, *Dr. Baldwin of Lahaina*, p. 147.

8 *Friend*, 1 June 1846; *Polynesian*, 17 January 1846.

9 Sir George Simpson, *An Overland Journey Round the World, during the Years 1841 and 1842*, vol. 2, p. 68.

10 John Cook, *Reminiscences of John Cook, Kamaaina and Forty-Niner*, pp. 4–6.

11 *Friend*, 3 April 1844.

12 BANC, "The Journal of Jotham Newton" (of the *Uncas*)

13 Ibid.

14 Ibid. One on-board, Lahaina preacher "drew many hearers from the seafaring community he being a man of much benevolence devotedness and of *somewhat* familiar style that is to say he is not unapproachable by reason of haughty pride."

15 Ibid.

16 *Friend*, 1 January 1847.

17 Alexander, *Dr. Baldwin of Lahaina*, p. 145.

18 Ibid., p. 148.

19 "Letter from Lahaina" (dated 17 December 1841), *Sailor's Magazine*, vol. 14, no. 12 (August 1842), p. 375.

20 *Polynesian* (New Series), 13 July 1844.

21 "Japan," *Putnam's*, vol. 1, no. 3 (March 1853), p. 248.

22 "The American Expedition to Japan," *North American Review*, vol. 83, no. 172 (July 1856), pp. 258–59.

23 Dwight Baldwin, "Shipwrecked Japanese," *Polynesian*, 1 August 1840.

24 Alexander, *Dr. Baldwin of Lahaina*, p. 119.

25 *Polynesian*, 1 August 1840; ibid., 17 October 1840.

26 *Friend*, 2 February 1846.

27 Amasa Delano, *A Narrative of Voyages and Travels, in the northern and southern hemispheres: comprising three voyages round the world; together with a voyage of survey and discovery, in the Pacific Ocean and Oriental islands . . .*, pp. 399–410; Kenneth Wiggins Porter, *John Jacob Astor: Businessman*, vol. 1, p. 199; Shunzo Sakamaki, "Japan and the United States, 1790–1853," *Transactions of the Asiatic Society of Japan*, 2nd series, vol. 18 (1939), p. 73.

28 *Polynesian*, 23 August 1845, p. 57.

29 Alfred L. Lomax, "Dr. McLoughlin's Tropical Trade Route," *Beaver* (Spring 1964), pp. 10–15.

30 "A Sailor's Attempt to Penetrate Japan."

31 Even David McLoughlin, MacDonald's childhood friend who had traveled across the Rockies with him, went there on Company business in 1847, holding out the possibility that the friends may have met.

32 J. S. Emerson, "The Shipwrecked Japanese," *Hawaiian Spectator*, vol. 1, no. 3, article 7 (July 1838).

33 Ball, *Born to Wander*, p. 67.

34 Simpson, *An Overland Journey Round the World*, vol. 1, pp. 240–42.

35 Ibid., vol. 2, p. 112.

36 Bernard, *The Life and Times of John Manjirō*, p. 34; Takashi Miyanaga, *Jon Man to yobareru otoko: Hyōryūmin Nakahama Manjirō no shōgai*, p. 109.

37 James J. Jarves, *Scenes and Scenery in the Sandwich Islands, and a trip through Central America: Being observations from my note-book during the years 1837–1842*, p. 54.

38 Simpson, *An Overland Journey Round the World*, vol. 2, p. 59.

39 Ibid., pp. 50–51.

40 Gustavus Hines, *A Voyage Round the World: with a history of the Oregon mission . . .*, p. 217.

41 "Chaplain's Study, Honolulu; Extract from Rev. Damon's Letter, October 1846," *Sailor's Magazine*, vol. 19, no. 8 (April 1847), p. 247.

42 "A Sailor's Attempt to Penetrate Japan," p. 91.

43 Ibid., 20 December 1849.

44 Jarves, *Scenes and Scenery in the Sandwich Islands*, pp. 77–86.

45 "Japan," *Polynesian*, 29 May 1847.

46 Sakamaki, "Japan and the United States, 1790–1853," pp. 33–35; *Polynesian*, 30 October 1847.

47 *Polynesian*, 19 September 1846.

48 "Commodore Biddle's Official Account of His Visit to Japan," ibid., 30 October 1847.

49 *Polynesian*, 6 November 1847 (reprinted article, dated Honolulu, 20 September 1846).

50 BCA, MS-1249, box 9, folder 13, MacDonald to McLeod, 4 June 1892.

51 *Polynesian*, 13 November 1847.

52 Ibid., 20 November 1847.

53 Ibid., 27 November 1847.

54 Ibid., 11 December 1847.

55 Ibid., 11 December 1847.

56 Ibid., 18 December 1847; 12 September 1846.

Chapter 8—Rishiri Island: The Adventure Begins

1 LMRM, pp. 150–51.

2 "A Sailor's Attempt to Penetrate Japan," *Friend*, 1 December 1848.

3 Ibid.

4 Gardiner, *In Pursuit of the Golden Dream*, ed. Dale L. Morgan, p. 14. Although the book was published many years later, Gardiner appears to be quoting from a then-contemporary source.

5   Ibid.

6   "A Sailor's Attempt to Penetrate Japan."

7   The *Plymouth* and *David Paddock* were two of the first New England whalers to discover the cost advantages of Hong Kong. A 29 January 1848 letter from Hong Kong (reprinted in the *Whalemen's Shipping List* of 2 May 1848), stated, "They came up from the Sandwich Islands, and are much pleased with our place; they consider it much cheaper, and in every respect better than the Islands. They think they can save 3 months of the most valuable time in the whaling season by coming here, as everything is much lower, and their bills can be negotiated at a reasonable rate."

8   *China Mail*, 3 February 1848.

9   BCA, MS-1249, box 9, folder 3, "Account of a Journey from the Sandwich Islands to Japan," p. 2. The "Whitny" MacDonald referred to is Asa Whitney, who in 1845 proposed to Congress that a transcontinental railroad be built to the Pacific.

10 BCA, MS-1249, box 9, folder 7, MacDonald to McLeod, 12 August 1899.

11 "Marine Intelligence," *Sag Harbor Corrector*, 17 January 1849 and 3 May 1849.

12 BCA, MS-1249, box 9, folder 3, "Account of a Journey from the Sandwich Islands to Japan," p. 2.

13 BANC, "The Journal of Jotham Newton" (of the *Uncas*).

14 Shusaku Endo's historical novel *The Samurai* (New York: New Directions Publishing, 1997) gives a good account of this trip. Its appendix, "Postscript: Fact and Truth in *The Samurai*," trans. Van C. Gessel, is particularly useful; see p. 268.

15 Derek Massarella, *A World Elsewhere: Japan's Encounter with Europe in the Sixteenth and Seventeenth Centuries* (New Haven: Yale University Press, 1990), p. 349.

16 LMRM, p. 162.

17 BCA, MS-1249, box 9, folder 1, "Adventure in Japan During Eleven Months" by Ranald MacDonald," p. 1.

18 BFO, "China Correspondence," F.O. 17/155, Visit of the U.S. Ship Preble at Nagasaki, Charles Gutzlaff to Foreign Office, 23 May 1849, p. 1.

19 *Whalemen's Shipping List*, 14 August 1849.

20 "A Sailor's Attempt to Penetrate Japan."

21 BCA, MS-1249, box 9, folder 1, "'Adventure in Japan During Eleven Months' by Ranald MacDonald."

22 HCMSL, Samuel C. Damon Papers, 1830–1890, Ranald MacDonald to Samuel C. Damon, 24 May 1849.

23 *Polynesian*, 20 November 1847.

24 *Friend*, 1 November 1848.

25 HCMSL, MacDonald to Damon, 24 May 1849.

26 "A Sailor's Attempt to Enter Japan," *Friend*, 1 December 1848.

27 BCA, MS-1249, box 9, folder 2, "Japan, Story of Adventure of Ranald McDonald, First Teacher of English in Japan, A.D. 1848–1849. The Gates, of Brass, Were Opened!' by Ranald MacDonald (with a Brief Sketch of His Life)," p. 44; BCA, MS-1249, box 8, folder 4, Miscellaneous Notes re: Japan by Malcolm McLeod.

28 LMRM p. 132.

29 Nichols, *Ranald MacDonald, Adventurer*, p. 55. I have never located the source of this quotation, but according to Nichols it comes from MacDonald's manuscript in the BCA. While Nichols is not always a reliable source, this section in her book was footnoted.

30 LMRM, p. 155.

31 Gardiner, *In Pursuit of the Golden Dream*, p. 14.

32 BCA, MS-1249, box 9, folder 7, MacDonald to McLeod, 12 August 1889.

33 LMRM, pp. 153–54.

34 LMRM, p. 155.

35 Masaki Takahashi and Yūji Ushiro, "Why on Rishiri? MacDonald's Landing Place in Japan," *Friends of MacDonald Newsletter* (Winter 1988–89), p. 4; Stephen Kohl, "In Ranald's Wake: Steve Kohl's FOM Experience in Japan," *Gates Ajar*, vol. 2, no. 1 (Fall 1989), p. 7.

36 NARA, Microfilm Publication M89, "Letters Received by the Secretary of the Navy from Commanding Officers of Squadrons ("Squadron Letters"), 1841–1886, Roll 4, East India Squadron, vol. 4, 12 February

1848–19 June 1850, "The Deposition of Ranald MacDonald, 30 April 1848."
37 HCMSL, MacDonald to Damon, 24 May 1849.
38 BCA, MS-1249, box 9, folder 3, "Account of a Journey from the Sandwich Islands to Japan," p. 5.
39 Ibid., pp. 5–6.
40 Ibid., pp. 5–6; LMRM, p. 158.
41 LMRM, pp. 168–69.
42 *The New Encyclopedia Brittanica*, vol. 13 (1997), p. 350.
43 LMRM, p. 168.
44 Isao Kikuchi, *Ainu minzoku to Nihonjin*, pp. 87–92.
45 *Sekai dai hyakkajiten*, vol. 1, p. 31.
46 *The New Encyclopedia Brittanica*, vol. 1, Micropaedia, p. 173.
47 LMRM, p. 166.
48 BCA, MS-1249, box 9, folder 3, "Account of a Journey from the Sandwich Islands to Japan," p. 9; ibid., box 6, folder 1, "'Japan, Story of Adventure of Ranald McDonald, First Teacher of English in Japan, A.D. 1848–1849. The Gates, of Brass, Were Opened!' by Ranald MacDonald (with a Brief Sketch of His Life)," p. 90.
49 Along with the other names of guards that MacDonald recorded, such as Kemon and Kechinza, Tangaro's name is rather odd sounding and has been the focus of intense debate among researchers in Japan. MacDonald's ear was not yet attuned to Japanese, and he had great difficulty transliterating what he heard. One man he met, "Meanjima," is fairly easy to identify from records as a foot soldier named "Miyajima." Torao Tomita, who translated the 1923 edition of MacDonald's autobiography, pored through Japanese records to try to determine if Tangaro was really a guard named "Zenjirō," "Kijirō," "Jūtarō," "Tajirō," or "Tadajirō," eventually concluding that "Tajirō" was the name.
50 LMRM, pp. 166–67.
51 Ibid., pp. 171–72.
52 Ibid., pp. 173–74.
53 Otowa Shigure, *Shima monogatari*, p. 569.
54 "Chiiki kara sekai wo manabi; sekai kara kyō do wo manabu" [Learning about the world from a locality; Learning about home from the world], *Seikyō Shinbun*, 29 September 1997.
55 Kyōji Furukawa, "Ranarudo Makudonarudo to no deai" [How I met Ranald MacDonald], *Rishirito hatsu Makudonarudo tsūshin*, vol. 5 (20 July 1996), pp. 4–6.
56 "Sakunen 11gatsu, kyōfū de taoreta Makudonarudo jōriku kinenhi, bungakuhi to shite saiken" [Monument commemorating MacDonald's landing destroyed by gale last November, to be rebuilt as a literary memorial], *Hokkaidō shinbun* (Rumoi-Sōya edition), 24 June 1996, p. 22.

Chapter 9—On Japan's Northern Frontier

1 BCA, MS-1249, box 9, folder 3, "Account of a Journey from the Sandwich Islands to Japan," p. 14.
2 Ibid.
3 Ibid., pp. 16, 19.
4 Ibid., p. 20.
5 N. Nozikov, *Russian Voyages Round the World*, p. 37.
6 Lensen, *The Russian Push Toward Japan*, pp. 123–25; Nozikov, *Russian Voyages Round the World*, p. ix.
7 Lensen, *The Russian Push Toward Japan*, p. 102 (quoting Polonski, p. 480).
8 Ryōhei Kisaki, *Kōdayū to Rakusuman: Bakumatsu nichiro kōshō shi no ichi sokumen*, pp. 128–34.
9 One castaway, that Laxman brought with him, Kōdayū Daikokuya, went on to make important contributions to Japanese knowledge of Russia and the outside world and is the subject of novels and a popular film. Upon his return to Japan, he was interrogated on his experiences and closely monitored for the rest of his life; he was never allowed to return home.
10 Kisaki, *Kōdayū to Rakusuman*, p. 114.
11 G. H. von Langsdorff, *Voyages and Travels in Various Parts of the World During the Years 1803, 1804, 1805, 1806 and 1807,* vol. 1, p. 208.
12 G. H. von Langsdorff, *Remarks and Observations on a Voyage Around the World, from 1803 to 1807,* vol. 1,

pp. 207–8.

13 Ibid., p. 174.

14 Langsdorff, *Voyages and Travels*, vol. 1, p. 31.

15 Langsdorff, *Remarks and Observations*, vol. 1, p. 223.

16 Langsdorff, *Voyage and Travels*, vol. 1, p. 225.

17 Ibid., p. 226.

18 Clarence Manning, *Russian Influence on Early America*, p. 54.

19 John A. Harrison, *Japan's Northern Frontier; A Preliminary Study in Colonization and Expansion with Special Reference to the Relations of Japan and Russia*, p. 21.

20 Ibid., p. 22; Hector Chevigny, *Lost Empire: The Life and Adventures of Nikolai Petrovish Rezanov*, p. 304.

21 Lensen, *The Russian Push Toward Northern Japan*, p. 167.

22 One captive, Gorōji Nakagawa, who knew some Russian and tried to talk to the men, was later taken back to Russia. There, he learned the secret of using cowpox for smallpox vaccination and after returning to Japan in 1812 helped mitigate several smallpox epidemics. *Konsaisu jinmei jiten: Nipponhen* [Concise biographical dictionary: Japan] (Tōkyō: Sanseido, 1978), p. 798.

23 W. C. Aston, "Russian Descents in Saghalien and Itorup in the Years 1806 and 1807," *Transactions of the Asiatic Society of Japan*, vol. 1 (1874), pp. 90–93; Lensen, *The Russian Push Toward Japan*, pp. 169–71. The famous explorer Rinzō Mamiya happened to be surveying in the area and was wounded in the buttocks by a bullet. He was later interrogated by the Shogunate for his role but absolved of blame.

24 Shigure, *Shima monogatari*, pp. 561–650. Khvostov and Davydov were later arrested in Okhotsk and thrown into jail, partly for their actions. They escaped and were rehabilitated in St. Petersburg, when authorities realized they had merely been overzealous in following Rezanov's orders. But in September 1809, after a dinner at Langsdorff's apartment in St. Petersburg, they may have imbibed too much alcohol with the former American owner of the *Juno*. On the way home, the two officers tried to cross the Neva River even though the drawbridge was raised, fell in, and drowned. Lensen, *The Russian Push Toward Japan*, p. 175.

25 Aston, "Russian Descents," pp. 92–93.

26 Shigure, *Shima monogatari*, pp. 562–63.

27 Kisaki, *Sendai hyōmin to Rezanofu*, p. 256.

28 Captain Golownin, *Japan and the Japanese: Comprising The Narrative of a Captivity in Japan, and an Account of British Commercial Intercourse with that Country* (1852 edition) vol. 2, pp. 42–43.

29 Shigure, *Shima Monogatari*, p. 566.

30 BCA, MS-1249, box 9, folder 3, "Account of a Journey from the Sandwich Islands to Japan," p. 15.

31 Ibid., p. 19.

32 Ibid., p. 18.

33 LMRM, p. 182.

34 Ibid., p. 162.

35 BCA, MS-1249, box 9, folder 3, "Account of a Journey from the Sandwich Islands to Japan," p. 17.

36 LMRM, p. 277.

37 Ibid., p. 132.

38 Clarence L. Andrews, *Sitka: The Chief Factory of the Russian American Company*, p. 48.

39 Langsdorff, *Remarks and Observations*, pp. xxv—xxvii; Adams was involved in negotiating boundaries in the Oregon Country with Russia and the fur trade connected to China. See Clarence Hines, "Adams, Russia and Northwest Trade, 1824," *Oregon Historical Quarterly*, vol. 36, no. 4 (December 1935), pp. 349–58.

Chapter 10—Under Control of the Matsumae Domain

1 LMRM, pp. 183–85.

2 Ibid., pp. 187–88.

3 BCA, MS-1249, box 9, folder 3, "Account of a Journey from the Sandwich Islands to Japan," p. 22.

4 Ibid.

5 Ibid., pp. 22–23.

6　Ibid., pp. 23–24.

7　Ibid., p. 24; LMRM, p. 194.

8　Yoshitaka Inoue, *Hakodate Eigakushi, Vol. 1: Hakodate eigaku no genten to sono shūen* [A history of English studies in Hakodate, Vol. 1: Origins and end of Hakodate English studies], Hakodate University Publication, no. 29, 1998, pp. 45–50.

9　Matsumae Township Local History Editorial Offices, *Gaisetsu: Matsumae no rekishi,* pp. 41–48.

10　Golovnin, *Japan and the Japanese,* vol. 1, pp. 164–70.

11　Ibid., p. 176.

12　Ibid., p. 181.

13　Ibid., p. 204.

14　Ibid., pp. 228, also 211, 232–34. The Shogunate sent Rinzō Mamiya up from Edo, as Golovnin's presence was a golden opportunity to learn about the outside world. The Russians thought of Mamiya as a "geometrician and astronomer," but he was the famous explorer of the north (including Rishiri Island) who had been shot by Khvostov's men in 1806. Mamiya hoped to learn the latest European methods of surveying and navigation, as well as other scientific advances, but he and the Russians deeply distrusted each other.

15　Ibid., p. 301.

16　Ibid., pp. 316–17.

17　Ibid., vol. 2, p. 10.

18　Tsutomu Sugimoto, *Nagasaki tsūji: Kotoba to bunka no honyakusha,* pp. 152–55; pp. 185–87; Lensen, *The Russian Push Toward Japan,* pp. 247–48.

19　Golovnin, *Japan and the Japanese,* vol. 2, pp. 98 and 74.

20　Torao Tomita, *Makudonarudo "Nippon kaisōki,"* p. 264.

21　For accounts of this, see *Friend,* May 1848; *New York Daily Times,* 15 June 1852; *Tsūkō ichiran zokushū,* vol. 4, pp. 262–88.

22　*Friend,* 1 May 1848.

23　Ibid.

24　Sakamaki, "Japan and the United States," pp. 50–55; *Tsūkō ichiran zokushū,* vol. 4, pp. 373–78.

25　U.S. Senate Documents, 32nd Congress, 1st session, *Executive Document,* no. 59, pp. 9–25.

26　*Whalemen's Shipping List,* 14 May 1849.

27　*Gaisetsu: Matsumae no rekishi,* pp. 82–83.

28　LMRM, pp. 194–95.

29　Ibid., pp. 199–200; NARA, Microfilm Publication M89, "The Deposition of Ranald MacDonald, April 30, 1848," p. 259.

30　LMRM, p. 200.

31　Matsumae Township Local History Editorial Offices, *Matsumae chōshi tsūsetsuhen,* vol. 1, part 1, p. 923.

32　BCA, MS-1249, box 9, folder 13, "Letters to Malcolm McLeod, 1889–1894," Ranald MacDonald to Malcolm McLeod, 4 December 1893.

33　HPL, *Kōshi nikki, kaei gannen* [Public and private diaries, 1848].

34　LMRM, p. 203.

35　Torao Tomita, ed., *Makudonarudo "Nippon kaisōki,"* pp. 262–64.

36　Ibid., p. 126.

37　LMRM, p. 207.

Chapter 11—Arrival in Nagasaki

1　In his 1849 deposition, MacDonald says he arrived on the 15th. But having been confined for nearly three months, his counting may have slipped a tad. Both Japanese records and a 10 January 1849 article in the Dutch newspaper *Javasche Courant* have him arriving on 11 October 1848, and they are presumably correct.

2　LMRM, p. 210.

3　NARA, Microfilm Publication M89, "The Deposition of Ranald MacDonald," 30 April 1848, p. 260.

4　LMRM, p. 210.

5   Chisato Ishihara, "Ranarudo Makudonarudo no seito-tachi," p. 76.

6   LMRM, p. 211.

7   Kenji Sonoda, "Makudonarudo no nichiei goishū kaitei," p. 65.

8   LMRM, pp. 211–13. The Dutch ship was the *Josephine and Catharine*, which sailed in mid-November. There were good reasons for the lack of curiosity among citizens. Nagasaki was one of the few places where commoners often glimpsed strange-looking foreigners, but it was also dangerous to have too much contact with them.

9   Ibid., p. 214.

10 Ibid., p. 216.

11 NARA, "The Deposition of Ranald MacDonald," 30 April 1848, p. 259.

12 LMRM, p. 217.

13 NARA, "The Deposition of Ranald MacDonald," 30 April 1848, p. 259.

14 LMRM, p. 218.

15 Ibid., p. 220.

16 *Tsūkō ichiran zokushū*, vol. 4, p. 386 (*Nagasaki tomegaki*).

17 MAT, Center for the Study of Kyūshū Cultural History, Department of Literature Matsuki Collection, nos. 139 & 140. Japanese written translations of the Dutch superintendent's transcription of oral testimonies by foreign castaways, hereafter referred to as "The MacDonald Interrogations." Handwritten transcription of original manuscripts, and information on originals provided by Torao Tomita, who first learned of the records' existence from historical novelist Akira Yoshimura. Tomita first read the originals in 1988. "I was amazed, and excited," he recounts, "for I realized I had the core materials to write a new biography on MacDonald." But he later misplaced copies of the documents he had made, during a house move, and did not rediscover them for fourteen years, when he finally began editing a new book on MacDonald, scheduled for publication in 2003.

18 MacDonald Interrogations, First Interrogation.

19 Ibid.

20 Ibid.

21 Ibid., Second Interrogation.

22 Ibid.

23 Ibid.

24 Ibid.

25 LMRM, p. 225.

26 Joseph Levyssohn, *Bladen over Japan*, p. 55. Levyssohn quotes an article from the *Javasche Courant*, 10 January 1849, trans. Francisca Tausk.

27 Grant K. Goodman, *Japan and the Dutch, 1600–1853*, pp. 18–23. Quotation is from Karl Pieter Thunberg, a Swedish botanist and physician stationed in Deshima in 1776.

28 For additional information on interpreters and translators, see Sugimoto, *Nagasaki tsūji*, p. 32; Kazuo Katagiri, *Hirakareta sakoku: Nagasaki Deshima no hito, mono, jōhō*, p. 22; Kazuo Katagiri and Masanobu Hattori, *Oranda tsūji no kenkyū*, pp. 22–60.

29 Nagasaki City Educational Commission, ed., *Deshima* [Nagasaki, 1997], pp. 19–22. Siebold is said to have been betrayed by Rinzō Mamiya, the explorer of Japan's northern frontier.

30 Sugimoto, *Nagasaki tsūji*, p. 156.

31 Sir Stamford Raffles, *Report on Japan to the Secret Committee of the English East India Company*, ed. M. Paske Smith, p. iii.

32 Langsdorff, *Voyages and Travels*, vol. 1, p. 287. When the Britisher, Commodore Elliot, took a castaway named Rikimatsu with him to Nagasaki in 1855, the man was described as having "rendered the substance of all conversations in such patches and shreds that it was an exercise in ingenuity to sew them together." See W. G. Beaseley, *Great Britain and the Opening of Japan, 1834–1858*, p. 120.

33 Langsdorff, *Voyages and Travels*, vol. 1, p. 240; idem, *Remarks and Observations*, vol. 1, pp. 170–71; idem, *Voyages and Travels*, vol. 1, p. 230.

34 Langsdorff, *Voyages and Travels*, vol. 1, p. 237.

35 Ibid., p. 238.

36 Sugimoto, *Nagasaki tsūji*, pp. 153–56.

37 Katagiri, *Hirakareta sakoku,* pp. 53–55.
38 Belcher, *Narrative of the Voyage of H.M.S. Samarang,* vol. 2, pp. 4, 471.
39 *Friend,* 2 February 1846.
40 Belcher, *Narrative of the Voyage of H.M.S. Samarang,* vol. 2, p. 471.

Chapter 12—Nagasaki Days: Teaching English and Learning Japanese

1 Kazuo Katagiri and Masanobu Hattori, *Nenban oranda tsūji shiryō,* pp. 311, 323; Nagasaki Suwa Shrine tourist pamphlet.
2 LMRM, pp. 220–21.
3 Ibid., pp. 221–22.
4 BCA, MS-1249, box 6, file 3, photocopy of Ranald MacDonald's "Japan," vols. 3 and 4, p. 186.
5 Richard Hildreth, *Japan: As It Was and Is,* pp. 503–4.
6 BCA, MS-1249, box 6, file 3, photocopy of Ranald MacDonald's "Japan," vols. 3 and 4, pp. 185–86.
7 LMRM, pp. 233, 243. In his diary entry for that day, Levyssohn did not mention the newspapers but wrote that "I sent a small quantity of coffee, sugar, butter, cigars, and four loaves of bread to the American Ronald MacDonald on the occasion of the New Year." See *Dag Register,* J. H. Levyssohn entry, 1 January 1849.
8 Levyssohn, *Bladen over Japan,* pp. 53–56.
9 Ibid., p. 53.
10 NARA, Microfilm Publication M89, p. 260, "Deposition of Ranald MacDonald," 30 April 1848.
11 Masami Obama, "Makudonarudo tomo no kai Nagasaki: Kessei made no keii" (unpublished paper, Nagasaki, 6 March 1998).
12 MacDonald later claimed to have taught French also to the Nagasaki interpreters. Either because it cannot be independently confirmed or the interpreters later found little need for it, that training is never mentioned in Japan. See "Hudson's Bay Company; Its Organization, and the Objects Contemplated," *Spokane Falls Review,* 26 October 1890.
13 Katagiri, *Oranda tsūji no kenkyū,* p. 623.
14 Ishihara, "Ranarudo Makudonarudo no seito tachi," p. 61.
15 LMRM, pp. 224–26, 244.
16 Ibid., pp. 227, 244.
17 Modern Japanese is replete with English and pseudo-English terms.
18 *Angeria gorin taisei,* pp. 61, 232, 492, 521, 673, 641.
19 LMRM, pp. 209–10.
20 BCA, MS-1249, box 9, folder 13, MacDonald to McLeod, 24 May 1889.
21 *Friend,* 2 February 1846.
22 Edward Yorke McCauley, *With Perry in Japan,* ed. Alan B. Cole, pp. 90–93, 103–4.
23 S. Wells Williams, "A Journal of the Perry Expedition to Japan (1853–1854)," p. 120.
24 BCA, MS-1249, box 6, file 3, photocopy of Ranald MacDonald's "Japan," vols. 3 and 4, p. 164.
25 U.S. Senate Documents, 32nd Congress, 1st session, *Executive Document,* no. 59, p. 57.
26 Osaka Women's University, ed., *A Critical Bibliography of Materials for English Studies in Japan,* p. 17.
27 In all fairness, it should also be noted that there was still no agreement on the spelling of many words in English-speaking nations, either. Those with a double "s" like "missed," for example, were still being rendered as both "mifsed" and "missed."
28 Yumiko Kawamoto, "Futatsu no 'Nichiei goishū'—Makudonarudo no genten to makuraudo no henshū ni yoru mono," *Kiyō,* p. 81.
29 Sonoda, "Makudonarudo no nichiei goishū kaitei," *Eigakushi kenkyū,* p. 64.
30 LMRM, pp. 227, 235.
31 BCA, MS-1249, box 6, file 3, p. 183.
32 LMRM, p. 230.
33 Ibid., p. 232.
34 Kenji Sonoda, "Nagasaki ni okeru Makudonarudo," *Nippon eigakushi kenkyū,* pp. 107–13.

Chapter 13—Leaving Nagasaki

1 LMRM, pp. 227, 232, 235–36, 242.
2 Langsdorff, *Remarks and Observations*, vol. 1, p. 174; idem, *Voyages and Travels*, vol. 1, p. 266.
3 Langsdorff., *Voyages and Travels*, vol. 1, pp. 235–36, 295.
4 Arlette Kouwenhoven and Matthi Forrer, *Seibold and Japan: His Life and Work*, pp. 45–46.
5 *Sekai dai hyakka jiten* [Heibonsha's world encyclopedia], vol. 19, p. 282.
6 LMRM, p. 225; BCA, MS-1249, box 9, folder 5, Malcolm McLeod, "R. McDonald, Part of journal," p. 35; ibid., folder 13, MacDonald to McLeod, 24 May 1889.
7 Kouwenhoven and Forrer, *Seibold and Japan*, p. 62.
8 "Correspondence between William II of Holland and the Shogun of Japan A.D. 1844," *Transactions of the Asiatic Society of Japan*, no. 34 (June 1907), pp. 99–123.
9 "Japan," *Friend*, 1 May 1848; "From St. Helena—Cruelty of the Japanese toward American Sailors," *New York Daily Times*, 15 June 1852. The British were on Japan's blacklist because of the *Phaeton* incident (see ch. 12).
10 Ibid.
11 Levyssohn, *Bladen over Japan*, p. 47; *Tsūkō ichiran zokushū*, vol. 4, pp. 262–88.
12 *Tsūkō ichiran zokushū*, vol. 4, pp. 262–88.
13 "Robert McCoy Deposition," U.S. Senate Documents, 32nd Congress, 1st session, *Executive Document*, no. 59, p. 12.
14 Levyssohn, *Bladen over Japan*, p. 52.
15 "Robert McCoy Deposition," p. 15.
16 Ibid.
17 Ibid., pp. 16, 18.
18 LMRM, pp. 234–36.
19 "From St. Helena," *New York Daily Times*, 15 June 1852.
20 *New York Courier and Enquirer*, 18 September and 24 August 1849.
21 Levyssohn, *Bladen over Japan*, p. 64.
22 "Narrative of the Shipwrecked Seamen in Japan," U.S. Senate Documents, 32nd Congress, 1st session, *Executive Document*, no. 59, pp. 38–39; ibid., "Deposition of John Bull," p. 19.
23 Tomita, *Makudonarudo—"Nippon kaisōki,"* p. 267; Tokutarō Shigehisa, *Nihon kinsei eigakushi*, p. 270.
24 *Friend*, May 1854.
25 An example is Dulles, *Yankees and Samurai*, which describes early shipwrecked American sailors (and MacDonald) in Japan. Of the *Lawrence* crew, the book only mentions that "[o]ne of their number died" without the men's claim that the man was murdered. See pp. 30–31.
26 Levyssohn, *Bladen over Japan*, p. 56, quoting an article in the *Javasche Courant*, January 1850.
27 LMRM, p. 197.
28 HCMSL, MacDonald to Damon, 24 May 1849.
29 Undated letter from John Waters and John Bawl to Joseph Levyssohn, U.S. Senate Documents, 32nd Congress, 1st session, *Executive Document*, no. 59, pp. 4–5.
30 Ibid., "Sailing Instructions to Commander Glynn," pp. 6–7.
31 BFO, "China Correspondence," F.O. 17/153 (microfilm), copies of letters enclosed in a communication from C. Gutzlaff to S. G. Bonham, 11 February 1849, pp. 294–307.
32 *Friend*, 20 December 1849.
33 "Visit of the U.S.S. Preble to Japan," *China Repository*, vol. 18, no. 6 (June 1849), p. 317.
34 "Memoranda of a Conversation between Commander James Glynn and a Japanese High Military Chief, Named 'Serai Tatsnosen,'" U.S. Senate Documents, 32nd Congress, 1st session, *Executive Document*, no. 59 [no. 1, B], pp. 29–31.
35 Ibid., p. 31.
36 In reality, because of poor communications, in the summer of 1846 Japanese officials in Edo probably had not yet heard of the *Lawrence* crew.
37 "Memoranda of a Conversation; Questions Asked by Commodore James Glynn of the High Mandarin or Chief, through the Interpreter, Who Spoke English," U.S. Senate Documents, 32nd Congress, 1st ses-

sion, *Executive Document,* no. 59 [no. 1, B], pp. 31.

38 Ibid., no. 59, pp. 43–44.

39 "Memorandum of an Interview between Commander James Glynn and a High Military Official of Nangasacki, Named 'Matsmora Schal,'" U.S. Senate Documents, 32nd Congress, 1st session, *Executive Document,* no. 59, p. 32.

40 "Memorandum of a Conference between Commander James Glynn with a High Military Official of Nangasacki, Named 'Matsmora Schal,' the Same Interpreter, 'Morreama Einaska' Acting," U.S. Senate Documents, 32nd Congress, 1st session, no. 59, p. 33.

41 Ibid., pp. 33–34.

42 Ibid.

43 "Visit of the U.S.S. Preble," *China Repository,* p. 318.

44 Levyssohn, Bladen over Japan, p. 58; NAN, Japans Dagh Register gehouden in't Comptoir Nagasackij, transcription, Levyssohn diary entry, 22 April 1849.

45 NAN, *Japans Dagh Register,* Levyssohn diary entry, 22 April 1849.

46 "Memoranda of a Conference Held in the Cabin of the Preble with 'Tatsnosen,' a Military Chief from Nangasacki," U.S. Senate Documents, 32nd Congress, 1st session, *Executive Document,* no. 59 [no. 4], p. 36.

47 Ibid., p. 36.

48 NPL, *Hankachō.*

49 LMRM, pp. 246–47.

50 NARA, microfilm RG 24, "USS Preble;" LOC 18W4 7/22/3, "Log book, U.S. Sloop Preble, 14 Guns, James Glynn Commander," 22 March 1849–26 May 1849, 27 April entry.

51 LMRM, pp. 260, 265.

52 BCA, MS-1249, box 9, folder 13, MacDonald to McLeod, 24 May 1889.

53 "Deposition of Ranald MacDonald," U.S. Senate Documents, 32nd Congress, 1st session, *Executive Document,* no. 59, p. 28.

54 Malcolm McLeod, "British Pacific Railway—An Imperial Necessity," *Ottawa Times,* 24 June 1869.

55 HCMSL, "Samuel C. Damon Papers 1830–1890," box 3, folder 1B, MacDonald to Damon, 24 May 1849.

56 Akira Yoshimura, *Umi no sairei,* p. 247.

57 "Deposition of Ranald MacDonald," U.S. Senate Documents, 32nd Congress, 1st session, no. 59, p. 28; Yuji Aisaka, a Japan FOM member, says: "MacDonald's words made me realize that the concept of 'the people first' even existed in those days. In Japan's samurai-dominated society, it would then have been unthinkable." Interview with Aisaka, Mihama, Japan, 20 September 1998.

58 U.S. Senate Documents, 32nd Congress, 1st session, *Executive Document,* no. 59, "Doc. C," pp. 57–62; ibid., "James Glynn to the President," 10 June 1851, pp. 74–78.

59 BCA, MS-1249, box 9, folder 13, MacDonald to McLeod, 24 May 1889.

60 Matthew C. Perry, *The Japan Expedition 1852–1854, The Personal Journal of Commodore Matthew C. Perry,* Roger Pineau, ed, pp. 14, 220–21.

61 Moriyama served as chief interpreter on Perry's return trip to Japan in 1854 and later interpreted the arduous negotiations with the first U.S. consul to Japan, Townsend Harris. These efforts resulted in a full commercial treaty in 1858. Moriyama also interpreted during the arrival of Russian Vice Admiral Putiatin in Nagasaki in 1853; in 1862 Moriyama accompanied Japan's first official mission to Europe. When the British Elgin mission worked with the interpreter in 1857–58, they referred to Moriyama as "a diplomat of the Talleyrand school," after the famous French statesman of the same name. See Beasely, *Great Britain and the Opening of Japan,* p. 189.

62 Ishihara, "Ranarudo Makudonarudo no seito tachi," p. 78.

Chapter 14—Creation of the Narrative

1 Williams, *A Journal of the Perry Expedition to Japan,* p. 120.

2 NARA, "Log Book of U.S. Sloop Preble (14 Guns), James Glynn Commander," entry for 22 May, 1849; ibid., "Consular Despatches, Hong Kong, 1849 Letter Book" (p. 355), Commander James Glynn (on

U.S.S. Preble) to U.S. Consul Bush at Hong Kong, 21 May 1849; HCMS, "Samuel C. Damon Papers, 1830–1890," MacDonald to Damon, 24 May 1849.

3   "Japan," *Putnam's Monthly*, vol. 1, no. 3 (March 1853), pp. 241–42.

4   LMRM, pp. 249, 199. The ship was reportedly the *Sea Witch* but it has never been positively identified. It was not the famous clipper of the same name, which sank much later near Havana.

5   In 2002, Japan FOM member Yūji Aisaka uncovered an 1855 miner's license issued to a "Ronald McDonald" in Ballarat, but there is no way today to determine if this was "Ranald MacDonald." While in Ballarat, MacDonald is also said to have defeated a local boxing champion. See LMRM, p. 45.

6   *Kettle Falls Pioneer*, 23 November 1893, p. 1; OHS, MSS 1089, box 1, Eva Emery Dye, "Letters from Ranald MacDonald," Donald Ross to Eva Emery Dye, 21 May 1904; BCA, MS-1249, box 9, folder 13, MacDonald to McLeod, 29 August 1891; BCA Microfilm, F919, "Ranald McDonald, Lands and Works Department, B.C.," Lt. Colonel Moody to Sir James Douglas, 4 January 1860.

7   Cole, *This Blessed Wilderness*, pp. 120, 255–56; see Archibald McDonald to Donald Ross, 1 May 1846.

8   HBCA, microfilm series 1, reel no. 428, ref. no. A.36/9, "Officers' and Servants' Wills," an 1852 will recorded at Superior Court of Lower Canada, 29 October 1853, transcription provided by Jean Murray Cole.

9   Archibald McDonald to Angus McDonald, 3 April 1852 (copy supplied by Jean Murray Cole from letter in possession of Eileen S. Decker, St. Ignatious, Montana).

10 BCA, MS-1249, box 9, folder 13, MacDonald to McLeod, 14 May 1892.

11 Records from London's Library and Museum of Freemasonry do indicate MacDonald was initiated on 21 June 1853, passed on 20 July, and raised on 17 August; Benjamin MacDonald, "Narrative of Benjamin MacDonald," *Washington Historical Quarterly*, vol. 16, no.3 (July 1925), p. 194; BCA, MS-1249, box 9, folder 1, "Adventure in Japan during Eleven Months by Ranald McDonald," p. 75.

12 PAC, C76, "Hargrave Collection" (microfilm), John Bell to James Hargrave, 1 July 1853.

13 BCA, MS-1249, box 9, folder 13, MacDonald to McLeod, 29 August 1891.

14 *Appleton's Cyclopaedia of American Biography*, vol. 4, pp. 146–47; DCB, vol. 7, 1836–1858, pp. 570–71; HBCA/PAM, film no. 4M101, E.4/Index E.5/10, "Red River Settlement Register of Baptisms, 1820–1841"; E4/1a, "Index to Register of Baptisms, 1820–1828" and E4/16, "Red River Settlement Register of Marriages and Funerals, 1820–1841 Index to Register of Marriages."

15 BCA, MS-1249, box 2, folder 1, "Recommendation from A. R. Carson, Rector of the High School," 10 January 1840.

16 Williams, *Hudson's Bay Miscellany*, p. 190.

17 EWSHS, box 1, MS 25 File 1/3, T. P. Foran to William S. Lewis, 28 March 1919.

18 BCA, MS-1249, box 8, folder 2, "Ranald MacDonald, Story of Adventure," p. 16.

19 Ibid., box 1, folder 4, McLeod to Edwards & Co., 18 March 1857.

20 Malcolm McLeod, *The Pacific Railway, Canada; Selection from Series of Letters by "Britannicus" (from 1869 to 1875) on the Subject, with Additional Remarks* (Aylmer County, Ottawa, Quebec, 1875), p. 18.

21 BCA, MS-1249, box 6, file 3, "Malcolm McLeod Papers," p. 188.

22 Malcolm McLeod, "British Pacific Railway—An Imperial Necessity," *Ottawa Times*, 24 June 1869; Ranald MacDonald, *Bentinck Arm and Fraser River Road Company Prospectus*.

23 BCA, MS-1249, box 8, folder 4, "Miscellaneous Notes re: Japan, by Malcolm McLeod."

24 Ibid., box 7, vol. 4, p. 224.

25 McLeod, *The Pacific Railway*, p. 2.

26 Malcolm McLeod, *Memorial to the Government and Parliament of Canada of Malcolm McLeod, Q.C., & c., for Indemnity for Service in Initiating the Canadian Pacific Railway, &c., &c.* (Ottawa [no publisher given], 1889), p. 15.

27 Ibid., p. 5.

28 Ibid., p. 1.

29 McLeod, "British Pacific Railway—An Imperial Necessity."

30 Malcolm McLeod, ed., *Peace River*, p. vii.

31 McLeod, *Memorial to the Government and Parliament of Canada of Malcolm McLeod, Q.C., & c., for Indemnity for Service in Initiating the Canadian Pacific Railway, &c., &c.* (Ottawa [no publisher given], 1889), p. 15; *Oregon Indemnity: Claim of Chief Factors and Chief Traders of the Hudson's Bay Company,*

thereto, as partners, under Treaty of 1846, ([No place, publisher given]: 1892).

32 Tomita, *Makudonarudo "Nippon kaisōki,"* pp. 220–21; BCA, MS-1249, box 1, folder 4, McLeod to Sandford Fleming, 5 August 1888; also box 7, ch. 12, "Explanatory Remarks by Editor and Author," p. 224.

33 BCA, MS-1249, box 8, folder 4, "M. McLeod, Misc., re: Japan," "Remarks on Manuscript."

34 BCA, MS-794, box 2, file 7, vol. 7, "Robert Brown Journal-Ranald MacDonald," "Ranald McDonald's Journal, V.I. Exploring Expedition, Victoria, V.I. 1864," 2 December 1864.

35 John Hayman, ed., *Robert Brown and the Vancouver Island Exploring Expedition*, p. 118.

36 Frederick Whymper, *Travel and Adventure in the Territory of Alaska*, pp. 64–71.

37 OHS, MSS 1089, Eva Emery Dye, "Letters from MacDonald, Ben, and Donald, and Duncan; and McCarthy," Ben McDonald to Dye, 29 November 1904; Christina M. M. Williams, "A Daughter of Angus MacDonald," *Washington Historical Quarterly*, vol. 13, no. 2 (April 1922), p. 117; OHS, MSS 1089, box 2, Eva Emery Dye, "Letters—Ranald McDonald," F. H. Grubbs to E. E. Dye (letter transcript, n.d.).

38 Ranald MacDonald to Benjamin MacDonald, 14 January 1874, courtesy of Jean Murray Cole.

39 BCA, MS-1249, box 9, folder 12, MacDonald to Mr. and Mrs. Archibald McKinlay, 2 June 1889.

40 BCA, MS-1249, box 9, folder 13, MacDonald to McLeod (n.d.). The "Colville Miner" referred to is presumably the *Steven's County Miner.*

41 Transcontinental letters, once requiring a year, now took only six days to reach a destination. In a 17 November 1889 letter, MacDonald joked about how in the old days of the HBC, the battle of Waterloo was celebrated at Ft. St. James in New Caledonia three years after it was fought, because of poor communications. See BCA, MS-1249, box 9, folder 13, MacDonald to McLeod, 17 November 1889.

42 BCA, MS-1249, box 7, ch. 14, "MacDonald Redivivus, His Letter and Life, Etc.," pp. 258–67.

43 Ibid., box 1, folder 4, "Malcolm McLeod: Correspondence and Personal Papers, 1880–1889," McLeod to Sandford Fleming, 4 May 1889.

44 Ibid., box 9, folder 12, MacDonald to Mr. and Mrs. Archibald McKinlay, 2 June 1889.

45 Ibid., box 1, folder 4, "Malcolm McLeod Papers, 1880–1889," Wm Drysdale & Co., to Malcolm McLeod, 23 July 1889.

46 Ibid., box 8, folder 4, "M. McLeod, Misc., re: Japan," copy of "Takahashi Critique," p. 3.

47 Ibid., p. 5.

48 Ibid., p. 6.

49 BCA, MS-1249, box 9, folder 13, MacDonald to McLeod, 11 August 1889.

50 Ibid., MacDonald to McLeod, 12 March 1894, 16 January 1893, 17 November 1889.

51 Ibid., MacDonald to McLeod, 10 August 1891.

52 Ibid., box 8, folder 4, "M. McLeod, Misc., re: Japan."

53 Ibid., box 9, folder 1, MacDonald to McLeod, 4 January 1892; ibid., box 8, folder 4, "M. McLeod, Misc., re: Japan," draft letter with remarks about manuscript.

54 Ibid., box 9, folder 13, MacDonald to McLeod, 11 April 1892.

55 Ibid., box 8, folder 2, "Ronald McDonald, Story of Adventure," draft letter from McLeod to MacDonald; also box 9, folder 13, MacDonald to McLeod, 5 September 1893.

56 Ibid., box 9, folder 13, MacDonald to McLeod, 5 September 1893.

57 Ibid., 24 October 1893.

58 Ibid.

59 "Early Settlements in Washington and Adventures in Japan," *Kettle Falls Pioneer*, 16 November 1893; BCA, MS-1249, box 1, folder 5, L. G. P. Hawkins to Malcolm McLeod, 2 December 1893.

60 BCA, MS-1249, box 8, folder 4, "M. McLeod, Misc re: Japan."

61 Ibid.

62 Eva Emery Dye to Rev. Otis Cary (in Kyōto, Japan), 31 May 1913, copy courtesy of Beth Cary.

63 Dye, *McDonald of Oregon*, p. v; BCA, MS-1249, box 9, folder 11, MacDonald to Eva Emery Dye, 24 July 1892 (typescript copy).

64 Thomas W. Prosch, "Review of *McDonald of Oregon*, by Eva Emery Dye," *Washington Historical Quarterly*, vol. 1, no. 2 (January 1907), pp. 66–70.

65 Ibid.

66 LMRM, p. 21.

67 Allen Sinclair Will, "A Review of *Ranald MacDonald, 1824–1894*," *New York Times*, 15 September 1923; F. W. Howay, "*Ranald MacDonald*," *Canadian Historical Review*, vol. 4, no. 4 (1923), pp. 349–50.

Chapter 15—The MacDonald Legacy

1 "From sticks to stone: Monuments tell MacDonald story," *Friends of MacDonald Newsletter* (Winter 1988–89), p. 1.
2 BCA, MS-1249, box 9, folder 13, MacDonald to McLeod, 5 February 1894. Benjamin was also married later to Elizabeth Pyke.
3 Even the date of MacDonald's death has been debated. The 31 August 1894 edition of Spokane's *Spokesman Review* reported his death as occurring on 26 August; but the same article inexplicably claims that he had left a "large family of grown children" and had been on a "fishing and hunting expedition." The McDonald family Bible lists his death as "March 1895," age 71. Lewis and Murakami claim that he died on August 5, and a deposition by Jennie Lynch claims that he was buried on August 7, so the August 5 date is most likely correct.
4 In the letter, McLeod asked MacDonald about the difference between the east and west sides of Japan. When MacDonald replied that he had sailed on the east side of Bonin Islands, McLeod misinterpreted this to mean the east side of the main Japanese islands. In one draft of the *Narrative,* the error was corrected but not in the edition published by Lewis and Murakami. See BCA, MS-1249, box 9, folder 7, MacDonald to McLeod, 12 August 1889.
5 In Japan, FOM member Mamoru Inagami keeps a database of articles on MacDonald, now numbering well over two hundred. Also, a new book on MacDonald by Japan FOM members, tentatively titled *Kujira no hiraita sakoku no tobira* [Doors of a Secluded Land, Opened by Whales], was scheduled for publication by the Hokkaidō Shinbunsha in late 2003.
6 Gretchen Murphy, "'A Home Which Is Still Not a Home,'" pp. 225–44.
7 John C. Jackson, *Children of the Fur Trade: Forgotten Métis of the Pacific Northwest*, p. 230.
8 William S. Lewis, *Dictionary of American Biography* (New York, C. Scribner's Sons, 1928-58), vol. 12, p. 19.
9 Interview with J. S. Brown, Winnipeg, 23 November 1999.
10 LMRM, p. 92.
11 BCA, MS-1249, box 9, folder 11, Ranald MacDonald to Mrs. C. H. Dye, 24 July 1892 (typescript copy).
12 Howay, "Review of *Ranald MacDonald*," pp. 349–50.
13 BCA, MS-1249, box 9, folder 13, Ranald MacDonald to Malcolm McLeod, 18 July 1892.
14 *Republic News-Miner*, 2 August 2001.
15 Broadcast on Seattle NPR station, KUOW 94.9, 18 August 2001.
16 BCA, MS-1249, box 9, folder 13, MacDonald to McLeod, 24 May 1889.

Appendix B—Ranald MacDonald and the Chinooks

1 BCA, MS-1249, box 9, folder 13, MacDonald to McLeod, 4 June 1891.
2 "The Oldest Living Astorian; A Brief Sketch of the Life of the Grandson of King Kumkumly, the Old Indian Chief," *Morning Oregonian*, 12 February 1891 (reprint of article in *The Astorian*).
3 HBCA D.4/5, f. 13, Governor George Simpson to Benjamin Harrison, 10 March 1825.
4 OHS, MSS 1089, "Eva Emery Dye," Letters from S—, box 1 of 24, Silas B. Smith to Dye, 20 October 1891.
5 OHS, MSS 5, "Chinook Indian Tribe vs United States" (21 January 1902).
6 BCA, MS-1249, box 9, folder 13, MacDonald to McLeod, 10 August 1891.
7 "Comcumly's Followers—Their Empire About the Mouth of the Columbia—How Princess Mary, Granddaughter of the Historic Red Chieftain, Lives on Elliott's Bay," *Oregonian*, 17 December 1899.

Bibliography

Unpublished Primary Source Materials

For a list of archives and libraries with unpublished primary source materials, please refer to *Abbreviations Used in Endnotes*.

Nineteenth-Century Periodicals

Alta California, China Mail, Chinese Repository, Friend, Harper's, Kettle Falls Pioneer, Living Age, Montreal Gazette, New York Courier and Enquirer, New York Daily Times/Evening Times, Oregonian/Morning Oregonian, Ottawa Times, Polynesian, Putnam's, Sag Harbor Corrector, Sailor's Magazine, Sandwich Island Mirror and Commercial Gazette, Sandwich Island News, Spokane Falls Review, Spokesman Review, Steven's County Miner, and *Whalemen's Shipping List.*

In understanding nineteenth-century North American media attitudes toward Japan in MacDonald's era, a web-based archive of periodicals—the *Making of America* Project, at Cornell University and the University of Michigan—proved to be a godsend.

A variety of modern periodicals in Hokkaidō, Nagasaki, Tōkyō, and the Pacific Northwest were also referenced, as well as back issues of the *Oregon*

Historical Quarterly, *Transactions of the Asiatic Society*, and *Washington Historical Quarterly*. *Gates Ajar* and the Japan *Makudonarudo Tsūshin* [Friends of Ranald MacDonald] newsletters, published by FOM societies in Astoria and Rishiri (Japan), respectively, were particularly helpful.

The U.S. Friends of MacDonald society is located at the following address: c/o Clatsop County Historical Society, 1618 Exchange Street, Astoria, Oregon 97103, U.S.A. The *Makudonarudo tomo no kai* [Friends of MacDonald] society is located at Rishiri Township Museum, 136 Honchō, Senbōshiji, Rishiri-chō, Rishiri-gun, Hokkaidō Prefecture 097–0311, Japan.

Books, Magazines, and Papers

(Publications with primary source materials are prefaced with an asterisk).

Abott, John S. C. "The People of the Red River." *Harper's Magazine* (January 1859), pp. 169–76.

Alexander, Mary Charlotte. *Dr. Baldwin of Lahaina*. Berkeley, California: [No publisher given], 1953.

Andrews, Clarence. *Sitka: The Chief Factory of the Russian American Company*. Caldwell, Idaho: The Caxton Printers, 1945.

Angeria gorin taisei [A compilation of English words]. Reprint of 1814 original, Tōkyō: Yūshōdō Shoten, 1976.

Arthur, M. Elizabeth, "General Dickson and the Indian Liberating Army in the North." *Ontario Historical Society*, vol. 62, no. 3 (September 1970), pp. 151–63.

Aston, W. G. "Russian Descents in Saghalien and Itorup in the Years 1806 and 1807." *Transactions of the Asiatic Society of Japan*, vol. 1 (1874), pp. 86–95.

*Ball, John. *Born to Wander: Autobiography of John Ball, 1794–1884*. Reprint of 1925 edition. Grand Rapids: Grand Rapids Historical Commission, 1994.

Bancroft, Hubert Howe. *History of the Pacific States of North America*. Vol. 23. *The North West Coast* 1800–1846. Vol. 2. San Francisco: A. L. Bancroft, 1884. P. 651.

*Barker, Burt Brown. *The McLoughlin Empire and Its Rulers: Doctor John McLoughlin, Doctor David McLoughlin, Marie Louise (Sister St. Henry)*. Northwest Historical Series 5. Glendale, California: A. H. Clark Co., 1959.

Barman, Jean, and Bruce M. Watson. "Fort Colvile's Fur Trade Families and the Dynamics of Race in the Pacific Northwest." *Pacific Northwest Quarterly*, vol. 90, no. 3 (Summer 1999), pp. 140–53.

Beasley, W. G. *Collected Writings of W. G. Beasley*. Vol. 5. *The Collected Writings of Modern Western Scholars on Japan*. Richmond, Surrey: Japan Library and Synapse Press, 2001.

———. *Great Britain and the Opening of Japan, 1834–1858*. London: Luzac and Co., Ltd., 1951.

Beaumont, Raymond M. "The Rev. William Cockran: The Man and the Image." *Manitoba History*, no. 33 (Spring 1997), pp. 2–15.

*Belcher, Sir Edward. *Narrative of the Voyage of H.M.S. Samarang, During the Years 1843–1846*. Vols. 1 and 2. London: Reeve, Benham, and Reeve, 1848.

Bernard, Donald R. *The Life and Times of John Manjiro*. New York: McGraw Hill, 1992.

Berney, Bruce. "Friends of MacDonald: A Brief History." Unpublished paper, Astoria, Oregon, 24 May 1999.

Bieder, Robert E. "Scientific Attitudes Toward Indian Mixed-Bloods in Early Nineteenth Century America." *Journal of Ethnic Studies*, vol. 8, no. 2 (Summer 1980), pp. 17–30.

*Bill, Erastus. *Citizen: An American Boy's Early Manhood Aboard a Sag Harbor Whale-Ship Chasing Delirium and Death Around the World, 1843, being the Story of Erastus Bill Who Lived to Tell About It*. Anchorage, Alaska: O. W. Frost, 1978.

Bishop, Charles. See Roe entry.

Bredin, Thomas F. "The Red River Academy." *Beaver* (Winter 1974), pp. 10–17.

Brown, Jennifer S. H. *Strangers in Blood: Fur Trade Company Families in Indian Country*. Norman: University of Oklahoma Press, 1980.

———. "Ultimate Respectability: Fur Trade Children in the 'Civilized World.'" *Beaver*, vol. 3 (1977), pp. 4–10; vol. 4 (1978), pp. 48–55.

——— and Jacqueline Peterson. *The New Peoples: Being and Becoming Métis in North America*. Winnipeg: University of Manitoba Press, 1985.

Burns, Robert Ignatius. *The Jesuits and the Indian Wars of the Northwest*. New Haven: Yale University Press, 1966.

Busch, Briton Cooper. *"Whaling Will Never Do for Me": The American Whaleman in the Nineteenth Century*. Lexington, Kentucky: University Press of Kentucky, 1994.

*Chapin, Jane Lewis, ed. "McLoughlin Letters, 1827–1849." *Oregon Historical Quarterly*, vol. 37, no. 1 (March 1836), pp. 45–75.

Chevigny, Hector. *Lost Empire: The Life and Adventures of Nikolai Petrovish Rezanov*. New York: MacMillan Co., 1937.

Clark and Lewis. See Thwaites entry.

*Cole, Alan B., ed. *With Perry in Japan: The Diary of Edward Yorke McCauley*. Princeton: Princeton University Press, 1942.

Cole, Jean Murray. *Exile in the Wilderness: The Biography of Chief Factor Archibald MacDonald, 1790–1853*. Seattle: University of Washington Press, 1979.

———, ed. *This Blessed Wilderness: Archibald McDonald's Letters from the Columbia, 1822–1844*. Vancouver: University of British Columbia Press, 2001.

———. "Ranald MacDonald—His Ancestry and Early Years." Paper delivered at the Annual Meeting of the Friends of Ranald MacDonald Society, Red Lion Inn, Jantzen Beach, Portland, Oregon, May 1989.

Cook, John. *Reminiscences of John Cook, Kamaaina and Forty-Niner*. Honolulu: The New Freedom Press, 1927.

*"Correspondence Between William II of Holland and the Shogun of Japan, A.D. 1844." *Transactions of the Asiatic Society of Japan*, vol. 34 (June 1907), pp. 99–132.

*Coues, Elliot, ed. *New light on the early history of the greater Northwest. The manuscript journals of Alexander Henry, Fur Trader of the Northwest Company and of David Thompson, Official Geographer and Explorer of the Same Company, 1799–1814*. Vol. 2. New York: F. P. Harper, 1897.

*Cox, Ross. *The Columbia River, or scenes and adventures during a residence of six years on the western side of the Rocky Mountains among various tribes of Indians hitherto unknown; together with "A Journey across the American Continent."* Edited by Edgar I. and Jane R. Stewart. Norman: University of Oklahoma Press, 1957.

*Custer, Elizabeth B. "An Out-of-the-Way 'Outing.'" *Harper's Weekly*, vol. 35, no. 1804 (18 July 1891), pp. 534–35.

Dale, Paul W., ed. *Seventy North to Fifty South: The Story of Captain Cook's Last Voyage*. Englewood Cliffs, New Jersey: Prentice-Hall, 1969.

Damon, Ethel. *Samuel Chenery Damon; Chaplain and Friend of Seamen, Historian-Traveler—Diplomat, Doctor of Divinity, Journalist, Genial Companion, Genealogist*. Honolulu: Hawaiian Mission Children's Society, 1966.

*Delano, Amasa. *A Narrative of Voyages and Travels, in the northern and southern hemispheres: comprising three voyages round the world; together with a voyage of survey and discovery, in the Pacific Ocean and Oriental islands. . . .* Boston: E. G. House, 1817.

Dictionary of American Biography. New York: C. Scribner's Sons, 1928–58.

Dictionary of Canadian Biography. Toronto: University of Toronto Press, 1966.

Drury, Clifford Merrill. *Elkanah and Mary Walker: Pioneers Among the Spokanes*. Caldwell, Idaho: Caxton Printers, 1940.

Dudley, William S., and Michael J. Crawford. See Mockford entry.

Dulles, Foster Rhea. *Yankees and Samurai: America's Role in the Emergence of Modern Japan*. New York: Harper and Row, 1965.

Dye, Eva Emery. *McDonald of Oregon: A Tale of Two Shores*. Chicago: A. C. McClurg and Co., 1906.

————. *McLoughlin and Old Oregon: A Chronicle.* Chicago: A. C. McClurg, 1900.

Ens, Gerhard J. *Homeland to Hinterland: The Changing Worlds of the Red River Metis in the Nineteenth Century.* Toronto: University of Toronto Press, 1996.

Ermatinger, C. O. *The Talbot Regime, or the First Half Century of the Talbot Settlement.* St. Thomas: Municipal World, Ltd., 1894.

Finkenor, George A. *Whales and Whaling: Port of Sag Harbor, New York.* Sag Harbor: William Ewers, 1975.

Fisher, Robin, and J. M. Bumsted, eds. See Walker entry.

Fitzhugh, William W., and Chisato O. Dubreuil, eds. *Ainu: Spirit of a Northern People.* Washington, D.C.: Arctic Studies Center, National Museum of Natural History, Smithsonian Institution, in association with University of Washington Press, 1999.

Flanagan, Thomas. *Louis 'David' Riel: 'Prophet of the New World.'* Toronto: University of Toronto Press, 1979.

Fogdall, Alberta Brooks. *Royal Family of the Columbia: Dr. John McLoughlin and His Family.* Portland: Binford and Mort, 1982.

*Franchère, Gabriel. *Adventure at Astoria, 1810–1814.* Edited and translated by Hoyt C. Franchère. Norman: University of Oklahoma Press, 1967.

Fraser, William J. *St. John's College Winnipeg, 1866–1966; A History of the First Hundred Years of the College.* Winnipeg: Wallingford Press, 1966.

Furukawa, Kyōji. *Ranarudo Makudonarudo to no deai* [How I met Ranald MacDonald]. *Rishirito hatsu Makudonarudo tsūshin,* 5 (20 July 1996), pp. 4–6.

Galbraith, John S. *The Hudson's Bay Company As an Imperial Factor, 1821–1869.* Berkeley: University of California Press, 1957.

————. *The Little Emperor: Governor Simpson of the Hudson's Bay Company.* Toronto: Macmillan of Canada, 1976.

*Gardiner, Howard C. *In Pursuit of the Golden Dream: Reminiscences of San Francisco and the Northern and Southern Mines, 1849–1857.* Edited by Dale L. Morgan. Stoughton: Western Hemisphere, 1970.

Giraud, Marcel. *The Métis in the Canadian West.* Vols. 1 and 2. Translated by George Woodcock. Lincoln: University of Nebraska Press, 1986.

*Golovnin, Captain Vasilii Mikhailovic. Japan and The Japanese: Comprising The Narrative of a Captivity in Japan, and an Account of British Commercial Intercourse with that Country. Vols. 1 and 2. London: Colburn and Co., 1852.

Goodman, Grant K. *Japan and the Dutch, 1600–1853.* Richmond, Surrey: Curzon Press, 2000.

Gowen, Herbert Henry. *Five Foreigners in Japan.* Reprint of 1936 edition. Freeport, New York: Books for Libraries Press, 1967.

Gregor, Alexander, and Keith Wilson. *The Development of Education in Manitoba.* Dubuque, Iowa: Kendall/Hunt Publishing Co., 1984.

Harden, Blaine. *A River Lost: The Life and Death of the Columbia.* New York: W. W. Norton and Co., 1996.

Harrison, John. A. *Japan's Northern Frontier: A Preliminary Study in Colonization and Expansion with Special Reference to the Relations of Japan and Russia.* Gainesville: University of Florida, 1953.

Haruna, Akira. *Nippon Otokichi hyōryūki* [The story of castaway Nippon Otokichi]. Tōkyō: Shōbunsha, 1979.

Harvey, A. G. "Chief Concomly's Skull." *Oregon Historical Quarterly,* vol. 40, no. 2 (June 1939), pp. 161–67.

Hayman, Joyhn, ed. *Robert Brown and the Vancouver Island Exploring Expedition.* Vancouver: University of Columbia Press, 1989.

*Heco, Joseph. *The Narrative of a Japanese; What he has seen and the people he has met in the course of the last forty years.* Vols. 1 and 2. Edited by James Murdoch. San Francisco: American-Japanese Publishing Association [1928].

Hildreth, Richard. *Japan: As It Was and Is.* Boston: Phillips, Sampson, and Co., 1855.

Hines, Clarence. "Adams, Russia and Northwest Trade, 1824." *Oregon Historical Quarterly,* vol. 36, no. 4 (December 1935), pp. 349–58.

*Hines, Gustavus. *A Voyage Round the World: with a history of the Oregon mission. . . . To which is appended a full description of Oregon Territory, its geography, history and religion; designed for the benefit of emigrants to that rising country.* Buffalo: G. H. Derby and Co., 1850.

Holman, Frederick. *Dr. John McLoughlin, the Father of Oregon.* Cleveland: Arthur H. Clark Co., 1907.

*Howay, Frederic W., ed. *Voyages of the "Columbia" to the Northwest Coast, 1787–1790 and 1790–1793.* Boston: Massachusetts Historical Society, 1941.

*Howay, F. W., William S. Lewis, and Jacob A. Meyers, eds. "Documents—Angus McDonald: A Few Items of the West." *Washington Historical Quarterly,* vol. 8, no. 3 (July 1917), pp. 188–229.

*Inagami, Mamoru. *Ranald MacDonald bunken mokuroku daiisshū* [A bibliography of materials on Ranald MacDonald, 1st collection]. Tōkyō: Makudonarudo tomo no kai, 1993.

Inoue, Yoshitaka. *Hakodate eigaku—mite arukimasu; Moshi kurobune ga konakattara* [English studies in Hakodate—a visual tour; What if the "Black Ships" had not come?]. Hakodate: Goryōkaku Tower, 2002.

Iritani, Evelyn. *An Ocean Between Us.* New York: William Morrow and Co., 1994.

Irving, Washington. *Astoria, or, Anecdotes of an Enterprise Beyond the Rocky Mountains.* Vols. 1 and 2. Introduction by William H. Goetzmann. Reprint of 1836 edition. New York: J. B. Lippincott Co., 1961.

Ishihara, Chisato. *Ranarudo Makudonarudo no seito-tachi* [Ranald MacDonald's pupils]. *Nippon Eigakushi kenkyū,* no. 23 (1 October 1990).

Jackson, John C. *Children of the Fur Trade: Forgotten Métis of the Pacific Northwest.* Missoula: Mountain Press Publishing Co., 1995.

Japans Dagh Register gehouden in't Comptoir Nangasackij, Hmo, 1843–1847, Door Den Opperhooden Pieter Albert Bik en `Henrij Levijssohn. Transcribed by Nichi-Ran Kōshōshi Kenkyūkai. From unpublished originals in The Hague, 1965.

*Jarves, James J. *Scenes and Scenery in the Sandwich Islands, and a trip through Central America: Being observations from my note-book during the years 1837–1842.* Boston: James Munroe and Co., 1844.

*Jesset, Thomas E., ed. *Reports and Letters of Herbert Beaver, 1836–1838.* Portland, Oregon: Champoeg Press, 1959.

*Jones, Robert F. *Annals of Astoria: The Headquarters Log of the Pacific Fur Company on the Columbia River, 1811–1813.* New York: Fordham University Press, 1999.

*———, ed. *Astorian Adventure: The Journal of Alfred Seton, 1811–1815.* New York: Fordham University Press, 1993.

Kaiho, Mineo, ed. *Bakusei shiryo to Ezochi* [Shogunate records and Ezo]. Sapporo: Miyama Shobō, 1980.

*Kane, Paul. "The Chinook Indians." *Canadian Journal of Industry, Science, and Art,* no. 7 (January 1857), pp. 12–23.

*———. "Notes of a Sojourn among the Half-Breeds, Hudson's Bay Company Territory, Red River." *Canadian Journal of Industry, Science, and Art,* no. 2 (March 1856), pp. 128–30.

Kaneko, Hisakazu. *Manjiro, the Man Who Discovered America.* Boston: Houghton Mifflin and Co., 1956.

Katagiri, Kazuo. *Hirakareta sakoku: Nagasaki Deshima no hito, mono, jōhō* (An open closed-country: The people, things, and information of Nagasaki's Deshima]. Tōkyō: Kodansha Gendai Shinsho, 1997.

——— and Masanobu Hattori. *Nenban oranda tsūji shiryō* [Materials on annual Dutch interpreters]. Tōkyō: Kondo Shuppansha, 1977.

———. *Oranda tsūji no kenkyū.* Tōkyō: Yoshikawa Kōbunkan, 1985.

Kawamoto, Yumiko. "Futatsu no 'Nichiei goishū'—Makudonarudo no genten to makuraudo no henshū ni yoru mono" [Two English-Japanese glossaries—MacDonald's original and McLeod's edited version]. Waseda Daigaku Nihongo Senta-Kiyō, no. 10 (1998).

———. "Makudonarudo to nihon to no deai" [1]. [MacDonald and an encounter with Japan]. *Yōgakushi kenkyū,* no. 12 (1995).

———. "Makudonarudo to nihon to no deai" [2]. [MacDonald and an encounter with Japan]. *Yōgakushi kenkyū,* no. 13 (1996).

———. "Ranarudo Makudonarudo no 'Nichiei goishū'—hatsuon to hyōki no kankei kara hōgengoi wo saguru" [On 'the glossary of English and Japanese words' by Ranald MacDonald—A phonological approach to determine dialect words]. *Eigakushi kenkyū.* no. 30 (October 1997).

*Kawasumi, Tetsuo, ed. *Nakahama Manjirō shūsei* [The Manjirō Nakahama collection]. Tōkyō: Shōgakukan, 1990.

Kikuchi, Isao. *Ainu minzoku to Nihonjin* [Japanese and the Ainu race]. Tōkyō: Asahi Shinbunsha, 1994.

Kisaki, Ryōhei. *Kōdayū to Rakusuman: Bakumatsu nichiro kōshōshi no ichi sokumen* [Kōdayū and Laxman: One aspect of Japanese-Russian history at the end of the Edo era]. Tōkyō: Tōsui Shobō, 1992.

———. *Sendai hyōmin to Rezanofu: Bakumatsu nichiro kōshōshi no ichisokumen* [The Sendai castaways and

Rezanov: One aspect of Japanese-Russian history at the end of the Edo era]. Tōkyō: Tōsui Shobō, 1997.

Kleinfeld, Herbert L., ed. *The Complete Works of Washington Irving: Astoria.* Boston: Twayne Publishers, 1976.

Koga, Jūjirō. Tokugawa jidai ni okeru Nagasaki no eigo kenkyū [English learning in Nagasaki during the Tokugawa era]. Fukuoka: Kyūshū Shobō, 1947.

*Koka zakki, Kaei zakki [Records from the Koka and Kaei eras]. Introduction by Kazuo Minami. Series: Naikaku bunko shozō shiseki sōkan, 35. Tōkyō: Shiseki Kenkyūkai: Kyūko Shoin, 1983.

Kokushi Daijiten Henshū Iinkai, ed. *Kokushi daijiten* [Dictionary of national history]. Tōkyō: Yoshikawa Kōdōkan, 1979.

Kouwenhoven, Arlette, and Matthi Forrer. *Siebold and Japan: His Life and Work.* Leiden: Hotei Publishing, 2000.

**Krusenstern, Captain A. J. *Voyage Round the World, in the Years 1803, 1804, 1805, 1806, by order of His Imperial Majesty Alexander the First, on Board the Ships Nadeshda and Neva, under the Command of Captain A. J. Von Krusenstern, of the Imperial Navy.* Vols. 1 and 2. London: 1813.

Lahaina Restoration Foundation, ed. *Story of Lahaina.* Lahaina: Lahaina Restoration Foundation, 1961.

**Langsdorff, G. H. von. *Remarks and Observations on a Voyage Around the World, from 1803 to 1807.* Vols. 1 and 2. Translated by Victoria Joan Moessner. Reprint of 1812 edition. Kingston, Ontario: Limestone Press, 1993.

*———. *Voyages and Travels in Various Parts of the World During the Years 1803,1804,1805,1806 and 1807.* Vols. 1 and 2. Reprint. New York: Da Capo Press, 1968.

Leckie, Shirley A. *Elizabeth Bacon Custer and the Making of a Myth.* Norman: University of Oklahoma Press, 1993.

Lensen, George. *The Russian Push Toward Japan; Russo-Japanese Relations, 1697–1875.* Princeton: Princeton University Press, 1959.

**Levyssohn, J. H. *Bladen over Japan* [Papers about Japan]. The Hague: Belinfante Brothers, 1852.

Lewis, William S. "Archibald McDonald: Biography and Geneology." *Washington Historical Quarterly,* vol. 9, no. 2 (April 1918), pp. 93-102

*——— and Naojirō Murakami, eds. *Ranald MacDonald: The Narrative of his early life on the Columbia under the Hudson's Bay Company's regime; of his experiences in the Pacific Whale Fishery; and of his great Adventure to Japan; with a sketch of his later life on the Western Frontier, 1824–1894.* Spokane, Washington: Eastern Washington State Historical Society, 1923.

"Long Live King Com-Comly." *Spokane Review,* 27 November 1893, p. 2.

Losey, Elizabeth Browne. *Let Them Be Remembered: The Story of the Fur Trade Forts.* New York: Vantage Press, 1999.

**MacDonald, Benjamin. "Narrative of Benjamin MacDonald." *Washington Historical Quarterly,* vol. 16, no. 3 (July 1925), pp. 186–97.

**MacDonald, Ranald, *Bentinck Arm and Fraser River Road Company Prospectus.* Victoria, V.I.: British Colonist Office, 1862.

Manning, Clarence A. *Russian Influence on Early America.* New York: Library Publishers, 1953.

Matsumae Township Local History Editorial Offices. *Gaisetsu: Matsumae no rekishi* [An outline of Matsumae history]. Matsumae: Matsumae Township, 1995.

*———. *Matsumae chōshi-shiryōhen* [Matsumae township history: Documents]. Vols. 1 and 2. Matsumae: Matsumae Township, 1974/77.

———. *Matsumae chōshi tsūsetsuhen* [Matsumae township history: A general history]. Vol. 1, part 1. Matsumae: Matsumae Township, 1988.

McCauley, Edward Yorke. See Alan B. Cole entry.

**McDonald, Lois Halliday. *Fur Trade Letters of Francis Ermatinger, written to his Brother Edward during his service with the Hudson's Bay Company, 1818–1853.* Glendale: Arthur H. Clark Co., 1980.

McLeod, Malcolm. *Oregon Indemnity: Claim of Chief Factors and Chief Traders of the Hudson's Bay Company, thereto, as partners, under Treaty of 1846.* [No publisher given]: 1892.

———. *Memorial to the Government and Parliament of Canada of Malcolm McLeod, Q.C., & c., for Indemnity for Service in Initiating the Canadian Pacific Railway, &c., &c.* Ottawa: [No publisher given], 1889.

———. *The Pacific Railway. Britannicus' Letters from the Ottawa Citizen.* Ottawa: "Citizen" Printing and Publishing Co., 1875.

———, ed. *Peace River: A Canoe Voyage from Hudson's Bay to Pacific by Sir George Simpson (Governor, Hon. Hudson's Bay Company) in 1828. Journal of the late factor, Archibald McDonald (Hon. Hudson's Bay Company), who accompanied him.* Reprint of 1872 edition. Rutland, Vermont: Charles E. Tuttle, 1971.

*McLeod, Margaret Arnett, ed. *The Letters of Letitia Hargrave.* Toronto: Champlain Society, 1947.

Melville, Herman. *Moby-Dick, or, The Whale.* New York: Penguin Books, 1992.

*Merk, Frederick, ed. *Fur Trade and Empire: George Simpson's Journal.* Cambridge: Harvard University Press, 1931.

Miller, Warren Cron, ed. *Vignettes of Early St. Thomas: An Anthology of the Life and Times of Its First Century.* St. Thomas: Sutherland Press, 1967.

Miura, Ayako. *Kairei* [Undersea ridge]. Vols. 1–3. Tōkyō: Kadokawa Bunko, 1983.

Miyanaga, Takashi. *Jon Man to yobareru otoko: Hyōryūmin Nakahama manjirō no shōgai* [A man named Jon Man: The life of drifter Manjiro Nakahama]. Tōkyō: Shūeisha, 1994.

Mockford, Jim. "The Lady Washington at Kushimoto, Japan, in 1791." In *The Early Republic and the Sea: Essays on the Naval and Maritime History of the Early United States.* Edited by William S. Dudley and Michael J. Crawford. Washington, D.C.: Brassey's Inc., 2001.

Morrison, Dorothy Nafus. *Outpost: John McLoughlin and the Far Northwest.* Portland: Oregon Historical Society Press, 1999.

*Mudge, Rev. Z. A. *A Memoir of Cyrus Shepard, Embracing a Brief Sketch of the Early History of the Oregon Mission.* New York: Carlton and Phillips, 1853.

Murphy, Gretchen. "'A Home Which Is Still Not a Home:' Finding a Place for Ranald MacDonald." *American Transcendental Quarterly,* vol. 15, no. 3 (1 September 2001), pp. 225–44.

Nagai, Mamoru. "Ranarudo Makudonarudo no kōken to wa?—Nagasaki de no rantsūji e no hajime no eigo kyōjū" [What was Ranald MacDonald's contribution?—The first teaching of English to the Dutch interpreters in Nagasaki]. *Eigo kyōiku kenkyū,* nos. 37 and 38, 1995.

Nagasaki Kenshi Henshū Iinkai, ed. *Nagasaki kenshi: Taigai kōshō shi* [Nagasaki prefecture: History of foreign relations]. Tōkyō: Yoshikawa Kōbunkan, 1985.

Nagasaki-shi Kyōiku Iinkai, ed. *Deshima.* Nagasaki: [Publisher unlisted], 1997.

Newman, Peter C. *Caesars of the Wilderness: Company of Adventurers.* Vol. 2. Toronto: Penguin Books, 1987.

———. *A Company of Adventurers.* Vol. 1. Toronto: Penguin Books, 1985.

Nichols, Marie Leona. *Ranald MacDonald Adventurer.* Caldwell, Idaho: Caxton Printers, 1940.

Nozikov, N. *Russian Voyages Round the World.* Edited by M. A. Sergeyev. London: Hutchinson and Co., [1944].

*Nute, Grace, ed. "Notes and Documents: Documents Relating to James Dickson's Expedition." *Mississippi Valley Historical Review,* vol. 10, no. 2 (September 1923), pp. 174–81.

*———, ed. "James Dickson: A Filibuster in Minnesota in 1836." *Mississippi Valley Historical Review,* vol. 10, no. 2 (September 1923), pp. 127–40.

Obama, Masami. "Makudonarudo tomo no kai Nagasaki: Kessei made no keii" [Events leading up to the formation of the Nagasaki Friends of MacDonald society]. Unpublished paper. Nagasaki, 6 March 1998.

Oliva, Peter. *The City of Yes.* Toronto: McClelland and Stewart, 1999.

Ōsaka Joshi Daigaku Fuzoku Toshokan, ed. *Nippon eigakushi kaidai* [A critical bibliography of materials for English studies in Japan]. Unpublished book. Compiled by Osaka Women's University, 1962.

*Parker, Rev. Samuel. *Journal of an Exploring Tour Beyond the Rocky Mountains, under the direction of A.B.C.F.M.* Ithaca, New York: Andrew, Woodruff and Gauntlett, 1844.

*Perry, Matthew C. *The Japan Expedition, 1852–1854, The Personal Journal of Commodore Matthew C. Perry.* Edited by Roger Pineau. Washington, D.C.: Smithsonian Institution Press, 1968.

Plummer, Katherine. *Saisho ni amerika o mita Nihonjin* [The first Japanese to see America]. Translated by Masako Sakai. Tōkyō: Nippon Hōsō Shuppan Kyōkai, 1989.

Porter, Kenneth Wiggins. *John Jacob Astor: Businessman.* Vol. 1. Cambridge: Harvard University Press, 1931.

*Pritchard, John. *Glimpses of the Past, in The Red River Settlement, From Letters of Mr. John Pritchard, 1805–1836.* Middle Church, Manitoba: Rupert's Land Indian Industrial Press, 1892.

Pritchett, John Perry. *The Red River Valley, 1811–1849: A Regional Study.* New Haven: Yale University Press, 1942.

*Raffles, Sir Stamford. *Report on Japan to the Secret Committee of the English East India Company.* Edited by M. Paske-Smith. London: Curzon Press, Ltd., 1971.

"Ranald MacDonald's Monument, Toroda Creek, State of Washington." *British Columbia Historical Society,* vol. 11 (July–October 1951), pp. 223–27.

Rich, E. E. *The Hudson's Bay Company, 1670–1870.* Vols. 1–3. New York: MacMillan, 1961.

*———, ed. *The Letters of John McLoughlin, from Fort Vancouver to the Governor and Committee, First Series 1825–1838.* Toronto: Champlain Society, 1941.

Roe, Jo Ann. *Ranald MacDonald: Pacific Rim Adventurer.* Pullman: Washington State University Press, 1997.

*Roe, Michael. *The Journal and Letters of Captain Charles Bishop on the North-West Coast of America, in the Pacific and in New South Wales, 1794–1799.* Published for the Hakluyt Society, Cambridge: The University Press, 1967.

*Rollings, Phillip Ashton, ed. *The Discovery of the Oregon Trail: Robert Stuart's Narratives of His Overland Trip Eastward from Astoria in 1812–13. From the Original Manuscripts in the Collection of William Robertson Coe, Esq., To Which is added: An Account of the* Tonquin's *Voyage and of Events at Fort Astoria* [1811–12] and *Wilson Price Hunt's Diary of His Overland Trip Westward to Astoria in 1811–12.* Translated from *Nouvelles Annales des Voyages,* Paris, 1821. New York: Charles Scribner's Sons, 1935.

*Ross, Alexander. *The Red River Settlement: its rise, progress, and present state.* London: Smith, Elder and Co., 1856.

Ruby, Robert H., and John A. Brown. *The Chinook Indians: Traders of the Lower Columbia River.* Norman: University of Oklahoma Press, 1976.

———. *Indian Slavery in the Pacific Northwest.* Northwest Historical Series 17. Spokane: The Arthur H. Clark Co., 1993.

Rupert's Land to Riel. Vol. 1. *Manitoba 125: A History.* Winnipeg: Great Plains Publications, 1993.

Saitō, Kōichi. "Ima, naze 'Nippon Otokichi' nanoka: Mihamachō kara sekai e no kakehashi" [Why Otokichi now? A bridge from Mihama Township to the World]. Unpublished paper, October 1996.

Sakamaki, Shunzō. "Japan and the United States, 1790–1853." *Transactions of the Asiatic Society of Japan,* 2d ser., vol. 18, 1939.

Schodt, Frederik L. *America and the Four Japans: Friend, Foe, Model, Mirror.* Berkeley: Stone Bridge Press, 1993.

———. "Ranald MacDonald, An Early American Adventurer in Japan." *Japan Related,* (May/June 1995) no. 12, pp. 39-42.

Scott, Harvey W. *History of the Oregon Country.* Vols. 1 and 2. Cambridge: Riverside Press, 1924.

Sekai dai hyakkajiten [Heibonsha World Encyclopedia]. Tōkyō: Heibonsha, 1975. Vols. 1–33

*Shigehisa, Tokutarō. *Nihon kinsei eigakushi* [Modern studies of English learning]. Kyōto: Kyōiku Tosho., 1941.

Shigure, Otowa. *Shima monogatari* [Story of the island]. Wakkanaichō: Sōya Kankō Kyōkai, 1948.

Simpson, Sir George. *An Overland Journey Round the World, during the years 1841 and 1842.* Vols. 1 and 2. Philadelphia: Lea and Blanchard, 1847.

Sleight, Harry D. *The Whale Fishery on Long Island.* New York: The Hampton Press, 1931.

Sonoda, Kenji. "Kasuta-fujin to makudonarudo" [Mrs. Custer and MacDonald]. *Nagasaki Dansō,* no. 76 (1 March 1990), pp. 55–70.

———. "Makudonarudo no nichiei goishū kaitei" [MacDonald's 'glossary of English and Japanese words' revised]. *Eigakushi kenkyū,* no. 21 (1 October 1988), pp. 61–75.

———. "Makudonarudo no Nichiei kaiwashū" [MacDonald's English-Japanese colloquial expressions]. *Nagasaki daigaku iryo tandai kiyō,* no. 2 (1988), pp. 57–63.

———. "Makudonarudo no oranda-go" [MacDonald's Dutch]. *Nichiran gakkai kaishi,* vol. 13, no. 2 (no. 26 in series) (March 1989), pp. 49–52.

———. "Makudonarudo no tanjōbi to shibōbi" [MacDonald's birth and death dates]. *Eigakushi kenkyū,* no. 23 (1 October 1990).

———. "Nagasaki ni okeru Makudonarudo" [MacDonald in Nagasaki]. *Nippon eigakushi kenkyū,* no. 24 (1 October 1991).

———. "Preble gō no Nagasaki-ko nyūkō to Makudonarudo" [MacDonald, and the entry of the Preble into the port of Nagasaki]. *Nagasaki dansō,* no. 75 (1 June 1989), pp. 28–46.

———. "W. S. Lewis and N. Murakami, eds., *Ranald MacDonald* ni tsuite" [About W. S. Lewis and N. Murakami, eds., *Ranald MacDonald*]. *Eigakushi kenkyū*, no, 22 (1 October 1989), pp. 33–45.

Starbuck, Alexander. *History of the American Whale Fishery, From Its Earliest Inception to the Year 1876.* Waltham, Massachusetts: [self-published], 1878.

Stuart, Robert. See Rollings entry.

Sugimoto, Tsutomu. *Nagasaki tsūji: Kotoba to bunka no honyakusha* [Nagasaki interpreters: Translators of language and culture]. Tōkyō: Kaitakusha, 1981.

Thomas, C. *History of the Counties Argenteuil, Quebec, Prescott, Ontario.* Belleville, Ontario: Mika Publishing Co., 1981.

*Thwaites, Reuben Gold, ed. *The Original Journals of the Lewis and Clark Expedition, 1804–1806.* Vols. 3 and 4. New York: Dodd, Mead and Co., 1905.

*Tolmie, William Fraser. *The Journals of William Fraser Tolmie, Physician and Fur Trader.* Vancouver, Canada: Mitchell Press, 1963.

Tomita, Hitoshi, ed. *Umi wo koeta Nihon jinmei jiten 1551–1897* [Biographical dictionary of Japanese travelers to the Occident, 1551–1897]. Tōkyō: Nichigai Associates, Inc., 1985.

Tomita, Masakatsu. "Ranarudo Makudonarudo ni takusuru yume" [My dreams for Ranald MacDonald]. Shisō no Kagaku (February/March 1993), pp. 70–71.

Tomita, Torao, ed. *Makudonarudo—"Nippon kaisōki"* [MacDonald's "recollections" of Japan]. (Translation of William Lewis and Naojirō Murakami's *Ranald MacDonald*). Tōkyō: Tōsui Shobō, 1979.

*Tyrell, J. B., ed. *David Thompson's Narrative of His Explorations in Western America, 1784–1812.* Publications of the Champlain Society. Vol. 12. Toronto: Champlain Society, 1916.

*U.S. House of Representatives. 31st Congress, 1st session. *Executive Document,* no. 84.

*U.S. Senate. 32nd Congress, 1st session. *Executive Document,* no. 59.

*Vancouver, George. *The exploration of the Columbia River by Lieutenant W. R. Broughton, October, 1792 : an extract from the Journal of Captain George Vancouver.* Longview, Washington: Longview Daily News (ca. 1927).

Van Kirk, Sylvia. *Many Tender Ties: Women in Fur Trade Society, 1670–1870.* Norman: University of Oklahoma Press, 1980.

*Walker, Alexander. *An Account of a Voyage to the North West Coast of America in 1785 and 1786, by Alexander Walker.* Edited by Robin Fisher and J. M. Bumsted. Seattle: University of Washington Press, 1982.

Warring, Mary. "Historical Fact or Fiction: Will the Real Ranald MacDonald Please Step Forward?" In *Leaves of History,* a Joint Publication of the Ferry County Historical Society and the Stonerose Interpretive Center, Curlew, Washington, May 2000.

*West, John. *The Substance of a Journal During a Residence at The Red River Colony, British North America.* London: L. B. Seeley and Son, 1824.

*Whymper, Frederick. *Travel and Adventure in the Territory of Alaska.* New York: Harper and Brothers, 1869.

Wiley, Peter Booth [with Korogi Ichirō]. *Yankees in the Land of the Gods: Perry and the Opening of Japan.* New York: Viking, 1990.

*Williams, Christina M. M. "A Daughter of Angus MacDonald." *Washington Historical Quarterly,* vol. 13, no. 2 (April 1922), pp. 107–17.

*Williams, Glyndwr. "Governor George Simpson's Character Book." *Beaver* (Summer 1975), pp. 4–18.

*———, ed. *Hudson's Bay Miscellany, 1670–1870.* Winnipeg: Hudson's Bay Record Society, 1975.

*Williams, S. Wells. "A Journal of the Perry Expedition to Japan (1853–1854). *Transactions of the Asiatic Society of Japan,* vol. 37, part 2 (1910), pp. 120–23, 220.

Willson, Beckles. *The Great Company.* Toronto: Copp, Clark Co., 1899.

Yamawaki, Teijirō. *Nagasaki no oranda shōkan: Sekai no naka no sakoku Nihon* [The Dutch factory at Nagasaki: Isolated Japan in the middle of the world]. Tōkyō: Chuōkōronsha, 1980.

*Yanai, Kenji, comp. *Tsūkō ichiran zokushū* [A summary history of passages]. Vols. 4 and 5. Ōsaka: Seibundō Shuppan, 1972.

Yoshimura, Akira. *Umi no sairei* [Festival of the sea]. Tōkyō: Bungei Shunjū, 1989.

Index